C000006616

Religion, Education and

SERIES EDITORS:

Professor Stephen G. Parker
The Rev'd Canon Professor Leslie J. Francis
Professor Rob Freathy
Professor Mandy Robbins

Volume 13

PETER LANG
Oxford • Bern • Berlin • Bruxelles • New York • Wien

Collective Worship and
Religious Observance in Schools

Collective Worship and Religious Observance in Schools

Religion, Education and Values

SERIES EDITORS:

Professor Stephen G. Parker
The Rev'd Canon Professor Leslie J. Francis
Professor Rob Freathy
Professor Mandy Robbins

Volume 13

PETER LANG
Oxford • Bern • Berlin • Bruxelles • New York • Wien

Collective Worship and Religious Observance in Schools

Peter Cumper and Alison Mawhinney (eds)

PETER LANG

Oxford • Bern • Berlin • Bruxelles • New York • Wien

Bibliographic information published by Die Deutsche Nationalbibliothek.
Die Deutsche Nationalbibliothek lists this publication in the Deutsche National-
bibliografie; detailed bibliographic data is available on the Internet at
http://dnb.d-nb.de.

A catalogue record for this book is available from the British Library.

Library of Congress Control Number: 2017963047

Cover image: © M.studio – Fotolia.com.

Series design by Peter Lang Ltd.

ISSN 2235-4638
ISBN 978-1-78707-655-6 (print) • ISBN 978-1-78707-656-3 (ePDF)
ISBN 978-1-78707-657-0 (ePub) • ISBN 978-1-78707-658-7 (mobi)

© Peter Lang AG 2018

Published by Peter Lang Ltd, International Academic Publishers,
52 St Giles, Oxford, OX1 3LU, United Kingdom
oxford@peterlang.com, www.peterlang.com

Peter Cumper and Alison Mawhinney have asserted their right under the
Copyright, Designs and Patents Act, 1988, to be identified as Editors of this Work.

This publication has been peer reviewed.

Printed in Germany

Contents

ROBERT JACKSON

Foreword

This important book is the first collaborative study focusing entirely on issues concerning religious worship in schools across the United Kingdom. Acts of worship and religious observance in schools need to be distinguished from religious education as a curriculum subject, although there is a relationship between the two. The research on which much of this book is based took on the task of evaluating systematically current law and policy related specifically to 'collective worship' in England, Wales and Northern Ireland, and 'religious observance' in Scotland. The book brings together the expertise of scholars working in education, law and a range of other relevant academic disciplines.

Speaking more generally, the place of religion in state-funded schools in different European countries – especially in relation to religious *education* – has changed significantly since the 1960s. The main drivers of change include secularization, characterized by a decline in religious belief and practice. A second influence for change is pluralization, especially through the migration to European states of people of various ethnic and religious backgrounds. A third is globalization, often connecting aspects of life in particular countries with events in other parts of the world. For young people, the revolution in communication represented by the internet, the mobile telephone and social media have been transformative. The changes resulting from these different influences have varied in a number of ways across countries, not least because of some very different national histories of religion and state, and some different experiences over time in relation to migration.

Thus, in various European states, there has been a shift in state education from so-called 'confessional' forms of religious education, in which religious beliefs and values are transmitted to young people, to forms of inclusive religious education, in which young people from a variety of

religious and non-religious family backgrounds learn together about religious and non-religious diversity, sometimes with opportunities for moder-
ated discussion and personal reflection. Issues related to the development
of workable methods for studying religions and beliefs in state schools
across the European continent are discussed in on-going work initiated
by the Council of Europe (Jackson, 2014).

The situation regarding religious education is complex in the United
Kingdom. Scotland has its own education system, and the education system
in Northern Ireland differs in some ways from that in England and Wales.
English and Welsh policies can also differ in certain respects. The compli-
cation is compounded by the fact that, in addition to religious education
in the classroom, there is also legal provision for what in England, Wales
and Northern Ireland is still called 'collective worship', and in Scotland is
called 'religious observance'.

To take the English case, the 1944 Education Act regarded what it
called 'religious education' as including *both* 'religious instruction' and
'collective worship'. Under the influences outlined above, religious instruction and collective worship as practised in state-funded schools have both
evolved.

'Bottom-up' changes in schools run in parallel with influences from
the academic world and the world of professional education. In England
and Wales, in the case of religious instruction, such influences eventually
resulted in changes to law. The 1988 Education Reform Act at last changed
the name of the curriculum subject from 'religious instruction' to 'religious
education', and acknowledged that its content should take account of the
country's religious diversity. However, the term 'collective worship' was left
in place, and academic argument – as reflected in John Hull's powerful book
School Worship: An Obituary (Hull, 1975) – made no impact on the law.

The legal requirement to maintain acts of collective worship in state-
funded schools with pupil and teacher populations from diverse religious
and secular backgrounds has presented schools with some serious challenges. As the present volume indicates, one response has been simply to
ignore the requirement. Another has involved interpreting the requirement
loosely, using the time and opportunity to bring the whole or parts of the
school together in order to pursue worthwhile collective activities, often

related to learning about religions and beliefs, spirituality, or exploring values issues as a school community. Creative and valuable as many of these activities are, it is clear that changes in law and policy are required urgently.

Maintaining the status quo would be a mistake, and arguably runs counter to the human rights principle of freedom of religion or belief. Abolishing the duty completely would remove opportunities for bringing the school population together as a community. Clearly, the name of the activity needs to be changed in law (since the 1950s, many schools have simply referred to it as 'Assembly'), and there needs to be some flexibility. For example, in the secondary school where I taught in the late 1960s, the whole school assembled once a week, on Monday; there was no assembly on Wednesday; and on the other two days three particular age ranges assembled (11–13, 14–16, over 16). Assemblies included listening to invited guests, sometimes from religious or humanistic communities or from caring professions, speak about their work or their world view, outlining their experience and opening up discussions about values and society. When guests came in, opportunities were always provided for students to ask questions and make contributions. Students sometimes performed short dramas on religious or philosophical themes that they had prepared in English or RE lessons; I recall one by third-year pupils exploring different kinds of truth – logical, scientific, aesthetic and religious. Sometimes, the whole school was brought together to acknowledge and reflect on a particular event, such as the death of a pupil or a member of staff. To move to the present day, in June 2017, a south London primary school had a whole school assembly which gave pupils an opportunity to reflect on an attack near the school on a seventeen-year-old Muslim boy, and also on the atrocities committed on London Bridge. The concepts of terrorism and extremism were explored, together with human rights values, as were the obligations on members of the school community to respect one another's rights to hold particular beliefs. The assembly was part of a series both exploring the school as a community, whose shared values enable celebration of differences in culture and religion, and providing pupils with time for reflection on the issues raised. These examples show how bringing the whole school community together, or bringing particular age groups together, can provide educational opportunities for exploring questions of value and spirituality, as well as enabling pupils to learn about the commitments of people from different backgrounds.

My personal view is that all students should study and try to understand worship and devotion in different religious traditions, just as they should gain an understanding of non-religious world views. This can be done, in part, through listening to explanations and personal accounts from visitors to the school, or through participating in educational visits to particular communities.

I have shared some anecdotes about what can be done creatively in the context of outmoded legislation. However, changes in law and policy in relation to collective worship and religious observance are needed urgently across the United Kingdom. The present book provides politicians and policymakers with the tools they need in order to do this, as well as providing detailed information for educators and parents.

In addition to valuable introductory and concluding chapters by the editors, Part I presents an analysis of law and policy across the nations of the United Kingdom, indicating policy options in each particular case.

Part II provides a variety of legal perspectives on collective worship and religious observance, focusing on the rights of children, parents and teachers, and giving due consideration to the interests of the state.

Part III is written by scholars working in education, and deals with issues such as the contribution that 'assemblies' can make to pupils' spiritual, moral, social and cultural development, to the nurture of their reflexive and philosophical skills, and to the need to take close account of the religious or world view background of children and teachers who participate. This Part concludes with a discussion of ways forward for policymakers, noting difficulties in reaching a broad consensus, and favouring a position requiring serious reform rather than total abolition.

Part IV provides a welcome international perspective from scholars working in the broad field of religions and education in the USA, the Netherlands and Scandinavia. Relevant concepts such as the cultivation of human integrity, holistic interreligious knowledge and experiential learning through dialogue are presented, together with the argument that the state school should be a community of persons and learning, reflecting a diversity of values, world views, religions and convictions.

This book will surely generate informed debate, leading to important educational reform.

References

Hull, J. (1975). *School Worship: An Obituary.* London: SCM Press.

Jackson, R. (2014). *'Signposts': Policy and Practice for Teaching about Religions and Non-Religious Worldviews in Intercultural Education.* Strasbourg: Council of Europe Publishing.

PETER CUMPER AND ALISON MAWHINNEY

Introduction: Collective Worship and Religious Observance in Context

This is a book about *collective worship* and *religious observance* in UK schools. At first glance one might assume that notions such as 'collective worship' and 'religious observance' would have little place in the classrooms of state-funded schools. Yet, on closer inspection, it soon becomes clear that this is not the case, on account of the fact that the vast majority of UK schools are required by law to organize acts of collective worship (England, Northern Ireland, Wales) or religious observance (Scotland) for their pupils.

In view of the historically close ties between Church and State in the United Kingdom, it is perhaps unsurprising that the duty on schools to make provision for acts of collective worship/religious observance has a long history. For example, in England, Northern Ireland and Wales, forms of religious observance in schools were commonplace even prior to the Education Act 1944 – the statute which, in relation to the introduction of the 'collective worship' requirement, represented the first instance of a legal duty in regard to such matters in schools. Likewise, in Scotland, religious observance can be traced back to the nineteenth century and the Education (Scotland) Act 1872, which gave schools the freedom to continue the customary practice of religious observance, subject to a resolution in favour of discontinuation by the local electorate.

Controversy and topicality

Just as acts of collective worship/religious observance have had a long history in schools in the UK, so too have these practices been synonymous with controversy for many decades. Today issues relating to collective worship/religious observance continue to generate controversy. There are a number of reasons for this state of affairs. They include: disagreement about the appropriateness of acts of collective worship/ religious observance in an increasingly pluralistic, multicultural UK; the degree to which the current system properly affords respect to the rights of those with no 'religious' faith; and concerns that the present arrangements do not adequately develop the spiritual/moral education of pupils, or promote a community spirit and shared values in schools. We will explore, in more detail, these and other such criticisms of the current collective worship/religious observance arrangements in the forthcoming chapters.

The controversy surrounding collective worship/religious observance has also led to such matters being highly topical. After all, matters pertaining to collective worship/religious observance have, in recent years, increasingly been associated with the debate about the appropriate place of religion and belief in contemporary public life. Thus, for example, there have been: calls for the collective worship requirement in law to be replaced with non-statutory guidance, as made by Charles Clarke and Linda Woodhead (Clarke & Woodhead, 2015); proposals for collective worship to be replaced with inclusive times for reflection, as put forward by the Commission on Religion and Belief in British Public Life (Report of the CORBBPL, 2015); concerns about the procedure of opting out from acts of collective worship/religious observance, similar to those expressed by the UN Committee on the Rights of the Child (Committee on the Rights of the Child, 2016); relevant initiatives from law and policymakers, as evidenced by a recent announcement from the Scottish Government that it plans to hold a consultation on aspects of the practice of religious observance in Scottish schools (BBC News, 2016); and finally, other recent developments, such as a YouGov poll which found that 38 per cent of adults in Scotland are against having a place for worship in the education system (Sanderson, 2016), and a petition that was launched in 2017 which called on the Welsh Assembly to reform the law on collective worship in schools (Wightwick, 2017).

Rationale, scope and remit

Even though the issue of collective worship/religious observance is topical there is also, perhaps surprisingly, a relative paucity of published material by scholars in this area. One possible explanation for this state of affairs is the tendency of some to view collective worship/religious observance as being less a specialized or stand-alone topic and one rather to be explored in the context of the more general issue of religious education. Instead of adopting this approach – which risks collective worship/religious observance being subsumed by its expansive sibling religious education – this book seeks to examine collective worship/religious observance (to the extent that it is appropriate to do so) as a topic that is worthy of analysis in its own right. Accordingly, this book aims to document the relevant law and policy governing collective worship/religious observance, whilst also aspiring to stimulate fresh thinking in this area.

By bringing together scholars from such a wide range of disciplines, this collection aims to demystify much of the uncertainty that currently surrounds the areas of collective worship/religious observance. It seeks to examine questions such as: what is the purpose of collective worship/religious observance? How should schools take account of the rights of children, parents and teachers when organizing such acts? And what are the legitimate interests of the state in such matters? Another important theme to be explored in the book is discussion of whether significant differences exist in the law and policy governing collective worship amongst England, Wales and Northern Ireland as well as comparing collective worship legal frameworks with that governing religious observance in Scotland. Finally, the book aims to foster debate on the extent to which acts of collective worship/religious observance are capable of helping to develop shared values in an increasingly plural and multicultural society.

The essays in this collection are based primarily on research that was recently undertaken as part of a two-year Arts and Humanities Research Council (AHRC) funded project (Grant Ref: AH/K006436/1, <http://collectiveschoolworship.com/>) on collective worship and religious observance in UK schools. The primary focus of this book, as well as the aforementioned AHRC project, is schools *without* a religious character. While many of the observations made in the forthcoming chapters apply to all schools, the primary focus of this edited collection is schools *without* a religious character – the rationale for this being that a proper analysis of schools with a designated religious character would require detailed and separate consideration.

Structure

This book is divided into four parts. The first of these – entitled 'Collective Worship and Religious Observance in the UK: a regional analysis' – consists of four chapters which analyse the law and policy governing collective worship in England, Northern Ireland and Wales, and religious observance in Scotland. They describe and comment on the situation pertaining to collective worship/religious observance in the country at issue, as well as touching on the merits of a range of options that are available to policymakers therein. With education being a devolved matter, these four chapters seek to highlight how each of the UK administrations may respond differently to issues of education generally and collective worship/religious observance in particular.

Collective Worship and Religious Observance in the UK: A Country Analysis

The first part starts with a chapter entitled 'Collective Worship in England' by Peter Cumper and Julia Ipgrave. In focusing primarily on community schools that are not of a designated religious character, Cumper and Ipgrave explore the duty on such schools to ensure that the majority of their daily acts of worship are 'wholly or mainly of a broadly Christian character'. Cumper and Ipgrave also discuss a number of issues of concern that are commonly associated with the provision of collective worship, including the practical difficulties of implementing the relevant guidance and legislation.

They contend that the law and practice which currently governs collective worship in England's schools can be seen as being characterized by confusion and inconsistency – and that the controversy which is commonly synonymous with acts of collective worship in England is symptomatic of a much wider problem of agreeing on the appropriate place of religion in that nation's public life.

In 'Collective Worship in Northern Ireland's Schools', Aideen Hunter and Norman Richardson start by offering a brief overview of Northern Ireland's school system, before commenting on the relevant legal framework. Hunter and Richardson point out that collective worship in Northern Ireland is largely influenced by the person who is delivering it and the ethos of a school, not least because there is no inspection or guidance on this process. As a result of this lack of direction there is considerable diversity across the educational sector in the overall standard and quality of collective school worship. In commenting on public attitudes to religion generally in schools and collective worship in particular, Hunter and Richardson identify a number of different perspectives. These range from a conservative perspective that wishes to maintain the status quo, to one that advocates change and the adoption of a more secular approach. For Hunter and Richardson there is a need for fresh empirical research so as to glean information about contemporary attitudes to school worship – information that could, in turn, lead to appropriate review and reform in this area.

The markedly different position of *religious observance* in Scottish schools is then examined by Claire Cassidy and Frankie McCarthy in 'Religious Observance in Scotland'. They discuss key policy and practice shifts in regard to religious observance and highlight a number of legislative provisions that are of relevance in this area. Consideration is given to the proposed move towards time for reflection as a more inclusive approach to the spiritual development of Scotland's children. The role of parents, statutory bodies and religious groups is explored, and the chapter highlights that children are marginalized in discussions about their religious observance. For Cassidy and McCarthy the increasing significance of children's rights demands that greater attention should be paid to the views of children in determining the appropriate place for religious observance in Scottish schools. In particular, they raise concerns that relate to the parental right to withdraw their children from religious observance, situating this within the context of children's rights. The statutory requirement for religious observance in Scotland may differ from the 'collective worship' duty that exists elsewhere in the UK but, as Cassidy and McCarthy acknowledge, many of the challenges faced in Scottish schools mirror those in the rest of the UK.

Finally, in 'Collective Worship in Wales', Alison Mawhinney and Ann Sherlock examine matters of principle and practice surrounding the statutory duty on schools (not of a designated religious character) to organize daily acts of collective worship that must be 'wholly or mainly of a broadly Christian character'. Mawhinney and Sherlock argue that there is limited data on attitudes to the duty and its implementation in Wales, and that this is a state of affairs which warrants further investigation. Moreover, mindful of such considerations, they contend that there is a pressing need to reconsider the aims of collective worship in today's diverse, multibelief Wales. This chapter concludes with Mawhinney and Sherlock observing that, while Welsh views and principles were easily ignored in the Westminster legislature when the current law was made, today Welsh institutions have the legal competence to respond to the complexities of collective school worship in an innovative manner that is appropriate for Welsh society in the twenty-first century.

Collective Worship and Religious Observance: Legal Perspectives

In the book's second part, in which various legal perspectives are offered on collective worship/religious observance, there are three chapters from scholars with expertise in the fields of law and human rights. Key themes in this part of the book include the challenge of taking account of the rights of all relevant parties (i.e. children, parents and teachers) and affording appropriate respect to the interests of the state.

In the first of these three chapters, 'The Law on Collective School Worship: The Rationale Then and Now', Alison Mawhinney interrogates the existence and nature of the rationale underlying the law on collective school worship. She draws on the Eliasian notion of the state as a survival unit to offer both an explanation and a justification for why a state might choose to impose a duty of collective school worship (i.e. from a need to organize an effective internal structure to assist in its defence and advancement in the 'survival game'). However, she argues that for any law to be coherent and effective a convincing rationale must exist that explains why a chosen means will fulfil an identified need. As Mawhinney points out, whilst the rationale for the law requiring collective school worship may have been relatively strong when it was first introduced in 1944, it has subsequently declined in plausibility as both the needs of the state have changed and the effectiveness of the means (worship) has declined in a less religious society. She argues that, in deciding whether to maintain, abolish or reform the current law, a state today must begin with consideration of the question of need. Only if a need is identified can it then sensibly decide whether that need is capable of being fulfilled by an act of worship. It may find that a revised need exists that requires an alternative means to fulfil it or, indeed, a state may conclude that no need exists that requires any such statutory duty of this nature. Finally, Mawhinney observes that education is a devolved matter in the UK, and it is for each constituent country to determine whether it has a need that requires schools without a religious character to hold daily acts of worship.

In the next chapter, 'Dynamic Self-determinism, the Right to Belief and the Role of Collective Worship', Frankie McCarthy considers the justification for the practice of collective worship in state schools. In examining this issue she employs the 'dynamic self-determinism' model of the jurist John Eekelaar to explore the connection between collective worship and the child's human right to belief. McCarthy's chapter first extrapolates the basic, developmental and autonomy interests protected within the right to belief as encapsulated within the tapestry of international legal instruments. It then argues that school worship could serve the child's interest in developing their capacity for spiritual and philosophical thought, although the absence of a clear policy on the type of capacity that schools should seek to develop prevents worship from fulfilling this role effectively. McCarthy also argues that the child's autonomy interest demands that 'mature minors' have the choice to 'opt out' of worship on conscience grounds. Finally, at the end of her chapter, McCarthy makes a number of recommendations for reform of worship in schools so as to ensure compliance with the UK's international human rights obligations.

This theme of human rights generally, and the rights of children in particular, is also a characteristic of the final chapter in this part of the book. In 'Religious Observance and Collective Worship in Schools: A Human Rights Perspective', Ann Sherlock examines whether the current law and practice governing religious observance and collective worship in schools complies with the UK's human rights obligations. She points out that were there not to be an opportunity for the withdrawal of children from these practices, there would be a breach of the right to freedom of religion or belief, as well as a violation of the right of parents/guardians to ensure that their personal convictions are respected in relation to the education of their children. Sherlock examines possible problems with the 'opt-out' procedure as a way of securing genuine respect for rights, and also considers whether the different treatment of Christian and non-Christian worship gives rise to discrimination on grounds of religion or belief. She also suggests that there should be a more rigorous and child-rights-centric scrutiny of the arrangements for opt-outs before they are accepted as a complete solution to respecting the rights of parents and children.

Collective Worship and Religious Observance: Educational Perspectives

Our analysis of collective worship/religious observance then moves from a legal to an educational perspective. In the third part of the book we have contributions from scholars from different parts of the UK who have expertise on a range of education-related issues.

In the first of this part's chapters the relationship between collective worship/religious observance and spiritual development is explored. In 'The Contribution of Collective Worship to Spiritual Development', Jacqueline Watson examines ways in which activities in this area (i.e. collective worship/religious observance/assemblies) have been identified as contributing to the spiritual, moral, social and cultural development of children and young people. Watson observes that spirituality in education has been strongly associated with a broad set of pedagogical values such as 'pupil voice', space for reflection, and the holistic education of the child, and notes the common assumption that activities such as collective worship/ religious observance can make a strong contribution to spiritual and moral development. For Watson the current model in Scotland, where religious observance is designed to follow the broad and inclusive understanding of spiritual development and seeks 'to promote the spiritual development of all members of the school community and express and celebrate the shared values of the school community' (Circular 1/2005) offers a particularly positive way forward. Her preference for this model is based on the fact that it is inclusive (i.e. it has the spiritual development of all members of the school as its primary aim) and that it seeks to celebrate the shared values of the school community.

In the next chapter, 'Philosophy with Children: An Alternative to Religious Observance', Claire Cassidy also makes a call for change. Cassidy starts by observing that in Scotland all schools must provide opportunities for religious observance. She argues that notwithstanding the proposal in 2004 from the Religious Observance Review Group that 'time for reflection' may be more appropriate for what is undertaken in some schools, neither religious observance nor time for reflection should support the spiritual development of the school community, and that little, if any, advice has been provided for teachers, pupils or their parents regarding what might count as religious observance/time for reflection if not an act of worship. Accordingly, Cassidy advocates Philosophy with Children as being a meaningful alternative to religious observance, and that it could be usefully and meaningfully employed in Scotland and the other jurisdictions in the UK, regardless of the curriculum followed. Cassidy makes the point that there is agreement that children should be taught to think philosophically in order that they can act positively in the world. Moreover, for Cassidy, Philosophy with Children would have a number of other benefits, including the fact that it would enable children to question and challenge themselves, as well as encouraging them to assess, probe and evaluate their thinking and behaviour.

From Philosophy with Children, we move to theology in the next chapter, 'Collective Worship and Theology: Issues and Questions', in which Julia Ipgrave and Farid Panjwani explore the relationship between collective worship and theology. Using *teacher perspectives*, Ipgrave and Panjwani investigate the difficulties entailed in retaining the benefits to the community of collective worship, while giving due consideration to the divergent religious (and non-religious) outlooks of pupils and the integrity of religious content. They argue that that a number of key questions and issues require consideration before recommendations can be made about the future of collective worship in non-religious and religiously plural schools. These include the appropriateness of a religiously informed collective worship to the religious backgrounds of pupils, the contribution of collective worship to the community of the school, and the extent to which collective worship can help to prepare pupils for wider society. For Ipgrave and Panjwani the challenges posed by collective worship do not, in themselves, provide sufficient reasons to abolish this requirement for schools. On the contrary, they contend that these challenges should help to stimulate a more detailed exploration of the practice of collective worship. In this regard Ipgrave and Panjwani maintain there is value in engaging with the theologically informed theories and practices of those who recognize the value (and parameters) of joint opportunities for worship in our religiously plural society – and that positive and valuable lessons for society may be derived from the process of such engagement.

This part on educational perspectives is then brought to a close by Norman Richardson and Aideen Hunter in 'Educational Perspectives on School Collective Worship: Beyond Obituary'. Richardson and Hunter take as their stating point societal, and more particularly educational, changes in the UK since the post-war Education Acts of the 1940s prescribed a daily act of collective worship in England, Wales and Northern Ireland. Given perceptions in some quarters that collective worship/religious observance requirements for schools are currently anachronistic, Richardson and Hunter review proposals for reform in this area. In particular, they investigate three different scenarios: the maintenance of the status quo; reform of the collective worship requirement; and abolition of the current requirement. Richardson and Hunter reach the conclusion that broad consensus does not appear to be possible, although they contend that many educational observers appear to favour what they term 'a moderate position' whereby acts of collective worship might incorporate opportunities for reflection and spiritual development in the classroom.

Collective Worship and Religious Observance: International Perspectives

In the final part of the book we then move beyond the United Kingdom. In this regard an international perspective is provided by three scholars from other jurisdictions, who offer their views on issues that are of relevance to current UK law and policy on collective worship/religious observance. Their views are especially insightful given that it is difficult to think of another comparable nation which has, within its educational system, arrangements that mirror those that exist on these shores in relation to collective worship/religious observance.

In 'Collective Worship and Religious Observance in UK Schools: Questions and Possibilities', Mary Elizabeth Moore argues that engaging communal religious practices is part of holistic learning. Recognizing the significance of contextual differences to collective worship and religious observance, she analyses, respectively, a number of diverse purposes and approaches. In relation to the former, the purposes she identifies include: the cultivation of human integrity; holistic interreligious knowledge; and human relationships with self and other. And in relation to the latter, the potential approaches that are highlighted by Moore are wide-ranging, and include the need to: engage practices of one tradition; offer choices to opt out of religious practices; develop collective experiences without religious content; engage in shareable practices from multiple traditions; and cultivate a sense of wonder. In the conclusion Moore includes her heuristic visions for UK schools which range from specific goals from personal development, to reflection and to collective sensibilities. Her chapter also culminates with reference to the qualities of holistic education which include: intersubjective learning, engaging religions religiously, ritualizing, moving from dominance to multiplicity, dignifying, and revering. For Moore the underlying hope is for a comprehensive, engaged education that is meaningful for human lives and communities, while preparing good citizens.

12

The role of education in preparing children for successfully engaging with strangers or those who might be regarded as 'the other' is an underpinning theme in the next chapter, 'Embracing Otherness in Supporting Community: A Plea from a Pedagogical Perspective for Experiential Learning in Dialogicality', by Ina ter Avest. In this chapter the British educational context is compared with the Dutch one in relation to the task of educators (typically parents and teachers) to promote 'living together in peace'. With such considerations in mind ter Avest proposes ways by which the skill of dialogicality – understood as meaning the competency to engage in a constructive and meaningful dialogue – may be developed, so the ability to embrace 'otherness' can be intensified. In this regard ter Avest also recommends that trainee teachers should be taught to support the community by means of experiential learning in dialogicality.

Finally, in 'Common Symbols in a Diverse School for All: Collective Worship Seen from a Scandinavian Perspective', Geir Skeie considers the role and function of schools both locally and nationally. In this chapter he identifies a number of parallel issues between the UK and Scandinavia. In particular he explores some relevant developments in Scandinavia, including changes in Norwegian schools to the place of religion based on human rights law, and considerations about collective celebrations in Swedish schools. Skeie argues that it is important for schools to have collective practices which reflect the general aims of education in ways that are accessible for students. In this regard he emphasizes that the local school ought to be a *community* of people and of learning, and that it should also function in the public sphere as representing a diversity of values, worldviews, religions and convictions.

Conclusion

The book ends with a brief concluding chapter by the editors. It touches briefly on some of the options for reform in terms of the ways that collective worship/religious observance might develop in the future.

References

BBC News (2016). 'Religious observance opt-out for pupils to be considered', November 5. Retrieved October 2, 2017, from <http://www.bbc.co.uk/news/uk-scotland-37883229>.

Clarke, C., & Woodhead, L. (2015). *A New Settlement: Religion and Belief in Schools.* The Westminster Faith Debates. Retrieved October 2, 2017, from <www.faithdebates.org.uk>.

Committee on the Rights of the Child (2016). *Concluding observations on the fifth periodic report of the United Kingdom of Great Britain and Northern Ireland*, June 3, 2016, CRC/C/GBR/CO/5. Retrieved October 2, 2017, from <http://www.crae.org.uk/media/93148/UK-concluding-observations-2016.pdf>.

Report of the Commission on Religion and Belief in British Public Life (CORBBPL) (2015). *Living with Difference.* Cambridge: The Woolf Institute. Retrieved October 2, 2017, from <http://www.areiac.org.uk/public/downloads/Livingwith Difference.pdf>.

Sanderson, D. (2016). 'Take religion out of the classroom'. *The Times*, December 29. Retrieved October 2, 2017, from <https://www.thetimes.co.uk/article/take-religion-out-of-the-classroom-9j6x06mzw>.

Wightwick, A. (2017). 'Two girls' bid to stop daily prayers in schools wins support of AMs'. *Wales Online*, June 27. Retrieved October 2, 2017, from <http://www.walesonline.co.uk/news/education/two-girls-bid-stop-daily-13248297>.

Collective Worship and Religious Observance in the UK:
A Country Analysis

PETER CUMPER AND JULIA IPGRAVE

1 Collective Worship in England

ABSTRACT

This chapter examines the legal obligation on state-funded schools in England to organize daily acts of collective worship. In focusing primarily on community schools – schools that operate under Local Authority control and are not of a designated religious character – the chapter explores the duty on such schools to ensure that the majority of their acts of worship are 'wholly or mainly of a broadly Christian character'. The chapter discusses some issues of concern that are commonly associated with the issue of collective worship, and concludes that the law on collective worship in England's schools is today characterized by confusion and inconsistency.

Introduction

This chapter explores the law and practice governing collective school worship in England. It starts by offering a concise overview of the demographics of belief in England before providing a brief summary of that nation's school system. The law pertaining to collective worship in England's schools is then described before attention is focused on the relevant situation in community schools – the rationale for this being that the challenges of implementing the law governing collective worship in these state-funded (local authority controlled) schools are not merely onerous in their own right, but that they also demonstrate many of the problems of agreeing on the appropriate place of religious practices in a nation that is, simultaneously increasingly secular yet ever more multifaith in nature. Furthermore, a number of contemporary concerns about school worship are explored – most notably, that a significant number of schools fail to comply with the obligation to organize acts of collective worship; and that, in the opinion of some, the law governing collective school worship discriminates in favour of religious forms of belief generally and Christianity in particular. In conclusion, it is argued that the position of collective worship in England's community schools is characterized by confusion and inconsistency, and that the controversy which is synonymous with the specific issue of collective worship is symptomatic of the wider problem of agreeing on the appropriate place of religion in contemporary public life.

The context: The demographics of belief in England

England is the home to a wide variety of religions and other forms of belief. Evidence of this can be seen from the results of the 2011 Census for England and Wales (Office for National Statistics, 2011), which posed the question, 'What is your religion?' The answers to this question reveal strikingly different patterns of belief throughout England.

Whilst Christianity remains the largest single religion today in England, a significant number of people also describe themselves as being Muslim, Hindu, Sikh, Buddhist, Jewish, or of no religion. Yet those who would so categorize tend not to be evenly spread throughout the land, being often concentrated in particular locations. For example, the 2011 Census found that two thirds of the population in the North East and North West of England identified themselves as 'Christian', with as many as 80.9 per cent of people in one area (Knowsley in Merseyside) so self-classifying. By way of contrast, the 'Christian' population was less than 40 per cent in other specific areas (e.g. Camden, Harrow, Hackney) and cities (e.g. Leicester), whilst in the East London Borough of Tower Hamlets only 27.1 per cent of respondents declared themselves as Christians, with the equivalent figure for Muslims being 34.5 per cent (Office for National Statistics, 2011).

One of the findings of the 2011 Census is that there is a high concentration of certain faith communities today in some English towns and cities. As a result, areas such as Blackburn (27 per cent Muslim), Brent (17.8 per cent Hindu), Slough (10.6 per cent Sikh) and Barnet (15.2 per cent Jewish) are commonly associated with the members of a particular minority faith tradition. In addition, there appears to be an interesting correlation between membership of certain faith groups and religious affiliation more generally. The 2011 Census found that parts of England which are home to some of the highest minority faith populations – including Newham (32 per cent Muslim), Harrow (25.3 per cent Hindu) and Slough (10.6 per cent Sikh) – were the areas that had the *lowest* proportions of the population reporting 'no religion'. By way of contrast, those places that had the *highest* proportion of people reporting 'no religion' – most notably Norwich (42.5 per cent) and Brighton and Hove (42.4 per cent) – have relatively small Muslim, Hindu and Sikh populations (Office for National Statistics, 2011).

Today England has a rich and varied tapestry when it comes to the demographics of belief. Beyond that it is possible to make a number of additional observations. First, recent decades have witnessed an increase in church attendance within certain minority Christian communities (e.g. Orthodox and Pentecostal groups), whereas there has been a decline in the numbers of those attending the services of more mainstream Christian denominations (Brierley, 2014). Secondly, immigration has had a signifi-cance impact on religious life in England as evidenced by claims that new arrivals from overseas have, for example, led to an increase in the numbers of Catholics taking mass (Bates, 2006) and have helped to create a situa-tion whereby black Christians in London are more likely to attend church services than their white counterparts (Brierley, 2013). Thirdly, the number of people – especially young people – declaring no religious affiliation has also increased, and, by way of example, a YouGov survey in 2013 found that religious leaders had less influence over the lives of 18- to 24-year-olds (with only 12 per cent feeling so influenced) than politicians (38 per cent) or even celebrities (21 per cent) (YouGov, 2013).

It is axiomatic that today England is the home of many different forms of religion, belief or lack thereof. However, what is much less clear is how law and policymakers should best respond to the challenge of accommo-dating this plethora of beliefs in the nation's schools and colleges. Few issues in the field of education illustrate this state of affairs more starkly than the challenge of ensuring that appropriate cognizance is taken of these disparate beliefs when it comes to implementing the law relating to collective worship in schools.

Schools in England: A brief summary

There are currently just over 8 million children are enrolled in England's 24,372 schools (Department for Education, 2014). Schools in England that receive funding from the state include:

- *Community* schools, which operate under Local Education Authority (LEA) control, so the LEA owns the school's land/buildings, employs school staff, and sets the admissions criteria.
- *Foundation* schools, which are controlled by a governing body that employs the staff and sets the entrance criteria, subject to rules imposed by central government.
- *Voluntary* schools, which are typically schools of a religious nature, that consist of *voluntary aided* (run primarily by the governing body) and *voluntary controlled* (run primarily by the LEA) schools.
- *Academies*, which are independent, self-governing schools that are approved and funded directly by central government (i.e. the Department for Education), rather than being subject to LEA management or control.

The 'state-funded' schools listed above, unlike their counter-parts in the privately funded independent sector, are required to comply with the law relating to collective worship. Yet whereas there have been significant changes to the educational system of late – most notably in relation to the establishment of new academies and faith schools, with more than 3,000 of the former and 800 of the latter having opened in recent years (Nash, 2013) – the law relating to collective worship appears to have been a low priority for law and policymakers. On those (admittedly rare) occasions where government ministers have been questioned about collective school worship, successive administrations have insisted that they have no plans to change the law (Truss, 2014; Lewis, 2002). This approach tends to imply that those in government believe that the law relating to collective school worship is operating clearly and efficiently. Mindful of such considerations, it is to the law in this area we now turn.

Collective school worship and the law

Schools in England have a long history of incorporating elements of religious worship into the classroom. Whilst acts of worship were common in England's schools in the late nineteenth and early twentieth centuries, it was not until the Education Act 1944 that all maintained schools were required to organize a daily act of collective worship for their pupils. The 1944 Act, which stipulated that 'the school day in every county school and in every voluntary school shall begin with collective worship on the part of all pupils in attendance at the school' (The Education Act 1944, s. 25(1)), was amended by the Education Reform Act 1988, which provided that 'all pupils in attendance at a maintained school shall on each school day take part in an act of collective worship' (The Education Reform Act 1988, s. 6). The law governing collective school worship in maintained schools is currently regulated by s. 70 of the School Standards and Framework Act 1998 (SSFA), which provides that 'each pupil in attendance at a community, foundation or voluntary school shall in each day take part in an act of collective worship'. As a result of these 1988 and 1998 statutes, schools today have a certain amount of flexibility when it comes to complying with the law in this area. After all, the act of worship need neither be held at any particular time, nor provided simultaneously to the entire school, so it can, for example, be offered to a particular year or tutor class.

Given the aforementioned legal obligations, it might, at first glance, appear that collective worship is compulsory in England's state-funded schools. However, on closer inspection, it soon becomes clear that attendance at an act of school worship is subject a number of important qualifications. First, parents retain the right to withdraw their children from collective worship at all state-funded schools (including faith schools) and, in so doing, are not required to provide any reasons for making such a request (SSFA, s. 71). Secondly, sixth-form pupils are entitled to withdraw themselves from acts of collective worship without having first to secure parental approval (The Education and Inspections Act 2006, s. 55). And thirdly, as a general principle, teachers and staff in community schools may not be compelled to lead (or even attend) acts of collective worship, although for some teachers in religious schools this may be a matter of contractual obligation, in the sense that their appointment to post may originally have been conditional on their willingness to participate in such 'religious' activities.

As noted above, English law requires that community, foundation and voluntary schools must ensure that their pupils 'each day take part in an act of collective worship' (SSFA, s. 70). The term 'collective worship' is not defined in the relevant legislation, but additional guidance can instead be found in the Department for Education's Circular 1/94 (DfE, 1994). The Circular states that 'Worship ... should be taken to have its natural and ordinary meaning ... [and that it] must in some sense reflect something special or separate from ordinary school activities ... [being] concerned with reverence or veneration paid to a divine being or power' (DfE, 1994, para. 65). The weight that should be attached to this Circular is however questionable, not just because it lacks the legal status of a statute, and was drafted twenty years ago, but on account of the fact that groups such as the National Association of Standing Advisory Councils on Religious Education and the Association of Religious Education Inspectors, Advisers and Consultants say the government now allows schools to be 'flexible' and 'imaginative' in their interpretation of the Circular (Walker, 2012). That said, frequent reference will be made to the Circular in this chapter, not just because of the absence of any other 'official' guidance on the matter, but because, in its stipulations and terminology, it demonstrates some of the problems of interpretation that are present in the collective worship debate more generally. The contemporary relevance of the Circular may be uncertain, but what seems beyond dispute is that the rules governing the provision of collective worship depend largely on the nature of a particular school.

In community schools, where responsibility for the provision of collective worship lies with the head teacher and the school's governors, a majority of the acts of collective worship should, in any given school term, be 'wholly or mainly of a broadly Christian character' (SSFA, Sch. 20, para. 4(a)). The term 'broadly Christian' suggests that the act of collective worship must relate to the traditions of Christian belief, such as affording a special status to Jesus Christ, although it may also contain 'some non-Christian elements' or 'elements common to Christianity and one or more other religions' (DFE, para. 63). However, with the Circular providing that consideration should be given to the 'circumstances relating to the family backgrounds of the pupils' (DFE, para. 64), there are obviously occasions where the composition of the student body would make it inappropriate to conduct an act of collective worship that is 'broadly Christian' – for example, in a community school that is, say, overwhelmingly Muslim or Hindu. In such circumstances the school can apply to the Local Authority's Standing Advisory Council for Religious Education (SACRE) for an exemption from the 'broadly Christian' requirement for some or all of their pupils. This is known as a 'determination', and it enables schools to provide alternative acts of worship that are based on non-Christian faiths, although the right of parental withdrawal continues to operate (SSFA, Sch. 20). In this context it is generally assumed that if schools are granted 'determinations', which allow them to organize acts of collective worship that are reflective of the faith backgrounds of their pupils, parents will be then less likely to withdraw their children from such worship. SACREs frequently have agreed determinations of multifaith worship for whole schools rather than, say, sections or groups of pupils, but there is a paucity of material on such matters because the government has acknowledged that it does not collect data on SACRE determinations 'or specify criteria that SACREs should use in making decisions' (Truss, 2014).

Faith schools – such as Voluntary Aided, Voluntary Controlled and Foundation schools *with* a religious character – are also legally obliged to provide an act of collective worship for their students (SSFA, s. 70 and sch. 20(4) and (5)). Perhaps unsurprisingly, in such schools the act of worship is expected to reflect the religious character of the institution (e.g. collective worship in a Church of England school is based on the tenets of Anglicanism), whilst Academies with a religious designation are similarly required to provide collective worship in accordance with the terms of each school's funding agreement. Where a school (including an Academy) is designated as having a denominational religious character, the content of collective worship may be examined by inspectors appointed by the school's governing body (or the foundation governors in a foundation school), with inspections being held approximately every five years (The Education Act 2005, s. 48).

In Academies *without* a religious designation, the source of the legal obligation to provide collective worship is not primary legislation, but is rather each school's funding agreement with the Secretary of State for Education (The Academies Act 2010, ss. 1–2). These funding agreements are typically drafted to mirror the requirements for acts of collective worship in maintained schools, so pupils are obliged to take part in a daily act of collective worship that is based wholly or mainly of a broadly Christian character. Moreover, just as a maintained school can request an exemption from its local SACRE from having to offer broadly Christian worship given the religious backgrounds of it pupils, so too can Academies apply to the DfE for a determination to ensure that collective worship which is more reflective of their pupils' traditions and beliefs will be provided.

Foundation schools that are *not* of a religious character, like the schools above, are required to provide a daily act of collective worship for their pupils (SSFA, s. 70). This must be in line with the trust deeds of the school and in accordance with the policy of the governors, following consultation with the head teacher (ibid. Sch. 20). As is the case with other kinds of school, parents may remove their children from acts of collective worship and sixth-form students may also so withdraw themselves without parental consent.

Notwithstanding the fact that state-funded schools in England are under a legal obligation to respect the law relating to collective worship there have, especially in recent years, been frequent claims that the law relating to collective worship is routinely ignored. Successive governments have tended to avoid commenting on such matters, with one former minister even acknowledging that the Department for Education 'does not itself make an assessment of the level of compliance with the provisions of the Standards and Framework Act 1998 for a daily act of collective worship' (McCarthy-Fry, 2009). It is against this backdrop that this chapter now examines collective worship in England, with particular reference to the schools that often lie at the very heart of the debate surrounding the future of collective worship – community schools without a designated religious character.

Responsibilities for collective worship in community schools

The School Standards and Framework Act 1998 (ss. 70 and 71) describes where responsibility lies for ensuring compliance with statutory requirements and for the arrangement and oversight of collective worship in maintained schools. As Circular 1/94 spelled out, collective worship (like RE) is 'properly a matter for local responsibility' (DfE, 1994, para. 6). Local Standing Advisory Committees (SACREs), representing faith groups, teachers and the local authority, have a monitoring and advisory[1] role for collective worship, as well as being responsible for the determination procedure by which individual schools can apply to opt out of the statutory 'mainly of a broadly Christian character' stipulation for acts of collective worship (DfE, 1994, para. 68f). The burden of responsibility for securing pupil participation in daily acts of worship is given to the head teacher and governing body (ibid. paras 52, 53). At the same time the Circular suggests reasons for the monitoring of collective worship at a national level, when it refers to the government's desire 'to encourage improved standards and secure comparable opportunities for all pupils in non-denominational schools' (ibid. para. 6) and, in particular, governmental concern that 'insufficient attention has been paid explicitly to the spiritual, moral and cultural aspects of pupils' development' (ibid. para. 1). In 1992 Ofsted was given

---

[1]   For examples see the SACRE guidance for collective worship from Warwickshire and Essex SACREs (links given in references at the end of this chapter).

responsibility for inspecting social, moral, spiritual and cultural development (SMSC) in schools, as well as being charged with reporting on how well each school meets its requirements for collective worship.

Among those with responsibility for collective worship, the churches and organized religion more generally are virtually absent. This absence may often go unnoticed in England, but it contrasts sharply with the close involvement of the churches in religious affairs in the state schools of many other European countries (Willaime, 2007, 60). In England, the churches, for many years, provided a model for school worship in terms of the hymn–reading–homily-prayer format. They have continued to offer guidance on school worship and, in several schools, local clergy are still invited in by head teachers to lead some acts of collective worship. Nevertheless, it is not uncommon today for school worship to be conducted without any reference to religious organizations. Although the Church of England, other churches and other faiths are represented (alongside teacher and local authority representatives) in the local authority's Standing Advisory Councils for Religious Education, in reality their role in determining the content and organization of collective worship is limited.

The history of religious education is closely tied to that of collective worship, and although RE and collective worship are represented separately in legislation, in practice it is often hard to explain trends in collective worship without acknowledging the close relationship between them. Indeed, in some cases, the boundaries have become blurred. For example, collective worship is commonly regarded as providing an opportunity to teach about different faiths, while the RE lesson may be used as an occasion for spiritual reflection. Yet irrespective of whether this happens, RE contributes to the climate for religion (e.g. multicultural, pluralist, private, constructed, pragmatic, critical) within the school, and to young people's (and their teachers') understanding of the same.

The working out, in reality, of responsibility for collective worship, differs from law and 'official' guidance. In practice there is a wide diversity of interpretations, as well as widespread ignorance of their stipulations. Weakness in structures of authority and accountability has enabled a very high level of non-compliance over a long period of time, particularly in the secondary education sector. For example, in 2004 the Chief Inspector of Schools, David Bell, drew Parliament's attention to the fact (evidenced from SACRE reports) that 76 per cent of secondary schools were breaking the law by failing to provide daily acts of worship (Curtis, 2004). A 2011 survey by Comres for the BBC found that out of 500 parents, 64 per cent reported that their children did not attend school worship (Comres, 2011). In recent years it seems there has been a lack of will on Ofsted's part to enforce statutory requirements in relation to collective worship. Ofsted's *Update 42* (2003) stated that a failure to provide a daily act of worship was a significant breach of statute, and should mean that the governance of a school would be judged 'unsatisfactory'. However, after complaints from schools, Ofsted, in *Update 43* (2004), reduced its requirement for statutory governance to evidence that the governing body had 'done all it reasonably could to ensure compliance'. Ofsted reports reveal not only a failure to encourage compliance but also a general lack of interest in collective worship. Where it does appear in the reports, it often does so as just one of several aspects of school life deemed to contribute to pupils' spiritual and moral development, but it very often fails to appear at all. Barbara Wintersgill's paper for Devon SACRE on 2012 Ofsted reports showed that out of forty school inspections, only eight commented on collective worship (albeit wrongly termed as 'assembly'), and that these comments were idiosyncratic, reflecting confusion about the purposes of collective worship (Wintersgill, 2012). SACREs rely on Ofsted reports to promote and monitor collective worship in their local schools, but the lack of information from this source, as well as a clear method of assessment, make it difficult for them, effectively, to carry out their responsibilities. The Qualifications and Curriculum Authority analysis of the 2000 SACRE reports found these bodies to be hampered by the 'uneven' Ofsted coverage, and the 2004 analysis recorded a feeling of impotence among SACREs with regard to monitoring collective worship (QCA, 2004).

With little accountability at national or local authority level those responsible for school management (head teachers and senior teachers sometimes in consultation with governors) have had largely unfettered control of collective worship arrangements. In other words, they have been free to make key decisions about how often, when and with which groupings collective worship should take place. This includes, for example, whether it be a whole school gathering held in the school hall or a short 'thought for the day' offered in tutor group settings. Indeed, it may even cover whether students should be offered worship in separate faith groups, as happens in a small minority of schools, although this arrangement is contrary to the ethos of the legislation and Circular 1/94 (DfE, 1994, para. 7). School policies and guidelines may be produced that give a particular slant to collective worship, and may vary in different directions from school to school. Thus, for example, the strong emphasis of one head teacher may be spiritual, guided by the hope that providing chances for reflection 'might encourage prayerfulness and lead [the children] into having a spiritual dimension' (Ipgrave, 2012, 37), while for another school it could be moral, 'providing a time to expose and reflect upon common values, including moral values' (Cheetham, 2004, 105).

The school management may also decide what recognition is given to God and religion within collective worship. For example, a guideline in one secondary school declared that 'the "thought-for-the-day" will be based upon general moral values and have no foundation or affiliation with any religion', a position that ignores the 'broadly Christian' requirement of the 1988 Education Reform Act (which is now found in the School Standards and Framework Act 1998), and avoids the 'reverence or veneration to a divine being or power' of Circular 1/94 (ibid. para. 105). Furthermore, research has found that two primary schools with significant Muslim populations may adopt contrasting approaches: at one, pupils are encouraged to address prayers to Allah and God ('Dear Allah, dear God, thank you for our families, thank you for our friends and help us achieve our targets this week'), while at the other a 'thought-for-the-day' is followed by quiet reflection and no prayers to God are voiced (Ipgrave *et al.*, 2010, 80).

Richard Cheetham's penetrating analysis of practice in twelve English schools found that this freedom over collective worship is not just institutional (at the school level) but is also personal (at the teacher level) (Cheetham, 2004). Considerable control over what happens in collective worship lies with the teachers who deliver the assemblies (a group largely ignored in Circular 1/94), and its content and style is shaped by these teachers' personal beliefs and educational philosophy (ibid. 81). Cheetham reports how teachers draw their inspiration from a multitude of sources (religious and non-religious) seasoned by their own thoughts, interests and experiences to construct a wide variety of collective worship formats (ibid. 82). The dominance of the teachers' perspective over any corporate religious tradition is evident in the use of material from holy scriptures and elsewhere to illustrate a theme already decided upon, and their preparedness to (in their own words) 'twist' this material to suit their purposes (ibid. 82–83). The freedom exercised by the teachers is evident in the statement of one secondary teacher, 'I have this philosophy that you can pick any theme out of the air and you can build something around it' (ibid. 82). The power that head teachers and teachers have over the style, focus, religious references and material of collective worship can be seen as a working out of Benjamin Disraeli's prediction, at the time of the 1870 Education Act, that the school teacher will become the 'new sacerdotal caste' (Disraeli, 1870).

The lack of accountability and freedom given to schools and teachers in collective worship has already been noted. However, claims of religious extremism in a few Birmingham schools in 2014, and public reaction to the same, have generated heated debate about the place of religion in education, and may well lead to greater scrutiny (Cannizzaro and Gholami, 2016). The so-called 'Trojan Horse' affair has created a climate of fear of extremist infiltration of Muslim majority community schools (Miah, 2017). What these events in Birmingham reveal is a lack of clarity about school governance and accountability, particularly where questions of religion are concerned. In press reports collective worship is commonly portrayed as being a concern, irrespective of whether it is governing bodies wanting assemblies to be more Islamic to reflect the school's population, head teachers using 'inappropriate material in assembly', or disagreements about recognizing the celebrations of other faiths (Clarke, 2014). Peter Clarke's report to Parliament (commissioned by the Secretary of State for Education) on the Trojan Horse controversy included the recommendation that:

> Ofsted should consider whether the existing inspection framework and associated guidance is capable of detecting indicators of extremism and ensuring that the character of a school is not changed substantively without following the proper process. This includes ensuring that the appropriate boundaries for a non-faith school are not breached. (Ibid. 99)

A wave of no notice inspections of schools followed Clarke's report with a particular view to investigating these issues.

Collective worship: Current issues of concern

In recent years there have been a number of reports on religion in schools in England that have included critiques of collective worship, focussing on the quality of its provision and on its appropriateness in modern British society. Thus, for example, in 2015 a report by the former Secretary of State for Education Charles Clarke and the sociologist Linda Woodhead, (*A New Settlement: Religion and Belief in Schools*) drew attention to the lack of consistency and compliance when it spoke of the '"nod and wink" culture around the nature of the act of collective worship in school', and included abolition of the current requirement for collective worship in its recommendations for reform (Clarke and Woodhead, 2015, 7). In the same year the Commission on Religion and Belief in Public Life, convened by the Woolf Institute, published its report, *Living with Difference* (2015), in which it expressed unease about the preferential status given to Christianity in the current arrangements. The Commission concluded that '[t]he arguments in favour of retaining compulsory Christian worship in UK schools are no longer … convincing.' Instead it gave its support to 'the joint initiative in Scotland between the Humanist Society Scotland and the Church of Scotland to work together for an inclusive "time for reflection"' – an approach which the Commission endorsed as offering 'an example for the rest of the UK', and being capable of building 'on the good practice of holding inclusive assemblies that already exists in many schools but remains technically unlawful' (CORAB, 2015, 35, para. 4.17). An article produced in response by Nigel Genders, the Church of England's Chief Education Officer, argued that 'if the [collective worship] requirement is removed, schools will be tempted to lose this vital element altogether and children will not have the opportunity for a different part of the day to pause and reflect'. His concern with the recommendation for 'inclusive reflection' is that attempts to provide this will fall at the impossibility of defining and of officially monitoring this 'inclusivity'. In support of his argument for collective worship, Genders linked a regular pattern of collective worship with schools' ability to respond to crises as they occur in the modern world. Making a link with a well-publicized terrorist outrage at that time he argued that '[m]ost schools' responses to the Paris attacks will have been in the context of collective worship' (Genders, 2015). More recently, in July 2016, a House of Commons briefing paper on religious education, though referencing the critiques in recent reports, maintained the status quo for collective worship and cited and referenced Circular 1/94 as the still current position on the subject (Long, 20–21). However, a very different approach was evident in March 2017, when the Liberal Democrats passed a motion at their party conference calling for the repeal of 'the existing legal requirement for all state-funded schools to hold acts of collective worship' (Accord, 2017).

It is significant that these discussions of collective worship are in the context of religion and belief in public life and the changing nature of British society. The question of collective worship is (to borrow Cheetham's phrase) 'the tip of the iceberg' (Cheetham, 2004, 12), for behind debates about its appropriateness and viability in modern Britain lie a range of issues and concerns about religion in the public sphere, about responses to plurality, about the remit of state-funded education, and about the forces that separate or bind our society. A frequent argument against the current arrangements for collective worship is the fact that the variety of religious and non-religious positions represented within a typical school community, makes a nonsense of the concept of *collective* worship. For example, the British Humanist Association argues that, in a context of plurality, collective worship discriminates in favour of religion and that the 'broadly Christian' stipulation discriminates in favour of Christianity in particular (BHA, *Collective Worship*). Viewed from the British Humanist perspective, however, schools' non-compliance in collective worship means that fewer non-Christians are being discriminated against in practice. Even with the narrowest interpretation of the religious elements of collective worship legislation and guidance, the disjuncture between statutory requirements and practice means that many schools have very little engagement with this activity that critics describe as discriminatory, and many others offer exactly the inclusive, non-religious assemblies that the British Humanist Association (BHA) and others advocate. Few, however, see non-compliance as a satisfactory answer to the issues collective worship raises. The BHA argues that 'determinations', which allow schools to amend their collective worship, that are granted on the basis of a school's religious demography, fail to cater for the needs of minorities within the school population, and do not give consideration to the non-religious (BHA, *Collective Worship*). Nor does the right to withdraw constitute a sufficient answer to the problem, for this leads to the exclusion of the individual child who is withdrawn from what may be a significant element in the life of the school community (BHA, *Collective Worship*).

Although the increasing diversity of society is often viewed as a modern challenge, acknowledgement of religious plurality was in fact embedded in collective worship from the start. It accorded with the non-confessional approach to religion in schools, established by the 1870 Education Act and embodied in the famous 'Cowper-Temple' clause (repeated in Circular 1/94, para. 32) stating that 'no religious catechism or religious formulary which is distinctive of any particular denomination' should be taught in the new board schools, which are the predecessors of today's community schools and are distinct from church schools.

In the 1944 Education Act (s. 25), and in subsequent legislation and guidance, the word 'collective' was used instead of 'corporate' to distinguish school worship from worship among a group that held beliefs in common. Thus, it was recognized that not all pupils would share the (Christian) belief being presented. The idea that all attend the same act of worship, but are free to respond differently to it, is present in Circular 1/94 and can be found in more recent guidance (Essex SACRE, 2013, 7). The Circular states that collective worship should 'provide the opportunity for pupils to worship God' (DfE, 1994, para. 50) but not dictate their response. In other words, collective worship should be 'capable of eliciting a response from pupils, even though on a particular occasion some of the pupils may not feel able actively to identify with the act of worship' (ibid. para. 59). Warwickshire SACRE, in its collective worship guidance for schools, reiterates this principle of freedom of response when it differentiates between pupils with faith who might consider the worship stimulus in the light of their religious beliefs and 'pray or worship internally', and those without who 'make a personal internalized response to the same stimulus' (Warwickshire County Council). Its approach allows for ambiguity, for it does not seek to know the religious position or faith of the pupil. Its assumption (disputed by the BHA paper cited above) is that it is possible, and desirable, to share the communal experience of worship without sharing the belief. This feeds into the important question that will be returned to later in this section about what constitutes community, collective experience and disposition, or collective beliefs and values. The theological questions surrounding these distinctions are explored further in Chapter 10 by Ipgrave and Panjwani.

There is an evident link in this view of collective worship to civic religion. The 1970 Durham Report, sponsored by the Church of England, described it as more akin to civic services which 'do not presume the individual commitment of all those who attend them; they have a symbolic significance, representing society's disposition towards religion' (National Society, 1970, 137–138). We may conclude that society's disposition towards religion has changed since the 1970s, but religion is still very often part of the ritual on state occasions, at public celebrations, commemorations and responses to times of crisis and sorrow at national, local and family level. At the national and local level the attendance of representatives from a variety of faiths has become established practice in many such civic services, though they are usually hosted by the Church. Collective worship can thus be seen both as a replication of this use of ceremony, as well as a ritual to strengthen the community (in this case the school), and as a preparation for such activity in wider society. A more recent combined churches position paper makes this point, noting that: 'it is important that children and young people become familiar with the language and silence common to many forms of public worship' (CJEP, 2006).[2] The eclectic mix which constitutes collective worship in many schools means that it may be hard to discern traditional patterns of public worship in them. Nevertheless, debates about collective worship fit within wider discussions about the

2   Churches Together in England is an ecumenical body with forty-four member churches from a wide variety of denominations.

role of religious ritual and ceremony in English public life more generally. Accordingly, questions about the value of collective worship need to be considered alongside contemporary controversies about faith in public life – controversies that range from the inclusion of prayers in town council business meetings to the presence of Church of England bishops in the House of Lords.

The classification of school worship as 'collective' and 'civic' puts an emphasis on the children's response to the external stimulus of collective worship. Demands that collective worship should 'be appropriate for' all pupils attending a school (DfE, 1994, para. 54), and that it should be 'appropriate to the family backgrounds of the pupils' (ibid. para. 64), lay emphasis on the response of providers and deliverers of collective worship to the personal religious (or non-religious) position of the child. Recognition of pupils' cultural (including religious) identity was a platform of the multicultural education of the 1980s and 1990s. Multiculturalism promoted collective experience and disposition above collective beliefs and values, encouraging a non-evaluative appreciation and active enjoyment of each other's traditions. This was the case in collective worship, as well as in other areas of the curriculum and school life, and in this context the catchphrase was 'celebrating diversity'. Multicultural education's foundational document, the Swann Report, advocated an education that would generate 'greater understanding and appreciation of the diversity of value systems and life styles now present in our society' (Swann, 1985, 5). The procedures for determination and withdrawal however tell another story, implying a need for the safeguarding of the child's religious (or non-religious) identity and integrity from other religious influences. While the expectation has always been that the vast majority of pupils from their varied religious backgrounds will be able to participate in collective worship, the longstanding withdrawal option has been utilized both by the members of religious communities who wish to protect their children from outside influence and 'erroneous' doctrines, as well as others who have a secular objection to collective worship, although such instances are rare. In relation to the latter, groups such as the British Humanist Association and the National Secular Society campaign on behalf of those non-religious parents who are concerned about their children's exposure to religious stories and teaching in collective worship (BHA, *Collective Worship*; NSS, *Collective Worship*). The issue raised here is the perennial question of how far one can engage with another's religion or belief without compromising one's own cherished views or opinions.

The tolerance of ambiguity contained in the coining of the term 'collective' (rather than 'corporate') worship is increasingly being challenged by the desire for a clearer definition, and an associated hardening of language to include words like, 'integrity', 'sincerity', 'honesty', 'hypocrisy', 'indoctrination' and 'imposition'. The ambiguity allowed in the use of the term 'worship' is likewise being challenged; or what constitutes the active participation required of the children (DfE, 1994, paras 50, 59, 65). In its 1995 paper on *Collective Worship in Schools*, the Churches' Joint Education Policy Committee engaged with these concerns pronouncing that the leader of collective worship 'must neither infringe the integrity of particular believers nor appear to require hypocritical responses from pupils and staff – sincerity and integrity are essential in the practice of worship' (CJEPC, 1995, 5.5). The BHA also uses the language of 'hypocrisy' for the existing 'broadly Christian' requirement for collective worship. Its current position is that 'no-one should feel that their own beliefs are being contradicted and that they are wrong for not sharing the religious views being presented by the teacher' (BHA). This statement is made in a context where pupils (partly influenced by humanist ideals of rational argumentation) are increasingly being encouraged to define, articulate and justify their own beliefs in school RE, as well as evaluate those of others (REC, 2013, 11). After all, Circular 1/94 speaks of the duty of religious education and collective worship 'to promote among pupils a clear set of personal values and beliefs' (DfE, 1994, para. 9).

At the same time, there has been an increased wariness about religion, which is partly a consequence of 9/11 and subsequent terrorist attacks (YouGov, 2013). This is evidenced by the fact that, in relation to RE, the 2007 Ofsted report declared 'we should dispense with the notion that we should encourage pupils to think uncritically of religion as a "good thing"' (Ofsted, 2007, 40). It is also partly due to the inclusion of secular worldviews in RE which have introduced a more critical and propositional, less communal and experiential interpretation of religion (Hand, 2004). By the same token, collective worship can no longer rely on the support of a positive disposition towards religion in school or in society. Even the Bishop of Oxford, the Chair of the Church of England's Board of Education, has recently suggested that while it once represented the mood of the nation, compulsory participation in collective worship could actually put people off religion; instead he advocates a time in the school day for 'spiritual reflection' (Pritchard, 2014). The challenge for those with an interest in religion is whether or not a strategic retreat from the public sphere is the best response to a less favourable climate.

Linked to this is the question of whether a retreat of religion, for fear of compromising the integrity of those of different belief systems, might result in an education that is increasingly segregated along religious lines with the more religiously inclined (where they are able) preferring schools for their children where there is some religious reference and practice over purely secular community schools. To some degree collective worship can possibly act as a bridge between the voluntary and community sectors of English education, providing opportunities for children of faith in both sectors to worship God (DfE, 1994, para. 50) and to venerate a divine being or power (ibid. para. 57) should they wish to do so. It could be argued that children without faith are given some idea, through the collective worship experience, of what it might be like for their fellow human beings to have faith and, in this regard, Essex SACRE's guidance speaks of 'learning about the nature or worship' (Essex SACRE, 2013, 12). Were these opportunities removed it is possible that those who view faith as an important element of one's identity would be more likely to seek places in schools of a religious character. After all, the number of Muslim families who already send their children to Catholic schools in preference to what many view as increasingly secular community schools supports this view, as can be seen from the fact that 10 per cent of non-Catholic children in Catholic schools are from Muslim families (Catholic Education Service, 2016). Accordingly, in the absence of collective worship in England, a gap of comprehension could possibly widen between what are increasingly being labelled 'faith' and 'non-faith' schools, and the internal religious diversity of the community school might be diminished.

Underlying so many of the issues that congregate around the collective worship debate is the distinction between 'corporate' and 'collective', made with reference to school worship in the 1944 Education Act, and the related question of what it is that constitutes community. The concept of *collective* worship relates to a community united by experience and activity, though beliefs and values may differ. It is challenged by a more corporate understanding of community where the beliefs and values presented by the institution are shared by all of its members. The Swann Report may have promoted a disposition of appreciation towards those with different values from oneself, but Circular 1/94 puts a strong emphasis on the 'shared values' of the school (ibid. paras 2, 3, 50). There has recently been a revival of interest in finding common values to unite communities, both at an institutional and also at a national level. As with beliefs (and so too with moral values) there are difficulties in finding agreement within our diverse society on emotive and highly controversial issues such as gender roles and homosexuality – issues that were, for example, prominent in the 'Trojan Horse' affair. In an effort to identify a set of commonly agreed norms, the UK Government has, in recent years, been keen to foster the notion of 'British values'. However, there is little agreement as to what constitutes 'British' values and (to the extent they can be quantified) their impact on collective worship in England's schools remains to be seen.

Conclusion

The position of collective worship in English community schools is today characterized by confusion and inconsistency. This is partly due to the practical difficulties of implementing the relevant legislation, prompting a widespread non-compliance among secondary schools in particular. In addition, it reflects the inherent tensions in the legislation and guidance between the promotion of a collective worship that is both in the main 'broadly Christian' whilst also being inclusive; between a collective worship that is appropriate to all yet has procedures for determination and withdrawal on the grounds that it may not be; between an approach which provides opportunities for students in collective worship to explore new realms of understanding, whilst also being responsive to their existing outlooks and religious identities; and finally, a collective worship model that celebrates diversity but also seeks coherence. Much of the confusion originates in differences of interpretation of terms such as 'collective' and 'worship' – a confusion that becomes more obvious when tolerance of ambiguity is replaced by a desire for definition. These issues are internal to the phenomenon of collective worship, but the debates have much wider implications and any decisions about its future need to take into consideration the big societal questions. These include: how do we meet and respect the religious requirements of communities and individuals in a context of plurality? What role does religion have in civic life and the collective life of the nation? And what are the essential points of commonalty on which the cohesion of our society depends? Definitive answers to these questions have yet to be found. There seems little doubt that the controversy which is associated with the specific issue of collective worship in England is symptomatic of a much wider problem of agreeing on the appropriate place of religion in that nation's public life.

References

Accord (2017). Retrieved May 14, 2017, from <http://accordcoalition.org. uk/2017/03/31/lib-dems-call-for-end-to-religious-discrimination-in-faith-school-admissions/>.

Bates, S. (2006). Devout Poles show Britain how to keep the faith, *The Guardian*, December 23. Retrieved May 14, 2017, from <https://www.theguardian.com/uk/2006/dec/23/religion.anglicanism>.

Bingham, J. (2014). Compulsory Christian school assembly should be scrapped – Church of England education chief. *The Daily Telegraph*, July 7. Retrieved May 14, 2017, from <http://www.telegraph.co.uk/education/educationnews/10951894/Compulsory-Christian-school-assembly-should-be-scrapped-Church-of-England-education-chief.html>.

BHA. *Collective Worship.* Retrieved May 3, 2017, from <https://humanism.org.uk/campaigns/schools-and-education/collective-worship/>.

Brierley, P. (2014). *UK Church Statistics, Number 2, 2010 to 2020.* Tonbridge: ADBC Publishers.

Catholic Education Service (2016). *The 169th Annual Report.* Retrieved October 20, 2017, from <https://www.catholiceducation.org.uk/images/AnnualZReportZ2016ZFinal_2.pdf>.

Cannizzaro, S., & Gholami, R. (2016). The devil is not in the detail: representational absence and stereotyping in the 'Trojan Horse' news story. *Race Ethnicity and Education, 21* (1), 15–29.

Cheetham, R. (2004). *Collective Worship: Issues and Opportunities.* London: SPCK.

Churches Joint Education Policy Committee (1995). *Collective Worship in Schools.* London: CJEP.

Churches Joint Education Policy Committee (2006). *The Churches and Collective Worship in Schools: a position paper.* London: CJEP. Retrieved May 5, 2017, from <www.churchofengland.org/media/1393062/churchesandcollectiveworshippositionpaper.pdf>.

Clarke, C., & Woodhead, L. (2015). *A New Settlement: Religion and Belief in School.* Retrieved May 5, 2017, from <http://faithdebates.org.uk/wp-content/uploads/2015/06/A-New-Settlement-for-Religion-and-Belief-in-schools.pdf>.

Clarke, P. (2014). *Report into allegations concerning Birmingham schools arising from the 'Trojan Horse' letter.* House of Commons. Retrieved August 24, 2014, from <https://www.gov.uk/government/uploads/system/uploads/attachment_data/file/340526/HC_576_accessible_-.pdf>.

Comres (2011). *Poll Digest – Social – BBC Collective Worship Poll.* Retrieved August 8, 2014, from <http://www.comres.co.uk/poll/523/bbc-collective-worship-poll.htm>.

CORAB (2015). *Living with Difference: Community, Diversity and the Common Good.* Cambridge: The Woolf Institute.

Curtis, P. (2004). End Daily Collective Worship in Schools says Ofsted Head. *The Guardian,* June 11. Retrieved October 20, 2017, from <http://www.theguardian.com/education/2004/jun/11/schools.uk>.

DfE (1994). *Religious Education and Collective Worship Circular 1/94.* London: Department for Education.

Disraeli, B. (1870). *Hansard,* 3rd series, ccii, 289.

Essex SACRE (2013). *Guidance on Collective Worship in Schools.* Essex County Council.

Genders, N. (2015). *Church Schools Make a Difference.* Retrieved May 5, 2017, from <http://cofecomms.tumblr.com/post/134520796697/church-schools-make-a-difference>.

Hand, M. (2004). Religious Education. In J. White (Ed.), *Rethinking the School Curriculum: Values, aims and purposes*. London: Routledge Falmer.

Ipgrave, J. (2012). Conversations between the Religious and Secular in English Schools. In *Religious Education, 107*(1), 30–48.

Ipgrave, J., Miller, J., & Hopkins, P. (2010). Responses of Three Muslim Majority Primary Schools in England to the Islamic Faith of their Pupils. In *Journal of International Migration and Integration, 11*(1), 73–89.

Lewis, I. (2002). HC Hansard, February 7, Column 1056W.

Long, R. (2016). *Religious Education in Schools (England)*. House of Commons Library Briefing Paper Number 07167, July 7, 2016.

McCarthy-Fry, S. (2009). HC Hansard, March 5, Column 1834W.

Miah, S. (2017). *Muslims, Schooling and Security: Trojan Horse, Prevent and Racial Politics*. Cham, Switzerland: Springer.

Nash, Lord. (2013). November 18, HL Hansard, c160W.

National Secular Society. *Collective Worship*. Retrieved June 6, 2017, from <http://www.secularism.org.uk/collective-worship.html>.

National Society (1970). *The Fourth R: The Durham Report on Religious Education*. London: SPCK.

Office for National Statistics, from <http://www.ons.gov.uk/ons/rel/census/2011-census/key-statistics-for-local-authorities-in-england-and-wales/rpt-religion.html>.

Ofsted (2003). *Update 43*, online newsletter. Retrieved May 3, 2005, from <http://www.ofsted.gov.uk>.

Ofsted (2007). *Making Sense of Religion*. London: HMI.

Pritchard, J. (2014). *Bishop John on Collective Worship*, Retrieved May 3, 2017, from <https://www.oxford.anglican.org/bishop-john-collective-worship/>.

QCA (2004). *Religious Education and Collective Worship: An Analysis of the 2004 SACRE Reports*. London: Qualifications and Curriculum Authority.

REC (2013). *A Curriculum Framework for Religious Education in England*. The Religious Education Council of England and Wales.

Swann Report (1985). *Education for All*. London: HMSO.

Truss, E. (2014). HC Hansard, March 24, Column 85W.

Walker, P. (2012). Schools can sidestep Christian worship rule, say religious education groups. *The Guardian*, November 9. Retrieved May 14, 2017, from <https://www.theguardian.com/education/2012/nov/09/schools-sidestep-christian-worship-rule>.

Warwickshire County Council. SACRE – Collective Worship. Retrieved August 24, 2014, from <http://www.warwickshire.gov.uk/sacrecollectiveworship>.

Willaime, J.-P. (2007). Different Models for Religion and Education in Europe. In R. Jackson, S. Miedema, W. Weisse, & J.-P. Willaime (Eds.), *Religion and*

Education in Europe: Developments, Contexts and Debates (pp. 57–66). Münster: Waxmann.

Wintersgill, B. (2012). *The Inspection Of School Provision For Pupils' Spiritual, Moral, Social And Cultural Development (SMSC) – A report to Devon SACRE.* Retrieved August 24, 2014, from <http://www.devon.gov.uk/sacre-ofsted-references-to-smsc-2012.pdf>.

YouGov (2013). *British Youth reject Religion.* Retrieved May 14, 2017, from <https://yougov.co.uk/news/2013/06/24/british-youth-reject-religion/>.

AIDEEN HUNTER AND NORMAN RICHARDSON

2 Collective Worship in Northern Ireland's Schools

ABSTRACT

Northern Ireland is a unique country within the United Kingdom, having a complex and highly contested cultural and civic identity. Religion plays a specific defining role within this context. While it has been argued that the Northern Ireland conflict was not religious (Barnes, 2005), religion as a social identity marker nevertheless plays a defining role in where people live, work, socialize and are educated. Religious education and collective worship in schools have become the elephant in the room, under-researched and under-addressed in the post-conflict narrative. Religious education has not been a major focus of community relations work or in shared education initiatives. Both historically and contemporarily in many schools there has been little distinction between religious instruction/education and participation in prayers and liturgical practices. Current legislative orders are inherited directives from the Education Act (Northern Ireland) 1947 and the Education and Libraries (Northern Ireland) Order 1986 which stipulate daily Christian collective worship that is not particular to any religious denomination. Collective worship is largely influenced by the ethos of a school and who is delivering it; there is no inspection or guidance on this process. This lack of direction results in considerable diversity across the sectors in the overall standard and quality of school collective worship.

Introduction

In setting out this overview of law and policy in relation to collective worship within the Northern Ireland education system, it has seemed important to present it in the broad context of the place of religion in education in that corner of the UK. In part this is because religion has played and continues to play a particularly significant role in shaping the nature of schooling, not least in its separateness, in Northern Ireland. It is also because in many people's minds collective worship and curricular religious education are inextricably linked, as indeed they are in legislation. The lack of any recent direct research and analysis on collective worship itself in this region also makes it advisable to present a broad overview which will hopefully set collective worship appropriately into its Northern Ireland context, as a preliminary to UK-wide comparative examination.

Belief demographics

Since its establishment as a separate legal entity within the UK in 1921, Northern Ireland has often been described in terms of its cultural-religious character and throughout its relatively short history these aspects of its identity have been very much in the public eye. The establishment of a region with a deliberately inbuilt majority and minority, and the responses of its various communities to this situation, has impacted on cultural, political, religious and educational experience in the region, and continues to do so to this day. Northern Ireland's well-known conflicts throughout the twentieth century, and especially the period of 'The Troubles' from the late 1960s to the mid-1990s, have significantly impacted all areas of public policy and governance. Religion, of itself and in relation to many aspects of public life, continues to play a role in people's sense of identity and their relationships to each other. While the 'tribal' divisions of Northern Ireland are also based on a range of social, economic, political and cultural factors, religious identity and religious belief continue to be significant, not least in the regular use of 'Protestant' and 'Catholic' as shorthand descriptors of community background.

According to the 2011 Census, 40.7 per cent of the population continue to describe themselves as Catholic, while 41.5 per cent describe themselves as Protestant. Other religions number just under 1 per cent, 'no religion' is at just over 10 per cent and just over 7 per cent did not state their religion. In terms of active church membership, however, statistics from other sources (Boal *et al.*, 1997; Richardson, 1998; Nic Ghiolla Phádraig, 2009) reveal that while church attendance remains relatively high in Northern Ireland by comparison with other UK regions and much of Europe, all the larger long-established denominations have experienced a decline in their numbers. At the same time, some of the smaller evangelical Protestant denominations have expanded, probably at the expense of the 'more traditional' churches. Although numbers claiming to belong to religions other than Christianity remain relatively small in comparison with many other parts of the UK, religious and ethnic diversity has very clearly increased in the years since the paramilitary ceasefires came into force.

The Northern Ireland school system

Schooling and education remain particularly impacted by religious differences and related factors. For both historical and contemporary reasons, the numerically larger churches have continued to exercise significant control and influence on the shape of education and on the demographics of school populations. While the Protestant denominations mostly transferred their schools to state control in the 1930s – thus the term 'controlled' schools – this was part of a deal in which they retained certain rights and privileges in relation to management, the inspection of RE and the right to withdraw pupils for denominational instruction (though this latter right is very seldom exercised now). Catholic schools remained under Church management, although since the early 1990s Catholic maintained schools have received full state-funding. Voluntary schools – mostly selective grammar schools and, in a few cases, their associated prep schools – are also very largely state-funded, though in a slightly different way. The province's integrated schools, emerging since the early 1980s, were initially self-funded but now receive full state funding. Northern Ireland has virtually no independent schools (the few exceptions mainly including a small number of Protestant 'independent evangelical Christian schools' plus a Steiner School and a tiny number of others). No state funding is requested or received by these schools. There are no 'faith schools' catering for religious groups outside the various Christian traditions.

Normal practice is for families from a Protestant background to send their children to controlled schools and for those from a Catholic background to send their children to Catholic schools. This practice continues to hold consistently for just over 90 per cent of the school-going population. Since the early 1980s integrated schools have set out to provide an alternative shared model of schooling for pupils from Catholic, Protestant and 'other' backgrounds on an intentional (though not always fully achieved) 40:40:20 ratio. There are now just over sixty such schools, about one third of them post-primary and two-thirds primary, but despite attempts to expand them (and apparent significant public support for the concept) numbers have settled at around 7 per cent of the school-going population. A small sector of Irish medium schools, mainly primary, has also been established and currently caters for about 4,600 pupils. A small proportion of pupils, for a mixture of historical and geographical reasons, could be described as 'cross-over' – Catholic pupils who attend controlled or (Protestant) grammar schools and a somewhat smaller cohort of Protestant pupils who attend Catholic schools.

Overall educational administration in Northern Ireland previously resided in five regional Education and Library Boards (ELBs), which were merged in 2015 into the Northern Ireland Education Authority (EA). The Catholic Maintained sector is managed by the Council for Catholic Maintained Schools (CCMS). Integrated schools are supported by the NI Council for Integrated Education (NICIE) and Irish Medium Schools by *Comhairle na Gaelscolaíochta* (CnaG). In 2016 a new body, the Controlled Schools' Support Council (CSSC), was established to provide services and represent the Controlled schools sector. The NI power-sharing Executive has given some official encouragement to arrangements for 'Shared Education' – short of full integration but making use of shared facilities, teachers and classes – and some well-funded experiments have indicated initially positive outcomes.

Various educational cross-community programmes designed to improve contact and community relations have been implemented over several decades in Northern Ireland, with variable impact on social cohesion (Richardson & Gallagher, 2011). Collective worship and religious education, however, have often appeared to be largely untouched by such activities and shared education programmes have also seldom ventured into the realms of religion. Religion has also sometimes proved divisive in integrated schools and it is not unusual to hear calls for 'taking religion out of education', as, for example, in the website of the Humanist Association of Northern Ireland (Humani, n.d.). For some teachers and others, religion is clearly a controversial 'no-go' area that is perceived to open up undesirable 'cans of worms'. Perhaps it is also partly due to the fact that the churches in Northern Ireland have had a considerable social and political voice (not least during the period of the Troubles) and that politicians and civil servants have preferred to keep all aspects of school religion at an arm's length, rather like a wasp's nest.

The legal framework

Arrangements for religious teaching and worship in schools go back to the nineteenth century, when various attempts were made by governments to regulate how religion was to be dealt with as the state gradually took on responsibility for providing public education. (During this period there was often little distinction in schools between religious instruction and participation in prayers and other liturgical practices.) An early attempt to educate children together from the 1830s onwards, with religion kept to the edges of the day, largely failed as Protestant and Catholic Churches aspired to different approaches and gradually established separate arrangements. A further attempt at a unified system in the early days following partition (the 'Londonderry Education Act' of 1923) also floundered due to the intense opposition of the churches who, in somewhat different ways, feared the imposition of a 'secular' system. The changes resulting from this took legal shape in the Education Act (Northern Ireland) 1930, establishing clearly the present separate systems and providing the framework for religion in county (later 'controlled') schools based on 'non-denominational Bible teaching' and on Catholic catechesis/faith formation in Catholic schools.

The post-war Education (Northern Ireland) Act 1947 – to a considerable degree prompted and shaped by the Education Act 1944 in England and Wales – perpetuated these arrangements, with some additional refinements. While acts of worship had been common practice in schools over many years, there had never been any legal requirement placed on schools until this point. In Paragraph 54 of its 1944 White Paper on Educational Reconstruction, however, the Northern Ireland Government had indicated its intentions on the grounds of what might currently be termed 'community cohesion':

> The government are in no doubt as to the widespread desire of the people of Northern Ireland that, in the future, greater prominence should be given to religious education in the schools, and they now propose to emphasize its paramount importance by including in the forthcoming Bill a definite requirement that religious instruction shall be given in every primary and secondary school and that the school day shall begin with collective worship on the part of the pupils. Exceptions will of course be allowed for individual children whose parents desire that they should be excused, and where the school premises render a single act of worship impracticable, suitable modifications will be permitted. (cited in Hyland *et al.*, 83)

In the Act it was thus specified that:

> ... the school day in every county school and voluntary school shall begin with collective worship on the part of all pupils in attendance at the school, and the arrangements made therefor shall provide for a single act of worship attended by all such pupils unless in the opinion of the local education authority, or, in the case of a voluntary school, the managers thereof, the school premises are such as to make it impracticable to assemble them for that purpose'. (Education Act (Northern Ireland) 1947, para. 21(1))

The Act further specifies that 'the collective worship required ... shall not, in any county school, be distinctive of any particular religious denomination'. Parental conscience clauses were included in relation to collective worship and the teaching of religious instruction (RI), but much to the irritation of the churches, teachers were also granted the right to request not to take part in worship or teach RI with the assurance that:

> A teacher in a county school who is excused from conducting or attending collective worship or from giving undenominational religious instruction shall not receive any less emolument or be deprived of, or disqualified for, any promotion or other advantage by reason of the fact that he does not conduct or attend collective worship or give undenominational religious instruction. (Ibid. para. 24(4))

While no stipulation appears to have been issued at any point in relation to a statutory or recommended length of time to collective worship, the Statutory Rules and Orders which followed the 1947 Act specified that:

> The time at which collective worship is held, and the time or times during which religious instruction is given, in any county school or voluntary school, shall be clearly shown on the time-table of the school. (Statutory Rules and Orders of Northern Ireland, 1948, 3(1))

The Statutory Rules also require that the timing of religious instruction in schools should be such as to cause 'as little inconvenience as possible' to pupils who have been excused from attending such instruction (ibid. 3(2)), and by implication this also appears to apply to the timing of collective worship.

Subsequent legislation (notably the Education and Libraries Order (Northern Ireland) 1986) has largely continued to reconfirm these arrangements, with the exception that in the Education Reform (Northern Ireland) Order (ERO) 1989 the term 'religious instruction' was changed to 'religious education'. The order also extended these provisions to Special Schools. From the 1980s onwards legislation also had to include and define the situation for the new integrated schools, and arrangements for the form of worship and RE were left to the discretion of governors in such schools. Specifically section 21 of the 1986 Order (which, in these areas, has not been modified by later legislation) specified that:

> (1) Subject to the provisions of this Article, religious education shall be given in every grant-aided school other than nursery school and the school day in every such school shall also include collective worship whether in one or more than one assembly on the part of the pupils in attendance at the school.
> (2) In a controlled school, other than a controlled integrated school, the collective worship required by paragraph (1) in any such school shall not be distinctive of any particular religious denomination.

(3) In
  (a) A controlled integrated school;
  (b) A grant-maintained integrated school; and
  (c) A voluntary school,
Collective worship required by paragraph (1) shall be under the control of the Board
of Governors of the school.
(4) ... Collective worship required by paragraph (1) shall be so arranged that -
  (a) The school shall be open to pupils of all religious denominations for education other than religious education;
  (b) No pupil shall be excluded directly or indirectly from the other advantages
  which the school affords.
                    (Education and Libraries (Northern Ireland) Order 1986, s.21)

All legislation in relation to collective worship and RE in Northern Ireland
has been premised on the assumption that it would inevitably be Christian,
and even though controlled schools must teach non-denominationally, this
has almost certainly been done largely in a confessional Christian context.
Gallagher and Lundy (2005, 175) have observed that '[t]he legislation does
not specify that worship must be Christian although such a requirement
might be inferred from the general context of the legislation and in particular the preceding references to religious education'. This is well illustrated by the fact that the major 1989 Education Reform Order legislation
(which established the introduction of the Northern Ireland Curriculum,
roughly following the pattern of the National Curriculum in England and
Wales) conferred the responsibility for designing a syllabus for RE on
'persons having an interest in Religious Education', but from the outset
the Department of Education assumed that this meant the four numerically largest Christian denominations (the Catholic Church in Ireland, the
Presbyterian Church in Ireland, the Church of Ireland [Anglican] and the
Methodist Church in Ireland). In the early 1990s an initial *Core Syllabus for
Religious Education* was drawn up which was overtly and unambiguously
Christian in content and tone, with no references to other religious faiths.
A revision of the Core Syllabus, eventually published in 2006 for use from
2007 (and currently in operation), made a small concession for the inclu-
sion of World Religions at Key Stage 3 only, but the churches continued
to emphasize their commitment to maintaining 'the essential Christian
character of Religious Education' (Churches Working Party, 2003, 4). The

Core Syllabus, however, is defined only as a 'core', and it does not preclude the teaching of other material (though the implication is that this should not be at the expense of the core content).

There have been no changes to legislation relating to collective worship for some decades, but the context of the RE Core Syllabus and the generally expressed views of the churches suggest that this is still intended to be exclusively Christian in nature.

Implementation of the legal requirements

Despite the ultimate responsibility of the four largest Christian Churches for the design, content and review of school worship and the RE Core Syllabus, the quality, nature and delivery of these areas in schools serving the Protestant community is relatively ungoverned, while the Catholic school authorities continue to take these responsibilities very seriously. The Protestant Churches continue to hold the position of inspectorate for this aspect of the curriculum in controlled schools but this has now largely fallen out of practice. While Protestant clergy regularly sit on boards of governors, occasionally visit RE classes and sometimes contribute to assemblies (mainly in the primary sector), their involvement in schools is generally limited to such activities. The Department of Education's Education and Training Inspectorate (ETI) have very limited jurisdiction over religious education and none at all over collective worship. Their remit extends only so far as the examination of school timetables to verify that RE and school worship are scheduled.

Since 1989 the ETI can be requested to inspect RE by a school's Board of Governors but this is a very rare occurrence. In effect, other than in the Catholic sector, daily collective worship and RE are not subject to any quality control and suffer from inadequate resourcing and virtually non-existent in-service support. Yet collective worship and RE remain as statutory requirements that all schools must provide at all stages of schooling and which all pupils must attend (unless withdrawn by their parents).

Evidence on the workings of conscience clauses (e.g. Mawhinney *et al.*, 2010) suggests that awareness among teachers and parents is very variable and often very vague. The Department of Education, when pressed, will provide figures about the withdrawal of pupils from RE, the numbers for which seem quite small. Related evidence seems to suggest that there are fewer requests for withdrawal from school worship than for RE. In relation to the clauses permitting teachers not to participate, it seems that few teachers choose to exercise this prerogative as it could be seen to disadvantage them in securing a teaching position – even though this would be illegal practice.

Collective (daily) worship usually takes the form of morning assembly although timing is not a stipulated requirement of current legislation and it can take place at any point throughout the day. Nevertheless, the 1947 Act specification that 'the school day in every county school and voluntary school *shall begin with collective worship* on the part of all pupils in attendance at the school' (current authors' emphasis) still appears to be regarded as the norm by many schools. In recent years, however, year group and key stage[1] assemblies have become more common with a whole school gathering difficult to facilitate in many school buildings, especially in post-primary and larger primary schools. While some schools do continue to observe the letter of the law by providing a brief daily act of worship, there seems little doubt that many schools, especially outside the faith-based sector, have reduced this to a weekly or twice-weekly provision (as evidenced by a poll carried out in England for the BBC in which 64 per cent of parents indicated that their children do not attend daily school worship (ComRes, 2011)). Involvement in leading acts of school worship appears to vary between formal leadership by head teachers or senior teachers, sometimes with participation by other teachers and pupils as readers, to rota arrangements for groups or classes to present a topic more informally. Input by school choirs and instrumental ensembles also appears to be

---

1   Key stages, used in the education systems in the UK regions except Scotland, are fixed stages into which the curriculum is divided, each having a prescribed course of study. Each key stage normally covers two or three year groups.

common although pupil participation in hymn singing appears to have declined significantly, especially at post-primary level.

The nature and format of these assemblies is normally in the hands of the head teacher and teaching staff, at least nominally guided by the Board of Governors who have legal responsibility that the legislation is observed. In terms of content the 1947 Act was explicit that worship in controlled schools should be non-denominational; schools in the maintained sector may have denominational content as appropriate; and more recent legislation indicates that integrated schools may well also include some denominational material subject to the agreement of governors. In the Catholic sector Diocesan Advisers have some responsibility for the quality of this daily worship and supporting teachers in its implementation, but this does not take the form of formal inspection. The general situation is now that collective worship in all kinds of schools (just like the approach to curricular RE) is largely influenced and determined by the school ethos and the individual who is delivering it and, to a much lesser extent, the composition of the Board of Governors. It is therefore inevitable that without guidance, consistency or critical review, there will remain considerable diversity across the sectors in the overall standards and quality of school collective worship.

Apart from very occasional references to school worship in reports from denominational Synods, Assemblies or Conferences, very little public comment appears to have been made in relation to the situation of collective worship in Northern Ireland. In its brief publication entitled *Design for Religious Education*, published in 1978 by the NI Religious Education Council (NIREC – a body appointed in 1966 by the Boards of Education of the three Protestant transferring denominations but now long since defunct), the final very short chapter looked at *The School Assembly*. It noted some current criticisms of collective worship, especially when enforced 'by the authority of an act of Parliament' and when it 'expresses commitment to one particular religious tradition', also noting observations about pupil reluctance and their sense of it being irrelevant. This publication also noted some arguments in favour of school worship and made brief recommendations, including that 'a reappraisal should be made of the purpose, structure and content of school assemblies' (NIREC, 1978, 53).

Almost certainly as a response to this the NIREC established a small working party in the early 1980s to examine 'the school assembly, with particular reference to its religious significance' in controlled and Protestant voluntary schools. One of the most useful tasks of this group was to commission a review of current thinking on school worship by Rev. Dr John Greer of the University of Ulster – probably the most important researcher and writer on RE and related matters in Ireland during the twentieth century (though disgracefully neglected or ignored by some members of the educational and religious 'establishment' at the time). Greer's 1980 paper (which was provided to members of the working party but not formally published) provides a résumé of research and academic writing about school worship over the period since the English 1944 Education Act, citing significant writers such as Harold Loukes, John Hull and others. But Greer noted that 'Little has been written about school assembly in Northern Ireland, so there the task of summarising the literature is a simple one' (Greer, 1980, 5). Decades later, that situation has barely changed. Quoting from his own 1968 study of sixth-form pupils in controlled or Protestant voluntary schools Greer indicated that adult (i.e. parental) attitudes towards school worship were much more positive and supportive than those of the pupils themselves. He also noted a Church of Ireland 1972 general synod report which discussed some of the issues but concluded that school assembly remained important in giving a sense of 'devotional practice' in religion, and that it might 'provide pupils with possibly their own regular opportunity of participating in the adoration of God through Christ'. Noting also the NIREC 1978 publication, Greer concluded with a number of open questions relating to the justification of compulsory school worship, its contemporary purpose and its regularity (daily or otherwise). He also suggested that the views of teachers, parents and pupils should be sought.

The Working Party initiated a detailed study of the attitudes of teachers (including head teachers) as well as of the experience of first-year student teachers in Stranmillis College and a report on the findings was issued in 1982. The conclusions from the research include details of practical issues (timing, whole school or groups, availability of resources, leadership of assemblies, involvement of clergy, teachers and pupils, etc.) and some observations on areas suggested by respondents for possible improvements (NIREC, 1982). There was a general favouring of more pupil involvement and some divisions over the desirability of daily observance or less frequent assemblies. A difference of views was also evident in relation to whether or not attendance for pupils and teachers should be obligatory or optional. When asked to rank the possible purposes of school assembly, a majority of all respondents favoured 'to give opportunity to worship God together'; also highly ranked by many was 'to present the Christian message' as well as 'to provide a focus for the corporate life of the school' (ibid.).

The authors of the report did not make any significant observations or proposals in relation to the desirability or otherwise of collective worship, largely restricting themselves to issues about the practicalities and organization. There is no evidence of the report being widely disseminated or of it having any impact on practice and it appears that no other research on school collective worship has been carried out since this was completed over thirty years ago. It seems clear that up-to-date empirical research is required for this area, in order to inform policy and implementation across Northern Ireland.

Areas of concern

While issues around the role of religion generally in Northern Irish education (and, though to a lesser extent, curricular RE) have been the focus of research and debate, it seems that in recent decades collective worship has somehow slipped by unnoticed and has not been examined in any systematic way. A letter to the Department of Education from the authors of this chapter to enquire about up-to-date official advice provided to schools on collective worship in Northern Ireland gained a very brief response and a referral to a document produced by an RE Adviser in one of the (former) Education and Library Boards with just a short section that sets out the formal legal requirements. Perhaps this paucity of information reflects the reluctance of statutory educational bodies to express a view on matters which have traditionally been the preserve of the churches. Undoubtedly there is in many people's minds a perception of a close association between school worship and RE as two sides of the same coin. But while the debate about RE can be presented as a professional and educational matter which does not necessarily need to rely on religious involvement or conviction for its educational credibility, it is much harder to make such a case for worship in school. The very term implies assumptions about the religious purpose of the activity and, indeed, about the intentions of those taking part, unrealistic as this may be.

The apparent official wariness and reluctance to comment on collective worship seems to leave it in a cold and uncomfortable place. Even those schools in Northern Ireland that have conformed most closely to the legal requirements have been left in the unfortunate position of good practice being uncelebrated and not disseminated and, perhaps more worryingly, of poor practice being overlooked and unaccountable. Guidance and leadership have been almost completely lacking in relation to the content, direction and progression of collective worship, raising serious questions about the quality and relevance of this experience for children and young people in schools.

Notwithstanding the observations above, a somewhat more positive tone was evident when the Department of Education for Northern Ireland was invited to respond to the Collective Worship project report in the Autumn of 2015. While noting that the department had 'not identified any pressing desire to amend existing legislation regarding collective worship', it was indicated that, subject to ministerial agreement, it would be 'willing to consider establishing a working group to examine these issues' (Fleming, 2015). Emphasizing the legal right of parents and teachers in relation to withdrawal from collective worship and RE, and that schools should make these provisions clear, the department acknowledged that it might be helpful to initiate 'a review of the information currently provided to see if greater clarity can be provided' (ibid.). The department also indicated that they would be prepared to consider a proposal in the report for the establishment of a monitoring mechanism to ensure that human rights standards are upheld (ibid.).

The need for further discussion and empirical work

Much has changed in Northern Ireland and globally since the early 1980s. Any attempt to revisit the issues tackled by the NIREC report will need to take into account changes in the educational context and the realities of an increasingly plural society. The ethical issues about compulsory worship must be included in any future survey of educational and public attitudes. Some small progress has been made in relation to broadening the scope, content and approaches to RE, but there is still a long way to go. The very nature of an activity defined as 'collective worship', and the inevitable assumptions about its purposes, make it much harder to present an inclusive and plural rationale. A conservative and cautious approach to issues around religion in schools still appears to prevail in Northern Ireland, but at the same time there are increasing calls for a more secular approach. Many view religion as the major obstacle to a more integrated system. These issues require empirical research and public discussion. Alongside any gathering of data from questionnaires and/or focus groups, a local conference or seminar for interested parties in Northern Ireland may well be a useful way of gleaning contemporary attitudes to school worship, leading to appropriate review and reform.

References

Barnes, L. P. (2005). Was the Northern Ireland Conflict Religious? *Journal of Contemporary Religion. 20*(1), 55–69. Taylor & Francis.

Boal, F. W., Keane, M., & Livingstone, D. N. (1997). *Them and Us? Attitudinal Variations among Churchgoers in Belfast.* Belfast: Queen's University Institute of Irish Studies.

Churches Working Party (2003). *Proposals for a Revised Core Syllabus in RE in grant-aided schools in Northern Ireland.* Belfast: The Churches' Religious Education Core Syllabus Review Working Party.

ComRes (2011). *BBC Collective Worship Poll.* Cobham: Communicate Research Ltd. Retrieved June 19, 2017, from <http://www.comresglobal.com/polls/bbc-collective-worship-poll/>.

Education Act (Northern Ireland) 1947. *Education in England* website. Retrieved June 11, 2017, from <http://www.educationengland.org.uk/documents/acts/1947-education-act-ni.html>.

Fleming, S. (2015). Presentation made on behalf of the Department of Education at the 'Collective Worship in Schools' conference, University of Leicester, November 13, 2015. (Copy with authors).

Gallagher, T., & Lundy, L. (2006). Religion, Education and the law in Northern Ireland. In J. L. Martinez López-Muñiz, J. De Groof, & G. Lauwers (Eds.), *Religious Education in Public Schools: Study of Comparative Law.* (pp. 171–175). Netherlands: Springer.

Greer, J. E. (1980). *The School Assembly.* Unpublished background paper presented to the NI RE Council working party on School Assembly.

Humani (n.d.). *Religion in Schools: Shared Education/Integrated Education.* Undated and unattributed article on the website of the Humanist Association of Northern Ireland. Retrieved May 22, 2015, from <http://www.humanistni.org/dynamic_content.php?id=125>.

Hyland, A., Milne, K., Byrne, G., & Dallatt, J. (1995). *Irish Educational Documents: Volume 3.* Dublin: Church of Ireland College of Education.

Mawhinney, A., Niens, U., Richardson, N., & Chiba, Y. (2010). *Opting Out of Religious Education: The views of young people from minority belief backgrounds.* Belfast: Queen's University.

Nic Ghiolla Phádraig, M. (2009). *Religion in Ireland: No longer an exception – Ark Research Update.* Londonderry: University of Ulster at Magee; Belfast: Queen's University.

NIREC (1978). *Design for Religious Education.* Belfast: Northern Ireland Religious Education Council/Christian Journals Ltd.

NIREC (1982). *Report of the Working Party on School Assembly.* Unpublished report. Belfast: Northern Ireland Religious Education Council.

Richardson, N. (1998). Introduction – Mixed Blessings: A View of Christian Practice in Northern Ireland. In Richardson, N. (Ed.), *A Tapestry of Beliefs: Christian Traditions in Northern Ireland* (pp. 9–24). Belfast: Blackstaff Press.

Richardson, N., & Gallagher, T. (2011). *Education for Diversity and Mutual Understanding – the Experience of Northern Ireland.* Oxford: Peter Lang.

CLAIRE CASSIDY AND FRANKIE MCCARTHY

3 Religious Observance in Scotland

ABSTRACT

While the countries that constitute the UK tend to refer to and practise collective worship, in Scotland, with its distinct education system, religious observance is undertaken in schools. The chapter discusses key policy and practice shifts in the area of religious observance and highlights a range of legislation relevant to religious observance. Consideration is given to the proposed move towards time for reflection as a more inclusive approach to the spiritual development of Scotland's children. The role of parents, statutory bodies and religious groups is explored, highlighting that children are marginalized in discussions about their religious observance. The chapter concludes by raising concerns relating to the parental right to withdraw their children from religious observance, situating this within the context of children's rights.

Introduction

The practice of religious observance is a requirement in Scottish schools. Historically, this requirement would have been fulfilled through acts of Christian worship. However, in recent years, recognition has increasingly been given to the diversity of faith and non-faith communities in Scotland. Policy guidance now recognizes that 'time for reflection' may more appropriately describe the process of personal search through which a child can discover his or her own moral and ethical values.

This chapter will explore the requirement of religious observance in Scotland by situating it within the current demographic, legal and educational context. It will identify key issues with the current practice of religious observance and call for further research to provide an evidence base on which recommendations for improvement can be based.

Context

Belief demographics of population

Questions on religion were introduced in the Scottish Census for the first time in 2001. In common with the approach in Northern Ireland, two questions were asked, namely 'what religion, religious denomination or body do you belong to?' and 'what religion, religious denomination or body were you brought up in?' In 2011, a sole question was asked in line with the approach taken in England and Wales, namely 'what religion, religious denomination or body do you belong to?' In both years, the question was voluntary, but the response rate was high, with 93 per cent of people responding in 2001 and 94 per cent in 2011 (Office for National Statistics, 2011).

The data suggest a period of significant change within the Scottish population. Of special note is the rise in the percentage of the population reporting no religion, an increase from 27.8 per cent in 2001 to 36.7 per cent in 2011. Affiliation with Christian denominations has fallen from 65.2 per cent to 53.8 per cent, although within that, membership of the Roman Catholic Church has remained static at 15.9 per cent, perhaps as a result of immigration from traditionally Roman Catholic countries in Eastern Europe. Affiliation with non-Christian religions remains small in percentage terms, however each minority religious affiliation (Buddhist, Hindu, Muslim, Sikh and Other religion) except Jewish has increased its share of the population since 2001. The 1.4 per cent of the population reporting affiliation with minority religions in 2001 had risen to 2.5 per cent in 2011.

A somewhat different picture is painted by the 2016 Scottish Social Attitudes Survey, in which 1,197 adults were asked about their religious affiliation. In it, 52 per cent of respondents did not consider themselves part of a particular religion, a considerably higher number than those reporting no religion in the most recent census (Montagu, 2017).

The Scottish school system

In 1998 the UK Government passed the Scotland Act which devolved powers to a new Scottish Parliament. Within the remit of those powers falls education. In fact, the education system in Scotland has always been different to that of its UK neighbours. According to Scottish Government figures, the vast majority of children in Scotland, approximately 95.5 per cent, attend state schools, with only about 4.1 per cent being educated in private (independent) schools and the remainder receiving their educational provision outside either context (Scottish Government, 2016). All children in Scotland are entitled to free nursery provision from the age of 3; that is up to 600 hours of pre-school education from August 2014. At the age of 5, children progress to primary school for seven years (primary one through to primary seven) and then move to secondary school around age 12. Children are permitted to leave school at 16, though they may remain in school until they reach 18.

All teachers in Scottish state schools are required to be registered with the General Teaching Council for Scotland (GTCS) and must meet Professional Standards as student teachers (Standards for Provisional Registration), as class teachers (Standards for Full Registration) (GTCS, 2012a) and as head teachers (Standards for Leadership and Management) (GTCS, 2012b). The Standard for Career-Long Professional Learning (GTCS, 2012c) was published in 2012 and makes teachers responsible for their own professional learning as they progress through their careers with monitored Professional Update being implemented from August 2014.[1] While teachers in private schools do not need to be registered with the GTCS, or even hold a teaching qualification, the majority of schools have embraced the notion of Professional Update for their teachers.

In a similar vein, Scottish state schools follow a curriculum, *Curriculum for Excellence* (CfE) (Scottish Executive, 2004a; Education Scotland, 2017), while the independent sector need not. CfE was introduced to all Scottish schools in 2010. The curriculum is for children aged between 3 and 18 years

---

1   General Teaching Council for Scotland, *Professional Update Microsite*, <http://www.gtcs.org.uk/professional-update/professional-update.aspx>, accessed May 2017

old. Following a National Debate on Education in 2002, five National Priorities were established: Achievement and Attainment; Framework for Learning; Inclusion and Equality; Values and Citizenship; and Learning for Life. These came together to provide the foundation upon which CfE would be built. They aimed to generate coherence and progression in children's educational experiences with a view of making 'our young people aware of the values on which Scottish society is based' (Scottish Executive, 2004a, 2011). These values would be evidenced through the children working towards what are known as the 'four capacities', where they will become responsible citizens, confident individuals, effective contributors and successful learners (Cassidy, 2013). The focus of the curriculum is on experiential learning with collaborative group work and cross curricular learning taking centre stage. Until children reach their third year of secondary schooling they should receive a broad, general education and afterwards specialize in subjects for which they will be assessed by national assessments.

Religious observance: Law, policy and practice

The legal framework

Human rights

The right to an education is contained within Article 2 of the First Protocol to the European Convention on Human Rights, incorporated into Scots law by way of the Human Rights Act 1998 and the Scotland Act 1998, section 57. This right is held by parents in respect of their children, and was ratified by the UK subject to the reservation that it would be adhered to only insofar as is compatible with the provision of efficient instruction and training, and the avoidance of unreasonable expenditure. Articles 28 and 29 of the United Nations Convention on the Rights of the Child (UNCRC) set out detailed provision as to the nature and goals of the education to which children are entitled. The UNCRC has not been directly incorporated into Scots law. However, children do hold a domestic right to education by virtue of the Standards in Scotland's Schools etc. Act 2000, section 1.

Freedom of thought, conscience and religion is protected for both parents and children under Article 9 of the ECHR, and freedom from discrimination is enshrined for both in Article 14. These protections are augmented domestically by the Equality Act 2010. The Act establishes nine protected characteristics (s. 4), including religion or belief (s. 10), and sets out prohibited conduct in relation to those characteristics (ss. 13–27) in various specific contexts, including education (ss. 84–99). Part 6 of the Act sets out what will be unlawful conduct in the context of schools (ss. 84–89). Amongst other things, a school must not discriminate against or victimize a pupil in the way it provides education for the pupil (s. 85(2)(a) and 85(5)(a)), by not providing education for the pupil (s. 85(2)(c) and 85(5)(c)) or by subjecting the pupil to any other detriment (s. 85(2)(f) and 85(5)(f)). Schools must also not harass a pupil (s. 85(3)(a)). A key caveat is that none of the provisions apply to anything done in relation to the content of the curriculum (s. 89(2)). The prohibition on discrimination in relation to the provision of public services (s. 29) is also excluded from application acts of worship or other religious observance organized by or on behalf of a school (Sch. 3, Part 2, 11).

Denominational schools are subject to special exemptions in relation to discrimination on the grounds of religion or belief (Sch. 11, paras 5 and 6). The prohibition on religious discrimination in relation to admissions and provision of education, benefits, facilities and services does not apply, allowing denominational schools to conduct themselves in accordance with the tenets of their faith.

Education law in Scotland

The law of education in Scotland has been bound up with religion since its inception (Scotland, 1969; Paterson, 2003; Stevenson, 2012). The earliest schools were connected to Christian churches or monastic institutions. The independence of the Scottish education system from England and Wales was secured by the Treaty of Union 1707, which included continuing national adherence to the Protestant faith as one of its central tenets. The

Education (Scotland) Act 1872, which laid the foundations for the modern education system by making schools the responsibility of a government department, allowed schools the liberty to continue with the practice of religious observance and instruction which had been customary up until that point (Scott, 2016, 7–10).

In the modern day, the principal obligations in respect of school education in Scotland are set out in the Education (Scotland) Act 1980, as substantially amended. The local authority, acting as an Education Authority, has an obligation to secure adequate and efficient provision of school education within its area (s. 1(1)). In performance of this obligation, pupils are to be educated in accordance with the wishes of their parents insofar 'as is compatible with the provision of suitable instruction and training' and the 'avoidance of unreasonable public expenditure' (s. 28). The Education Authority has a duty to provide schools (s. 17(1)), and it is lawful for the Authority to provide denominational schools where representations are made by members of the denomination to the effect that such a school is needed to accommodate their children s. 17(2)). The rules as to management of denominational schools are set out in section 21 of the 1980 Act, providing amongst other things that the religious beliefs and character of a teacher must be approved by representatives of the denomination.

Scottish state schools are non-denominational by default but, as noted above, the Education Authority is empowered to provide denominational schools where there is sufficient demand from members of the denomination in question. Information given on the Education pages of the Scottish Government website at the time of writing confirms that there are 370 state-funded denominational schools, 366 of which are Roman Catholic, three Episcopalian and one that is Jewish.

In all state-funded schools, both the practice of religious observance and instruction in religion should be made available (s. 8(1)), unless a resolution to discontinue this has been passed by the Education Authority and approved by electors in that local authority area (s. 8(2)). No explicit guidance is provided within the legislation as to what observance or instruction should entail. However, reference is made to the 'custom of public schools in Scotland'. Customarily, Scottish schools were Presbyterian in character, which offers implicit guidance as to what the legislation was intended to encompass (Scott, 2016). Scott notes that framing the provision in terms of custom, without an express connection to a particular religious tradition, has allowed for changes in practice to develop gradually without the need for legislative amendment. This may go some way to explaining why the Scottish legislation seems to have elicited little of the vigorous debate in Parliament which marked the passage of equivalent provisions for other areas of the UK.

Implementation of the statutory requirements

It is worth noting, as a precursor to the discussion which follows, that the majority of parents in a 2014 survey by the Scottish Parent Teacher Council (SPTC, 2014) strongly believed their child should have an opportunity during school hours for spiritual or moral reflection, in addition to believing that it was important for children to learn about different faiths (SPTC, 2014b). Although these principles seem to be broadly accepted, their practical implementation gives rise to some dispute.

Instruction in religion

Two terms are employed within the Scottish education system in relation to religious instruction. Religious and moral education (RME) is taught in non-denominational schools, while denominational schools teach religious education (RE). CfE content is framed around what are called Experiences and Outcomes. For RME, the Es and Os (as they are known) are presented under the following headings: beliefs relating to Christianity; Christian values and issues; Christian practices and traditions; beliefs of other world religions; other world religions' values and issues; other world religion practices and traditions; and the development of beliefs and values. For RE in Catholic schools, under the banner of Catholic Christianity, the headings are: the mystery of God; in the image of God; revealed truth of God; son of God; signs of God; word of God; hours of God; and reign of God. In addition, pupils will learn about the beliefs of other world religions; the values and issues as considered by other world religions and the practices and traditions of other world religions (Scottish Executive,

2004a). There are no expressly stated Es and Os for the small number of denominational schools which are not Catholic. Other religious schools are free to deliver religious instruction in their own faith and are also permitted to create their own RME syllabus. This, though, is not available through Education Scotland.

For RE and RME it is clear that children should learn both from and about religious and non-religious traditions (Nixon, 2013). This is a shift, asserts Nixon, from the Education Act of 1872 where what was then known as 'religious instruction' was used to ensure Protestantism could be safeguarded. Either way, the Scottish Government's advice to head teachers notes that children have an 'entitlement to have this [RE/RME] taught in a meaningful and progressive way' (Scottish Government, 2011a, para. 5).

Religious Observance

In Scotland, the notion of collective worship does not exist. Instead, the term religious observance is favoured. The two terms are philosophically distinct. Observance and worship were historically linked in the context of Scottish education as an obvious consequence of the religious roots of Scottish schools discussed above. This connection continued into the relatively recent past. In policy guidance issued in 1991, the Scottish Office Education Department (SOED) identified religious observance as referring to 'occasions set aside for different forms of worship' (SOED, 1991), with the curriculum at that time explaining that religious observance was reserved for 'something akin to worship' (SOED, 1992).

The position changed at the start of this century. In 2001, concerns were expressed by Her Majesty's Inspectorate of Education (HMIe) to the effect that non-denominational secondary schools were failing to provide appropriate opportunity for religious observance as required by the legislation. In response, Scottish ministers established a panel of representatives from education, religious organizations and parents' groups to review the provision for religious observance in all schools, to consider the current guidance on arrangements for religious observance and to make recommendations for the future (Scottish Executive, 2004b).

In its 2004 report, the Religious Observance Review Group set out a revised definition of religious observance as comprising 'community acts which aim to promote the spiritual development of all members of the school's community and express and celebrate the shared values of the school community' (Scottish Executive, 2004b, 12). In contrast to the historical position, the report makes a clear distinction between religious observance and acts of worship that are organized:

> Worship is a free response of an individual and community to what is considered worthy of worship. This response involves three elements: belief in the reality of the focus of worship, the desire to offer worship to the focus of worship and the commitment to life stances related to the focus of worship. (Scottish Executive, 2004b, 15)

The report states explicitly that when an organized act of worship is planned, it assumes that those attending the event share the elements noted above. On the other hand, this is not the case for religious observance. For denominational schools the notion of religious observance should be contiguous with the dominant faith of that community. In the non-denominational setting, with its arguably more diverse population, opportunities for religious observance via acts of worship should revolve around events within the informal curriculum such as those organized by various groups or chaplains, for example. religious observance is not simply the domain of the R(M)E portion of the curriculum but should be evident through the rest of children's school experience with a focus on supporting children in the development of their spirituality. At the same time, the Review Group recognize the importance of carefully planning for acts of worship with the norm being that schools would hold at least six such opportunities per year. (In the most recent March 2017 guidance, it is stated that opportunities for religious observance should be provided 'several times in a school year' and that 'parents and carers should be involved in making decisions about frequency' (Scottish Government, 2017, 3)). This would be over and above the school's traditional celebrations and aside from assemblies where children learn about news and events within the school community. The overall goal of the inclusion of religious observance in Scottish schools is that of supporting every child to 'reach his or her potential' – whatever that may mean – through personal search that allows the child to develop his or her values.

Following the report from the Religious Observance Review Group, in 2005 the Scottish Government issued new policy guidance on religious observance based on the Group's recommendations (Scottish Executive, 2005; Scottish Government, 2011b). Although schools are encouraged to draw upon the 'rich resources' of Scotland's Christian heritage, the guidance notes that (Scottish Government, 2011b, 10)

> Many school communities contain pupils and staff from faiths other than Christianity or with no faith commitment, and *this must be taken fully into account in supporting spiritual development*. It is of central importance that all pupils and staff can participate with integrity in forms of Religious Observance without compromise to their personal faith. (Emphasis included in original)

This paragraph does not appear in the most recent guidance from March 2017, though the sentiment is retained in the assertion that 'Religious Observance is a "whole school activity"' in which everyone within the school community might participate (Scottish Government, 2017, 1). The guidance recognizes that a term such as 'time for reflection' might be a more appropriate description of the activities carried out in fulfilment of the requirement of religious observance in some schools (Scottish Government, 2017, 6). The guidance recognizes that Scotland has a 'longstanding Christian tradition', but that it welcomes diversity and urges schools to recognize that increasing diversity by being 'sensitive' in meeting the 'spiritual needs and beliefs' of all children (Scottish Government, 2017, 6).

It is worth mentioning at this point that the Es and Os for religious and moral education make no reference to children participating in religious worship within the school setting. There is, though, specific mention that children will be 'discovering how Christian communities demonstrate their beliefs through prayer, worship and special ceremonies (RME 1-03a)', that they will be 'increasing my knowledge and understanding of different forms of Christian worship and artefacts and can explain their importance for Christians (RME 2-03a)', that they should be 'discovering how followers of world religions demonstrate their beliefs through prayer/meditation, worship and special ceremonies (RME 1-06a)' and that they are 'increasing my knowledge and understanding of different forms of worship and artefacts within world religions and can explain their importance for followers of world religions (RME 2-06a)' (Scottish Executive, 2004). The suggestion is that pupils will learn about and understand the lives of others, but there is no allusion to the children engaging in any communal religious activity themselves. It seems odd that advice is given from Education Scotland and the Scottish Government regarding religious observance when there is little in the more specific RME Experiences and Outcomes that children should have around worship and nothing at all about religious observance in the school setting.

In the Experiences and Outcomes for Catholic schools, however, the notion of religious observance is, as one might expect, more explicit. While the documentation allows for exploring the traditions and practices of religions other than Catholicism, children will also be able to say, from Primary one (age 5) upwards, that 'I have, through liturgical experiences, reflected on an ability to respond to symbols and take part in rituals in order to worship God (RERC 1-17a / RERC 2-17a)' (Scottish Executive, 2004a). Additionally, the Principles and Practices around RE in Catholic schools state that 'Young people in schools will also benefit from the experience of faith which they gain through acts of prayer, worship, celebration and loving service to others'. Children are also to be encouraged to question in order to reflect on their lives. Teachers are encouraged to ensure that time is given for reflection around moral issues and that they should 'incorporate experiences of prayer, liturgy and reflection and other opportunities for spiritual growth, enabling children and young people to experience the life of faith' (Scottish Executive, 2004a).

Inspection and accountability requirements

Education Scotland

It is worth making clear that within the Scottish education system, schools do not have a Board of Governors. The body with most influence in Scottish schools is Education Scotland. In 2011, the curriculum body in Scotland, known as Learning and Teaching Scotland (LTS), merged with HMIe to create Education Scotland. Education Scotland is an Executive Agency and, therefore, part of the Scottish Government. One arm of Education Scotland has responsibility for supporting teachers in their day-to-day roles in relation to curriculum and practice, while the other has school inspections as its remit.[2] The core principle espoused by Education Scotland is that 'all learners and users [are] at the heart of inspection and review' (HMIe, 2011: 6). The ethos of inspections in Scotland is focused on self-assessment by the relevant institution and Education Scotland inspectors should perform the role of supporting and challenging staff within establishments. The inspection considers all aspects of the school, including the formal and informal curricula and ethos. There is no specific remit to consider aspects of R(M)E or RO aside from how they might review any other aspect of the school.

The General Teaching Council for Scotland

The main body with ultimate responsibility for teachers is the General Teaching Council for Scotland (GTCS). Established in 1965, it is the oldest such organization in the world and achieved full self-regulating status independent of Government and HMIe in 2012. As noted earlier in the chapter, the GTCS sets the Professional Standards that teachers are expected to meet to teach in Scottish schools. While these Professional Standards make mention of the expectations of teachers in terms of the ways in which they conduct themselves, the values they hold and the knowledge and skills they should have, there is no mention of their duties in relation to religious observance. Teachers are expected to implement, to the best of their abilities, the Scottish curriculum. It is in breaches of their duties that the GTCS would become involved. It is, therefore, the class teachers and the head teacher within a school that have overall responsibility for ensuring that all children have full access to the curriculum. At present, this means that all children should, unless their parents choose otherwise, be involved in religious observance.

---

2   There is some debate around the group with responsibility for school inspections also being the same organization with responsibility for curricular development.

Religious bodies

In Scotland, religious bodies or organizations do not have responsibility for inspecting or reviewing practice in relation to religious observance. This does not mean that views are not expressed or that such bodies are not consulted in curriculum design and development, but teachers and head teachers are not held to account by these groups or organizations. One factor that is key in Catholic schools is that all teachers, particularly those in primary schools, must be in possession of a Catholic teaching qualification. In addition to this, in order to gain approval to teach in a Catholic school, the Scottish Catholic Education Service makes clear that teachers must produce a statement that demonstrates 'how his/her personal "religious belief and character" enables him/her to undertake the duties of the particular teaching post within the context of a Catholic school, with its particular mission, values and ethos' (Scottish Catholic Education Service, 2017). This is required in conjunction with a reference, preferably from the teacher's parish priest. In December 2016, however, the Equality and Human Rights Commission (2016) urged the Scottish Government to bring legislation relating to religious restrictions on teacher recruitment in line with the EU Employment Equality Directive.

Pupils and parents

Both pupils and their parents play a role in bringing schools to account in respect of their statutory obligations. Following the Scottish Schools (Parental Involvement) Act 2006, all schools must provide opportunities for parents to be involved in the life of the school (s 1), and they should provide equal opportunities for this involvement that do not discriminate against parents on account of a range of factors, including their 'beliefs or opinions, such as religious beliefs'. Each state school in Scotland must have a Parent Forum (s 5), constituted by the parents of all children attending that school (s. 5(1)), who have the right and the obligation to air their views on the operation of the school. The Forum may establish a smaller body, known as a Parent Council, to represent them (s. 5(2) and 6). The legislation does not specify how frequently either the Forum or the Parent Council should meet and practice varies, often depending on the issues to be considered. In some cases, Parent Council meetings are held monthly with Forum meetings occurring much less frequently. Indeed, the timing and frequency of meetings appear to be in the hands of each school's senior management team. At meetings of the Forum and/or the Parent Council, parents are entitled to air their views in relation to any aspect of the particular school's policy and practice, and these views can be aired to the head teacher, the local authority or Education Scotland's inspectors as appropriate (s 8). The 2006 Act, taken together with the Standards in Scotland's Schools etc. Act 2000, have the result that education authorities must consult with parents when reviewing the performance of schools. Indeed, the 2006 Act makes clear that the opportunities for the involvement of parents in the education of their child should be assessed when monitoring schools (2000 Act, s. 7(3)).

In addition, the Standards in Scotland's Schools etc. Act 2000 is explicit in stating that children should be consulted by the head teacher on the School Development Plan, with the head teacher seeking ways to involve the children 'when decisions require to be made concerning the everyday running of the school' (s. 6(3)). It is evident that both the notion and practice of religious observance are matters 'concerning the everyday running of the school', therefore implying that children should be consulted on the manner in which religious observance is carried out.

Evidence about implementation from inspection reports

In sampling a wide range of denominational and non-denominational primary and secondary school inspection reports from the thirty-two Scottish local authorities, the same bland and uninformative statements about religious observance can be seen. The denominational schools make specific reference to aspects of school life where religious observance is clear, as might be expected. Examples of common comments include: 'Assemblies and daily prayers provided appropriate opportunities for Religious Observance'; and 'There remains scope for some children to achieve more'; and 'Children have good opportunities for Religious Observance through daily prayers, regular assemblies and attendance at Mass for special celebrations'. In non-denominational schools the statements are considerably vaguer and give no clear impression as to what, if anything, the inspectors observed and the children experience. Comments appear to be drawn from a pool of statements since the same phrases and sentences appear repeatedly, including the likes of: 'There were appropriate arrangements for Religious Observance'; 'Regular assemblies provided good opportunities for Religious Observance and celebrating pupils' successes'; 'The school has suitable arrangements for Religious Observance'; 'Recent links with the local church had improved opportunities for Religious Observance'; 'There were very effective arrangements for Religious Observance, including a monthly assembly led by the school chaplain'. Further, the religious observance, when noted, appears to be Christian in nature, though some schools evidently involve those of other faiths in speaking to the children.

An issue worthy of discussion is that it is not clear what is considered appropriate in terms of religious observance and by whom it may be considered appropriate. Progress and children's learning in the likes of Mathematics or Physical Education can easily be seen and assessed, but it is not at all clear what would constitute a satisfactory experience or piece of learning in relation to religious observance.

Evidence about implementation from academic research

Little research has yet been carried out as to how the guidelines on religious observance are being implemented. An initial study does, however, give rise to some concerns that would benefit from further investigation. Gilfillan, Aitken and Phipps (2013) employed a case study method to gather original empirical evidence on the experiences of head teachers, practitioners and pupils with regard to the new guidelines. Research was carried out in four non-denominational state schools (three primary and one secondary) in central Scotland. Amongst practitioners there was confusion as to what the policy actually was and anxiety about how best to deliver it, along with a 'malaise surrounding RO as if it was a subject area of the curriculum that was destined to decline in significance' (Gilfillan *et al.*, 2013: 102). Amongst pupils, there was confusion about the concept of spirituality, uncertainty about whether school was the appropriate place to explore this aspect of life and, in the secondary school, a culture of 'anti-learning' around religious observance meaning that pupils considered themselves forced to pay attention to an activity from which they did not expect to learn anything (Gilfillan *et al.*, 2013).

The authors conclude that incoherence in the non-denominational understanding of religious observance lies at the root of the problems of implementation (Gilfillan *et al.*, 2013). In their view, there are few or no practitioners or practices available to enact policy in this area, with the result that a non-religious model of spiritual development remains out of reach. They recommend that further empirical research be conducted to confirm the findings of this pilot study, noting that any such research should try to include a greater number of secondary schools, and a greater number of schools with some presence of non-white ethnic minority pupils and teachers, although the difficulty with finding schools willing to participate in this type of research is acknowledged (Gilfillan *et al.*, 2013).

Areas for discussion

Appropriate terminology: 'Religious Observance' vs 'Time for Reflection'

Early in 2014, the Church of Scotland and Humanist Society Scotland (HSS) jointly called on the Scottish Government to amend the 1980 Act to replace references to 'Religious Observance' with 'Time for Reflection' (Fulton & McLellan, 2014). The call was made in a statement submitted to the Public Petitions Committee in respect of the petition on the parental opt-out from religious observance (PE01487: Religious Observance in Schools (20 June 2013)). The letter supports 'the opportunity for schools' communities to experience shared community acts of reflection and collective exploration of values and beliefs', and considers that a change in terminology would bring legislation into line with modern views by celebrating diversity, whilst 'removing the current focus on religion, with which many non-religious people struggle'.

Some support for this change in terminology can be found in the *Curriculum for Excellence* Experiences and Outcomes for R(M)E, which use the term 'reflection' more frequently than either 'worship' or 'observance'. Guidance for Catholic schools is that they should develop in children skills for reflection, though this need not pertain exclusively to one's religious beliefs since it is closely tied to comments around critical thinking, discernment and moral decision-making. In non-denominational schools there is a focus on children reflecting on their own moral values, though this is again linked with critical evaluation and critical thinking. However, the Es and Os for children in non-denominational schools suggest that children in the upper stages of secondary school are able to reflect on their responses to issues surrounding the likes of cultural and religious diversity. In articulating reflection in the same context as critical thinking, the notion of reflection in the Es and Os is more about evaluation rather than inner search, which appears only minimally in the section on principles and practice with some reference to children developing their own beliefs and attitudes.

The change in terminology proposed by the Church of Scotland and HSS received no direct comment from the Public Petitions Committee (SP M PPC 28 Jan 2014 2013–2014), or from the Education and Culture Committee to whom the Petition was subsequently referred SP M EC 6 May 2014 4139–4142). The most likely explanation for this absence of comment is that the terminology was not the focus of the petition, although subsequent public disagreement between the two groups as to what precisely had been meant by the letter may also have played a part (McLellan, 2014). The Church of Scotland's General Assembly report (2014) shows that the topic of religious observance was discussed broadly, and also in relation to the move towards time for reflection and the association with HSS. Under Section 16.3, in reference to media reporting of the HSS and Church of Scotland proposals, the report states that 'There was sadly, a great deal of misinformation in the coverage and commentary on that statement' (Church of Scotland, 2014, section 3/58, p. 97). The

Church stresses that it remains committed to religious observance, notably in relation to the Christian heritage to which the Scottish Government referred in their guidance to head teachers, but that they acknowledge the need for an inclusive approach. The Church and Society Council and the Standing Committee on Education had developed a training programme for those delivering religious observance/time for reflection. As part of this work they promote 'six core principles for Religious Observance/ Time for Reflection', the fourth of which being 'Religious Observance is not, and should never be confessional in nature (it is not worship nor can it be)' (section 3/60, p. 99). The report fails to elucidate on what the philosophical problem was with time for reflection given that it states that religious observance is not worship, that a name change may be helpful in advancing their work in schools, and that they had received feedback from people responsible for leading religious observance who said that time for reflection felt more inclusive and allowed all pupils and staff to participate, as the Scottish Government guidance states, 'with integrity in forms of religious observance without compromise to their personal faith stances' (section 3/60, p. 99). There seems to have been an assumption on the part of the Church that HSS had designs on removing any religious element from time for reflection, though this proposal is not recorded publicly by the Church or HSS. Section 16.3.9 makes clear that 'The Council emphasises that its understanding of the agreement reached with the Humanism Scotland [*sic*] was solely on the issue of the name change and not on any other aspect of Religious Observance' (section 3/60, p. 99) and there had been

> no intention of calling for a removal of religious content from Religious Observance/ Time for Reflection: such a call would in fact breach the guidelines. The Council remains committed to including faith, God and the insights of the Christian tradition in Religious Observance; we simply believe also that a change of name to Time for Reflection will help those guidelines – and our ministers and chaplains in schools – work even more effectively. (Section 3/60, p. 99)

The terminology has remained a focus of discussion, however. In April 2014, a petition (PEO1514: Making Time for Reflection representative of all beliefs (17 April 2014)) was lodged, criticizing a lack of diversity amongst speakers leading the Scottish Parliament's own time for reflection. Of the 1,309 parents who responded to the SPTC survey mentioned above (SPTC, 2014), 68 per cent of parents with children in denominational schools disagreed with the suggestion that RO should be changed to time for reflection. Amongst parents of children in non-denominational schools, 39 per cent agreed with the proposal, while 25 per cent disagreed (SPTC, 2014b). While it is difficult to predict how the Scottish public as a whole might feel about such a change, a 2016 YouGov survey for *The Times* newspaper found that 38 per cent of Scottish adults surveyed thought there should be no place for worship in the education system (*The Times*, 2016). This, though, is problematic since religious observance need not mean acts of worship as the notion of time for reflection demonstrates.

Right to withdraw

Difficulties with the accommodationist model

Parents have the right to withdraw their children from both religious observance and R(M)E (Education (Scotland) Act 1980, s. 9). The policy guidance makes clear that parents should be made aware of this right, that in no circumstances should a pupil be disadvantaged as a result of withdrawing, and that arrangements should be made for them to participate in a 'worthwhile alternative activity' (Scottish Government, 2011a: 14–17).

This mechanism for protecting the rights of parents who do not share the belief system espoused in religious observance is sometimes referred to as an 'accommodationist' model, and is recognized to be imperfect (McCarthy, 2011). A child who does not participate in the same activities may feel singled-out and be stigmatized by her peers (Canadian Civil Liberties Association, 1990; Zylberberg, 1988; McCollum, 1948). From a practical perspective, it can be extremely difficult for teachers to find something else for the child to do (Mawhinney, 2006). In recent jurisprudence in respect of Article 9 of the ECHR, the European Court of Human Rights has moved some way towards suggesting that, outside of faith schools, only secular education can meet the demands of Article 9 in religiously pluralist European society to avoid the difficulties which attend the accommodationist model, (Folgero, 2008; Zengin, 2008; Lautsi, 2010, 2011) but this attitude has also been criticized for equating 'secular' with 'neutral' rather than recognizing it as a (non-)faith-based approach in its own right (Ahdar & Leigh, 2005; Leigh, 2010).

Awareness of these difficulties was recently heightened in Scotland by a petition (PEO1487: Religious Observance in Schools (20 June 2013)) urging the Government to amend the Education (Scotland) Act 1980 by making religious observance opt-in rather than opt-out. The petition makes note of a 2012 YouGov poll commissioned by Humanist Society Scotland in which 1,000 parents of Scottish children aged 5–16 were asked about their understanding of the right to withdraw pupils from RO and RME (<https://www.humanism.scot/what-we-do/research/religion-and-education-2012/>). In all, 39 per cent indicated that they were not aware this right existed. The petition also asserts that the requirement that a 'worthwhile alternative activity' be made available was not always fulfilled. The petitioner, Secular Scotland member Mark Gordon, noted his own experience:

> My daughter is made to sit in the school office with paper and pencils to draw with and is 'looked after' by the school secretary since there are usually no teachers available.

In its response to the petition, the Scottish Government took the view that the policy and underlying legislation on this issue was relevant and up-to-date based on the evidence provided, but that work could be done on improving communication and implementation (McKechnie, 2013). It indicated that it would continue to work with Education Scotland, faith and non-faith groups to 'identify examples of good practice and areas needing support'. The Education and Culture Committee, to whom the petition was subsequently referred, were in general agreement with the Government position, and identified communication with parents both as to the existence of the right and the types of 'meaningful activity' which could replace participation in religious observance as the heart of the issue (SP M EC 6 May 2014 4139–4142). The legislation accordingly remains unchanged. It is not clear whether communication with parents has, in fact, improved, though the most recent guidance on the provision of religious observance makes it very clear that schools 'are expected to set a clear rationale for the approach taken' in the school towards religious observance and that parents and carers must be informed of their right to withdraw their child from religious observance (Scottish Government, 2017, 4). Further, guidance is provided for schools about what should appear in school handbooks regarding the right to withdraw by the first schedule to the Education (School and Placing Information) (Scotland) Regulations 2012. Humanist Society Scotland, as part of their Enlighten Up campaign, has also produced two books offering advice for non-religious parents and their children (Humanist Society Scotland, 2016).

From the Scottish inspection reports, it is rarely if ever clear what arrangements are in place for those children not participating in religious observance. This seems to pass without comment. Indeed, the heading under which religious observance is considered in the inspection reports is an interesting one: 'Climate and relationships, expectations and promoting achievement and equality'. Of the other headings, known as aspects, about which the inspectors comment, 'pastoral care' or 'partnership with parents and community' may seem more appropriate than something that conflates achievement and equality with children's religious practices and faith. Several of the inspection reports state that assemblies are used for religious observance and to celebrate pupils' successes. This would imply, therefore, that a child withdrawn from religious observance does not have the opportunity to have her successes celebrated by her peers in the wide forum of an assembly. This, it appears, is inequitable; ironic, given the rhetoric around '... promoting achievement and equality' and unacceptable given that guidance makes explicit that assemblies that celebrate successes should be distinct from those designed for religious observance (Scottish Government, 2017).

Parents' rights vs children's rights

A further potential issue with the right to withdraw which is beginning to receive attention in Scotland is the fact that the right can be exercised only by parents. The legislation makes no provision for the right to be exercised by the child herself, in contrast with the position south of the border, where sixth form pupils may exercise the right to be excused from worship on their own behalf (School Standards and Framework Act 1998, s 71(1B)). Humanist Society Scotland's on-going campaign has resulted in a judicial review of the decision by the Scottish Government not to extend the parental right of withdrawal to children. Their case is built on the assertion that the refusal to allow children to opt-out of religious observance breaches the European Convention on Human Rights and that the society is willing to test this.

Together, the Scottish Alliance for Children's Rights, has also recommended that the Scottish Government review their policy on religious observance. The most recent Concluding Observations from the United Nations Committee on the Rights of the Child, published in July 2016, make it clear that in order to satisfy children's rights legal provision must be repealed to ensure that 'children can independently exercise the right to withdraw from religious worship at school'. It is worth noting that children in Scotland have the right to be heard in respect of decisions affecting their lives, both by their parents (Children (Scotland) Act 1995, s. 6) and at school (Standards in Scotland's Schools etc. Act 2000, s. 2(2)), with a child presumed sufficiently mature to form a view at age 12. The question arises as to what effect this may have in a situation where the child's view conflicts with that of her parents.

Some assistance may be obtained through consideration of the position on minority medical consent, where under-16s seek medical advice or treatment against the will of their parents. In Scotland, the Age of Legal Capacity (Scotland) Act 1991, s. 2(4) provides that a child under 16 may consent to surgical, medical or dental treatment where, in the opinion of the treating practitioner, the young person understands the nature and possible consequences of the treatment. Authority exists for the proposition that once the child has established such understanding, her parent will no longer have any veto in respect of medical decisions (Houston, 1997). If this approach is correct in terms of physical health, it seems logically consistent to suggest a similar approach should be employed for questions of spiritual well-being or faith-based practices. If there comes a point at which a child is deemed sufficiently mature to have her own understanding of faith, there seems to be no reason why this should not be respected within her educational provision notwithstanding that it may be contrary to her parents' views. Indeed, it could be argued that the test of maturity should be less stringent in the educational religious context, since the impact of any decision taken is less likely to be immediately life-threatening than in the medical context. Whether this is the position in law currently is doubtful, however: the legislative provision recognizing the capacity of a mature minor to make medical decisions is not replicated for religious or educational decisions. On this point see also Chapters 6 and 7.

Concluding Remarks

The position on collective worship in Scotland is distinct in some key respects from elsewhere in the UK. Most obviously, the statutory requirement for religious observance in schools is interpreted through policy guidance which states that account must be taken of all faiths and none, recognizing that time for reflection may be a more accurate description of the practice than religious observance in some schools. In other respects, the challenges faced in Scotland mirror those through the UK. While religious observance is built within *Curriculum for Excellence*, it is not clear what form it does or should take across the various school contexts for those CfE serves. Evolving belief demographics raise difficult questions about how to implement RO in an educational system where Christian culture has historically been dominant. Perhaps most importantly, the increasing significance of children's rights demands greater attention be paid to the views of children, not just their parents or teachers, in determining the appropriate place for religious observance in Scottish schools.

It is clear that further research is required in Scotland in relation to religious observance, with children's voices heard alongside those of their parents and teachers. In the first place, research to establish current practices undertaken under the guise of religious observance, building on the pilot study conducted by Gilfillan *et al.* (2013), seems an essential step towards proposing resolutions to some of the issues outlined above. In conducting such research, particular attention should be paid to: (i) the views of children; (ii) the experiences of children of non-Christian faiths or of no faith; (iii) the arrangements in place for children who do not wish to participate in Religious Observance; and (iv) the differences in practice (if any) between denominational and non-denominational schools.

References

Ahdar, R., & Leigh, I. (2005). *Religious Freedom in the Liberal State*. Oxford: Oxford University Press.
Canadian Civil Liberties Association v Ontario (Minister of Education) (1990) 65 DLR (4th) 1.
Cassidy, C. (2013). Scottish Primary Education: Philosophy and Practice. In T. G. K. Bryce, W. M. Humes, D. Gillies, & A. Kennedy (Eds.), *Scottish Education Fourth Edition: Referendum* (pp. 39–49). Edinburgh: Edinburgh University Press.
Church of Scotland (2014). *The Church of Scotland General Assembly. Hands Across the World*. Edinburgh: The Church of Scotland Assembly Arrangements Committee 2014.
Education Scotland (2017). What is Curriculum for Excellence? Retrieved May 2017, from <https://education.gov.scot/scottish-education-system/policy-for-scottish-education/policy-drivers/cfe-(building-from-the-statement-appendix-incl-btc1-5)/What%20is%20Curriculum%20for%20Excellence?>.
Equality and Human Rights Commission (2016). *Religion or Belief: is the Law Working?* Manchester: Equality and Human Rights Commission.
Folgero and Others v Norway (2008) 46 EHRR 47.
Fulton, S. F., & McLellan, D. (2014). Letter to David Stewart MSP, Convenor of the Public Petitions Committee (January 24). Retrieved May 2017, from <http://www.scottish.parliament.uk/S4_PublicPetitionsCommittee/General%20Documents/PE1487_KK_Church_of_Scotland-Humanist_Society_24.01.14.pdf>.
General Teaching Council for Scotland (GTCS) (2012a). *The Standards for Registration: Mandatory Requirements for Registration with the General Teaching Council for Scotland*. Edinburgh: GTCS.

General Teaching Council for Scotland (GTCS) (2012b). *The Standards for Leadership and Management: Supporting Leadership and Management Development.* Edinburgh: GTCS.

General Teaching Council for Scotland (GTCS) (2012c). *The Standards for Career-Long Professional Learning: Supporting the Development of Teacher Professional Learning.* Edinburgh: GTCS.

Gilfillan, P., Aitken, E., & Phipps, A. (2013). A research report on the reception of the 2005 *Religious Observance Guidelines* in Scotland. *British Journal of Religious Education, 35*(1), 98–109.

Her Majesty's Inspectorate of Education (2001). *Standards and Quality in Secondary Schools: Religious and Moral Education 1995–2000.* London: TSO.

Her Majesty's Inspectorate of Education (2011). *Principles of Inspection and Review.* Retrieved May 2017, from <http://www.educationscotland.gov.uk/Images/PrinciplesofInspectionandReview2010_tcm4-683703.pdf>.

Houston, Applicant 1996 SCLR 943.

Humanist Society Scotland (2016). *A Guide for Non-religious Parents: Know your Rights.* Edinburgh: Humanist Society Scotland.

Lautsi v Italy (2010) 50 EHRR 2 (Chamber), (2011) 54 EHRR 60 (Grand Chamber).

Leigh, I. (2010). New trends in religious liberty and the European Court of Human Rights. *Ecclesiastical Law Journal,* 266–279.

McCarthy, F. (2011). Prayers in the playground: religion and education in the United Kingdom and beyond. In J. Mair & E. Orucu (Eds.), *The Place of Religion in Family Law: A Comparative Search* (pp. 235–262). Cambridge, OR: Intersentia.

McCollum v Board of Education 333 US 203 (1948).

McKechnie, K., Curriculum Unit, Scottish Government. (2013). Letter to the Public Petitions Committee (December 18, 2013). Retrieved May 2017, from <http://www.scottish.parliament.uk/S4_PublicPetitionsCommittee/General%20Documents/PE1487_II_Scottish_Government_18.12.13.pdf>.

McLellan, D. (2014). Letter to David Stewart MSP, Convenor of the Public Petitions Committee (January 28, 2014) Retrieved May 2017, from <http://www.scottish.parliament.uk/S4_PublicPetitionsCommittee/General%20Documents/PE1487_PP_Humanist_Society_Scotland_28.01.14.pdf>.

Montagu, I. (2016). Is Scotland Losing its Faith? Retrieved May 2017, from <http://www.natcen.ac.uk/blog/is-scotland-losing-its-faith>.

Nixon, G. (2013). Religious Education in Scottish schools. In T. G. K. Bryce, W. M. Humes, D. Gillies, & A. Kennedy (Eds.), *Scottish Education Fourth Edition: Referendum* (pp. 492–496). Edinburgh: Edinburgh University Press.

Office for National Statistics (2011). *Statistical Bulletin – 2011 Census: Key results on population, ethnicity, identity, language, religion, health, housing and accommodation*

in Scotland – release 2A. Retrieved May 2017, from <http://www.scotlandscensus.
gov.uk/documents/censusresults/release2a/StatsBulletin2A.pdf>.

Paterson, L. (2003). *Scottish Education in the Twentieth Century.* Edinburgh: Edinburgh University Press.

Scotland, J. (1969). *The History of Scottish Education.* London: University of London
Press

Scott, J. (2016). *Education Law in Scotland.* Edinburgh: W. Green.

Scottish Catholic Education Service (2017). *Guidance on Approval.* Retrieved May
2017, from <http://www.sces.uk.com/Approval.html>.

Scottish Executive (2004a). *A Curriculum for Excellence.* Edinburgh: Scottish
Executive.

Scottish Executive (2004b). *Report of the Religious Observance Review Group.* Edinburgh: Scottish Executive.

Scottish Executive (2005). *Circular 1/2005: Provision of religious observance in
Scottish schools.* Retrieved May 2017, from <http://www.scotland.gov.uk/
Publications/2005/03/20778/53820>.

Scottish Government (2011a). *Curriculum for Excellence – Provision of Religious and
Moral Education in Non-denominational Schools and Religious Education in
Roman Catholic Schools.* Edinburgh: Scottish Government.

Scottish Government (2011b) *Curriculum for Excellence – Provision of Religious
Observance in Scottish Schools – March 2017* Edinburgh: Scottish Government.
Retrieved May 2017, from <http://www.gov.scot/Resource/Doc/920/0113849.
pdf>.

Scottish Government (2016). *High Level Summary of Statistics Trends: Pupil Numbers.* Retrieved May 2017, from <http://www.scotland.gov.uk/Topics/Statistics/
Browse/School-Education/TrendPupilNumbers>.

Scottish Government (2017). *Curriculum for Excellence – Provision of Religious Observance in Scottish Schools – March 2017.* Retrieved May 2017, from <http://www.
gov.scot/Resource/Doc/920/0113849.pdf>.

Scottish Office Education Department (SOED) (1991). Circular 6/91: Provision
of Religious Education and Religious Observance in Primary and Secondary
Schools. Edinburgh: SOED. Retrieved May 2017, from <http://www.scotland.
gov.uk/Publications/2001/06/14871/File-1>.

Scottish Office Education Department (SOED) (1992). *Religious and Moral Education: 5–14 National Guidelines.* Edinburgh: SOED.

Scottish Parent Teacher Council (2014). *Parents' Voice – Religious Observance, May 2014.* Retrieved May 2017, from <http://www.sptc.info/
parents-voice-religious-observance-may-2014>.

Scottish Parent Teacher Council (2014b). *Parents' Voice Survey Report on the Place of Religion in Schools*. Retrieved May 2017, from <http://www.sptc.info/parents-voice-survey-report-on-the-place-of-religion-in-schools-may-2014>.

Stevenson, J. (2012). *Fulfilling a Vision: the Contribution of the Church of Scotland to School Education 1772–1872*. Eugene, Oregon: Pickwick Publications.

The Times (2016). YouGov Poll: The Times Results Scottish Education. Retrieved May 2017, from <https://d25d2506sfb94s.cloudfront.net/cumulus_uploads/document/2qc10iw573/TimesScotlandResults_November2016_Education_W.pdf>.

The Times (2017). Take Religion out of the Classroom. Retrieved May 2017, from <https://www.thetimes.co.uk/article/take-religion-out-of-the-classroom-9j6xo6mzw>.

United Nations Committee on the Rights of the Child. (2017). *Concluding Observations on the Fifth Periodic Report of the United Kingdom of Great Britain and Northern Ireland*. Geneva: United Nations. Retrieved July 2017, from <http://www.togetherscotland.org.uk/pdfs/2016%20Concluding%20Observations%20-%20Final.pdf>.

Zengin v Turkey (2008) 46 EHRR 4.

Zylberberg v Sudbury Board of Education (1988) 65 OR (2d) 641 (CA).

ALISON MAWHINNEY AND ANN SHERLOCK

4 Collective Worship in Wales

ABSTRACT

Legislation places an explicit duty on state-funded schools in Wales to organize daily acts of collective worship. For schools without a 'designated' religious character, the majority of these acts of worship during any school term must be 'wholly or mainly of a broadly Christian character'. This chapter examines the principle and practice surrounding this statutory duty. It argues that there is limited data on attitudes to the duty and its implementation in Wales: this warrants further investigation. It contends that there is a pressing need to reconsider the aims of collective worship in today's diverse, multibelief Wales. The chapter concludes by observing that, while Welsh views and principles were easily ignored in the Westminster legislature when the current law was made, today Welsh institutions have the legal competence to respond to the complexities of collective school worship in an innovative manner appropriate for Welsh society in the twenty-first century.

Introduction

Legislation requires state schools in Wales to hold daily acts of collective worship. This chapter explores the complexities and challenges relating to this requirement; the equivocal legal provisions, the uncertain manner of its implementation and its contradictory conceptual underpinnings. To contextualize the duty within contemporary Welsh society, the chapter begins with an overview of the country's belief demographics and its education system before presenting the general legal framework and examining the specific legal provisions. Exploring existing evidence that points to concerns in the practice and appropriateness of the current legal obligation, the conclusion identifies areas of challenge and opportunity for the Welsh Government and the Welsh Assembly.

The context

Contemporary belief demographics

There are potential dangers of ambiguity and misrepresentation in gathering and interpreting statistical data about religion. However, the inclusion of the same voluntary question in the 2001 and 2011 Welsh censuses – 'what is your religion?' – allows for the identification of some emerging trends in belief demographics in Wales. It sought to measure the concept of religious affiliation that is, the connection or identification with a religion irrespective of actual practice or belief, rather than the extent of any religious belief or practice (Office for National Statistics (a)).

The data shows Wales as a country experiencing significant change in its belief affiliation demographics (Office for National Statistics, 2011). In 2001 individuals affiliating with Christianity formed the largest group in the country, representing 71.9 per cent of the population. In 2011 this group, still the largest category, had dropped to 57.6 per cent. In 2001 the second largest response group for the question relating to religious affiliation was no religion, 18.5 per cent of the population. In 2011 the 'no religion' group increased to 32 per cent. This 14 per cent rise was larger than in any England region. In addition, a further 7.6 per cent did not state a religion. In 2001, 1.5 per cent of the population in Wales self-affiliated with a minority religious group (Muslim, Hindu, Buddhist, Sikh, Jewish, Other religion). By 2011, this figure had risen to 2.7 per cent.

Statistics from the Integrated Household Survey (Office for National Statistics (b)) for the period April 2010 to March 2011 show that in Wales, 66.1 per cent of people stated they were Christian, 30.6 per cent stated that they had no religion, 1.2 per cent of people stated they were Muslim whilst other religions accounted for 2.2 per cent of people. The group stating they had no religion was 7.4 percentage points higher for Wales than Great Britain as a whole. The question asked in this survey measured religious affiliation irrespective of actual belief or practice: 'what is your religion, even if you are not currently practising?'

The census question measures the number of people who indicate an affiliation with a religion irrespective of the extent of their religious belief or practice. Arguably, to gain an insight into the appropriateness or likely public acceptance of requirements for collective worship in schools, measuring religious *behaviour* might provide more useful data. Specifically, attendance rates at religious services, a practice closely aligned to the idea of worship, is a common indicator of what sociologists of religion term 'behaving' (see e.g. Voas, 2007, 128–150). A 2007 survey sought to measure the number of regular churchgoers in Wales, a pertinent behaviour to measure given the emphasis on Christianity in the statutory provisions. It found that the percentage of regular churchgoers in Wales was 12 per cent, contrasted with Northern Ireland (45 per cent), Scotland (18 per cent) and England (14 per cent) (Ashworth and Farthing, 2007). The survey concluded that 'Wales is arguably the most secular nation' with 78 per cent either 'de-churched [had been to church in the past] or non-churched [never having attended church apart from weddings, baptisms or funerals]' and only 12 per cent regular churchgoers.

A more recent survey on religious service attendance in the UK also noted Wales as having the highest proportion in any area (78.5 per cent) who reported they did not attend religious services (Clements, 2014). The non-attendance rate in Wales in 1983 was 46.5 per cent.

Statistical data on religious affiliation and practice clearly indicate that Wales is a country with a high and growing number of persons who do not affiliate with Christianity and who do not participate in traditional Christian practices, such as attending church services. No data is available to indicate what percentage of Christians would, despite being practising followers of Christianity, expect a Welsh state school to provide Christian worship to their children on a daily basis. Neither is official data available to indicate pupils' views on this activity. Indeed, there is relatively little survey data from Wales on attitudes to collective worship in schools, since surveys on the topic by the British Social Attitudes and other organizations do not disaggregate Welsh data from English data. However, a small YouGov online survey, conducted in 2012 with 1,047 adults, did attempt to explore attitudes amongst the Welsh adult population to collective school worship in relation to one specific question (British Humanist Association, 2012).

Respondents were asked to what extent they would support or oppose a change of law to replace the current collective daily worship obligation with 'a requirement that schools hold assemblies which consider moral and ethical issues shared by a range of different religious and non-religious beliefs'. The poll found that 41 per cent supported such a change, while 36 per cent did not. While a number of petitions presented to the Welsh Assembly demonstrate an interest and concern in the issue of collective worship in schools, they cannot be regarded as representative of attitudes in Wales (National Assembly for Wales, 2012).

The school system

In Wales, the vast majority of schools (approximately 98 per cent), at both primary and secondary level, are in the state, or 'maintained', sector. These are the schools covered by the legislative requirements on collective worship. The schools may be divided into four main categories which are set out in the School Standards and Framework Act 1998 (s.20): community schools (1,271 in 2015/16), voluntary controlled schools (86 in 2015/16), voluntary aided schools (153 in 2015/16), and foundation schools (12 in 2015/16) (Welsh Government, 2016). (The Education (Wales) Measure 2011 prohibits the creation of any new foundation schools although existing foundation schools remain in existence.) Community and foundation special schools (39 in 2015/16) exist for children whose special educational needs make attendance at a mainstream school impossible.

The various categories of schools enjoy varying degrees of autonomy and financial support from the local authority. Only voluntary and foundation schools may be designated as having a religious character: this designation has implications for the rules applicable in relation to religious education and collective worship, school admissions and the appointment of staff on the basis of religious beliefs.

The designation of schools as having a religious character is carried out by the Welsh Government (SI 2016/1144 (W. 275)): the most recent order of 2014 (SI 2014/3261 (W. 332)) lists those voluntary aided, voluntary controlled and foundation schools which have been designated as having a religious character. The only denominations designated are Church in Wales, Roman Catholic, and one school whose religious character is Roman Catholic and Anglican. The Welsh Government states that schools with a religious character in Wales represent 14 per cent of all maintained schools in Wales (Welsh Government, 2011, 16).

Legal framework

The legal framework in Wales surrounding collective school worship is shaped by domestic and international law. Domestically, the School Standards and Framework Act 1998 sets down the current requirements surrounding the duty to provide a daily act of collective worship, an obligation first introduced in the Education Act 1944 and further defined in the Education Reform Act 1988. Each of these statutes was passed when legislative competence for education rested with the UK Parliament. Under the Government of Wales Act 2006, the National Assembly for Wales now enjoys full primary law-making powers in the area of education. However, thus far, none of its education legislation has dealt with collective worship in schools.

In addition to domestic education law, the legal framework relevant to the requirement and practice of acts of school worship includes relevant norms of domestic and international human rights law. Domestic standards binding the Welsh authorities are located in the Human Rights Act 1998 and the Rights of Children and Young Persons (Wales) Measure 2011. The Human Rights Act incorporates the rights of the European Convention on Human Rights into domestic law, including the right to freedom from discrimination (Article 14), the right to freedom of religion or belief (Article 9) and the right to education (Article 2 of the First Protocol). Freedom of conscience and religion requires respect for the rights of children and parents who wish to participate in collective worship and of those who do not. The right to education includes the right of parents to ensure that the education of their children conforms with their own religious and philosophical convictions. The Rights of Children and Young Persons (Wales) Measure 2011 places a specific duty on the Welsh Government to have 'due regard' to the UN Convention on the Rights of the Child in all its decisions (s.1). The Convention is underpinned by a number of key guiding principles, including the principle of non-discrimination (Article 2), the 'best interests of the child' principle (Article 3(1)), and the right of children to express views in all matters affecting them (Article 12). It contains a specific right to freedom of thought, conscience and religion (Article 14) and Article 29 details the aims of education which a state's education system must deliver to children.

In addition to ensuring respect for domestic human rights standards, the Welsh Government is also required to uphold the UK's obligations under a number of international human rights treaties, notably the International Covenant on Civil and Political Rights (ICCPR) and the International Covenant on Economic, Social and Cultural Rights (ICESCR). Article 18(3) of the ICCPR protects against indoctrination in schools against parental wishes while Article 13(1) ICESCR sets out the standards and goals that must be realized in relation to education.

Chapter 7 of this volume examines in detail the human rights issues and challenges raised by the practice of collective school worship in Welsh schools. The following section focuses on the domestic provisions that set out the statutory duty for all state schools to hold acts of daily worship.

School Standards and Framework Act 1998

The School Standards and Framework Act 1998 (SSFA) places a legal obligation on the local education authority, school governing bodies and head teachers to ensure that 'each pupil in attendance at a community, foundation or voluntary school shall on each school day take part in an act of collective worship' (s. 70(1)).

Schedule 20 of the SSFA sets out further provision on the organization and the nature of the worship (s. 70(3)). In providing directional regulations on these aspects, Schedule 20 draws upon the provisions of earlier statutes, namely the Education Act 1944 and, in particular, the Education Reform Act 1988.

Assistance on interpreting the duty is also found in Circular 10/94, a document issued by the Welsh Office Education Department in 1994 to provide guidance on the provisions of the Education Reform Act 1988 (Welsh Office, 1994). Its contents are broadly similar to Circular 1/94 which applies in England and was issued eight months earlier by the Secretary of State for Education. While influential in shaping understandings of the nature of the statutory obligation in the minds of some teachers, schools and inspection bodies, the circular lacks legal status. The document itself stipulates that its guidance does not constitute an authoritative legal interpretation of the provisions of the legislation, which is a matter exclusively for the courts. However, the influence of the circular – and its English equivalent – has led some to seek confirmation that the circular has indeed no legal, semi-legal status or quasi-legal status. For some, this has been deemed essential given its controversial interpretation of the legal provisions. Indeed, in assessing the near-identical English Circular 1/94, the National Association of Standing Advisory Councils on Religious Education, with a remit for England only (hereafter NASACRE),[1] and the Association of Religious Education Inspectors, Advisers and Consultants, whose membership includes professionals from Wales (hereafter AREIAC), have described it as 'one of the most significant stumbling blocks to success' in organizing and conducting periods of collective worship (NASACRE & AREIAC, 2012). In August 2012, NASACRE and AREIAC, which had been pressing for the withdrawal of Circular 1/94, received confirmation of the non-legal status of the Circular in a letter from the Department for Education in England:

> The original circular 1/94 contained a statement that 'This guidance does not constitute an authoritative legal interpretation of the provisions of the Education Acts or other enactments and regulations; that is exclusively a matter for the courts.' This

---

1   NASACRE's equivalent in Wales is the Welsh Association of Standing Advisory Councils on Religious Education (WASACRE).

was and still is the position of the Department regarding the circular. Schools can use it or not as they see fit.

In response to this, NASACRE and AREIAC issued a joint statement to their members advising them to encourage schools to set aside the circular when planning for collective worship (NASACRE and AREIAC, 2013).

A similar confirmation as to the status of Circular 10/94 has not been sought from the Department for Education and Skills in Wales. It would, however, be difficult to imagine Circular 10/94 having a different legal status to Circular 1/94 given their common origins. Despite this, a recent publication from Estyn, the Inspectorate for Education and Training in Wales, seemed to suggest that it understood Circular 10/94 to have legal status, incorrectly noting that 'The Education Reform Act 1988 and the Welsh Office Circular 10/94 set out the legal requirements for collective worship in schools in Wales' (Estyn, 2013, 1).

Procedural arrangements

The SSFA is clear on the arrangements for conducting acts of collective worship in schools. In schools without a religious designation, responsibility for making and monitoring these arrangements rests with the head teacher after consultation with the governing body. In schools with a religious character, responsibility lies with the governing body after consultation with the head teacher. A single act of worship for all pupils may be provided or, alternatively, separate acts of worship may be held for pupils in different age groups or in different school groups (SSFA, Schedule 20). The act should normally take place on school premises. Parents have the right to withdraw their children from attendance at acts of religious worship, a right extended to sixth-formers themselves in 2009 (SSFA, s.71 as amended). The legislation is silent on the nature of the alternative provision to be provided for children who are withdrawn from acts of collective worship. Staff at community, secular foundation or voluntary or special schools who choose not to attend religious worship may not as a result be 'disqualified' nor 'receive any less remuneration or be deprived of, or disqualified for, any promotion or other advantage' (SSFA, s. 59).

Nature of collective worship

Schedule 20 of the SSFA attempts to describe the nature of the collective worship to be provided. For schools with a religious character the matter is relatively straightforward and uncontroversial in that the collective worship will be in accordance with the school's trust deed or religious designation (SSFA, Schedule 20, para. 5).

A significant challenge arises, however, in relation to schools without a religious designation, the vast majority of schools in Wales. It is in these schools where the concept of collective worship becomes highly problematic at a conceptual and practical level. The attempt by Schedule 20 of the SSFA and Circular 10/94 to bring clarity to the requirements of the statutory duty serves only to highlight the inherent difficulties in conducting collective worship in state schools and, as a consequence, the impossibility of the act achieving certain of its professed aims (as discussed below).

The conceptual problems begin with the idea of worship in a non-religious school setting. Neither the SSFA nor any of its predecessor Acts offers a definition of worship. Circular 10/94 attempts to do so and in the process illustrates the impossibility of finding an appropriate definition that will make sense of the phrase 'collective worship' in a school setting. While initially noting that, in the absence of any legislative definition, 'worship' should be taken to have its 'natural and ordinary meaning' and 'should be concerned with reverence or veneration paid to a divine being or power', it then states that 'worship in schools will necessarily be of a different character from worship amongst a group with beliefs in common'. As John Hull has observed 'if it will necessarily be of a different character, then the natural and ordinary meaning of "worship" cannot be relevant' (Hull, 1995, 27–40, 30). He argues that 'the collective side of the expression [collective worship] gives weight to the variety of beliefs held by the participants. If that is the case, reverence or veneration paid to a supreme-being or power ceases to be a relevant factor in assessing the character of collective worship in schools.' Hull concludes that in the expression 'collective worship' 'an impossible situation has been apprehended through a self-contradictory concept', hence the unsurprising confusion that ensues as to what is required and the validity of the suggestion that the term *collective assembly* should replace 'collective worship'.

The contradictory nature of the phrase 'collective worship' is further compounded by the requirement that the worship in state schools without a religious character must be 'broadly Christian in nature' (SSFA, Schedule 20, para. 3(2). The original duty in the Education Act 1944, to begin each school day with an act of collective worship on the part of all the pupils (s. 25(1)), deliberately omitted the word 'Christian' in its provisions, the government having resisted demands during the parliamentary debates on the Act to specify *Christian* collective worship. The Earl of Selborne, for the government, explained that to require 'Christian worship' might only lead to legal complications in the future involving disagreement as to what was, or was not, in accordance with the requirements of Christianity (Selborne, HL Deb, 21 June 1944). However, he gave repeated assurances that it was the intention of the government and the bill that 'the corporate act of worship shall be an act of Christian worship'. This understanding was made explicit in section 7 of the Education Reform Act 1988 which introduced the wording now found in the SSFA that worship should be of a broadly Christian character.

The inclusion of the stipulation 'of a broadly Christian character' in the 1988 Act was the result of an amendment tabled in the House of Lords, an inclusion that has been described as a victory for religiously conservative groups where the lines of division were drawn not between Christians and secularists but rather 'between theologically liberal Christians and theologically conservative or establishment-minded Christians' (Bates, 1994). According to Freathy and Parker (2013) it was the latter group that managed to persuade the Conservative government to support the continuation of '"traditional English Christian culture" through the religious clauses of the 1988 Education Reform Act'. The supporters of the amendment argued for the need to maintain the place of Christianity in the country, citing the existence of an established religion as sufficient to impose a duty of Christian worship on all state schools (MacLeod, HL Deb, 26 February 1988). This claim failed to acknowledge the irrelevance of such an argument for Wales, a country without an established church.

Schedule 20 of the SSFA explains that collective worship will be of a broadly Christian character 'if it reflects the broad traditions of Christian belief without being distinctive of any particular Christian denomination'. In paragraph 63, Circular 10/94 offers a more detailed explanation, requiring that an act must 'contain some elements which relate specifically to the traditions of Christian belief and which accord a special status to Jesus Christ'. In other words, the act of collective worship on these occasions must contain elements which are distinctive of, and not merely consonant with, Christianity and of the place of Jesus Christ within that belief system. This understanding is confirmed in a letter from the Secretary of State for Education to the Board of Deputies of British Jews who had sought clarification on the meaning of 'broadly Christian' (Hull, 1995, 47).

Having stipulated the need for the majority of acts of collective worship to involve the worship of a Christian understanding of God, the Circular then advises that 'pupils who do not come from Christian families should be able to join in the daily act of collective worship even though this would, in the main, reflect the broad traditions of Christian belief'. It is difficult to understand how this could be considered rationally possible given the Circular's specific conception as to the nature of a broadly Christian act of worship. The human rights implications are considered in Chapter 7 of this volume.

Not every act of worship must be entirely 'broadly Christian' in nature. Schedule 20 provides for three exceptions. First, although acts may be 'wholly' of a broadly Christian nature, they may also be 'mainly of a broadly Christian character' (SSFA, Schedule 20, para. 3(2)). Circular 10/94 suggests that a 'mainly' broadly Christian act of worship is one that contains some non-Christian elements alongside the specifically Christian worship (para. 63).

Secondly, not every act of collective worship need be broadly Christian provided that 'taking any school term as a whole, most such acts which take place in the school' comply with this requirement (SSFA, Schedule 20, para. 3(4)). Schools may provide some acts of worship that are not 'broadly Christian' if there are 'circumstances relating to the ages, aptitudes and family backgrounds of the pupils which are relevant for determining the character of the collective worship' (SSFA, Schedule 20, para. 3(6)).

Circular 10/94 explains that an act of worship could be 'broadly in the tradition of another religion' or might contain 'elements drawn from a number of different faiths' (para. 62). The Circular confines itself to the terminology of religion and faith, rather than, for example, including the possibility of non-religious life stances or philosophies. If non-Christian acts of worship are held, the majority of acts of collective worship in any one term must, nevertheless, remain 'broadly Christian'.

Finally, a school may apply for a disapplication of the Christian collective worship requirement to allow a school or a group within it to hold a separate form of collective worship (SSFA, Schedule 20, para. 4). This provision allows a standing advisory council on religious education (SACRE) to determine that the Christian collective worship requirement is not appropriate in a particular school or to a 'class or description of pupils' in a school. When such a determination is made an act of collective worship must still be conducted for pupils. It should not be 'distinctive of any particular Christian or other religious denomination' yet this should 'not be taken as preventing that worship from being distinctive of any particular faith'(SSFA, Schedule 20, para. 4(2)(b)). John Hull has argued that '[T]he whole notion of these determinations is incompatible with the concept of collectivity' – one of the government's stated aims in introducing the legislation.

Requirements regarding inspection

Section 28 of the Education Act 2005 requires that schools are inspected at regular intervals. For schools without a religious character, the inspection of collective worship takes place as part of the normal inspection under this provision.

Collective worship is inspected by Estyn, the schools inspectorate in Wales, in two contexts. Firstly it examines whether a school complies with the statutory requirements regarding daily collective worship. Since 2010, inspectors will report only on instances where a school does *not* so comply (Estyn, 2016a & 2016b, para. 2.3.1). Silence on this aspect in an inspection report will therefore indicate compliance. Secondly, collective worship is also inspected in the context of the wider judgements that are made about the strength of the school's outcomes, provision, and leadership and management – in particular in relation to the spiritual, moral, social, and cultural development of pupils. School inspection reports may therefore make comments on collective worship in these contexts which are separate from the particular issue of compliance with the statutory requirements. Indeed, Estyn's guidance (Estyn, 2013) indicates that collective worship which does not comply with the legal requirements might still contribute to pupils' spiritual and moral development, while, conversely, worship complying with the legal requirements might make little contribution to that development.

Estyn's guidance requires that inspectors consider acts of collective worship 'in their own right and in the context of planning over a period of time'. They are to consider the spirit as well as the letter of the law, and minor or occasional breaches should not lead to an overall judgement that the school is not complying with the law. The inspection guidance reiterates the requirement set out in the Circular that more than 'passive attendance' is needed: mere attendance by pupils is not sufficient and it is up to inspectors to ensure that the person leading the worship 'at least prepares pupils appropriately and encourages them to listen to, watch or reflect on the worship offered'. The guidance acknowledges that it can be difficult for the inspectors to judge whether pupils are engaged and 'so inspectors may need to satisfy themselves that a reasonable attempt was made by the school to provide the opportunity for collective worship'. However, pupils' failure to bow their heads, respond at the end of a prayer, or sing hymns should not be taken as evidence that the act of collective worship fails to meet the legal requirements. Indeed, the guidance indicates that 'the law does not require schools to make pupils worship'. However, if pupils are observed very obviously *not* listening (for example playing cards during worship) this would not be acceptable and inspectors would need to consider whether this was an isolated incident before determining whether the legal requirements had been complied with.

The guidance notes that it would be acceptable for an individual act of worship not to make any reference to the Christian faith but inspectors would need to check the school's record of recent themes for collective worship in order to determine whether there is compliance with the legal requirement that the worship should be 'wholly or mainly of a broadly Christian nature'. As to how collective worship could be 'broadly Christian' in a school with a high proportion of Muslims, the guidance advises that:

> Those leading collective worship should be sensitive to the range of beliefs held by pupils in the school. Collective worship should give pupils the opportunity to worship without encouraging them to do something that is against the teachings of their religion. For example, times of prayer may be left open-ended for pupils to say their own prayers silently. (Estyn, 2013, 5)

In making a judgement on whether a school complies, the guidance indicates that:

> Unless an inspector is confident that the school is not providing pupils with the opportunity to worship then the judgement should be that the school meets the legal requirements. (Estyn, 2013, 5)

A striking aspect of the Estyn advice is its heavy focus on the worship component of the term 'collective worship'. Thus, in its 'Frequently Asked Questions' section, the questions relating to the content of the worship deals primarily with religious practice – for example, as to whether pupils should bow their heads and close their eyes during prayer, or respond at the end of prayers, or sing hymns and/or worship songs. No question draws the attention of an inspector to the stated aims of collective worship which relate to its community-building ambitions – for example, whether the act of collective worship developed a community spirit, promoted a common ethos and shared values, or reinforced positive attitudes. The approach of Estyn may be contrasted with the emphasis placed by the Welsh Association of SACREs (WASACRE) in its guidance document (WASACRE, 2012). WASACRE has chosen not to emphasize (or indeed mention) an aim of collective worship being 'to provide the opportunity for pupils to worship God', the primary aim of collective worship listed in Circular 10/94. In listing the benefits of collective worship, WASACRE talks, inter alia, of promoting 'spiritual development' but does not list or focus on 'the opportunity to worship' as a benefit of collective worship.

Implementation of the legal requirement

One of the challenges in attempting to capture an accurate picture of the practical implementation of the legal requirements in Wales is the dearth of Wales-only sources. Most pre-devolution studies of the law's implementation were conducted on an England and Wales basis, and there is a lack of disaggregated material for Wales alone. Accordingly, this section deals with the post-devolution period, for which Wales-only sources include the reports of Estyn, the reports of the SACRES in Wales, and publications by the Welsh Government or National Assembly for Wales. There is little independent empirical research on this area, but we refer to one study which is reported by Sandberg and Buchanan (2011).

Findings in Estyn reports

An examination of the Annual Reports of Estyn from 2004–2005 to 2015–2016 provides a small number of references to schools failing to comply with their statutory obligations regarding collective worship. All recordings of a failure to comply relate to secondary schools. The 2004–2005 report notes that 'many more schools' were providing daily collective worship but 'more than one in six schools' inspected did not 'fully keep to the law on daily collective worship' (Estyn, 2006, 63). The following year, it was recorded that one in six of the thirty-seven secondary schools inspected did not hold a daily act of collective worship. That report noted that many schools, due to lack of space to hold all pupils, arranged collective worship by tutor group with varying quality between the tutor-group sessions: sometimes the guidance for tutors was poor; and some form tutors were half-hearted in their approach because they did not consider the sessions to be important; while others were 'unwilling to lead acts of worship at all, because their personal beliefs [were] at odds with what they [had] to do' (Estyn, 2007, 16).

In the 2006–2007 report, of the forty-three secondary schools inspected, it was found that 'a few schools' did not meet the legal requirements for daily collective worship (Estyn, 2008, 24). In 2007–2008, when thirty-five secondary schools were inspected, Estyn reported that there were 'significant shortcomings in the curriculum offered by a quarter of schools', including 'a failure to meet statutory requirements for a daily act of collective worship for all learners' (Estyn, 2009, 34). Thirty-three secondary schools were inspected in 2008–2009 and Estyn reported 'important shortcomings in the work of governing bodies in a quarter of schools inspected': in these schools, 'the governors often failed to ensure that the school met all statutory requirements, such as providing a daily act of collective worship …' (Estyn, 2010, 14). The 2009–2010 Annual Report noted that 'a few' secondary schools did not meet the statutory requirement for a daily act of collective worship (Estyn, 2011, 14), and found shortcomings in a quarter of Pupil Referral Units inspected, the shortcomings 'almost always' including 'no collective worship or time for reflection' (Estyn, 2011, 19).

In the six most recent available Estyn annual reports, the only reference is in the 2015–2016 report regarding a Pupil Referral Unit failing to conduct daily collective worship (Estyn, 2017, 89). However, it is clear from our examination of local SACRE reports that individual secondary schools had been found during that period to have failed to comply with their statutory duties. Equally, the annual reports make no reference to non-compliance in primary schools but, again, the local SACRE reports refer to individual school inspection reports where non-compliance had been reported in primary schools.

Where a failure to meet the statutory requirements has been noted, no details are given as to the essence of the non-compliance, but sometimes the language suggests that it is largely a failure to hold a *daily* act of worship that is at issue. In terms of the content of the worship, in a thematic report of 2005, Estyn observed that while most schools complied with the legal requirement that worship should be broadly Christian, they also included other beliefs so that pupils from different religions did not feel excluded. However, 'a few schools hold purely Christian assemblies that do not enable pupils to explore other religions' (Estyn, 2005, para. 5.5).

Annual reports of SACREs

Under the Education Act 1996 (s. 390), each local authority in Wales is required to set up a local standing advisory council on religious education (hereafter SACRE). There must be representatives of Christian denominations and other religions and denominations that will represent the area's principal religious traditions. Also required are persons representing teachers' associations and a group to represent the local authority. There is no provision made for the direct election of persons with non-religious beliefs. The SACREs are required to advise the local authority regarding collective worship in schools without a religious character. They are also entrusted with determining any applications by a head teacher to lift the requirement for worship to be of a broadly Christian nature. Each SACRE must publish an annual report on how it has exercised its functions, and these are available on the WASACRE website (<http://www.wasacre.org.uk/publications/reports.html>). These reports provide an opportunity to gain some insight into the operation of the collective worship requirement in practice.

An examination of the annual reports of the local SACREs from 2008/9 until 2014/15 (where available) indicated that no school had requested a determination from its local SACRE that the requirement of broadly Christian worship be lifted. Reviews by the Welsh Government of SACRE reports from 2004/5 until 2010/11 found the same (Welsh Government, 2011b & 2013). One may speculate on the reasons for this: it might indicate that there is no great dissatisfaction with the implementation of the requirement or no feeling that is impossible to comply with the requirement. Alternatively, it might indicate that in some instances the legal requirements are simply being ignored, or are being interpreted in a very flexible manner, or, indeed, schools may be unaware of the possibility to request a determination.

The SACREs in their annual reports examine the Estyn reports on inspections that have taken place within their local authorities. An examination of these SACRE reports for the years 2010/11, 2011/12 and 2012/13 indicates the level of non-compliance with the statutory requirements in those schools which were inspected in those years by Estyn: instances of non-compliance were proportionately higher in secondary schools, but there were some failures to meet the requirements in primary schools. However, these findings do not report the overall picture at any one time as the SACRE reports refer only to those schools within their areas which have been inspected during a particular year.

In addition to our direct examination of SACRE reports, a survey of SACRE reports is also conducted by the Welsh Government. Both the 2011 and 2013 reviews observe some secondary schools failing to meet the statutory requirements on collective worship: these schools were either not providing a daily act of worship, or were providing sessions which had a 'primarily moral focus' but which contained little spiritual or religious content. Where this was the case, support had been offered to the non-compliant schools (Welsh Government, 2011b & 2013).

In the 2011 Review, of the twenty-two SACRES, only three indicated full compliance with the statutory requirements by those schools which had been inspected within their areas for all four years: in the 2013 Review, all but six local authority areas were in compliance in the three years (Welsh Government, 2013, Annex 9). However, even where there had been compliance with the statutory requirements, the reports indicated that there had been concerns with the quality of the collective worship provided in some schools (Welsh Government, 2011b, Annex 10). On the other hand, many of the reports noted the positive comments in inspection reports on the contribution made by collective worship to the spiritual, moral, social and cultural development of the pupils.

The Buchanan study

In their examination of collective worship in Wales, Sandberg and Buchanan (2011) present the findings of an empirical study undertaken in 2008 by Buchanan[2] (hereafter the Buchanan study) who sent a questionnaire to 209 schools, 172 primary schools and 37 secondary schools. These represented

---

2   We are grateful to Anna Buchanan for also allowing us access to the original unpublished work.

10 per cent of the schools in Wales. Responses resulted in the findings being based on a sample of 5 per cent of the schools in Wales, with primary schools dominating the study.

In the Buchanan study, all schools with a religious character indicated that they had met the statutory requirement for collective worship at their most recent school inspection. Of primary schools without a religious character, all but one had met the requirements: the head teacher of the school which failed (apparently on the basis that worship was three times a week rather than daily) was reported to feel strongly against compulsory worship in non-faith schools. However, of the secondary schools without a religious character that responded, nine reported that they had met the requirements while eight indicated that they had not. One of the schools which had failed considered that it was now complying with the statutory requirements, while one which had passed anticipated that it would fail the next inspection. Of those that did not comply, four head teachers considered that collective worship had no place in secondary schools. The other four non-complying schools' head teachers did not disagree with the principle of collective worship but made a variety of comments concerning the need for flexibility, professional judgement and practical issues – some of which led Buchanan to consider that there was some misunderstanding of the requirements. Sandberg and Buchanan note that the Estyn figures for 2001 to 2005 indicated that 81 out of 149 schools inspected in Wales failed to meet the statutory requirements for collective worship. Responses to other questions suggested that, while the legal requirements were generally understood, a number of misunderstandings existed.

The general finding was that schools with a religious character, and most primary schools (with or without a religious character) complied with the daily worship requirement, but that a majority of secondary schools did not. Of the primary schools that did not comply, they tended to have a number of acts of worship every week rather than nothing at all: the same could not be said about non-complying secondary schools. Interestingly, some responses suggested that a number of schools which had passed their inspection did not in fact hold a daily act of worship for all pupils.

The study found that very few parents had withdrawn their children from collective worship. No pupil had been withdrawn in fifty-one out

of seventy-one primary schools without a religious character, in nineteen
out of twenty-one primary schools with a religious character, in ten of the
eighteen secondary schools without a religious character or in any of the
secondary schools with a religious character.

Finally, as to whether head teachers believed that collective worship
had a place in Welsh schools, those in all but one of the schools with a religious character did believe this, as did all but five of the heads of primary
schools without a religious character. In contrast, ten out of eighteen heads
of secondary schools without a religious character considered it did not
have a place. In the primary schools, there was some difference of opinion
as to whether collective worship should be Christian in nature.

Sandberg and Buchanan concluded from the study that 'collective worship is a truly divisive issue in Welsh schools'. This is particularly the case
in secondary schools without a religious character. Interestingly, however,
they considered that many of the objections to collective worship were
actually objections to *daily* worship. And, significantly, the requirement
that the worship be 'of a broadly Christian character' was not singled out
for particular criticism: Sandberg and Buchanan consider that 'any criticism is levelled at religious content in general and not at Christianity in
particular'. They consider that further empirical work is needed to reveal
the extent to which worship is 'broadly Christian' in schools without a
religious character. This is undoubtedly true.

Implementation: A complex picture

As noted earlier, the Estyn and SACRE reports do not provide an overall picture of schools in Wales in any one year as they refer only to those
schools which have been inspected in the particular year. Without examining the individual school inspection reports over a period of years, it is
impossible to determine whether there are schools which are continually
non-compliant, although a few of the SACRE reports indicate instances of
successful resolution after a report of non-compliance. More information
on similar cases would provide some indication of whether non-compliance

is a deliberate policy to flout the requirements or results from falling short of the school's intended goals.

There are limits to what we can tell from the evidence reported in this section. Nonetheless, some tentative remarks may be made. The non-compliance instances appear to consist of instances of a failure to hold a daily act and instances where the worship does not meet the required Christian or religious character: however, as to which is more prevalent is not clear from the reports. Buchanan's study suggests that more criticism is directed at the requirement of daily worship rather than at worship *per se*.

Furthermore, while there are some instances of non-compliance in primary schools, the majority of the non-compliance appears to take place in secondary schools. One may speculate on why this might be the case: a less pressured timetable in primary schools; smaller, and therefore possibly less diverse, primary schools; greater engagement with, or less hostility to, worship by the pupils; leading appropriate worship being less challenging at the primary level? The existing available evidence raises many questions, but further empirical research is needed to find clearer answers.

Areas for enquiry

The limited data which exists on practice in Wales means that great cau-tion must be exercised in drawing conclusions on the extent to which there are problems relating to the principle and practice of collective worship in Welsh schools. However, the available data certainly suggests that it is worth pursuing further research in order to determine whether there are particular problems and of what nature. At the level of principle, there are contradictions and a lack of clarity and it would be surprising if these did not lead to challenges in terms of the implementation of the requirements in schools: further empirical research is necessary to explore the extent to which such challenges are a problem in Wales and, if so, the way in which schools are dealing with them. The remaining section outlines issues of concern which are deserving of further investigation.

Appropriateness of a statutory duty to conduct worship

The purpose and appropriateness of placing a statutory duty on state schools
to hold acts of collective worship has been consistently questioned since
the introduction of the duty under the 1944 Education Act. It was a duty
fiercely opposed by certain Welsh MPs at the time of its introduction
when it was rightly noted that the requirement represented a 'revolution
in British educational history' through the sanctioning of state compulsion in religious matters in schools (Cove, HC Deb, 10 March 1944). Up
until this point, acts of religious observance took place in many schools
but were not made compulsory by the state.

The debates during the passage of the 1944 Act suggest that the duty's
proponents wished to secure the place of Christianity in the life of the country,
particularly at a time when a war was being fought against totalitarian regimes
in Europe and beyond. Many interventions made during the reading of the
bill in the House of Lords focussed on a declared nexus between Anglo-Saxon
values, democracy and a future prosperous England. For example, the Earl of
Selborne, for the government, expressed his personal belief that 'the Anglo-
Saxon conception of democracy' could not function unless it was 'based on
the Christian ethic' (Selborne, HL Deb, 18 July 1944). He concluded his
speech with an expansive statement on the potential beneficial effects of the
bill on England. No reference was made to any possible impact on Wales.

Objections by Welsh MPs to the impropriety of the state in imposing
a duty of collective worship on schools went entirely unheeded. There was
also strong opposition by the National Union of Teachers. No account was
taken of the different religious and social context pertaining in Wales, a country where the Anglican Church had been disestablished and where a large
number of the population were non-conformists with distinct views on the
need for separation between Church and State, particularly in the field of
education. Mr William Cove, the Labour MP for Aberavon, declaring himself
to be a Non-conformist, argued that the state had always 'kept out outside
the religious field in schools' and that this principle ought to be upheld:

> We believe that religious teaching in the schools should be voluntary. Give it every
> facility certainly, and let the State provide facilities for the development of religious

knowledge, emotion and feeling; but do not, I beg hon. Members, bring the State in, to establish compulsion for any act of religious worship in the schools of this country. (HC Deb, 10 March 1944)

Mismatch between aims and methods

The rationale for placing a statutory duty on schools to hold daily acts of collective worship has typically been explained by the perceived ability of such an act to achieve a number of diverse aims. Circular 10/94 sets these out as follows:

> To provide the opportunity for pupils to worship God, to consider spiritual and moral issues and to explore their own beliefs; to encourage participation and response, whether through active involvement in the presentation of worship or through listening to, watching and joining in the worship offered; and to develop community spirit, promote a common ethos and shared values, and reinforce positive attitude.

Setting aside the principle of non-state compulsion in matters of religious practice, it may be possible to fulfil these aims through an act of collective worship in a society where the entire population adheres to the tenets of Christianity. However, in a diverse, multibelief country such as Wales, the stated aims cannot be achieved simultaneously through the tool of collective worship. Most markedly, the aim 'to develop community spirit, promote a common ethos and shared values, and reinforce positive attitude' is unlikely to be achieved through an act of worship in a situation where significant numbers of the school population may not be Christian and may not identify with Christian worship. Furthermore, the legislation itself undermines the aim of developing community spirit and ethos through providing for the right of withdrawal and the right of schools to seek determinations to allow groups within a school to hold a separate form of collective worship. Given this reality, it is appropriate and timely for education authorities in Wales to revisit the aims of collective worship in its state schools and to explore whether alternative options might be more effective in achieving the desired outcomes for Welsh society.

It is also appropriate to note that the Welsh Circular differs significantly from the English Circular in its statement of the government's aim in regulating collective worship in schools. The English version emphasizes the desirability of the *collective* nature of the act while ensuring the appropriateness of the content for the pupils taking part (paras 7–9). In contrast, the Welsh Circular does not focus on this idea of sharing and inclusion. Rather it chooses to underscore the duty to ensure pupils take part in an act of *worship*, and draws attention to the requirement that the majority of such acts each term must be wholly or broadly Christian in character (paras 8–10). This suggests some value in further research on Estyn's understanding of the legal framework for collective worship and the appropriate emphasis to be placed on the different aspects. Likewise, Estyn's attribution of legal status to Circular 10/94 deserves further investigation.

Concerns relating to implementation of the current duty

A number of procedural and legal issues of concern arise in relation to the implementation of the current statutory duty. On some of them, there is limited data to indicate whether there is a problem or its extent: for example, while it appears that there is limited take-up of the parental and sixth-former right to withdraw, further research is needed to determine whether this is due to a wish to participate in collective worship, a lack of awareness of the existence and content of collective worship, a lack of awareness of the right to withdraw or a fear of stigmatizing the pupil. Equally research is needed to assess whether those considering withdrawal are provided with adequate information on the content of the school's collective worship, and to evaluate the quality of alternative provision for pupils who have been withdrawn. Moreover, as is discussed later in this volume (see Chapter 6), there is a question of principle as to the whether the right to withdraw, or to resist parent withdrawal, should be extended to younger pupils.

The data indicates that no SACRE in Wales has ever received a request for a determination to disapply the requirement for worship of a broadly Christian character: again, further research might usefully pursue whether this is due to satisfaction with the requirements, a lack of concern about compliance or a lack of awareness of the procedure for applying for a determination.

Finally, there is a lack of information on the views of parents, teachers and pupils on the issue of compulsory collective worship. If the system is to work in an inclusive manner that respects diversity, the dearth of information on how it is currently perceived, including any problems it gives rise to, appears to be an undesirable state of affairs.

Conclusion

The areas of concern discussed above are indicative of the areas of future research needed. Conceptually, there is an urgent need for a reconsideration of the aims of collective worship. In light of this process, it would then be appropriate to consider how best to meet any revised aims that emerge. In the interim, there is a range of areas that demand investigation to understand more fully how the current statutory duty is understood and accepted by pupils, parents and schools, and to investigate to what extent the current arrangements comply with domestic and international human rights obligations. It is opportune to conclude by noting that the current law dates from a time when Welsh views and principles were easily subsumed by its dominant partner in the Westminster legislature. The Welsh Government and Welsh Assembly now have the legal competence to reconsider the practice of collective school worship and hence the opportunity to respond to its complexities in an innovative manner appropriate for Welsh society in the twenty-first century.

References

Ashworth, J., & Farthing, I. (2007). *Churchgoing in the UK: A research report from Tearfund on church attendance in the UK*. Teddington: Tearfund.

Bates, D. (1994). Christianity, Culture and Other Religions (Part 1): The Origins of the Study of World Religions in English Education. *British Journal of Religious Education, 17(6)*, 5–18.

British Humanist Association (2012). New survey on Collective Worship and RE in Wales finds more support than oppose legislative reform. Retrieved April 18, 2017, from <https://humanism.org.uk/2012/04/30/news-1030/>.

Clements, B. (2014). Changes in attendance at religious services in Britain. Retrieved April 18, 2017, from <http://www.brin.ac.uk/news/2014/changes-in-attendance-at-religious-services-in-britain/>.

Cove, W. (1944). HC Deb, 10 March 1944, vol. 397, cc. 2395–2427, 2402, 2403. Retrieved April 17, 2017, from <http://hansard.millbanksystems.com/commons/1944/mar/10/clause-24-general-provisions>.

Estyn (2005). *Equal opportunities and diversity in schools in Wales.* Cardiff: Estyn.

_____ (2006). *Annual Report for 2004–2005.* Cardiff: Estyn.

_____ (2007). *Annual Report for 2005–2006.* Cardiff: Estyn.

_____ (2008). *Annual Report for 2006–2007.* Cardiff: Estyn.

_____ (2009). *Annual Report for 2007–2008.* Cardiff: Estyn.

_____ (2010). *Annual Report for 2008–2009.* Cardiff: Estyn.

_____ (2011). *Annual Report for 2009–2010.* Cardiff: Estyn.

_____ (2013). *Supplementary guidance: collective worship in non-denominational schools.* Cardiff: Estyn.

_____ (2016a). *Guidance for the inspection of primary schools from September 2010 (updated in 2016).* Cardiff: Estyn.

_____ (2016b). *Guidance for the inspection of secondary schools from September 2010 (updated in 2016).* Cardiff: Estyn.

_____ (2017). *Annual Report for 2015–2016.* Cardiff: Estyn.

Freathy, R., & Parker, S. G. (2013). Secularists, Humanists and religious education: religious crisis and curriculum change, 1963–1975. *History of Education: Journal of the History of Education Society, 42: 2,* 222–225.

Hull, J. (1995). Collective Worship: The Search for Spirituality. In *Future Progress in Religious Education* [The Templeton Lectures] (pp. 27–40). London: Royal Society of Arts.

Macleod, E. (1988). HL Deb, 26 February 1988, vol. 493 cc. 1453–1486 (1475). Retrieved April 17, 2017, from <http://hansard.millbanksystems.com/lords/1988/feb/26/christian-teaching-in-schools>.

National Association of SACREs and the Association of Religious Education Inspectors, Advisers and Consultants (2012). Collective Worship Revisited: A Paper for all who are or *should* be interested in collective worship.

National Association of SACREs and the Association of Religious Education Inspectors, Advisers and Consultants (2013). *SACRE NEWS. Spring Issue.* National Assembly for Wales. (2012). E-petition. Retrieved April 18, 2017, from <http://www.senedd.assemblywales.org/mgIssueHistoryHome.aspx?IId=4420>, <http://www.senedd.assembly.wales/mgIssueHistoryHome.aspx?IId=3637>.

Office for National Statistics (a). Retrieved April 18, 2017, from <http://www.ons. gov.uk/ons/guide-method/measuring-equality/equality/ethnic-nat-identity-religion/religion/index.html>.

_____ (b). Retrieved April 18, 2017, from <http://wales.gov.uk/statistics-and-research/ sexual-identity-ethnicity-religion/?lang=en>.

_____ (2011). *Statistical bulletin: 2011 Census: Key Statistics for Wales.* Retrieved April 18, 2017, from <http://www.ons.gov.uk/ons/rel/census/2011-census/key-statistics-for-unitary-authorities-in-wales/stb-2011-census-key-statistics-for-wales. html#tab---Religion>.

Sandberg, R., & Buchanan, A. (2011). Religion, Regionalism and Education in the United Kingdom: Tales from Wales (pp. 107–132). In M. Hunter-Henin (Ed.), *Law, Religious Freedoms and Education in Europe.* Surrey: Ashgate.

Selborne, Earl (1944). HL Deb, 21 June 1944 vol. 132 cc. 306–370, 368. Retrieved April 17, 2017, from <http://hansard.millbanksystems.com/lords/1944/jun/21/ education-bill>.

_____ (1944a). HL Deb, 18 July 1944 vol. 132 cc. 950–982, 970, 971. Retrieved April 17, 2017, from <http://hansard.millbanksystems.com/lords/1944/jul/18/ education-bill>.

Voas, D. (2007). Surveys of Behaviour, Beliefs and Affiliation. In J. Beckford & N. J. Demerath (Eds.), *Handbook of the Sociology of Religion* (pp. 144–166). London: Sage.

Wales Association of SACRES (2012). Guidance on Collective Worship. Retrieved April 27, 2017, from <http://www.wasacre.org.uk/publications/GUID ANCE%20ON%20COLLECTIVE%20WORSHIP_FINAL_JUNE_2012_ ENGLISH.pdf>.

Welsh Government (2011). *Faith in Education.* Retrieved April 27, 2017, from <http:// gov.wales/docs/dcells/publications/130425-faith-in-education-en.pdf>.

_____ (2011b). *Review of SACRE Reports 2004–2005, 2005–2006, 2006–2007 and 2007–2008.* Retrieved May 8, 2017, from <http://learning.gov.wales/docs/learn ingwales/publications/131121-review-of-sacre-reports-2004-2008-en.pdf>.

_____ (2013). *Review of SACRE Reports 2008–2009, 2009–2010, 2010–2011.* Retrieved May 8, 2017, from <http://learning.gov.wales/docs/learningwales/ publications/131121-review-of-sacre-reports-en.pdf>.

_____ (2016). School Statistics. Retrieved April 18, 2017, from <https://stat swales.wales.gov.uk/Catalogue/Education-and-Skills/Schools-and-Teachers/Schools-Census/Pupil-Level-Annual-School-Census/Schools/ Schools-by-LocalAuthorityRegion-Governance>.

Welsh Office (1994). *Religious Education and Collective Worship*, Circular 10/94. Cardiff: Welsh Office Education Department.

Collective Worship and Religious Observance:
Legal Perspectives

ALISON MAWHINNEY

5 The Law on Collective School Worship: The Rationale Then and Now

ABSTRACT

The introduction and continued practice of collective worship as a compulsory activity in schools in England, Northern Ireland and Wales confound the dominant secularization narratives of the twentieth century. In an attempt to understand the origin of the legal obligation and to evaluate its contemporary rationale, this chapter draws on the work of Norbert Elias and Niels Reeh. In particular, it employs the Eliasian concept of the *survival unit* to argue that, for the state, the statutory duty to hold compulsory acts of school worship can be viewed as a valuable tool in its quest to ensure its continued existence, particularly at times when significant threats are considered to exist. While not denying the legitimacy of the state in devising such instruments, this chapter questions the rationale behind a duty of collective school worship in the context of today's multibelief society.

Introduction

The vast majority of schools in England, Northern Ireland and Wales are required by law to organize daily acts of collective worship (School Standards and Framework Act 1998, ss. 70–71; The Education and Libraries (Northern Ireland) Order 1986, Arts 21–22).[1] In England and Wales worship

---

1   In Scotland, the Education (Scotland) Act 1872 gave schools the freedom to continue the customary practice of religious observance and today all state-funded schools must make the practice of religious observance available, unless a resolution to discontinue the practice has been passed by the local education authority (Education (Scotland) Act 1980, ss. 8–9). While this chapter focuses on the duty of collective worship, considerations around the contemporary rationale for collective school

in schools without a religious character must be 'wholly or mainly of a broadly Christian character' (School Standards and Framework Act 1998, Sch.20. s. 3(2)). The desirability of a statutory duty of collective school worship has long been questioned (See, e.g., Hull, 1975; Swann Report, 1985; Hamilton & Watt, 1996; Cumper, 1998). A fundamental concern has to do with the appropriateness of a duty to hold acts of worship in non-faith state schools. The nature of the non-statutory guidance is a further source of unease (Department for Education, Circular 1/94; Welsh Office Education Department, Circular 10/94). Its provisions stress the need for the worship to 'be concerned with reverence or veneration paid to a divine being or power' and stipulate that 'a broadly Christian act' must 'contain some elements which relate specifically to the traditions of Christian belief and which accord a special status to Jesus Christ' (ibid. para. 6). Furthermore, its stated aims for the duty, which speak of providing an opportunity to worship God whilst simultaneously developing a community spirit and common ethos, appear incoherent and oblivious to the reality of a multibelief school environment.[2] Additional concerns include weaknesses in accountability structures leading to a wide diversity of practices, non-compliance with the duty and human rights issues surrounding the operation of opt-out provisions, including the right of pupils to have their views respected (Committee on the Rights of the Child, 2016).

A number of recent reports have highlighted these concerns (Clarke & Woodhead, 2015; Cumper & Mawhinney, 2015; Dinham & Shaw, 2015; Commission on Religion in Public Life, 2015). Several have called for a repeal of the law, with some suggesting that the nature of school assemblies should be left to the governors of individual schools (Clarke & Woodhead, 27). This chapter argues that, while the concerns and recommendations highlighted have validity and deserve attention, any consideration of the future direction of the law in this area must be preceded by an explicit discussion of the state's rationale in imposing the legal duty in the first place. In the absence of such a discussion it is impossible to weigh up coherently the

---

worship are relevant to debates concerning the practice of religious observance in Scottish schools today.

2   Where 'multibelief' refers to both religious and non-religious belief systems.

merits of maintaining, abolishing or reforming the current law. Moreover, a considered and balanced debate on the past and any present rationale for the duty may encourage politicians to engage more openly in discussions about the duty. To date they have shown an unwillingness to participate in these conversations.[3] An opportunity to begin with the question of rationale rather than a demand to react to recommendations may prompt greater engagement.

In examining the existence and nature of the rationale underlying the law on collective school worship, the chapter argues that the introduction of the duty in England and Wales in 1944 (Education Act 1944, ss. 26–28)[4] cannot be explained simply as an outcome of the agreement reached between the state and the churches during the negotiation of the 1944 Education Act nor by the perceived religious needs of the population at the time.[5] Indeed the introduction of the compulsory practice of collective school worship and its subsequent consolidation in the Education Reform Act 1988 confounds the dominant secularization narratives of the twentieth century. To explore this paradox and to identify the specific need of the state in introducing and continuing the duty, this chapter draws on the work of Norbert Elias and the concept of the state as a 'survival unit' (Elias, 1978). It employs the Eliasian concept to argue that a statutory duty to hold acts of school worship can be viewed as a potentially valuable tool for the state legitimately to use in its quest to ensure its continued existence, particularly at times when significant threats are considered to be present. It was this specific need of the UK state during the Second World

---

3   It has been suggested that the lack of political will for reform of the duty may be linked to a fear that any moves would 'likely be portrayed in certain newspapers as a "secular" or "multiculturalist" attempt to dilute Britain's Christian heritage. Fears of a media backlash may make politicians very hesitant to engage in discussion about statutory change' (*A New Settlement: Religion and Belief in Schools*, A St George's House Consultation, 15–16 February 2016, para. 116).

4   The duty was introduced in Northern Ireland under the Northern Ireland Act 1947, s. 21.

5   The Education Act 1944 established the current school system in England and Wales. The Act involved the state reaching a settlement with the main Christian Churches on key issues such as finance, governance and the place of religion in schools.

War that prompted it to impose the duty in the 1944 Education Act, a duty that simultaneously fulfilled the separate need of its partners in education at that time, the main Christian churches. The question that arises, however, is two-fold: first, did this need result in a coherent law with a plausible rationale and, secondly, does a need exist today that produces a convincing rationale for the continuation of a statutory duty of collective school worship.

In order to establish a process for identifying and evaluating the rationale underpinning the duty of collective worship, the first part of the chapter considers the relationship between the three components of a coherent law: needs, means and rationale. It argues that the task of producing a coherent law begins with the identification of a need. The second part introduces the Eliasian notion of the survival unit as a way of identifying the interests and needs of a state. In particular, it provides a summary of Niels Reeh's application of the concept to illustrate how the Danish state, acting as a survival unit, influenced the teaching of religion in state schools in order to protect its vital interests and to meet specific needs at particular points during the twentieth century. The third part of the chapter argues that the UK state acted in a similar manner in introducing and maintaining the duty of collective school worship in England and Wales. It draws on Reeh's analytical framework to argue that the state sought to use the education system to protect or improve its position in the 'survival game' at times when it perceived itself to be under threat. Evidence of this approach – and of the needs that the state sought to fulfil through a duty of collective worship – is drawn from the parliamentary debates at two specific points in time: in 1944 when the statutory obligation to hold daily acts of worship in schools was introduced in England and Wales; and in 1988 when the obligation was further defined. The fourth and final part assesses the plausibility of the rationale for a duty of collective worship, both historically and today. In so doing, it argues that an Eliasian notion of the state as a survival unit usefully highlights the legitimacy of the state in devising such instruments in response to perceived needs that must be met if the state, as a survival unit, is to exist and flourish. However, it notes that while a state may legitimately articulate such needs and develop statutory mechanisms to fulfil them, this does not necessarily guarantee that any resulting duty will have a plausible and convincing rationale. A duty that lacks a strong rationale cannot produce a coherent law. This chapter concludes that an appraisal of the future direction of the existing law must begin with identifying any contemporary needs of the state that require to be met through the holding of acts of worship in schools. It argues that if such needs do not exist then there can be no satisfactory rationale for continuing the duty of collective school worship.

A coherent law: Needs, means and rationale

Three elements should be present for a law to be considered coherent. First, a need must exist which the state believes should be fulfilled through imposing a legal duty. Secondly, the means to fulfil the need must be identified. Finally, a convincing rationale must exist that explains the reason why the chosen means will fulfil the need. None of these three elements is fixed; each may alter in response to changing circumstances. The nature of the need may change over time or become redundant. The means may become less effective in fulfilling the original need, or a new means may be required as a result of a change in the need. In response to a changed context, including, for example, a changed need and/or a changed means, the rationale may require re-articulation so that the legal duty imposed by the state continues to be seen as coherent. If a convincing rationale cannot be found in the wake of changed circumstances, then the law lacks coherence and the justification for the state in continuing to impose the legal duty becomes weak.

At the most basic level a need must be identified in order for a rationale to exist for a legal duty. Any appraisal of a law and its rationale should begin, therefore, with identifying the nature of the need that is sought to be fulfilled by the law. Only then can an examination be made to determine whether the means chosen to satisfy that need is appropriate and effective. If the need and the means to fulfil it correspond then a satisfactory rationale can be established for imposing the legal duty. It should be noted that the question of the justifiable nature of any need articulated by the state is a separate concern and independent of the question as to the plausibility of the rationale. It is entirely possible for a law to be supported by a strong rationale and thus coherent, yet for it to be disputed on grounds of the reasonableness of the underlying declared need.

An appraisal of a rationale for a law may lead to one of a number of conclusions. In the case of the law on collective school worship the outcome could be that the original need remains and can continue to be fulfilled by the current means, that is, daily acts of worship in schools. In the absence of any changes in other circumstances, the rationale for the duty would remain strong. However, while the need and the means could remain unchanged, a change in other circumstances in society could render the link between the need and the means incoherent, thus leading to a much weaker rationale for imposing the duty. For example, a significant change in the religious demographics of the population may mean that the notion of worship is alien to many pupils: a weakening of the positive correlation between the need and the chosen means. It is also possible that the need may remain the same but the decision is taken to change the means to fulfil that need. Thus a new duty is imposed. This duty may take the form of a collective activity (albeit not an act of collective worship) during a designated period of the school day; or perhaps the chosen means might take a completely different form, for example, amending the syllabus of a current curriculum subject. Whatever the means chosen, the strength of the rationale for any such duty will again depend on the relationship between the need and the means.

In contrast to the above scenarios where the original need remains unchanged, a review of the law and its rationale may lead to a re-articulation of the original need, resulting in one of the following three outcomes. First, the revision of the need may be such that it can be fulfilled by the current means, that is, daily acts of school worship. In the absence of any changes in other circumstances, the rationale for the duty could remain valid. However, a re-articulation of the original need may require a different means to fulfil that revised need. As noted above, any new means may take the form of an alternative collective activity during a designated period of the school day; or perhaps the chosen means might take a completely different form depending on the nature of the new need. Again, any new means chosen would have to correspond to the revised need in a manner that would provide a convincing rationale for the imposition of any revised duty. Finally, it may be found that the original need no longer exists in any form. In this case, it would become impossible to identify a cogent rationale for a statutory duty to hold daily acts of worship in schools.

Given the centrality of need in establishing a rationale, the rest of the chapter explores the original rationale for the introduction of the law on collective school worship through identifying the need that a daily act of worship was designed to satisfy. In so doing, it provides a starting point for an evaluation of the current rationale for the duty, namely, can the need and the means to fulfil that need provide a convincing rationale for imposing the duty of daily collective worship in schools today? It is not the intention of the chapter to question or to evaluate the existence and/ or nature of a need that may be identified by the state. As argued below, an Eliasian notion of the state as a 'survival unit' accepts the legitimacy of a state in asserting any such needs and in devising mechanisms to protect itself. Rather the focus is on the argument that the need and the chosen means must correspond if a plausible rationale is to exist. If a rationale is not convincing then the state's needs, be they justifiable or not, are not sufficient to create a coherent law.

The state as a survival unit: Denmark, religion and schools

The German sociologist Norbert Elias argues that from earliest times human societies have been divided into survival units (Elias, 1978; Elias & Schröter, 1991; Elias, 2008). Only the survival unit with the ability to defend a domain of sovereignty will survive (Kaspersen and Norman Gabriel, 2008). Elias considered the state to be a survival unit 'that participates in a survival game with other states in which all means appear to be employed' (Reeh, 2013, 238). These means include not only the maintenance of a military force but also the organization of an effective internal structure that, for instance, draws on economic development, the education of the citizen, and culture and religion in the quest for survival (ibid.). As Niels Reeh puts it, 'the defence of the State should be seen in very broad terms, namely as all the resources that a State can muster in order to maintain or increase its position in the survival "game"'(ibid.).

In Reeh's view, classic theories of secularization pay insufficient attention to the notion of state agency and as a result would struggle to render an intelligible account of the treatment of religion in schools by the Danish state during the twentieth century (ibid. 237). Instead, he argues that use of the Eliasian concept of the survival unit places an appropriate focus on the agency of the state in forming a comprehensible narrative:

> A different narrative of the historical process emerges once the State is put at the centre of analysis. Instead of a narrative in which the secular and religious spheres of society are differentiated into separate realms as the process of modernization unfolds, we see one in which the State has used the teaching of religion as an instrument to further its interests. (Ibid. 247)

From an analysis of primary sources relating to the political decisions behind Danish religious education policies in the twentieth century, Reeh reaches the conclusion that important developments in this account cannot be separated from the perceived needs of the Danish state, acting as a survival unit. His examination begins by noting the long history of intervention by the Danish state in the religious education of the population. Compulsory confirmation was introduced in 1736 and when compulsory schooling was introduced in 1739 schools were almost exclusively devoted to the confessional teaching of Christianity. From 1814 onwards, the Danish state became gradually less interested in the teaching of religion in schools and eventually in 1975 the confessional teaching of religion ended. Nevertheless, the state's interest in religious educational policies increased at two points during the period from 1814 up to the present day thus challenging a simple, linear narrative of secularization. These two points occurred during the Second World War and during the so-called War on Terror.

Prior to the Second World War and in the face of an increasingly aggressive posturing by Germany, the Danish Government realized that the organization of Danish society, including its culture in its entirety, needed to be regarded as a part of the Danish defence strategy. The political leaders considered an intimate connection to exist between defence policy and the internal affairs of the state and an explicit aim became the need 'to create a fellow feeling within the Danish people' to ensure that national life would endure even if the country was invaded by the Germans (ibid. 239). The creation of a 'fellow feeling' meant ensuring that personal freedom and intellectual liberty were recognized throughout society, including in schools which were recognized as important sites in the cultivation of this sense of societal cohesiveness. This need led to the lessening of control by the state in religious matters in schools to ensure that citizens did not feel alienated from the state. Parents were allowed to exempt their children from religious teaching and teachers were also allowed to be exempted from the teaching of religion.

However, changes in circumstances during the wars years of 1940–1945 led the Danish Government to move away from this 'hands-off' approach and caused it to adopt an increasingly directive role in influencing how religion should be taught in schools. In 1940 Denmark surrendered to and was occupied by Germany. The Danish Government was permitted to continue to govern during this period under strict conditions set by the Nazi regime. When the Nazi occupying powers pushed for cooperation between schools in Germany and Denmark, the Danish Government feared an attempt at the Nazification of its schools. It rejected the Nazi proposition and issued a departmental order clarifying how the rather general provisions of the School Act 1937 dealing with religious education ought to be interpreted. The order directed the teaching to focus on the formation of the moral character of children with a particular emphasis placed on the values of respect and solidarity.[6] As Reeh notes,

> the values of respect and solidarity were considered by Danish politicians also to apply to Christianity, although this term is so broad that it could be supposed to include the *Glaubensbewegung Deutsche Christen*, which supported the Nazi regime.

6   The order stated that the school should 'develop and strengthen children's sense of ethical and Christian values and give them respect for human life and nature, love of home and kin and country, respect for the opinions of others, and a sense of solidarity between peoples and with the other Nordic peoples.' Departmental Order, 24 May 1941.

However, in its Danish context Christianity was generally believed to be antithetical to Nazism. (Ibid. 242–243)

Reeh argues that the order can be seen as 'part of an overall political strategy that was directed at the survival of the Danish State under occupation' where the state influenced how religion should be taught in a bid to secure its vital interests (ibid. 242). The rationale for this proactive approach by the Danish state to religious education policy in schools was provided by the need to promote a common set of Danish values, something that could be achieved by focusing on these particular qualities in the religious education curriculum.

In the post-war years, and within the context of the Cold War and Denmark's membership of NATO, widespread political consensus led to the passing of the School Act of 1975. This act abolished the confessional teaching of Christianity in schools and, instead, provided that students should acquire knowledge of – but not faith in – the Christianity of the Danish Evangelical-Lutheran Church. Here again, in response to a fresh set of political threats, the needs of the state can be seen to prompt and provide a rationale for a change in its approach to the teaching of religion in schools. During the passing of the Act the overall aim of the Danish public school system was set out against the backdrop of the need to defend the values of democracy, intellectual liberty and tolerance – values considered to be absent in the USSR, the major military threat at the time. Given this context, a continuation of confessional teaching in state schools 'was seen by the government as just another type of indoctrination and therefore incommensurable with the logic of the welfare state, which was to provide a maximum of personal freedom and liberty to the individual citizen' (ibid. 247).

The next key period when the Danish state becomes interested in the teaching of religion in schools began in 2001 and remains to the present day. This period has seen the Danish People's Party gain considerable influence through its position as a coalition partner following the election of 2001. Against a backdrop of considerable immigration in the previous twenty years, the party has been explicit in conceptualizing the state and its culture in terms of 'the Danish people's history, experiences, beliefs, language and customs' and has forcefully argued that 'the protection and development of this culture is a precondition for the country's survival as a free and enlightened society'.[7] In addition to the perceived threat to Danish society caused by immigration, Denmark experienced considerable anti-Muslim feeling during 2005–2006 following the publication of caricatures of the Prophet Muhammad in the media, an event that led to fears that acts of terrorism might be carried out in the country by Danish Muslims. Reeh notes that the effect of these developments could be seen in 2007 when the decision was taken to turn the existing optional subject, 'Christianity/Enlightenment of Life', into a compulsory subject called' Christianity/Enlightenment of Life/Citizenship'. The move suggests that in the face of perceived threats – internal and external – to the values of Danish society, the Danish Government and politicians in general began 'to value education in the Danish national heritage, including Christianity. The teaching of Christianity was from this point in no danger of complete abolition, as it had been in the 1970s … the new school subject could be seen as an attempt to counter anti-democratic forces (especially Islamic terrorism)' (ibid. 247). In other words, the Danish state aimed to meet its perceived survival needs through a renewed emphasis on professed traditional Danish values, including those stemming from Christianity, thus providing a convincing rationale for the change in the state's religious educational policies in schools.

Collective school worship: The need of the UK state

Reeh's account of the influence of the Danish state in the teaching of religion in state schools provides an innovative explanation as to why, during a period of growing secularization within society, a state may choose to

7   Danish People's Party (2002), *Principprogram 2002*, translated and cited by Reeh (2013, 245).

encourage and control the form of religion taught in schools, namely, to meet an internal or external threat to its security and survival. The examination below explores the extent to which the introduction and continued practice of the obligation to hold acts of collective worship in schools in Wales and England, and later in Northern Ireland, can be said to be an attempt to fulfil a similar 'survival' need. In this exploration reference is made to relevant primary source material, particularly the parliamentary debates at the time of the passing of the two key pieces of legislation regulating collective school worship: the Education Act 1944 and the Education Reform Act 1988.

The Education Act 1944

In contrast to the experience of many countries in Continental Europe, including Denmark, the state came relatively late to playing a role in education in the United Kingdom. In England and Wales state provision of education began with the 1870 Elementary Education Act and in the 1880s with the establishment of Local School Boards. Prior to this involvement, schools were overwhelmingly run by religious bodies, the vast majority of them Christian. The lack of a historical state involvement in education makes it surprising that in the mid-twentieth century the state should choose to become so directly involved in the question of religion in schools through setting down the explicit duty on schools to hold daily acts of collective worship.

The duty was strongly opposed at the time of its introduction by the National Union of Teachers and a substantial number of Members of Parliament. It was rightly noted that the requirement represented a 'revolution in British educational history' through the sanctioning of state compulsion in religious matters in schools (Cove, HC Deb, 10 March 1944, 2403). Up until this point national legislation had not required schools to provide worship. Religious observances, such as Bible reading, took place in many schools but were not made compulsory by the state. The Elementary Education Act of 1870 permitted religious education but there was no obligation to provide it. If it was provided, it had to be voluntarily funded, exclude the catechism of any particular religious denomination and take place outside of normal curriculum time, in other words, at the beginning or end of a school session. As Mr William Cove, the Labour Member for Aberavon, noted during the Bill's passage in 1944:

> Hitherto, as I have understood it, the State has kept outside the religious field in the schools of our country ... A collective act of worship has been carried on in almost all the schools of the country, but now it will be compulsory; the State enters into it. (HC Deb, 10 March 1944, 2403)

The debates during the parliamentary passage of the 1944 Act suggest that there were two proponents of the duty: the government and the main Christian churches. While each had their own distinct need, a common means to fulfil those needs was agreed upon. The churches wished to revive and secure the place of Christianity in the life of the country at a time when concern surrounding declining participation and membership rates of the main Christian churches, including the decline in Sunday school attendance, had been growing (see e.g. Freathy & Parker, 2013, 223–227). In 1941 the Anglican archbishops published a document setting out five points that they considered necessary to follow to ensure that Christian values would be restored and protected in the country. The Archbishop of Canterbury had discussed these points with the government at the earlier stages of the bill. Point Five of the document was that all schools should start the day with an Act of Worship. In his contribution to the debates, the Earl of Selborne (for the government) confirmed that 'the collective act of worship was one of what were known as the Archbishop's five points, and this is the place where that point is embodied in this Bill. I think that is probably why the phrase which appears in the Bill is used' (HL Deb, 21 June 1944, 347).

While it is clear that the duty of collective worship was prompted by the desire of the Anglican Church to revive the religious life of the nation, it was, however, closely coupled to an argument that a strengthening of Christian values was particularly needed at a time when a war was being fought against totalitarian regimes. Arguably, this perceived threat to the nation's future well-being and survival encouraged the government to acquiesce to the Church's demands on collective worship and explains why the state, for the first time in its modern history, demanded compulsion in religious matters in schools. Freathy and Parker (2013, 223) note that it was within this context of mutual need that 'the churches and the State collaborated in passing the 1944 Education Act'. They observe that:

> The Second World War was frequently portrayed by British clerics and politicians as a spiritual and moral crisis threatening the Christian foundations of civilisation, freedom and democracy. Such rhetoric was repeatedly coupled with an assertion that Britain's social and political tradition and values could only endure the threat of idolatrous totalitarianism abroad and pre-war trends towards faithlessness at home if the nation's Christian identity was reinforced and reinvigorated. (Ibid.)

References to the close relationship between supporting Christianity and ensuring the well-being of the nation were evident in parliamentary exchanges made during the reading of the bill in the House of Lords. An emphasis on Anglo-Saxon and English traditions was particularly noticeable. In his concluding speech for the government, the Earl of Selborne noted that the new education system should aim 'first and foremost to give the children the right standard of values and conduct, to teach them their civic responsibilities, to give them the power of continuing to learn, and to equip them for the battle of life', noting that 'none of these things can be achieved unless the children have a firm religious foundation. I, personally, believe that it is impossible for the Anglo-Saxon conception of democracy to function unless it is based on the Christian ethic' (HL Deb, 18 July 1944, 970). He was specific in relating the proposed duty to hold acts of collective worship in schools with the need to ensure the survival of the nation and argued that collective worship would allow for a new approach that would allow the country to confront

> the real enemy [that] is the naked materialistic paganism which has reared its head in Europe to a height unknown for a thousand years, and which threatens Christendom to-day, and with it our civilization, our homes, our people. (Ibid.)

The link between the need to defend the nation and the need to ensure the place of Christianity in schools was also explicitly made by the Archbishop of Canterbury during the debates. The Archbishop urged the Chamber to never forget that freedom here, and also in Holland, began with the sense that men must obey God rather than man. Freedom was primarily understood in this country as freedom to worship God in accordance with the dictates of conscience. It is from that root that English freedom has sprung; ... At a moment, therefore, when we are fighting for liberty, it is a great thing we should also more firmly than ever before establish the religious foundation of the education of our children. That is secured by this Bill, provided that what it enacts is carried out in the spirit of the Bill itself. (HL Deb, 18 July, 972)

Once the principle of non-state compulsion in religious matters in schools was put to one side, it is not surprising that, in the context of the religious composition of the United Kingdom of the 1940s, the government was prepared to accept, as part of a wider agreement on educational reform, the proposition and rationale that the need to secure the morality and well-being of the nation and its children could be achieved through the means of a daily act of worship in schools.

The Education Reform Act 1988

More than forty years after the introduction of the law on collective school worship, the UK state explicitly chose to continue the duty of collective school worship in the Education Reform Act of 1988. Furthermore, it introduced an additional stipulation: that the act should be 'wholly or mainly of a broadly Christian character' (s. 7(1)). In other words, what previously had been an implicit understanding as to the content of an act of collective worship under the 1944 Act was made explicit in the 1988 Act. The copper-fastening of the duty to provide collective worship and the demand for it be Christian in nature appears unexpected given the educational and social developments that formed the backdrop to the 1988 Act. During the decades following the 1944 Act the cultural climate had become 'less conducive to the State-sponsored Christianization envisaged by those who were responsible for' that Act (Freathy & Parker, 2013, 224). Richard Cheetham (2004, 23–25) notes that by the 1960s key areas of change were emerging that challenged the acceptability of compulsory Christian school worship: non-Christian immigration; decline in religious adherence to Christianity as illustrated by a sharp decline in Sunday School attendance; greater tendency on the part of humanists, secularists, atheists and agnostics to express their views; increased concerns about the ability of school children to understand the religious concepts implicit in an act of worship, and the tension between the aims of worship and the aims of education. These factors contributed to an increasingly widespread view that the obligation to hold acts of worship in schools should be abolished or substantially modified in character (see e.g. Schools Council, 1971; Hull, 1975; Jones, 1969; Hirst, 1971).

During the early 1980s a number of parliamentary and government bodies expressed similar views. In 1981 the Select Committee on Education, Science and Arts (1982, HC116 II) recommended that the statutory obligation to hold acts of collective worship should be removed and instead made voluntary. A major government report, the Swann Report of 1985, had also given detailed consideration to the appropriateness of collective worship in an increasingly diverse society.[8] It reached the conclusion that due to the 'multiplicity of beliefs and non-beliefs now present in our society' (ibid. 397) compulsory daily collective worship could not continue to be required of schools for a society with a diverse range of beliefs. The report recommended that the government should 'look afresh' at the issue with a few to considering whether changes were needed after the passage of forty years from the earlier Act.

In parallel with these developments, a number of significant voices remained in favour of the obligation, a group that Cheetham describes as 'essentially a combination of the Christian religious and the political "right"' (2004, 32). Each had a need which could be satisfied through the continuation of the duty of collective school worship. The Christian element wished

---

8   The report, *Education for All*, was the final report of the Committee of Inquiry into the Education of Children from Ethnic Minority Groups, established in 1979 and chaired by Michael Swann. The Swann Committee's terms of reference relate only to England and hence its evidence gathering was restricted to England. However, its conclusions and recommendations were seen to have an importance for education across England and Wales, and were to influence discussions around the 1988 bill which was to have applicability to both Wales and England.

to use acts of collective worship to promote Christian confessional belief in schools,[9] while the political element, which was principally drawn from the Conservative Party, aimed to use the acts to advocate 'a common moral and cultural basis for life based on the Christian heritage of the country' (ibid.). The lobby was highly effective: the government firmly committed to ensuring that collective worship continued in the 1988 Act. Moreover, as noted above, the lobby succeeded in changing the wording of the duty in the original bill with respect to the nature of the worship: it now had to be wholly or mainly broadly Christian in nature.

The success is difficult to comprehend within a classic secularization narrative, particularly in light of the steady stream of opposition to the duty since the 1960s. However, applying the Eliasian concept of the survival unit leads to a greater analytical emphasis being placed on the role and agency of the state at this time, and on its need to maintain and strengthen its position in the 'survival game'. In particular, it highlights why the state would choose to organize its internal structure, including its education system, in a specific way in response to perceived threats to its continual well-being. Developments within the state since the 1960s – including the emergence of what may be described broadly as a more multicultural and permissive society – were perceived by certain politicians, principally those within the governing party, as a threat to both the well-being of the nation and its Christian heritage. In parliamentary debates, Kenneth Baker, the Secretary of State for Education, referred to the first of these concerns when he spoke of how the bill's amendments would help to promote values that would benefit and fortify society:

> We believe that there must be a bedrock in the basic teaching of Christianity in our schools, in both religious education and worship, because in that way our society is strengthened in a tolerant, humane and spiritual way. (HC Deb, 18 July 1988, 841)

---

9   Freathy and Parker (2013, 251) note the consistent advocacy of this lobby. For example, during the 1970s, when twenty-six questions and debates in the Westminster Parliament focused on religious education/religious instruction a majority of participants asserted 'an inextricable association' between traditional Christian instruction and the 'moral development of young people, the quality of national life, and (in the view of some) the very survival of Britain.'

With respect to the second concern – the need to safeguard the country's Christian heritage – Mr Baker stressed the important role the amendments would play in strengthening 'the Christian background and tradition' of the nation, something he argued to be of importance to the 'framework of this country' (ibid.). Thus, in partnership with those from the Christian right who felt threatened by the multicultural approach being taken to religious education and collective worship, the state as a survival unit, turned to collective school worship as an instrument to employ to protect its vital concerns.

The partnership between the state and the Christian religious right was particularly evident in debates in the House of Lords where the amendment requiring that worship be 'wholly or mainly of a broadly Christian character' was introduced.[10] Of note is the approach taken by the Christian group which chose not to rely on the arguments that would have explicitly articulated their views, namely, that the act of worship should be used 'as a vehicle to promote Christian belief' because 'the Christian faith is true and therefore it is right and proper to seek to nurture children into that faith' (Emery, HC Deb, 18 July 1988, 836). Instead the group expressed fears that 'moral and ethical standards have declined and are still declining' (Halsbury, HL Deb, 26 February 1988, 1469) and frequently aligned its views with those of the government in arguing that, in what was portrayed as a changing and increasingly permissive society, acts of school worship were 'vital to our national well-being' and to protecting 'the moral health of the nation' (Ashbourne, HL Deb, 26 February 1988, 1468). The contribution of Lord Swinfen was typical of those who sought to link the country's values to those of Christianity and, in turn, to the need to impose a duty of Christian worship in schools:

10   This was the wording subsequently found in Section 7(1) of the 1988 Act. When the bill was initially introduced and debated in the House of Commons no change had been proposed to the wording of the original duty found in the 1944 Act. However, when the bill reached the House of Lords what ultimately became Section 7 of the Education Reform Act was moved in the House of Lords at the third reading stage by the Bishop of London.

Over the past 30 years of so we have had a terrific influx of people into this country of religions which are other than Christian. Yet this country has been basically Christian for something like 1,400 years ... Our law, toleration, customs, culture and the way we organise ourselves in society, are all based upon Christianity. (HL Deb, 26 February 1988, 1473)

In common with Kenneth Baker's comments in the House of Commons, the role of collective Christian school worship in helping preserve the Christian heritage of the country was also frequently referenced. Baroness MacLeod, for example, argued that 'The Christian religion is part of our country, part of our heritage, with the Queen as head of the Church and the nation' (HL Deb, 26 February 1988, 1475). Meanwhile Baroness Strange, failing to appreciate that an argument premised on the existence an established church had no relevance outside of England, claimed that the existence of an established religion in England was sufficient reason to impose a duty of Christian worship on all state schools in England and Wales: 'Great Britain is supposed to be a Christian country. We have an established Christian religion' (HL Deb, 26 February 1988, 1476).

A number of peers did raise concerns about the introduction of the amendment and its segregating impact. The Labour peer Lord Morton of Shuna hoped that the provisions would 'do nothing to damage the furtherance of a collective community spirit in any school' (HL Deb, 7 July 1988, 435). He also pointed out that it 'would be unfortunate if the effect of the amendments was in any way to separate off people of different religions into different camps, so to speak' (ibid.).[11] When the bill returned to the House of Commons for consideration of the House of Lords amendments, Jack Straw, the Labour Shadow Minister on Education, expressed strong dissatisfaction with the time allotted (two hours) to the discussion of the amendments on religious education and worship. He also objected to the

---

11　Lord Morton was also concerned with the democratic process by which the amendment had been introduced. He inquired as to '[W]hy have the government changed their attitude during the Bill's progress through Parliament? In another place [the House of Commons] the government's attitude, as I understand it, was that the 1944 Act needed no amendment. Perhaps we may have some indication of why there was that change.'

bundling of a wide range of amendments, including the one dealing with collective worship, into a single package on which one vote would be taken (HC Deb, 18 July 1988, 819). He viewed the issue as one of tolerance and respect for minority beliefs, noting that the Religious Education Council of England and Wales was of the view that the proposed amendment was 'not the appropriate way to proceed' (ibid. 823). Non-Christian MPs argued that the amendment would not provide the proper basis for what was now a multi-religious society and that it was 'extraordinary that a new religious settlement should have been reached in haste and in dark corners ... The result is impoverished, impractical and unprincipled amendments' (Sedgemore, HC Deb, 18 July 1988, 837). The amendment was passed in the House of Commons by a vote on a block of amendments by 372 votes to 108.[12]

A plausible rationale: Then and now?

The use of an Eliasian approach to an examination of the law on school worship highlights the agency and legitimacy of the state in employing such tools if it believes that to do so will strengthen its position in the 'survival game'. The duties imposed under the 1944 and 1988 Acts demonstrate an acceptance of the role of the state in using the education system as a tool of socialization in this way and as a means of ensuring the continued well-being of the state. Indeed, the argument can be made that this is a proper role for schools and that the educational system 'as the single most important institution outside government' should be used more intensively in creating a strong democratic state (Gutman & Thompson, 1996, 359).

A strengthening of the parental right to educational authority in recent decades has led to suggestions that there is a growing reluctance to utilize

---

12   Given that the amendment on collective worship was just one in a set of amendments voted upon, it is impossible to analyse the number of MPs who would have supported or opposed this particular amendment. For a detailed account of the passing of the bill, see C. Alves (1991).

the education system as an institution for cultivating mutual values, leading to a neglect of this democratic potential of schools. Arguably an increased focus on the rights of parents and pupils may cause the state to act cautiously in this area. Nevertheless it does not reduce the legitimacy of the state in turning to the country's education system in its quest to devise strategies that will assist the state's continued survival in its desired form. However, to be coherent and effective, a statutory measure taken as part of this quest must not simply be a response to a particular need. It must also have a convincing rationale that explains the reason why the chosen means will fulfil the need. It is argued below that the introduction of the statutory duty of collective school worship in 1944 not only responded to clearly articulated needs but, crucially, it also had a cogent rationale. In 1988 when the legislators also articulated a set of needs for the duty, the changed nature of these needs in an altered environment produced a weak rationale for the duty. Today, in light of further transformations in society, a plausible rationale for the continuation of the duty is completely absent.

The history of collective school worship as outlined shows that the original 1944 duty was designed to meet two separate needs – the need of the state and the need of the main Christian churches. Each sought to protect their own survival. The state wished to instil standards and values in the population which would equip it to withstand foreign totalitarian forces, while the churches wanted to restore the place of Christianity in the life of the nation. Accommodation of the need of the churches was considered legitimate given the wider compromise agreement that was being negotiated between the state and the churches during the passing of the 1944 Act. The religious demographic of society at the time meant that the distinct yet contemporaneous needs of State and Church could reasonably be thought to be satisfied through a common means. Thus, the imposition of a duty on all schools to hold daily acts of collective worship had a credible rationale and the 1944 law could be viewed as coherent.[13]

---

13   As previously noted, despite a rationale existing, it is still possible to oppose a law on other grounds. As was noted above this was the case with the introduction of the law on the collective worship where a significant number of MPs argued strongly

By 1988 many circumstances in society had changed. In an increasingly diverse society, the duty was viewed by many as out of place. An Eliasian notion of the state as a survival unit suggests that its retention and increased Christian emphasis under the Education Reform Act 1988 can best be explained as an attempt by the state, as personified by the government of the day, to protect itself from what it saw as threats to its essential interests at a time of change. While debate exists around the existence and nature of any such threats – increased immigration and an increasingly permissive society – the needs they produced are nevertheless a manifestation of how the government of the day perceived these changes in society. The identification of these needs legitimately led the state to employ its internal resources to protect itself and ensure its survival in its preferred form.

However, more contentious and dubious – and central to the argument of this chapter – is the means chosen by the state to meet its identified needs of promoting democratic values and protecting the country's Christian heritage. The decision by the state to continue to use daily acts of collective school worship as its chosen means was flawed and incapable of providing a convincing rationale for the duty for two reasons. The first reason relates to a change in the nature of the needs. In 1944 two legitimate needs existed – those of the Church and the State. The Christian churches were explicit about their desire to re-establish Christianity in the life of the nation's population and therefore could provide a logical link between their stated need and means sought to achieve this aim, namely a daily act of collective worship in schools. Crucially, and conveniently, this means also had the potential to satisfy the needs of the state at that time, namely to bolster the nation's moral fibre during a period of crisis. However, by 1988, accommodating the needs of the churches through the use of state educational policies could no longer be considered legitimate. Indeed, recognizing this changed circumstance, those elements within the Christian churches that sought to continue the duty chose not to be explicit in expressing their specific need of promoting Christian confessional belief in schools. Instead, they relied on 'state survival' arguments that expressed

against it on the grounds that the state should not become involved with compelling a particular religious practice in schools.

the need to protect the country's Christian culture and those values deemed desirable in a healthy democratic society. Hence by the time of the 1988 bill, the only legitimate needs that existed to be fulfilled were those of the state and, in contrast to the situation in 1944, these did *not* include the need to 'establish the religious foundation of the education' (Archbishop of Canterbury, HL Deb, 18 July 1944, 972) of the nation's children.

The second factor that challenges the state's choice of means relates to changed social circumstances and specifically the changed religious composition of society. Society had undergone transformation to such an extent that, as Anthony Bradney (2008, 145) notes, 'the respect that the statute accords to Christianity [was] not to be found in the population at large'. The relationship between the need (the promotion of values that underpin democratic society and the protection of the country's Christian heritage) and the means designed to fulfil it (an act of mainly Christian worship) was illogical in a society where Christianity as a practised faith was no longer dominant. The result is a law where the needs and means do not correspond and where a convincing rationale for the duty is absent. The reason for its retention in the 1988 Act, in spite of the lack of such a rationale, can be explained by the extent of the constituency shared by the membership of the Christian right lobby and the government of the day.

The societal changes witnessed in the latter half of the twentieth century have intensified in the first decades of this century and serve to heighten the lack of a credible rationale for the duty today. While an Eliasian conception of the state recognizes that a state may need to develop statutory mechanisms of this nature as part of its wider 'defence strategy', if a measure lacks a plausible rationale then it becomes incoherent and the justification for the state in continuing to impose the duty becomes highly questionable. The law on collective worship has reached this point. To assess its future direction, policymakers must begin by reviewing the need that prompted the law. A review may find that the needs articulated at the time of the passing of the 1988 Act, namely, the promotion of democratic values and the preservation of the country's Christian heritage, continue to exist. Alternatively, it may be shown that new threats or circumstances give rise to additional or different needs on the part of the state. As the experience of Denmark illustrates, states periodically reshape educational policies in response to fresh political challenges in recognition of the close nexus between a state's defence policy and the organization of its internal affairs, including its education system. Thus, for example, if the state needs to reduce any sense of alienation from the state felt by certain sections of society and to encourage what the Danes call 'fellow feeling' amongst the population, it may elect to loosen its control on religious matters in schools and instead focus on measures to promote greater social cohesiveness.

In reappraising the duty of collective worship the critical stage is that of deciding how any identified need – new or old – should be met today. This in turn will drive the decision as to whether the current duty of collective school worship should be maintained, abolished or reformed. Here the central question for policymakers becomes one of rationale: is there an identified need that requires to be met through an act of collective school worship or is there an alternative means that more effectively fulfils any need that has been identified? For example, the state may well have a need to improve religious literacy or develop common values amongst its school population, but arguably these needs are more effectively met through amending existing activities and subjects within the curriculum rather than through an act of worship. Similarly, a need may relate to developing greater school and community cohesion in an increasingly fragmented society that has seen a rise in the politics of identity. However, it would seem strongly counter-intuitive to expect that this can be achieved through an act of worship from which significant numbers of pupils would be disaffected. Arguably school assemblies – understood as regular, non-religious collective school gatherings where news of activities and successes by pupils are shared and celebrated – offer a sufficient and inclusive opportunity to promote positive attitudes and develop a community spirit within the school and wider society. It is possible, therefore, that a review of the rationale of the duty today may confirm that the original needs continue to exist and/ or may identify new needs; but nevertheless conclude that these needs should be met through a means other than an act of collective worship. In this situation, where an act of collective worship is not considered as an effective means to fulfil any identified need, there can be no rationale for continuing the duty in schools.

Concluding remarks

This chapter has argued that an Eliasian notion of the state as a survival unit offers an explanation as well as a justification for why a state may choose to impose a duty of collective worship on its schools. However, it has also contended that the identification of a need on the part of the state is insufficient to create a coherent law: a convincing rationale must exist that can explain why the chosen means will fulfil the need. The strength of a rationale for a law is not fixed. It varies depending on whether the nature of the original need changes or disappears, and whether societal changes take place that are germane to the chosen means. Either occurrence can reduce the effectiveness of the chosen means in meeting the identified need thereby weakening the plausibility of any rationale. A need articulated by the state may be disputable but, as noted earlier, this issue is independent of the question as to the strength of the rationale.

The rationale for the law requiring collective school worship was relatively strong when first introduced in 1944 but has since steadily declined in plausibility. A changed need, which no longer includes the aim of restoring Christian belief amongst the population, coupled with a marked drop in affiliation to Christianity amongst the population makes an act of collective worship an improbable means by which to fulfil the stated needs of the 1988 Act, namely, the promotion of values that underpin democratic society and the protection of the country's Christian heritage. The options available to policymakers are thus three-fold: abolish the duty and prohibit the holding of acts of worship in schools; abolish the duty but allow schools to hold acts of worship if they so desire; or replace the current duty with a duty to organize an alternative activity during the designated period of the school day previously given over to collective worship.

In considering each of the three options the state must begin with the question of need. If a state considers it has no fresh need that demands to be fulfilled by an act of worship or, indeed, that the existence of a duty of collective school worship is detrimental to its other interests, it should abolish the current duty. The decision as to whether to replace it with a duty on schools to carry out an alternative collective activity will rest on whether there is a specific and well-articulated need that requires a collective act to take place during a brief, designated period of the school day and, moreover, one that cannot be sufficiently met through (amending) existing activities and subjects within the curriculum or through the holding of a regular school assembly. Finally, the option of amending the law to allow schools to choose whether to hold acts of collective worship brings with it a distinct and separate consideration in addition to that of rationale. An Eliasian perspective offers a justification for why a state may choose to impose a duty of collective worship in its schools: a need to organize an effective internal structure to assist in its defence and advancement in the 'survival game'. In contrast, however, the justification for allowing a non-religious state school to decide for itself whether it should conduct acts of worship is much less clear. An argument for giving this kind of latitude to non-religious state schools would need to be carefully considered and constructed by the state if it were to be persuasive. Furthermore, should the state choose to allow schools this freedom, any school that elects to hold an act of worship would have to clearly articulate the need that it is aiming to so fulfil in order to ensure the existence of a strong rationale for the activity.

Education is a devolved matter in the United Kingdom and it is for each constituent country to determine whether it has a need that requires schools without a religious character to hold daily acts of worship. The response may differ amongst countries according to the circumstances of each, and the aims and aspirations of its society and education system. In sum, this chapter has argued that any choice made by a state with respect to the future direction of the law must be an outcome of a process where the existence of a need has been considered and, if identified, matched with an appropriate means to produce a solid rationale. In the absence of such a focus on need and rationale, there is a substantial risk that one incoherent law could end up being replaced by another.

References

Alves, C. (1991). Just a matter of words? The Religious Education Debate in the House of Lords. *British Journal of Religious Education 13*(3), 168–174.

Archbishop of Canterbury (1944). (HL Deb, 18 July 1944) vol. 132, cc. 950–982, 97. Retrieved April 17, 2017, from <http://hansard.millbanksystems.com/lords/1944/jul/18/education-bill>.

Ashbourne, Lord (1988). (HL Deb, 26 February 1988) vol. 493, cc. 1453–1486 (1468). Retrieved April 17, 2017, from <http://hansard.millbanksystems.com/lords/1988/feb/26/christian-teaching-in-schools>.

Baker, K. (1988). (HC Deb, 18 July 1988) vol. 137 cc. 816–848 (841). Retrieved April 17, 2017, from <http://hansard.millbanksystems.com/commons/1988/jul/18/duties-with-respect-to-the-curriculum>.

Bradney, A. (2009). *Law and Faith in a Sceptical Age*. Oxford: Routledge-Cavendish.

Cheetham, R. (2004). *Collective Worship: Issues and Opportunities*. London: SPCK.

Clarke, C., & Woodhead, L. (2015). *A New Settlement: Religion and Belief in Schools*. The Westminster Faith Debates. Retrieved April 17, 2017, from <www.faithdebates.org.uk>.

Commission on Religion in Public Life (2015). *Living with Difference: Community, Diversity and the Common Good*. Cambridge: The Woolf Institute.

Committee on the Rights of the Child (2016). *Concluding observations on the fifth periodic report of the United Kingdom of Great Britain and Northern Ireland*. Retrieved April 17, 2017, from <CRC/C/GBR/CO/5.http://tbinternet.ohchr.org/Treaties/CRC/Shared%20Documents/GBR/CRC_C_GBR_CO_5_24195_E.docx>.

Cove, W. (1944). HC Deb, 10 March 1944, vol. 397, cc. 2395–2427, 2402, 2403. Retrieved April 17, 2017, from <http://hansard.millbanksystems.com/commons/1944/mar/10/clause-24-general-provisions>.

Cumper, P. (1998). School Worship: Praying for Guidance. *European Human Rights Law Review, 1*, 44–60.

Cumper, P., & Mawhinney, A. (Eds.) (2015). *Collective Worship and Religious Observance in Schools: An Evaluation of Law and Policy in the UK*, ISBN 978-1-84220-138-1. Retrieved April 17, 2017, from <http://collectiveschoolworship.com/>.

Department for Education (1994). *Circular 1/94: Religious Education and Collective Worship*. London: Department for Education Publication Centre.

Dinham, A., & Shaw, M. (2015*). RE for REal: The Future of teaching and learning about religion and belief*. Goldsmiths, University of London. Retrieved April 17, 2017, from <https://www.gold.ac.uk/media/goldsmiths/169-images/departments/ research-units/faiths-unit/REforREal-web-b.pdf>.

Elias, N. (1978). *What is Sociology?* New York: Columbia University Press.

Elias, N. (2008). *Essays II: On Civilising Processes, State Formation and National Identity*. Dublin: University College Dublin Press.

Elias, N., & Schröter, M. (1991). *The Society of Individuals*. Oxford: Basil Blackwell.

Emery, P. (1988). HC Deb, 18 July 1988, vol. 137. cc. 816–848 (836). Retrieved April 17, 2017, from <http://hansard.millbanksystems.com/commons/1988/jul/18/ duties-with-respect-to-the-curriculum>.

Freathy, R., & Parker, S. G. (2013). Secularists, Humanists and religious education: religious crisis and curriculum change, 1963–1975. *History of Education: Journal of the History of Education Society, 42*(2), 222–256.

Gutman, A., & Thompson, D. (1996). *Democracy and Disagreement*. Cambridge, MA: Belknap Press.

Halsbury, Earl. (1988). HL Deb, 26 February 1988, vol. 493, cc. 1453–1486 (1469). Retrieved April 17, 2017, from <http://hansard.millbanksystems.com/lords/1988/ feb/26/christian-teaching-in-schools>.

Hamilton, C., & Watt, B. (1996). A Discriminating Education – Collective Worship and Religious Education in British Schools. *Comparative Family Law Quarterly, 8*, 28–40.

Hirst, P. (1971). *Knowledge and the Curriculum*. London: Routledge and Kegan Paul.

Hull, J. M. (1975). *School Worship: An Obituary*. London: SCM Press.

Jones, C. M. (1969). *Worship in the Secondary School: An Investigation and Discussion*. Oxford: Religious Education Press.

Kaspersen, L. B., & Gabriel, N. (2008). The importance of survival units for Norbert Elias's figurational perspective. *Sociological Review, 56*(3), 370–387.

MacLeod, Baroness (1988). HL Deb, 26 February 1988, vol. 493, cc. 1453–1486 (1475). Retrieved April 17, 2017, from <http://hansard.millbanksystems.com/ lords/1988/feb/26/christian-teaching-in-schools>.

Reeh, N. (2013). Towards a New Approach to Secularization: Religion, Education and the State in Denmark, 1721–1900. *Social Compass 60*(2), 236–250.

Schools Council (1971). *Religious Education in Secondary Schools (Working Paper 36)*. London: Methuen Educational & Evans Bros.

Sedgemore, B. (1988). (HC Deb, 18 July 1988) vol. 137 cc. 816–848 (837). Retrieved April 17, 2017, from <http://hansard.millbanksystems.com/commons/1988/ jul/18/duties-with-respect-to-the-curriculum>.

Selborne, Earl (1944). (HL Deb, 21 June 1944) vol. 132 cc. 306–370 (347). Retrieved April 17, 2017, from <http://hansard.millbanksystems.com/lords/1944/jun/21/ education-bill>.

_____ (1944a). (HL Deb, 18 July 1944) vol. 132 cc. 950–982 (970). Retrieved April 17, 2017, from <http://hansard.millbanksystems.com/lords/1944/jul/18/education-bill>.

Select Committee on Education, Science and Arts (1982). *Second Report, 1981–1982: The Secondary School Curriculum and Examinations*. HC 116 II. London: HMSO.

Shuna, Lord. (1988). (HL Deb, 07 July 1988) vol. 499 cc. 420–454 (435). Retrieved April 17, 2017, from <http://hansard.millbanksystems.com/lords/1988/jul/07/education-reform-bill-1>.

Strange, Baroness (1988). (HL Deb, 26 February 1988) vol. 493, cc. 1453–1486 (1476). Retrieved April 17, 2017, from <http://hansard.millbanksystems.com/lords/1988/feb/26/christian-teaching-in-schools>.

Straw, J. (1988). (HC Deb, 18 July 1988) vol. 137 cc. 816–848 (819). Retrieved April 17, 2017, from <http://hansard.millbanksystems.com/commons/1988/jul/18/duties-with-respect-to-the-curriculum>.

Swann, M. (1985). *Education For All: The Report of the Committee of Inquiry into the Education of Children from Ethnic Minority Groups*. London: HMSO.

Swinfen, Lord (1988). (HL Deb, 26 February 1988) vol. 493, cc. 1453–1486 (1473). Retrieved April 17, 2017, from <http://hansard.millbanksystems.com/lords/1988/feb/26/christian-teaching-in-schools>.

Welsh Office (1994). *Circular 10/94: Religious Education and Collective Worship*. Cardiff: Welsh Office Education Department. Accessed April 17, 2017.

FRANKIE MCCARTHY

6 Dynamic Self-determinism, the Right to Belief and the Role of Collective Worship

ABSTRACT

The practice of collective worship remains mandatory in state schools throughout the UK. What justification exists for this practice? This chapter employs Eekelaar's 'dynamic self-determinism' model to explore the connection between collective worship and the child's human right to belief. The chapter first extrapolates the basic, developmental and autonomy interests protected within the right to belief as encapsulated within the tapestry of international legal instruments. It argues that school worship could serve the child's interest in development of the capacity for spiritual and philosophical thought. However, the absence of clear policy on the type of capacity schools seek to develop prevents worship from fulfilling this role effectively. It also argues that the child's autonomy interest demands that 'mature minors' have the choice to 'opt out' of worship on conscience grounds. The chapter concludes with recommendations for reform of school collective worship to ensure compliance with the UK's international rights obligations.

Introduction

What is the purpose of collective worship in UK schools? The practice of collective worship, most commonly taking the form of participation in assemblies where hymns are sung and passages from religious texts discussed, remains mandatory in state schools throughout the United Kingdom. In most areas, statute provides that worship must be 'wholly or mainly of a broadly Christian character'. Today the rationale and justification for 'the practice of collective worship' (a phrase originally taken from the Education Reform Act 1988, ss. 6–7, which applied to England and Wales) is less than clear. Teaching is no longer the province primarily of the clergy, and

members of the Christian church no longer form the majority of the UK
population. Despite this, collective worship retains its place, and parents
and governments continue to express support for its inclusion. What justification can be found for this practice in a religiously plural society?

In this chapter, I argue that collective worship can contribute to the fulfilment of the child's right to belief, by developing her capacity for religious
or philosophical thought. The right to belief is analysed through the lens
of John Eekelaar's model of dynamic self-determinism. Eekelaar, a former
director of the University of Oxford Centre for Family Law and Policy,
proposed a normative framework in which children's rights are understood
as a means of protecting and promoting a child's basic, developmental and
autonomy interests (Eekelaar, 1986a). These interests should be ordered as
a hierarchy, so that the autonomy interest need only be satisfied where it
does not conflict with the child's basic or developmental needs (Eekelaar,
1994). Adopting this framework in relation to the child's right to belief
allows me identify the interests collective worship might serve, the methods
by which it might do so, and the extent to which current law and practice
meet these ambitions.

The chapter is divided into three parts. In the first, I outline the dynamic
self-determinism model. Eekelaar developed this model in response to two
ostensibly conflicting theories of human rights, combining elements of both
to produce a theory which gives recognition to the evolution of capacity
over the course of childhood. In the second part, I use the dynamic self-
determinism model to unpick the interests comprised within the child's
right to belief. In the third part, I make some suggestions as to the role
school collective worship might play in protecting or promoting these
interests, and explore whether, as currently practised, collective worship
does play that role. In closing, I make three principal recommendations for
reform of collective worship applicable in each country in the UK: first,
that the government of each sets out a clear policy statement as to the type
of capacity for belief that the school system intends to develop; second,
that schools adopt a practice of worship that develops that capacity in line
with international human rights obligations, which is likely to require a
secular approach in non-faith schools; and thirdly, that the autonomy

interest of mature minors be respected through the ability to opt out of worship which conflicts with their beliefs or values.

The term collective worship is used throughout the United Kingdom other than in Scotland, where the term religious observance is preferred. In this chapter, for the sake of brevity, the term collective worship will be used to mean the practice in all four countries. Where specific jurisdictional practices are relevant, this will be made clear in the text and the correct terminology will be used.

Children's rights and dynamic self-determinism

Eekelaar's model of children's rights, which he termed 'dynamic self-determinism', arose from a larger debate about the normative underpinning of human rights in general (Choudhry and Herring, 2010, 97–139). The discussion focused on two competing justifications for human rights. Will theorists focused on autonomy, asserting that the purpose of human rights was to protect the choices made by an individual in respect of her own life. Interest theorists, by contrast, focused on welfare, arguing that rights existed to protect the interests of the holders by placing duties on others to respect those interests.

The position of children became central to this debate following Neil McCormick's argument to the effect that children, as non-autonomous actors, are incapable of making choices in most spheres of life. Accordingly, in his view, if the will theory of rights were correct, children would not be able to benefit from human rights protection. Interest theory should therefore be preferred, since children undoubtedly have interests that merit protection. Although a child would be unable to enforce the duties placed on others in recognition of her interests, enforcement could be carried out on her behalf by another person, such as a parent (MacCormick, 1976).

A central critique of interest theory, which carries particular weight where children are concerned, relates to how the protected interests are identified. Who has the right to decide? This was of concern to Eekelaar, who warned:

> Powerful social actors could proclaim what they deem to be in the interests of others, establish institutional mechanisms for promoting or protecting those interests, and claim to be protecting the rights of others, whether or not the others approved or even knew their interests were being constructed in that way. (Eekelaar, 2007, 336)

With this concern in mind, Eekelaar set out to develop a model that incorporated aspects of both potential normative underpinnings of children's rights. Key to this model was his proposition that supporting children to develop the capacity for autonomous decision-making is, in itself, an interest deserving of protection. Eekelaar (1986a, 169) started from the premise that, if rights are intended to protect interests, they must only protect 'the interests that the subject might plausibly claim in themselves'. He identified three categories of interest that a child might claim. In the first place, a child would seek protection of her basic interests, meaning general physical, emotional and intellectual care within the social capabilities of her caregivers (Eekelaar, 1986a, 170). This would include such things as food, shelter and clothing along with love and nurturing. The primary provider in respect of basic interests would likely be the child's parents or guardians. In the second place, the child would seek protection of her developmental interests, which are defined as the opportunity to have her capabilities developed to their best advantage within the constraints imposed by the economic and social structure of society (Eekelaar, 1986a, 170). This would include chiefly the provision of education and training, and as such these interests would be fulfilled by the state or society as a whole in conjunction with the child's parents. Lastly, the child would claim protection of her autonomy interest, meaning the freedom to choose her own lifestyle and to enter social relations according to her own inclinations uncontrolled by the authority of the adult world, whether parents or institutions (Eekelaar, 1986a, 171).

The potential for these interests to conflict is obvious. An infant child may refuse to wear warm clothes when going outside in winter. To support the child's autonomy interest in choosing her own clothes here would likely harm her basic interest in physical health. Eekelaar recognized this potential for conflict, and proposed that it be resolved by ordering the three categories of interests in a hierarchy:

> The problem is that a child's autonomy interest may conflict with the developmental interest and even the basic interest. While it is possible that some adults retrospectively approve that they were, when children, allowed the exercise of their autonomy at the price of putting them at a disadvantage as against other children in realizing their life-chances in adulthood, it seems improbable that this would be a common view. We may therefore rank the autonomy interest subordinate to the basic and developmental interests. However, where they may be exercised without threatening these two interests, the claim for their satisfaction must be high. (Eekelaar, 1986a, 171)

If we accept that the development of autonomy forms part of a child's interests, albeit a part that, at times, must be subordinated to more fundamental interests, what effect should that have on the treatment of children within the law? Eekelaar's view was that legal assessments of the best interests of the child did not do enough to take into account the development of childhood autonomy. He proposed that a dynamic self-determinism model be adopted by decision-makers to ensure that all three categories of interest were appropriately recognized in their decisions (Eekelaar, 1994). Within this model, the goal of the decision is to ensure that the child is placed in an environment that is reasonably secure, but which exposes her to a wide range of interests (Eekelaar, 1994, 47–48). As she develops, the child would be encouraged to draw on these influences in such a way that she contributes to the outcome. The overarching ambition is for the child to reach adulthood fully equipped to make autonomous choices for herself (Eekelaar, 1994, 48).

For assistance in determining the extent to which a child should be viewed as legally competent to make autonomous decisions, Eekelaar (1994, 50) looked to the understanding of autonomy elaborated by Joseph Raz (1986, 369) in his monograph *The Morality of Freedom*. In Raz's theory, first, an autonomous decision is viewed as one wherein the desires chosen to be followed are (intentionally) consistent with the individual's ultimate goals. The goals in which these desires are realized must be achievable within attainable social forms. Finally, a decision may be autonomous even if inconsistent with the decision-maker's self-interest (Eekelaar, 1994, 55–56).

Eekelaar was cognizant that applying this definition to decisions made by children would not always be straightforward. The requirement that a decision be reconcilable with the individual's life goals might be hard to assess for children, since the child's personality or identity might not yet be fully formed. As a solution, Eekelaar (1994, 55) suggested that we may say a decision is not autonomous if it reflects a feeling or aspiration which is so seriously unstable, or where there is such a grave disjunction between it and others held by the child, that to give effect to the decision risks serious conflicts within the individual at a later stage of development. For example, a five-year-old child may wish to exist on a diet of chips and chocolate, but may also wish to be sufficiently nourished to play with her friends, grow tall, and become a champion athlete in adult life. To accept the child's decision on her diet would conflict so gravely with her other ambitions that it could not be considered an exercise of autonomy. The social form requirement provides a safeguard that is easier to apply. Children's decisions may be considered non-autonomous because whatever goal they aspire to may simply be unrealistic, at least at present. Assessing the probability of an outcome may be beyond the cognitive capacity of a child at that point (Eekelaar, 1994, 55). For example, a child may wish to live in an ice palace with an animate snowman for companionship, but the prospect of achieving such an ambition must be vanishingly small.

Eekelaar's desire to marry protection of welfare and promotion of autonomy within a single justification for children's rights is not unique amongst academic commentators. Michael Freeman (1983) developed a typology with similar ambitions, which he described as 'liberal paternalism'. Here, the interests of children are divided into four categories – the right to welfare, the right of protection, the right to be treated like adults and rights against parents – which broadly cover the same ground as the three interests in Eekelaar's model (Freeman, 1983, 57). Freeman also recognized the need for balance between protection of welfare and promotion of autonomy.

> The question we should ask ourselves is: what sort of action or conduct would we wish, as children, to be shielded against on the assumption that we would want to

mature to a rationally autonomous adulthood and be capable of deciding on our own system of ends as free and rational beings? We would choose principles that would enable children to mature to independent adulthood. One definition of irrationality would be such as to preclude action and conduct which would frustrate such a goal. (Freeman, 1983, 57)

Joel Anderson and Rutger Claassen (2012) conceptualized the issue somewhat differently in their exploration of a 'regime of childhood' which recognized that the status of being a child plays out within a certain set of rules. They explain a regime as being a normative status, constituted by institutionally and culturally backed understandings of what this status licenses bearers of the status to do, and obligations and prohibitions it places on others. Their focus is on four distinct but interlocking aspects of the modern regime of childhood, namely: (i) an orientation towards autonomy development; (ii) limited liability for children; (iii) parental supervisory responsibilities and (iv) age-based demarcation (Anderson & Classen, 2012, 508–512). When determining the appropriate limits to be placed on individuals participating in certain activities based on age, the question to ask is what scheme of supervisory responsibility on the part of parents and what duration of the period of childhood tutelage best serves to realize the fundamental interest in autonomy development (Anderson & Classen, 2012, 511). They describe situations in which individual children may be exempted from a general prohibition on making autonomous decisions prior to the age of majority, for example in relation to medical treatment, as examples of 'local emancipation' (Anderson & Classen, 2012, 512). In determining whether such emancipation should be allowed, they suggest it is necessary to consider the current and future welfare of the child, and the current and future agency interests of the child (Anderson & Classen, 2012, 512–513).

Other models offering a synthesis of protection of interests and promotion of autonomy could no doubt be proposed. In the context of the discussion in this chapter, however, I have preferred Eekelaar's approach, not only because it is arguably the most influential within discussion of children's rights in the UK, but also because it offers the most useful insights into the right to belief and its relationship to the practice of collective worship. It is to this discussion that the chapter will now turn.

The child's right to belief and dynamic self-determinism

In Eekelaar's model, children's rights in general are designed to protect their basic, developmental and autonomy interests. In this part of the chapter, that general outline will be applied in relation to the specific example of the child's right to belief. What basic, developmental and autonomy interests can we identify within this right?

The first step in answering this question is to define what is meant by 'the child's right to belief'. It is not possible to find a definition by simple reference to one international treaty or piece of domestic legislation. Children's rights are contained within a number of overlapping instruments which vary in their content, their jurisdictional extent and their enforcement mechanisms. Additionally, rights designed to protect the interests of the child at this complex intersection of belief, education and family life may be held by the child's parents rather than the child herself, in recognition of the age-related limitations on the child's capacity to enforce her own rights. The detail of the various rights and freedoms accorded in relation to children's beliefs is set out in full in Chapter 7, and I will not rehearse that material again here. However, a short summary of the key protections is necessary before Eekelaar's basic, developmental and autonomy interests can be identified.

As a general point, it is helpful to clarify that the rights of the child in relation to belief are not confined to religious belief in a strict sense. Article 9 of the European Convention on Human Rights provides for freedom of thought, conscience and religion. The European Court of Human Rights has understood this to cover, in essence, all spiritual and philosophical convictions (*Kokkinakis*, 1993), including atheism (*Angelini*, 1986), pacifism (*Arrowsmith*, 1978), veganism (*W*, 1993) and political value systems such as communism (*Hazar*, 1991). The same approach was adopted in the United Kingdom by the House of Lords (*R (Williamson)*, 2005, especially Lord Nicholls at [15] and Lord Walker at [55]). Accordingly, the right of the child under discussion here is not necessarily a right to adhere to a particular religion, but the right to identify with a system of values that allows her to understand the world and her place in it. That understanding may emerge partially or wholly through the child's membership of a religious faith, but it may equally emerge through atheism or a non-theological set of philosophical convictions.

Several specific rights can be enumerated in relation to children's beliefs. In common with all human beings, the child has an absolute right to freedom of thought, conscience and religion, together with a qualified right to manifest those beliefs, limited on various public interest grounds including public safety and protection of the rights and freedoms of others (ECHR, art 9; UNCRC, art 14). The United Nations Convention on the Rights of the Child explicitly recognizes the right of parents to be free from state interference in directing the child in the exercise of this right in line with her evolving capacities (UNCRC, art 14(2)) – a proviso not included in respect of other specific rights where a parent might be expected to offer direction, such as the rights to freedom of expression or freedom of assembly. The child also has a right to determination and preservation of her identity, including nationality, name and family relations (UNCRC, art 8 [right of the child to preserve her identity]; United Nations International Covenant on Civil and Political Rights, art 1(1) [right to self-determination]; Mair, 2015). Although belief is not specifically mentioned in the provisions related to identity, both international and domestic legal instruments (UNCRC, art 20; United Nations Declaration on the Elimination of All Forms of Intolerance and Discrimination Based on Religion or Belief, art 5(4); Adoption and Children Act 2002, s 1(4)-(5); Adoption and Children (Scotland) Act 2007, s 14(4)(b)) do recognize that the child's religious identity should be taken into account when, for example, she is to be adopted or otherwise separated from her birth family. Although a child has an independent right to education (ECHR, Protocol 1, art 2; UNCRC, art 28–30), the state must respect the right of parents to ensure that education is in conformity with the parents' religious and philosophical convictions (ECHR, Protocol 1, art 2. This does not provide a positive right to have a child educated in accordance with parental beliefs at state expense, but a parent must have the ability to withdraw a child from teaching which conflicts with parental religious or philosophical convictions).

Identifying the interests of the child protected by these various belief rights is complicated by the fact that the rights often serve more than one master. This is so both in cases where the child holds a right directly, and where a right is held by the parent in respect of their child. Take, for example, the right of a parent to direct their child in the exercise of her right to freedom of thought, conscience and religion. To some extent, this right can be seen to derive from the child's interests. A young child has no capacity to guide the early formation of her values, but such values will inevitably form – even a toddler can understand basic moral ideas, like the fact it is generally wrong to hit others. It is in the interests of the child to be assisted in forming these values, which we might consider a type of intellectual and emotional nurture. The unarticulated assumption within the human rights instruments is that parents are the appropriate people to perform that role in the interests of the child. They are provided with the right to direct the child's exercise of her right to belief to protect them, and in turn their child, from unjustified interference by a state that might seek to impose values of its own. However, this parental right does not derive solely from the child's interests. Parents have an independent interest which is also protected through this provision.[1] As Rachel E Taylor notes:

> For devout parents, the proper religious upbringing of their children is often a core religious obligation of the parent themselves and a protected manifestation of the parent's own right to religious freedom. (Taylor, 2015, 18)

A further level of complexity may be added by the interests of specific religious communities. Anat Solnicov notes that parental rights in respect of religious education were not initially based on the interests of either the parent *or* the child, but intended rather for protection and preservation of religious minorities, by helping to ensure their continued existence into the next generation (Solnicov, 2007, 10).

---

1   It should be kept in mind, however, that this parental right under ECHR, article 9 to manifest religious belief is relative, and can be limited where necessary, amongst other things, to protect the rights and freedoms of others.

A further difficulty with identifying the interests of the child protected by the various belief rights is that the interests protected by the right to religious freedom for adults can be disputed. The primary justification relied upon in the jurisprudence of the European Court of Human Rights is the promotion of autonomy. In the leading decision of *Kokkinakis v Greece*, the court found:

> Freedom of thought, conscience and religion is one of the foundations of a 'democratic society' within the meaning of the Convention. It is, in its religious dimension, one of the most vital elements that go to make up the identity of believers and their conception of life, but it is also a precious asset for atheists, agnostics, sceptics and the unconcerned. The pluralism indissociable from a democratic society, which has been dearly won over the centuries, depends on it. (*Kokkinakis*, 1994, at [31])

Support for autonomy as the relevant normative value can also be found in the academic literature (Evans, 2001; Laycock, 1996). However, doubt has been cast on whether autonomy can provide a complete explanation for the full range of activities protected by this right (Ahmed, 2017), and competing justifications, such as liberty of conscience, have also been put forward (Koppelman, 2009; Nussbaum, 2008).

For children, the argument that the interests protected by belief rights must include more than simply the promotion of autonomy is of particular relevance. This is, of course, because children are not autonomous for much of their childhood. This reality does not render autonomy irrelevant as an interest during childhood (LaFolette, 1989) – all children have an interest in developing the capacity for autonomy, and some children ('mature minors', discussed further below) will be capable of autonomous decision-making in relation to belief prior to reaching the age of majority. Sylvie Langlaude argues, however, that to focus solely on the autonomy aspects of the child's right to belief is to misunderstand the important family and community interests which are also protected by this right (Langlaude, 2008, 494–497). Children brought up within a system of values are nurtured by families and communities that care about the transmission of those values. The interest of the child, in her view, is 'to grow up as a religious being and to be nurtured into a religious faith by parents and religious community' (Langlaude, 2008, 477). Since the right to belief protects all systems of values, religious and non-religious, this assertion can perhaps be opened out. The interest of the child is to be nurtured in her development as a moral or philosophical person, regardless of whether that system of values is theologically based.

How, then, does this complex web of rights around children's beliefs map onto Eekelaar's dynamic self-determinism model? In the first place, I would argue that the child has a basic interest in the initial formation of her religious or philosophical identity. Since it is not possible to avoid forming an identity of some kind, protection and nurturing of this aspect of her identity may be considered to fall within Eekelaar's category of emotional needs, best fulfilled by her parents or caregivers (Eekelaar, 1986a, 170). Conceptualizing the child's basic interest in this way is coherent with the rights of the child herself, and with the legal rights of parents in respect of their children in this context: parents have a right and responsibility in respect of her religious or philosophical nurture just as they would do in respect of her physical and emotional nurture.

Secondly, I would assert that the child's developmental interest might best be summed up, to paraphrase Eekelaar's terms, as the opportunity to have her capacity for religious and philosophical thought and action developed to its best advantage (Eekelaar, 1986a, 170). This includes the development of the capacity for autonomous religious and philosophical thought and action. As an essentially educational interest, it might be expected that both the child's parents and the state would play a role here. Again, this conceptualization is consistent with the international rights framework described above.

Finally, I would argue that the child's autonomy interest requires that she has the maximum freedom possible to make her own choices in terms of her religious and philosophical beliefs. It is worth reiterating at this point that the dynamic self-determinism model posits these interests as a hierarchy, meaning that the child's freedom of choice in relation to belief must be subordinated to her developmental and basic interests where they would otherwise be harmed. However, where the exercise of a child's autonomy would not be harmful, her interest in doing so should be respected by both her parents and the state (Eekelaar, 1986a, 171). Additionally, where a child's capacity for religious and philosophical thought has been developed to the level of maturity of a competent adult, in Eekelaar's model, there can be no basis on which to argue that she should be prevented from exercising that autonomy (Eekelaar, 1994, 47–48). When a child reaches this stage, the role of the state may be most accurately characterized as protecting her interests from interference *by her parents.*

The dynamic self-determinist right to belief and the role of collective worship

In the second part of the chapter, I set out the basic, developmental and autonomy interests that are, in my analysis, served by the child's right to belief. In this section of the chapter, I analyse how the practice of school collective worship does or could contribute to the protection or promotion of these interests. In short, I argue that collective worship can play a role in fulfilling aspects of the child's developmental and autonomy interests in relation to the formation and exercise of a personally meaningful system of religious or philosophical beliefs. However, reforms to current practice are needed before collective worship can play that role effectively. Specific recommendations for reform are included within my concluding section.

My focus is on the developmental and autonomy interests served by the right to belief. By the time the child reaches school age and takes part in collective worship for the first time, around the age of 5 or 6, she will already have a basic understanding of the world and her place in it. This may include understanding of a supreme being, or an alternative philosophical take, but the roots of some system of values – an ability to tell 'right' from 'wrong', perhaps – will be present. I would assert, then, that collective worship has no real role to play in fulfilling the child's basic interest here. Once at school, the developmental interest of the child comes to the forefront. Just as the academic elements of school are intended to develop the child's intellectual capacity, I would argue that collective worship is one mechanism for developing the child's capacity for religious or philosophical thought. Finally, collective worship can be seen as having two roles in relation to the autonomy interest. First, it should assist the child in becoming an autonomous actor in matters of religious and philosophical belief. Second, it should respect her existing autonomy where it is possible to do so without harming her developmental interest.

In this section, the role of collective worship in relation to the child's developmental and autonomy interests in religious or philosophical belief will be considered.

The Developmental Interest

How can collective worship contribute to the child's developmental interest in the right to belief?

This question is at the heart of much of the debate around the place of religion in the context of education. In terms of academic education, there is basic consensus within society about the type of adult we want the school system to help develop – an adult who has key literacy and numeracy skills, for example. In terms of religious or philosophical belief, however, the nature of any consensus is unclear.

Eekelaar's model helps to define the parameters within which consensus must be achieved. He argues that the developmental interest of a child demands that she be placed in an environment which is reasonably secure, but which exposes her to a wide range of interests, with the aim of her becoming a good 'chooser' (Eekelaar, 1994, 47–48). Liberal philosophy tends to the argument that, in the context of belief, development towards autonomy demands that the child be furnished with the ability to reflect critically on the beliefs with which they were raised, alongside exposure to other modes of belief or ways of understanding the world (Arneson & Shapiro, 1996; Macleod, 1997). An alternative argument can be made that this approach to development of autonomy during childhood actually results in closing off certain choices. Devotion and constancy towards one system of values in the formative period of our lives can provide the option of a form of adult religious life that is not otherwise possible, in the same way that dedication to the practice of a sport or musical instrument during childhood can provide the option of elite performance in adulthood which is otherwise virtually impossible (Callan, 2002, 134–135). In this conceptualization, development of the capacity for autonomous revision of inherited beliefs should be subordinated to the opportunity to develop the devotion which will allow for autonomous *adherence* to a belief system in adult life (Callan, 2002, 137–139).

Reasonable people may well disagree about the form of capacity for autonomy that should be preferred in relation to belief, in much the same way as they may disagree about the developmental goals of our school system in relation to other types of capacity. These disagreements are socio-political and cannot be resolved by law. What is needed is a statement of governmental policy which makes clear the ambitions underlying collective worship in the UK. Do we, as a society, seek to develop adults with the capacity for autonomous revision, or the capacity for autonomous adherence? Are there other aspects of this capacity we seek to develop?

Any such policy must, however, adhere to the limitations placed on it by our human rights obligations. As discussed in more detail in Chapter 7, the European Court of Human Rights has broadly taken the view that, in a society with a plurality of religious and philosophical beliefs such as the United Kingdom, the state may choose to provide faith schools in line with parental demand, but is not under an obligation to provide a school of any particular religious or philosophical character (*X*, 1978; followed in the UK courts by *R (on the application of K)*, 2002; *R (on the application of R)*, 2006). Outwith the faith school sector, the court has tended increasingly to the view that the state's duty of neutrality requires education to be secular. Aspects of education which could be considered to have a proselytizing or indoctrinating effect, such as participation in religious activities, run counter to this duty in the eyes of the court (*Lautsi*, 2012). An accommodationist model, by which children (or their parents on their behalf) may opt out of activities which do not accord with their beliefs, has been accepted by the court as an appropriate mechanism for respecting the religious rights of all parties in a school where various belief systems are represented (*Kjeldsen, Busk Madsen and Pedersen*, 1979–1980; *Folgero*, 2008; *Zengin*, 2008; McCarthy, 2011), although difficulties arise where confessional religious aspects of education cannot easily be separated out from the remainder of the curriculum (*Folgero*, 2008). The jurisprudence here, in particular the extent to which secularism is equated with neutrality, is not uncontroversial (Leigh & Adar, 2012; Kyritsis &Tsakyrakis, 2013; Neha, 2013). It does, however, represent the current position on interpretation of human rights in this context.

Taking the previous paragraphs together, two models of rights-compliant collective worship which serve the developmental interest present themselves. First, for advocates of the autonomous adherence approach, confessional religious worship in a particular faith would fulfil the child's developmental interest without contravening human rights requirements, provided that all children in the school shared the same faith. Alternatively, for advocates of the autonomous revision approach, a non-confessional, secular practice of philosophical belief would again meet the child's developmental interest without contravening human rights, on the assumption that the beliefs of a religious child are not disrespected by participation in non-confessional activities. (As Leigh & Adar (2012) note, this assumption may not be correct in all cases.) A model that is arguably ruled out, however, is an accommodationist approach to collective worship, whereby a child whose beliefs do not allow her to participate in confessional activities simply opts out. This model may be appropriate by the time the child has sufficient capacity to make an autonomous decision on participation in worship – in other words, once the child is a mature minor whose developmental interest, at least in so far as belief is concerned, has been fulfilled – which I will return to below. For a less mature child, however, the difficulty is that her developmental interest is neglected if she simply opts out of the activities designed to improve her capacity for religious or philosophical thought, assuming that a meaningful alternative is not provided (Mawhinney, 2006).

Does the current practice of collective worship serve the child's developmental interest?

To what extent does law and practice in UK schools match up with the models of collective worship outlined above? In faith schools throughout the UK, where collective worship takes the form of confessional practice in line with the religious character of the school, the child's developmental interest is arguably satisfied on the autonomous adherence model.

In relation to non-faith schools, the position varies across the three jurisdictions. Scotland may come closest to realizing a non-confessional model of development of the capacity for autonomous revision. Scottish governmental policy guidance makes explicit that the overall goal of religious observance is to ensure that every child 'reaches his or her potential' through personal search that allows her to develop her own values (Scottish Executive, 2004). It is explicitly noted that non-denominational schools must support the development of children of all faiths or none through religious observance, with the suggestion that 'time for reflection' may be a more apposite title for the practice (Scottish Government, 2011, para. 10). As discussed in Chapter 2, however, it is not always clear that this guidance is followed in practice, where schools may tend to fall back on primarily Christian activities.

In both England and Wales, schools without a religious character are under a statutory obligation to provide acts of worship 'of a broadly Christian character' (School Standards and Framework Act 1998, s. 70 and sched. 20, para. 3(2) and 3(3)), with policy guidance elaborating that acts of worship 'must contain some elements which relate specifically to the traditions of Christian belief and which accord a special status to Jesus Christ' (for England, see Department for Education, 1994, para. 62; for Wales, see Welsh Office Education Department, 1994, para. 65). As discussed in Chapters 1 and 4, the policy guidance as to the purpose of including collective worship within the school day is inconsistent and contradictory. It is difficult to see how this can appropriately fulfil the child's interest in development of her religious or philosophical capabilities on either the adherence or revision model, other than, perhaps, where a child has been raised as a member of the relevant Christian faith. The position in Northern Ireland is perhaps even more confused since the legal provisions on collective worship and guidance on its implementation in practice have been elided with the provisions and guidance on religious education (Education and Libraries (Northern Ireland) Order 1986, art 21(1)). What is clear from Chapter 3, however, is that worship is intended to be both Christian and confessional, which again suggests that the development interest is not being satisfied at least for non-Christian children. In summary, the current provision of collective worship in the UK outside of the faith school sector does not, as a general rule, serve the child's developmental interest in relation to belief, where development is understood, as in Eekelaar's terms, to have the goal of producing an autonomous adult. To remedy the issues here, what is needed in the first place is a clear statement of the policy goal collective worship seeks to serve – for example, whether the school system aims to produce adults capable of autonomous adherence or autonomous revision. Only then can meaningful consideration be given to moulding the practice of worship in line with these goals and in compliance with international human rights obligations.

The Autonomy Interest

How should collective worship respect the child's autonomy interest in relation to belief?

In the previous section, I discussed the role of collective worship in developing the child's capacity for belief, including the development of autonomy in relation to belief. Once a child's capacity has been sufficiently developed – that is to say, once the child's capacity for autonomous decision-making on belief is equivalent to that of an adult – the child's developmental interest can no longer be harmed. At this stage, when the child becomes a 'mature minor', respect for the child's autonomy interest demands that she be entitled to withdraw from participation in worship where it conflicts with her independently determined religious or philosophical beliefs.

In the United Kingdom, the general rule is that individuals are viewed as autonomous actors on reaching the age of majority. However, in recent times the law has begun to recognize that children may also have the capacity for autonomous decision-making in certain contexts, with the age at which such capacity is obtained varying from child to child. The leading authority for this concept is *Gillick v West Norfolk and Wisbech Area Health Authority* (1985). The case arose when Victoria Gillick applied to the English courts for a determination as to whether a notice issued by the Department of Health and Social Security was lawful. The notice advised doctors that when persons under 16 sought contraceptive advice and treatment, it was desirable for their parents to be consulted; however, in exceptional circumstances, a doctor might treat such a child alone so long as she did so in good faith and with regard to the child's best interests. Mrs Gillick argued that a child under 16 had no common law right to consent to treatment. The only person competent to consent was the child's parent or guardian by virtue of their parental rights. Accordingly, she argued that a doctor would be acting illegally if he treated a child without the consent of her parent or guardian.

By a narrow margin, the House of Lords disagreed with Mrs Gillick. It was held that children under 16 could consent to receiving medical treatment, including contraceptive treatment, provided they had reached a certain degree of maturity and understanding. The exact criteria for such '*Gillick*-competence' did not emerge clearly from the judgement. Lord Scarman expressed the view that, that for a child to be competent, she should understand the nature of the medical treatment and have sufficient maturity to understand what was involved, including moral and family questions and the risks to health and emotional stability. Lord Fraser, on the other hand, emphasized that along with other factors, a doctor should only regard a child as competent *if the treatment requested was in that child's best interests*. The difference in these two approaches has the result that *Gillick* cannot be said to have unambiguously recognized the autonomy of the child in law (Eekelaar, 1986b; Bainham, 1988; Gilmore, 2009; Fortin, 2011), but as has been noted, it 'undeniably placed the idea of children's autonomy rights in the legal consciousness in a way that had not previously existed' (Gilmore, Herring and Probert, 2009, 6).

Subsequent legal developments have varied in the different UK jurisdictions. In Scotland, the Age of Legal Capacity (Scotland) Act 1991 gave specific statutory recognition to the autonomous capacity of children in relation to writing a will (s. 2(2)), instructing a solicitor (s. 2(4A)) and consenting to medical treatment (s. 2(4)), amongst other things. This exceptional capacity is usually presumed to arise at age 12, but in the case of medical treatment, it arises when the child is assessed by the practitioner as capable of understanding the nature and possible consequences of the treatment.[2] There is no requirement for treatment to be in the child's best interests: the Scottish Law Commission, after extensive consultation on this point, came to the conclusion that if a child was deemed to have sufficient maturity then it should not matter if the treatment was for her benefit or not (Scottish Law Commission, 1987, 3.61-3.77). In the sole Scottish authority commenting on the issue, *Houston, Applicant* (1996), the sheriff was satisfied that a mother could not give consent to medical treatment of her fifteen-year-old son, who had been assessed as capable of understanding the decision and had clearly refused treatment. The decision in the case did not turn on this issue, however, meaning the views of the court have less force than they might have had. Scottish academic commentators tend to the view that the right to consent carries with it the right to refuse (Edwards, 1993; Elliston, 2007, 112) and current National Health Service guidance to medical professionals in Scotland recommends that where a competent person under 16 refuses treatment, the refusal must be respected (Scottish Executive Health Dept, 2006, Chapter 2).

In England and Wales, recognition of the potential autonomy of children has been more restricted. *R (Axon) v Secretary of State for Health* (2006) confirmed that the law in *Gillick* should also apply in relation to abortion, but found that treatment without parental consent requires a high level of understanding on the part of the child along with being in the best interests of the child. In *Re R (A Minor)* (1991), Lord Donaldson suggested that a mature minor and her parent were both 'keyholders' to consent, and either might use her key regardless of the position of the other. This view was reiterated in *Re W* (1992). Accordingly, although both a child and her parent may have the right to consent, it seems only a parent has the right to refuse treatment on her child's behalf. It is worth noting,

---

2   The section reads: 'A person under the age of sixteen shall have legal capacity to consent on his own behalf to any surgical, medical or dental procedure or treatment where, in the opinion of a qualified medical practitioner attending him, he is capable of understanding the nature and possible consequences of the procedure or treatment.'

however, that children under 16 are given a specific statutory right to refuse medical procedures ordered by the court in relation to a child protection order (Children Act 1989, s. 44(7)), in addition to a more general right to have their views heard when the court is taking decisions in relation to their upbringing (Children Act 1989, s 1(3)(a)). Although less developed than in Scotland, then, the concept of autonomy for the child nevertheless has a hold in English and Welsh law.

In Northern Ireland, the position is similar to that of England and Wales. Although the decision in *Gillick* is nor directly applicable, there is no reason to think that it would not be followed there. It is not clear how subsequent decisions such as *Re R* would be viewed. Children under 16 are again given a specific statutory right to refuse medical procedures ordered by the court in relation to a child protection order (Children (Northern Ireland) Order 1995/755, art 62(8)), and have a right to be heard in relation to decisions affecting their upbringing (Children (Northern Ireland) Order 1995/755, art 3(3)(a)).

Although recognition of the autonomy of the child within the UK jurisdictions remains restricted, I would argue that the existing precedents support the requirement of respect for the child's autonomy in relation to collective worship. The position in relation to medical decisions is particularly salient. In this area, two significant, related concerns animate constraints on the exercise of autonomy. First, the consequences of a child's decision can be extremely serious. Refusal of medical treatment may result in death. By contrast, refusal to participate in collective worship cannot cause harm where the child's developmental interest is already fulfilled, and even if a child who was not sufficiently mature was in error permitted to excuse herself from worship, the harm caused would be limited. In the second place, decisions taken in the medical context may be irreversible. Even where the outcome of a medical decision is less dramatic than death, it may still represent a door being closed on a line of treatment that was only available at a particular time or in particular circumstances, for example if a child were to refuse an organ transplant. By contrast, refusal to participate in worship at one time by no means precludes a change of heart at a later time. The nature of religious or philosophical identity is that it evolves over the course of a lifetime. At least in the UK, it is common to hear of adults leaving and returning to faiths at different life stages. The decision taken by a child here is far from determinative or irreversible. In fact, the opportunity to visit and revisit beliefs is an integral aspect of autonomous adult life.

In assessing whether a child has reached the level of maturity required to allow her to make an autonomous decision on participation in worship, some guidance can be gleaned from current practice in the courts. Throughout the UK, children have the right to be heard in court proceedings where the outcome will have an effect on their lives, with the most common examples being residence and contact disputes (Children Act 1989, s. 1(3)(a) (England and Wales); Children (Scotland) Act 1995, s. 11(7)(b); Children (Northern Ireland) Order 1995/755, art 3(3)(a)). The court will consider the child's views subject to the child's age and level of understanding. In Scotland, a presumption of maturity at age 12 is contained in statute (Children (Scotland) Act 1995, s. 11(10)). Research into the various mechanisms by which the child's capacity is assessed and her views recorded (Parkinson and Cashmore, 2008, Chapter 4; Barnes, 2008a; Barnes, 2008b; Raitt, 2007; Kay, Tisdall *et al.*, 2004) tends to suggest that, for most children, the best approach is through face-to-face conversation with the person who will make the decision on her capacity, preferably in a neutral venue (Barnes, 2008b, 141). The purpose of the conversation should be made clear to the child, and all children should be treated in the same way (Barnes, 2008b, 140). Decision-makers should be given appropriate training on working with children and assessing their maturity relevant to the particular context (Raitt, 2007, 218). It seems reasonable to suggest that a teacher tasked with assessing the maturity of a child in order to determine whether the child has sufficient maturity to opt out of collective worship is in a stronger position than a judge or other professional making such assessments in court: teachers have extensive training in dealing with children and may have had the opportunity to come to know the child in question fairly well over several years of school. Against that background, there seems no reason to doubt that a teacher would be capable of making an assessment of the child's maturity in this context.

Does the current practice of collective worship respect the child's autonomy interest?

I argued in the preceding section that, where a child is sufficiently mature to make her own decisions on matters of religious or philosophical belief, respect for her autonomy interest demands that she be entitled to opt out of worship where it conflicts with her values. Support for the argument that an 'opt-out' is necessary to meet our international obligations in terms of the child's right to belief can be found in the United Nations Committee on the Rights of the Child's *Concluding Observations on the Fifth Periodic Report of the United Kingdom*, published in July 2016. To what extent is an opt-out already available in the various UK jurisdictions?

The position varies. Scotland, in contrast with its approach in relation to medical treatment, offers the child no real autonomy here. Parents have the right to withdraw their children from religious observance (Education (Scotland) Act, s. 9), but the child has no independent entitlement to do so (McCarthy, 2017). The position is the same in Northern Ireland, where parents can withdraw their children 'on grounds of conscience' (Education and Libraries (Northern Ireland) Order 1986, art 21(5)). Parents in England and Wales may also withdraw their children from collective worship, in addition to which, sixth-form children in these jurisdictions have an independent entitlement to do so without the need for parental agreement (School Standards and Framework Act 1988, s. 71).

Conclusion and recommendations

My intention in this chapter has been to offer a novel understanding of the role of collective worship by using Eekelaar's model of dynamic self-determinism as a mechanism for breaking down the different elements of the child's right to belief. I have argued that collective worship, or at least some form or religious or philosophical practice, may make a valid and important contribution to the development of a child's capacity for autonomous religious and philosophical belief. However, reform of current law and practice is necessary to ensure that collective worship does so in a way that protects the child's developmental and autonomy interests to the maximum extent possible whilst also adhering to international human rights standards.

In the first place, I consider it critical for a clear governmental policy to be articulated as to the type of religious or philosophical capacity we, as a society, seek to develop in our children. This will be no easy task. However, it is clear that the historical reasons for the practice of collective worship have become outdated and without clear guidance on what we, as a society, consider the child's developmental interest to be here, it is not possible to ensure that interest is being met.

With that policy statement in place, I argue that the practice of worship should be revised to meet those policy ambitions within the human rights framework. At present, the primarily Christian practice of worship in non-faith schools does not appear to support the development of autonomy on either the adherence or revision models, in addition to which it contravenes the European Court of Human Rights guidance on neutrality in the classroom. These difficulties are not insurmountable, and Claire's Cassidy's discussion of philosophy with children in Chapter 9 offers a useful starting point for consideration of models of collective worship (or 'time for reflection') which might meet these tests.

Finally, where the practice of worship contradicts the values of a Gillick-competent child, I have argued that respect for the child's autonomy interest in relation to belief demands that an opt-out be made available to her. A right to withdraw here would not impact on the child's developmental interest, since for a Gillick-competent child, this interest has already been met. It is worth noting, however, that an inclusive model of worship, such as the practice of philosophy suggested above, is likely to avoid the need for an opt-out to be exercised since the practice is unlikely to conflict with any child's particular beliefs.

With these reforms in place, a clear answer can be given to the question posed at the start of this chapter. Collective worship (or time for reflection) will contribute to the fulfilment of the right to belief of every child within a religiously plural society.

References

Ahmed, F. (2017). The autonomy rationale for religious freedom. *Modern Law Review, 80*(2), 238–262.

Anderson, J., & Claassen, R. (2012). Sailing alone: teenage autonomy and regimes of childhood. *Law and Philosophy, 31*, 495–522.

Angelini v Sweden, Application no. 10491/83, (1986) DR 51, 41.

Arneson, R. J., & Shapiro, I. (1996). Democratic Autonomy and Religious Freedom. In I. Shapiro & R. Hardin (Eds.), *Political Order* (pp. 365–410). New York: New York University Press.

Arrowsmith v United Kingdom, Application no. 7050/75, (1978) DR 19, 5.

Bainham, A. (1988). *Children, Parents and the State*. London: Sweet & Maxwell.

Barnes, L. A. (2008a). 'A child is, after all, a child': ascertaining the ability of children to express views in family proceedings. *Scots Law Times* 121.

Barnes, L. A. (2008b). 'Moral actors in their own right': consideration of the views of children in family proceedings. *Scots Law Times* 139.

Callan, E. (2002). Autonomy, child-rearing and good lives. In D. Archard & C. M. Macleod (Eds.), *The Moral and Political Status of Children* (118–139). Oxford: Oxford University Press.

Choudhry, S., & Herring, J. (2010). *European Human Rights and Family Law*. Oxford: Hart.

Department for Education (1994). *Collective Worship in Schools*. Circular 1/94. London: HMSO.

Edwards, L. (1993). The right to consent and the right to refuse. *Juridical Review, 1*, 52–73.

Eekelaar, J. (1986a). The emergence of children's rights. *Oxford Journal of Legal Studies, 6 (2)*, 161–182.

Eekelaar, J. (1986b). The eclipse of parental rights. *Law Quarterly Review, 102*, 4–9.

Eekelaar, J. (1994). The interests of the child and the child's wishes: the role of dynamic self-determinism. *International Journal of Law, Policy and the Family, 8*, 42–61.

Eekelaar, J. (2007). *Family Law and Personal Life*. Oxford: Oxford University Press.

Elliston, S. (2007). *The Best Interests of the Child in Healthcare*. London: Routledge Cavendish.

Evans, C. (2001). *Freedom of Religion under the European Convention on Human Rights*. Oxford: Oxford University Press.

Folgero and Others v Norway (2008) 46 EHRR 47.

Fortin, J. (2011). The *Gillick* decision – not just a high water mark. In S. Gilmore, J. Herring, & R. Probert (Eds.), *Landmark Cases in Family Law*. Oxford: Hart.

Freeman, M. (1983). *The Rights and Wrongs of Children*. London: Pinter.

Gillick v West Norfolk and Wisbech Area Health Authority [1985] 3 All ER 402.

Gilmore, S. (2009). The limits of parental responsibility. In R. Probert, S. Gilmore, & J. Herring (Eds.), *Responsible Parents and Parental Responsibility* (pp. 63–84). Oxford: Hart.

Gilmore, S., Herring., J., & Probert, R. (2009). Introduction: Parental responsibility – law, issues and themes. In R., Probert, S., Gilmore, & J. Herring (Eds.), *Responsible Parents and Parental Responsibility* (pp. 1–20). Oxford: Hart.

Hazar, Hazar and Acik v Turkey, Application no. 16311/90-6313/90, (1991) DR 72, 200.

Houston, Applicant, 1996, SCLR 943.

Kay, E., Tisdall, M., *et al.* (2004). Children's participation in family law proceedings: a step too far or a step too small? *Journal of Social Welfare and Family Law, 26*(1), 17–33.

Kjeldsen, Busk Madsen and Pedersen v Denmark, A-23 (1979–1980) 1 EHRR 711.

Kokkinakis v Greece (1993) A 260-A.

Koppelman, A. (2009). Conscience, Volitional Necessity and Religious Exemptions. *Legal Theory, 15*, 215.

Kyritsis, D. and Tsakyrakis, S. (2013). Neutrality in the classroom. *International Journal of Constitutional Law, 11*(1), 200–217.

LaFollette, H. (1989). Freedom of religion and children. *Public Affairs Quarterly, 3*, 75–87.

Langlaude, S. (2008). Children and religion under Article 14 UNCRC: A Critical Analysis. *International Journal of Children's Rights, 6*(4), 474–504.

Lautsi v Italy (2012) 54 EHRR 3.

Laycock, D. (1996). Religious Liberty and Liberty. *Journal of Contemporary Legal Issues, 7*, 313–356.

Leigh, I., & Ahdar, R. (2012). Post-secularism and the European Court of Human Rights: or how God never really went away. *Modern Law Review, 75*(6), 1064–1098.

MacCormick, N. (1976). Children's rights: a test case for theories of rights. *Archiv fur Rechts-und Sozialphilosophie, 32*, 305.

Macleod, C. (1997). Conceptions of Parental Autonomy. *Politics and Society, 25*(1), 117–141.

Mair, J. (2015). Born or becoming: Children, religion and identity. In Jänterä-Jareborg, M. (Ed.), *The Child's Interests in Conflict* (pp. 31–54). Cambridge: Intersentia.

Mawhinney, A. (2006). The Opt-out clause: imperfect protection for the right to freedom of religion in schools. *Education Law, 7*(2), 102–115.

McCarthy, F. (2011). Prayers in the playground: religion and education in the United Kingdom and beyond. In Mair, J., and Orucu, E. (Eds.) *The Place of Religion in Family Law: A Comparative Search* (pp. 235–262). Cambridge: Intersentia.

McCarthy, F. (2017). Children's rights in action: reforming religious observance in Scottish schools. *Edinburgh Law Review, 21* (2) 257–261.

Neha, T. (2013). Religion without God: philosophical misconceptions in the European Court of Human Rights' evolution of a 'right to practice and preach atheism'. *European Human Rights Law Review*, 412–418.

Nussbaum, M. (2008). *Liberty of Conscience: In defence of America's tradition of religious equality.* New York: Basic Books.

Parkinson, P., & Cashmore, J. (2008). *The Voice of a Child in Family Law Disputes.* Oxford: Oxford University Press.

Raz, J. (1986). *The Morality of Freedom.* Oxford: Oxford University Press.

Solnicov, A. (2007). The child's right to religious freedom and formation of identity. *International Journal of Children's Rights, 15*, 1–17.

R (Axon) v Secretary of State for Health [2006] EWHC 37 (Admin).

R (on the application of K) v Newham LBC [2002] ELR 390.

R (on the application of R) v Leeds City Council [2006] ELR 25.

R (Williamson) v Secretary of State for Education and Employment [2005] UKHL 15.

Raitt, F. (2007). Hearing children in family law proceedings: can judges make a difference? *Child and Family Law Quarterly, 19*(2), 204–224.

Re R (A Minor) [1991] 4 All ER 177.

Re W [1992] 4 All ER 62.

Scottish Executive (2004). *Report of the Religious Observance Review Group.* Edinburgh: Scottish Executive.

Scottish Executive Health Dept (2006). *A Good Practice Guide on Consent for Health Professionals in NHS Scotland.* Edinburgh: Scottish Executive.

Scottish Government (2011). *Curriculum for Excellence – provision of religious observance in schools.* Edinburgh: Scottish Government.

Scottish Law Commission (1987). *Report on the Legal Capacity and Responsibility of Minors and Pupils.* Scot. Law Com. No.110.

Taylor, R. E. (2015). Responsibility for the soul of the child: the role of the state and parents in determining religious upbringing and education. *International Journal of Law, Policy and the Family, 29*, 15–35.

W v United Kingdom, 18187/91 (10 February 1993).

Welsh Office Education Department (1994). Religious Education and Collective Worship. Circular 10/94. Cardiff: HMSO.

X v United Kingdom 7782/77, (1978) 14 DR 179.

Zengin v Turkey (2008) 46 EHRR 4.

ANN SHERLOCK

7 Religious Observance and Collective Worship in Schools: A Human Rights Perspective

ABSTRACT

This chapter examines whether the current law and practice in the UK on religious observance and collective worship in schools meets the UK's human rights obligations. Without an opportunity for the withdrawal of children from these practices, there would be breaches of the right to freedom of religion or belief, and the right of parents to ensure that any education received by their children does not conflict with their own convictions. The chapter examines possible problems with opt-outs as a means of securing genuine respect for rights. It also considers whether the different treatment of Christian and non-Christian worship gives rise to discrimination on grounds of religion or belief.

Introduction

This chapter examines the law on collective worship and religious observance in schools within the UK from a human rights perspective. It focuses on schools without a designated religious character, those frequently referred to as 'non-faith schools', although, as explained in earlier chapters, they are not religion-free. In Wales and England, worship of a 'broadly Christian character' is expressly required by statute. In Northern Ireland, the Christian nature of worship is implicit in the requirements. The position in Scotland appears to allow greater flexibility to cater for children of all faiths and none, with guidance suggesting that 'time for reflection' may be a more suitable title for the activity in non-denominational schools than 'religious observance' (see Chapters 1–4).

This area is rich with tensions between different groups of rights-
holders – parents, families, and children – and between different rights –
freedom of religion or belief, education, and the rights of different family
members to be treated as autonomous decision-makers. ('Child' is used in
this chapter in the UN Convention on the Rights of the Child sense of a
person under 18 years of age.) The state's obligations require not only that
it refrains from direct acts infringing these rights but also that it secures an
appropriate balance between the rights of the different groups of rights-
holders. In addition the state has its own interests, such as producing well-
informed and tolerant citizens, and making best use of limited resources.
Balancing parents' and children's rights, and determining the appropriate
place for religion in the public sphere, individually raise many contested
issues: when they intersect, it is unsurprising that there are strong conflicting views.

Overview of relevant human rights

The UK is bound by a number of international human rights treaties.
Freedom of religion or belief is guaranteed in Article 18 of the International
Covenant on Civil and Political Rights (ICCPR), Article 9 of the European
Convention on Human Rights (ECHR) and Article 14 of the UN
Convention on the Rights of the Child (UNCRC). The following provi-
sions on the right to education bind the UK: Article 13 of the International
Covenant on Economic, Social and Cultural Rights (ICESCR), Articles 28
and 29 UNCRC, and Article 2 of Protocol No 1 to the ECHR (P1-ECHR).
A prohibition on discrimination is found in all the key treaties, either as
a free-standing right (Article 26 ICCPR, Article 2(2) UNCRC) or as a
right to enjoy the other human rights guarantees without discrimination
(Article 14 ECHR, Article 2 ICCPR, Article 2(1) UNCRC, Article 2(2)
ICESCR). Some rights are explicitly guaranteed to *either* parents or children, for example, the parents' right in relation to their children's education. However, the other rights in the treaties are guaranteed to 'everyone':

therefore both parents and children enjoy these rights, although there may be practical issues regarding their independent enforcement in relation to children. While parents' and children's views will usually converge, that may not always be so. In that case it is necessary to determine whose right should prevail (Lundy, 2005). The UNCRC is focused on the rights of the child, although the rights of parents to give direction and guidance are protected (Articles 5 and 14 UNCRC). Only the UNCRC expressly guarantees children a right to be heard, and have their views given due weight (Article 12).

These treaties' different systems for securing state compliance is relevant to how accessible the rights are for individuals. The UK has not accepted the individual complaints systems under the ICESCR, ICCPR or UNCRC, so its performance under these treaties is monitored by a 'reporting' system whereby it submits periodic reports on its progress under the treaties to committees of independent experts who examine and issue 'observations' on its performance. These committees also issue 'General Comments' providing guidance on the requirements of particular provisions. Reporting systems provide the opportunity for issues to be commented upon in the absence of a specific individual complaint, but, given the range of issues under consideration, something as specific as collective worship in schools may receive less attention if there are more serious failings to be dealt with (but see below for the attention given to the issue by the Committee on the Rights of the Child in 2016). Individual cases from other states to the monitoring bodies are of course relevant in relation to the provisions' interpretation. In contrast, under the ECHR, individual complaints may be submitted to the European Court of Human Rights (ECtHR) by 'victims' once domestic remedies have been exhausted. Thus, the interpretation and application of the law is developed by the ECtHR adjudicating on concrete cases. The absence of a reporting system under the ECHR means that if there are no individual complaints, the issues will not be examined, although relevant normative standards may be derived from cases dealing with related matters.

Of the international treaties binding the UK, only the ECHR's provisions are enforceable in the UK courts, under the Human Rights Act 1998 (HRA), although the courts may choose to have regard to other treaties in interpreting domestic law. The HRA therefore provides the most accessible enforcement system to individuals within the UK and, accordingly, this chapter focuses primarily on the ECHR. While placing no limits on the legislative competence of the UK Parliament, the HRA allows the courts in the UK to rule that there has been an unlawful act and to provide a remedy if a 'public authority' has acted incompatibly with a 'Convention right' unless that action was required by an Act of the UK Parliament (HRA, s. 6(2)). If an Act of the UK Parliament cannot be interpreted in a way which is compatible with the Convention rights (HRA, s3), it remains valid and enforceable but may be declared 'incompatible' (HRA, s. 4) thereby triggering a system under which it may be repealed or amended by ministerial order (HRA, s. 10). Unlike the UK Parliament, the legislatures of the devolved jurisdictions are bound to comply with the Convention rights on issues within their competence, and their legislation may be declared invalid if successfully challenged. If, as with education, the area is one of devolved competence, correcting any incompatible UK pre-devolution legislation which applies within their jurisdiction is the task of the devolved institutions. Thus far, apart from a judicial review case in Scotland which was subsequently withdrawn (BBC, 2016; Humanist Society Scotland, 2017), there has been no domestic or international human rights litigation against the law or practice on collective worship or religious observance within the UK.

Education rights

Human rights provisions on education have two main aspects: a right to education for the child and the right of parents to have their beliefs respected in their child's education. While the ECHR makes no provision regarding the goals of education, both the ICESCR and the UNCRC state the aims at some length, emphasizing that education should be directed towards the development of the child's personality and strengthening respect for human rights. Article 29(1) UNCRC provides that another aim is developing 'respect for the child's parents, his or her cultural identity, language and values' as well as respect for the values of the child's countries of residence and origin and for other civilizations. While exposure to knowledge about other religions and cultures is wholly consistent with these aims, one may question whether requiring a child to participate in worship in another faith, or having to opt out, serves to develop respect for the child's parents or cultural identity.

Under Article 2 P1-ECHR, the child's right to education is relatively limited: it involves the right to access the available education and have those studies officially recognized, but not to be provided with any particular type of education (*Belgian Linguistic case No. 2*, para. 4). Harris therefore concludes that, even if collective worship were regarded as an element of 'education', the state is under no obligation to provide it within the education system (Harris, 2007, 440). Repeal of the current requirements for collective worship/religious observance would not therefore pose a problem regarding the child's ECHR right to education. It is equally unlikely that, claims of discrimination aside, the UK would be found, by virtue of Article 2 P1-ECHR, to be obliged to provide additional collective worship for those not currently catered for by the current law.

Regarding the parents' rights, with the treaties' drafting having taken place against memories of the second world war and the background of totalitarian regimes, it is unsurprising that protecting the family against state interference and the child against possible indoctrination was deemed valuable. Article 18(4) ICCPR and Article 13(3) ICESCR are in identical terms and provide that the states 'undertake to have respect for the liberty of parents ... to ensure the religious and moral education of their children in conformity with their own convictions.' Article 2, P1-ECHR guarantees that '[i]n the exercise of any functions which it assumes in relation to education and to teaching, the State shall respect the right of parents to ensure such education and teaching in conformity with their own religious and philosophical convictions.' Not only religious views are protected but also those of parents who have no religion, and it will not be difficult to bring views about collective worship within their scope.

Article 5 UNCRC requires states to 'respect the responsibilities, rights and duties of parents ... to provide, in a manner consistent with the evolving capacities of the child, appropriate direction and guidance in the exercise by the child of the rights recognized in the present Convention.' It is notable that the only provision in the UNCRC which repeats the respect for the rights of the parents to provide direction is Article 14(2) on religion which provides that 'State Parties shall respect the rights and duties of the parents ... to provide direction to the child in the exercise of his or her right in a manner consistent with the evolving capacities of the child.'

The UK entered a reservation to the right of parents under Article 2 P1-ECHR, accepting the obligation 'only in so far as it is compatible with the provision of efficient instruction and training, and the avoidance of unreasonable expenditure'. The HRA gives effect to this reservation in domestic law. How much impact this reservation could have is unclear: there remain questions over whether it would survive a challenge to its validity on the grounds that it is overly broad and general (*SP v UK*) and, if valid, whether it would be applicable given that reservations are not intended to apply to statutory provisions which pre-date them. While the requirement to hold collective worship predates the reservation, the specific requirement of 'broadly Christian worship' was not introduced until 1988 although may have been implicit before then.

In the ECHR context, in cases involving the place of religion in schools, the ECtHR has treated Article 2 P1-ECHR as the relevant '*lex specialis*' and tackled it first and often to the exclusion of other provisions. While the ECtHR has recognized that Article 9 (the right to freedom of religion or belief), along with Article 8 on family life, includes a general right to pass on one's belief to one's children (*Vojnity*, para. 37) it is hard to see that making this case under Article 9 would add much to what is offered by Article 2 P1-ECHR. Similarly, the focus of the Human Rights Committee (HRC) tends to be on Article 18(4) ICCPR when freedom of religion arises in schools, rather than the general right in Article 18(1).

Thus far, most attention in individual cases has been on religious education, although some cases have involved religious practices to some extent. The crucial line that is drawn in all cases is between objective information being provided *about* religions and beliefs, and instruction or practice *in* a particular belief. It is not just the state's *law* which may cause problems: the ECtHR has also indicated that problems can arise in *practice* due to 'carelessness, lack of judgment or misplaced proselytism' (*Kjeldsen, Folgerø, Köse*). While compulsory instruction *in* a particular belief would offend against the human rights guarantee, objective and unbiased education about religions and beliefs has not only been held to be compatible with the parents' rights, but regarded as something to be encouraged in order to produce informed and tolerant citizens (OSCE /ODIHR, 2007).

In its first case on parents' rights under Article 2 P1-ECHR, the ECtHR held that parents could not object to the communication of objective material in a pluralistic manner: what was prohibited was 'indoctrination' (*Kjeldsen*), a position also taken by the HRC under the ICCPR (HRC, 1993). The ECtHR has also indicated that states are under an obligation to ensure that information is conveyed in 'a calm atmosphere free of any misplaced proselytism' (*Zengin*, para. 52). In relation to the teaching of a compulsory subject on religious education in Norway, the state's intentions were found to be 'clearly consonant' with Article 2's objectives of pluralism and objectivity, and the Court found no indoctrination (*Folgerø*, paras 88–89). However, in favouring Christianity in the curriculum, in a *qualitative* rather than merely *quantitative* sense, and in involving the children in *participation* in religious activities, there was a failure to respect the parents' religious convictions (*Folgerø*, paras 90–95). Yet, this case shows how there may be diverging views on the appreciation of the facts and the application of the legal principles as it was decided by a 9 to 8 majority, with the dissenting judges finding no qualitative favouring of Christianity. Unusually, the same facts were the subject of a complaint to the HRC which also found that the state had failed to comply with the parents' rights. Like the ECtHR, the HRC also considered it problematic that religious practice and education in religious knowledge were not separated in the module (*Leirvåg*, paras 14.3 & 14.6).

In contrast, in the *Lautsi case*, the Grand Chamber of the ECtHR found that the presence of a crucifix in Italian state school classrooms did not fall foul of the guarantee in Article 2 P1-ECHR: given the context, in which various religious traditions were respected and celebrated in school life, the presence of the crucifix in the classroom represented only a 'passive symbol' and its presence fell within the 'margin of appreciation' enjoyed by the state in determining what was appropriate (*Lautsi*, para. 72).

While drawing the line between what is neutral and what is not can be finely balanced, it would be difficult to categorize a requirement to participate in worship as anything other than a confessional activity and one which could not be regarded as the kind of 'passive' element that the ECtHR would accept. Accordingly, without some form of exemption, this would breach the parents' rights under Article 2 P1-ECHR. On the other hand, an invitation to participate in quiet reflection might more easily be regarded as an activity which could be undertaken by pupils in line with the guidance given to them by their parents. An activity of this nature would be considered to be objective and pluralistic, and thus the existence of an opt-out provision would not be required. For some parts of the UK such an approach would require a change in the law.

Right to freedom of religion or belief

Under the treaty provisions which bind the UK (Article 9 ECHR, Article 18 ICCPR and Article 14 UNCRC), a range of beliefs, religious and non-religious, and the right not to hold or manifest a belief, are protected (HRC, 1993; *Kokkinakis*, para. 31). Accordingly, these provisions will apply to those who wish to attend school worship as well as to those who do not.

As to the preferred constitutional structures for protecting freedom of religion or belief, international human rights law is flexible and accepts a range of different Church-State relationships as long as they produce no negative effects for members of minority belief systems. For example, within Europe, some states have established/official churches (e.g. UK, Sweden, Norway), while others require very strict separation between Church and State (e.g. France, Turkey).

As noted before, children as well as adults enjoy the right to freedom of religion or belief. However, by choosing to examine cases concerning religion in schools under Article 2 P1-ECHR, the interests of the children are often subsumed within the consideration of their parents' interests. Frequently, the views and rights of children may converge with those of their parents but there may be situations where they do not. Exactly what the child's rights involve will depend on the age, maturity and understanding of the child. A younger child's rights to religion or belief are described by Langlaude as the right 'to be unhindered in their growth as an independent autonomous actor in the matrix of parents, religious community and society'. This requires respect for the child's interest to 'be brought up as a religious being, to belong to a religious community, and to interact with parents and religious community' (Langlaude, 2008). On the other hand as the child matures, the right to make autonomous choices arises and must be protected not only against state interference but also, by the state if necessary, against parental overbearing. However, it is unclear how far the ECtHR would go in respecting the child's right to freedom of religion or belief if it conflicts with that of the parent. The *Vojnity* case appears to indicate a very strong recognition of the rights of the parents to pass on their religion to their children: finding a violation due to an absolute ban on a father's access to his son because of the father's religious convictions, the ECtHR held that under Articles 8 and 9 ECHR and Article 2 P1-ECHR, parents had the right to promote their religious convictions in rearing their children, even in 'an insistent or overbearing manner unless this exposes the [child] to dangerous practices or psychological harm ...' In some areas, the ECtHR has taken a child-rights approach to interpreting the ECHR, using the UNCRC to assist in the process (Kilkelly, 2001). Whether this would be the case regarding a child's right to freedom of religion or belief – whether to attend or to absent himself from worship in school – has yet to be determined.

Each of the different treaty provisions on religion and belief provides that the *manifestation* of a belief (referred to as the *forum externum*) may be subject to limited restrictions whereas the *holding* of a belief (referred to as the *forum internum*) is subject to no such qualifications. In a number of cases, the ECtHR held that a requirement to disclose one's religion or belief was a concern that fell within the protection of the *forum internum* of each individual (e.g. *Sinan Işık*, para. 42). However, as noted elsewhere (e.g. Taylor, 2005), monitoring bodies may be reluctant to interpret the *forum internum* too widely as it is not then possible to justify any limitations. For example, in *Buscarini*, which Taylor views as a clear case of compulsion (Taylor, 2005, 130), the ECtHR did not regard requiring the applicants to swear an oath on the Christian Gospels before taking their seats in the state's legislature as falling within the *forum internum*, but rather as a violation of the right not to manifest a religion or belief. Earlier, the European Commission of Human Rights held that the requirement to pay a church tax fell within the *forum internum* which protected every-one 'from being compelled to be involved directly in religious activities against his will without being a member of the religious community carry-ing out those activities' (*Darby*, paras 50–51). On the other hand, when the ECtHR ruled on the case, it did not consider the Article 9 aspect, perhaps an indication that it had no wish to contemplate an extended concept of the *forum internum*. Some of the academic literature takes the view that as long as one is not prevented from holding one's own beliefs, 'the *forum internum* remains untouched' (M. Evans, 1997, 295). In one of the few cases not focused specifically on religious education, Jehovah's Witnesses pupils were required to participate in a school parade which they perceived to have militaristic overtones. Carolyn Evans considered that: '[t]hey were in effect being asked to recant, by their behaviour, their religion' (C. Evans, 2001, 77–78). The ECtHR, however, did not perceive this as an aspect of the *forum internum*, and indeed went on to find no breach of Article 9 at all. Overall, in the absence of severely repressive measures to coerce someone into denying their beliefs, it seems likely that the ECtHR will consider requirements to attend worship as an interference with the right to manifest, or not manifest, a belief, rather than a requirement which is prohibited in absolute terms. In any case, the UK would point to the option for withdrawing children from worship or observance as a response to any human rights claim. Only if the opt-out systems were found wanting (as discussed below) would the UK be required to justify its action under Article 9(2). This would require it to show that the interference pursued a legitimate aim, was provided for in law which was clear and accessible, and was a proportionate response to the legitimate aim being pursued.

Without the availability of an opt-out, it would be difficult to justify compulsory participation in worship in a faith that is not one's own in these terms. Even if there are generally good intentions about cultivating spiritual and moral development, it would require an extremely generous margin of appreciation for the state – one that bucks the trend of the stricter scrutiny in cases such as *Folgerø* – to require children to participate in the prayer and practices of another faith. It is true that in relation to religious education, favouring the majority or traditional religion of a state was not in itself a breach of Article 2 P1-ECHR, but that was in the context of material *about the* religion being conveyed in an objective and pluralistic way. While the Grand Chamber in *Lautsi* was content that a crucifix on classroom walls did not breach Article 2 P1-ECHR, the applicability of its ruling (which is not uncontroversial) is constrained by the characterization of the crucifix as a purely 'passive' symbol, something which could not be said of compulsory participation in worship. While faiths other than Christianity may be included in worship, in England and Wales the legislative requirement is for worship that is 'wholly or mainly of a broadly Christian character'. A neutral 'time for reflection', would more easily meet the requirement of showing a proportionate response to a legitimate aim. On the other hand, if the *practice* does not measure up to this neutrality, then it is still problematic. Once again, the existence of a satisfactory option for withdrawal is crucial and is discussed below.

The child's right to autonomous decision-making

Article 12 UNCRC provides that when decisions are being taken in relation to a child, that child has the right to be heard and have her views given due weight (see further UNCRC, 2009). In terms of how the balance between parental and child rights is to be determined, this links with the stipulation in Article 5 UNCRC that the parents' right to direct the child shall wane in line with the 'evolving capacities of the child'. There is no equivalent explicit protection of this autonomy right in the other treaties binding the UK, although it could be argued that the child's right to be consulted on how she would choose to manifest her beliefs in school might be implicit in the provisions on freedom of religion or belief as a matter of procedural fairness. Such an approach has been taken in relation to the rights to family life under Article 8 ECHR (e.g. *T. P. and K. M*, para. 72).

As the child becomes more mature, this right to make an autonomous decision on religion or belief arises. This is a right in itself *and* an aspect of the right to freedom of religion or belief. The general issue of a child's capacity to make decisions independent of her parents, especially in relation to consent to medical treatment, has been dealt with in case law and legislation within the UK and is discussed in detail in Chapter 6. The extent to which the current arrangements in the UK respect the right of the child under Article 12 UNCRC is considered in the next section of this chapter.

Opt-outs as a means of respecting children's and parents' rights

Where schools cross the line from the mere transmission of objective knowledge into confessional religious activity, a right of withdrawal from the relevant practice has traditionally been seen as a means of ensuring human rights compliance. States may make any doctrinal religious education classes completely optional or provide an exemption mechanism or offer an alternative subject (e.g. *Zengin*, para. 71). The General Comments issued by the HRC (HRC, 1993, para. 6) and the Committee on the Economic, Social and Cultural Rights (CESCRC, 1999) specify that instruction in a particular religion or belief will be a breach of the parents' right to respect for their convictions *unless* 'provision is made for non-discriminatory exemptions or alternatives that would accommodate the wishes of parents' (see also *Hartikainen*, para. 10.4). In addition to withdrawing individual children from worship, in England and Wales, a school, rather than the parents or pupils, may seek a determination that the 'broadly Christian character' of worship be lifted for all or a group of pupils within the school. Schools would be thus well advised to consider their obligations under the Human Rights Act to respect parents' and children's Convention rights in deciding whether to apply for a determination, as would the local SACRE in deciding on whether it should be granted.

In relation to children's rights, the focus has tended to be on whether children can exercise a right of withdrawal independently of their parents. The law in England and Wales provides that a sixth-former may exercise the right of withdrawal independently of the parents (School Standards and Framework Act 1998, s. 71, as amended) but this is not available to a younger pupil, even one of sufficient maturity to be judged competent to consent to medical treatment, the so-called 'Gillick-competent' child. In Scotland and Northern Ireland, the relevant legislation allows parents to withdraw their children (Education (Scotland) Act 1980, s.9; Education and Libraries Order (Northern Ireland) 1986, Article 21(5)), but makes no provision for pupils of any age to withdraw themselves although guidance from the Scottish Government in March 2017 requires that children should be involved in discussions about this. In response to the revised guidance, a judicial review case challenging the absence of an opt-out for children was withdrawn (BBC, 2016; HSS, 2017).

The limited availability of an independent opt-out opportunity for mature pupils has been criticized within the UK and outside. The UK Parliament's Joint Committee on Human Rights (JCHR), considered that to comply with the State's human rights obligations the law should give the right to 'any pupil of sufficient maturity, understanding and intelligence to make an informed decision about whether or not to withdraw' from collective worship. The JCHR referred to the '*Gillick*-competent' child as the child who would be so entitled. Any administrative burdens this entailed for schools would not justify the interference with child's Article 9 rights (JCHR, 2006 and 2008).

In June 2016, the UN Committee on the Rights of the Child expressed concern that there was no independent right of withdrawal for children in the UK, other than for sixth-form pupils in England and Wales. It recommended that the UK should ensure the right of withdrawal for children to exercise independently of their parents (UNCRC, 2016).

These points are important in relation to respecting the autonomy of the child and the right to be heard and to influence decisions. However, the discussion tends to frame the child's interests purely as an autonomy issue regarding opting out, to the exclusion of the child's right to respect for their freedom of religion or belief. If there are significant disadvantages associated with withdrawal, does the right to be withdrawn fully 'respect' the child's right to freedom of religion or belief?

It has been observed that, in the past, the mere existence of an opt-out was regarded as sufficient to protect the rights of parents and children (Mawhinney, 2006 & 2015). For example, Mawhinney draws attention to the *CJ* case where an exemption from religious instruction was available but the exempted pupil had to spend the time alone in the corridor, and appeared to be subject to pressure from her peers and teachers regarding her absence from the course, eventually returning to the classes as a result. Yet the European Commission on Human Rights found that the pupil's attendance at religious instruction was voluntary (Mawhinney, 2006, 104). However, more recent cases have subjected exemptions to greater scrutiny.

In *Folgerø*, a partial exemption system failed to ensure respect for the parents' rights. It required parents to be sufficiently aware of what was being taught so as to identify the elements incompatible with their own beliefs and request their child's exemption from those parts: the ECtHR considered this to be unduly burdensome on parents, a view shared by the HRC in the equivalent *Leirvåg* application (*Leirvåg*, para. 14.6). Reasonable grounds had to be given unless the exemption request concerned clearly religious activities, a requirement which the ECtHR considered to give rise to the risk that the parents might feel obliged to disclose aspects of their own religious beliefs. Furthermore, a request regarded as reasonable would not necessarily lead to the full withdrawal of the pupil from the activity since, for some activities such as religious services, it was proposed that the child's *participation* could be replaced with *observation* by the child, a distinction which the ECtHR considered to be 'complicated to operate in practice' but also undermining the effectiveness of the exemption as a means of protecting the parents' convictions. These factors led the ECtHR to conclude that the partial exemption system had failed to avoid a violation of the parents' rights under Article 2. (In contrast, the dissenting judges found the system to be neither unduly burdensome nor overly intrusive.) The failure of the system to separate education of religious *knowledge* and religious *practice* was also considered by the HRC in *Leirvåg* to make the exemption scheme impracticable. Rejecting the option which had been floated in *Kjeldsen* (para. 54), the ECtHR held that the obligation to safeguard pluralism was not fulfilled by the opportunity for children to attend alternative private schools, even if heavily subsidised by the state (*Folgerø*, para. 101). Elsewhere, an exemption available only to parents of particular faiths was found wanting in relation to its availability and its requirement for parents to disclose details of their beliefs (*Zengin*, para. 76).

The *Folgerø* and *Zengin* cases indicate that the mere existence of some procedure for withdrawing children is not enough. To be an acceptable solution, an exemption must be available to parents of all religions and beliefs without discrimination, must not place undue burdens on them, and must not require parents to reveal information about their own beliefs. A breach may also arise from the way in which the exemption provisions are applied in practice in a school (*Zengin*, para. 53). McCarthy concludes that 'accommodationist approaches *can* still meet the required human rights standards' but 'the form of accommodation will be more stringently controlled than ever' (McCarthy, 2011, 245).

Despite the ECtHR's acceptance of opt-outs in principle, some academic research has concluded that opt-outs are an inherently flawed and divisive approach which fails to accord genuine respect to the rights of parents and children (Bradney, 1993, 63; Cumper, 2011, 217). Existing empirical research focuses mainly on opt-outs from religious education, but the concerns expressed about opt-out mechanisms are in principle applicable to worship too. Mawhinney, Niens, Richardson and Chiba identified parents' and teachers' low levels of awareness of the legal position on opt-outs as a particular problem. Even where there is awareness, parents fearful of stigmatizing their children are reluctant to withdraw them. Some children considered that opting out of worship conducted at school assembly was impossible since the worship was mixed with school news, and parents may be influenced by such fears of their children missing out. The research found that the pupils did not feel that their religion or beliefs were 'acknowledged and respected' by the school through opt-outs. Parents feared that younger children were unable to understand and cope with being separated from their peers during the school day. While some young people were satisfied with the opt-out experience, others felt excluded by being separated from the rest of their class when religious education took place. The lack of consultation regarding alternative arrangements led some opted-out pupils to feel that their beliefs were not of interest or concern. The authors of the research concluded that international human rights bodies should recognize that opt-outs might 'formally protect against unwanted indoctrination' but did not constitute respect for the beliefs of those children (Mawhinney, Niens, Richardson, Chiba, 2010 and 2011).

Other jurisdictions have seen the pressure on a child in withdrawing as a problem. In the *Zylberberg case* in Ontario, despite the opportunity for withdrawal, school prayer was found to violate religious freedom. Rejecting the Attorney General's submission that while requesting an exemption might be embarrassing, it was not coercive, the Ontario Court of Appeal held that this did not reflect the situation faced by members of religious minorities: '[w]hether or not there is pressure must be assessed from their standpoint and, in particular, from the standpoint of pupils in the sensitive setting of a public school' (*Zylberberg*, 645). Others have considered that even if there is no coercion, having to be opted out of prayer labels the pupil as an outsider, and that '[s]uch disparagement is a constitutionally cognizable harm' (Eisgruber and Sager, 2007). In contrast, the German Constitutional Court has found voluntary school prayer not to violate the Basic Law (Lock, 2011).

McCrea questions whether this 'sense of alienation or inferiority is itself a rights violation or whether it is problematic for other reasons', for example as a breach of the US constitutional principle of separation of Church and State (McCrea, 2017; see also Adhar and Leigh, 2013). In this regard McCrea quotes Laborde's statement that 'hurt feelings or a sense that the state does not share one's values are inevitable parts of democratic life' (McCrea, 2017, 1013–1028). Others point to case law of the Commission and the ECtHR as supporting the position that 'having the right to freedom of thought, conscience and religion does not mean that its enjoyment need be without cost' unless it involves discrimination for the purposes of Article 14 ECHR (M. Evans, 1997, 300).

While this may be convincing in the adult context, it may not be appropriate in relation to children. Where no meaningful alternative activity is provided, and at present there is no legal obligation to do so, the experience may imply some form of exclusion. While parents may be able to cope with a sense of being different, it is arguable that, viewed from a child-rights-centric perspective, some attempt at parity of esteem may be necessary to provide genuine respect for the rights of children, particularly those of younger children who are unable to understand fully the basis for their perceived exclusion from a school event or make sense of the conflict between their family's belief system and the mainstream. Learning about one's differences from the mainstream may be valuable at some point as the young person matures, but for younger children it is suggested that, to be respectful of a child's religion or belief, any exemption should be accompanied by some meaningful alternative activity whose nature, timing and location do not involve the child missing out on, for example, general school news and announcements, or being sent to a location normally used for punishment or feeling stigmatized as an 'outsider'. Thus far, this type of child-centric scrutiny has not been undertaken by any of the treaty monitoring bodies. Indeed, while the difficulties for parents in opt-outs are considered in case-law, the interests and rights of children tend to receive little or no attention, being held to raise no separate issues (*Lautsi*, para. 79) or not being not addressed at all (*Zengin*).

It is unclear how severe the negative impacts or practical difficulties would need to be to render an exemption system unacceptable to the ECtHR. For example, would the circumstances surrounding the availability of an exemption in the *CJ* case discussed earlier now be regarded by the ECtHR as problematic? It may be that, in the sensitive area of parents, children and religion, the ECtHR will be wary of venturing too far into what it regards as the state's margin of appreciation in requiring positive action on the part of the state. In turn, any such reticence may guide the UK courts who will not seek to limit the other organs of government more than it believes the ECtHR would do.

Discrimination

Protection against discrimination on grounds of religion is guaranteed in a number of international treaties which are binding on the UK, including Article 14 ECHR, Articles 2 and 26 ICCPR, Article 2 ICESCR, and Article

2 UNCRC. Of these, Article 14 ECHR is enforceable as a 'Convention right' in the UK courts and ultimately in the ECtHR. It is not a freestanding right but must be linked with another right in order to bring a claim. In the context of collective worship, this is not a problem as the argument would be that there has been discrimination in relation to the enjoyment of the right to religion or belief, or the parents' rights regarding their child's education. As long as one of these rights is *applicable*, it is not necessary that there is a *breach* of the substantive right itself. Under Article 14, a difference in treatment is not prohibited in itself but will constitute unlawful discrimination if it does not pursue a legitimate aim or if the difference in treatment is not proportionate to that aim (*Belgian Linguistics case*, para. 10). This does not mean identical treatment is either required or even appropriate in all cases: a breach of Article 14 could lie in the failure to distinguish appropriately between the persons to whom the national law is applied, if this results in substantive inequality (*Thlimennos*). While discrimination might not be intentional, it is the effect rather than the motive behind the action which is crucial.

As regards domestic legislation, the Equality Act 2010, which applies to most of the UK, includes religion among the individual characteristics which must be protected against discrimination. However, the Act expressly excludes collective worship and religious observance in schools from this protection. The question remains however whether providing state-funded collective worship for some but not others may be found to violate the UK's human rights obligations not to discriminate.

Of course, in England and Wales where there is the explicit requirement for 'broadly Christian' worship, it is the case that only a majority of acts of worship each term must fall into this category. There is therefore some flexibility for schools to minimize different treatment of different faiths, although it is doubtful that schools can accommodate students of no faith while still delivering 'worship'. Where a 'determination' lifts the requirement of 'broadly Christian' worship, worship suitable for the group in question will be provided. However, if there are insufficient pupils for such a determination, the only alternative is for a minority belief pupil to be withdrawn from worship. In that case, alternative worship is not legally required and is permitted only if it involves no cost to the school

(Circulars 1/94 and 10/94, see Chapters 1 and 4). The funding of worship for one group but not another raises questions under Article 14 ECHR (Hamilton, 1996).

A difference in treatment will breach Article 14 ECHR if it lacks a legitimate aim or if the difference is not a proportionate response to that aim. Given the lack of clarity and consistency regarding the rationale and aims of worship discussed in earlier chapters, identifying a legitimate aim might be a challenge. However, the approach of the ECtHR tends to be most 'light-touch' in relation to states' assertions of legitimate aims, and it might accept a general assertion of the value of the pupils' spiritual development. The most contentious point is likely to be whether the difference in treatment is a proportionate response to this aim. The UK would undoubtedly point to the financial cost and administrative burden of providing worship for all other faiths within a school, and to the reservation it entered in relation to Article 2 P1-ECHR limiting its obligations under that provision to what could be provided without unreasonable expenditure. However, that reservation does not apply to Article 9 on freedom of religion or belief which may be used jointly with Article 14 ECHR, and in any case it may be argued that if the UK *chooses* to fund worship in one faith, it must be alive to its obligations not to discriminate. The decision is likely to come down to whether the burden on resources is regarded as an acceptable justification, a question on which there are diverging views.

When the HRC was drafting the General Comment on freedom of religion there was disagreement among committee members on whether funding religious education for one faith and not for others would amount to discrimination (HRC, 1993, paras 20–36). The General Comment, as adopted, states that the fact that a faith is recognized as a state religion should not result in any discrimination against members of other faiths and that 'measures ... such as ... giving economic advantages' to members of the predominant religion would constitute discrimination on the grounds of religion or belief (HRC, 1993a, para. 9). In an individual case, the HRC held that while a state is not obliged to fund schools established on a religious basis, if it chooses to do so then it must make the funding available without discrimination (*Waldman*, para. 10). Any difference in such funding must be based on reasonable and objective criteria, and enshrining a distinction between religions in a state's constitution 'does not render it reasonable and objective' (*Waldman*, para. 10.4).

In contrast, Adhar and Leigh have argued that the 'majority status of Christianity and the cost to the state of providing a comprehensive range of alternative forms of collective worship could plausibly be argued' to constitute a reasonable and objective justification for the purposes of Article 14 ECHR (Adhar & Leigh, 2013, 260). On the other hand, the CESCR states that 'a lack of available resources is not an objective and reasonable justification unless every effort has been made to use all resources that are at the State party's disposition in an effort to address and eliminate the discrimination, as a matter of priority' (CESCR, 2009, para. 13). If the ECtHR took this view, it would need to examine whether alternatives had been explored within the UK jurisdictions for achieving the aims of supporting pupils in developing their belief systems without discriminating against minority pupils.

If the current position were to be found to constitute a breach of Article 14 ECHR, Harris considers that the abolition of the requirement of collective worship might be the only means of resolving the problem (Harris, 2007, 440) although, as he notes, schools wishing to continue with worship would then have to be even more careful about their obligations in the absence of a statutory framework. An alternative approach might be to explore whether a quiet time for reflection could be used to accommodate all faiths and none, while still serving the goals of developing a sense of community within the school.

Conclusion

At present, the case law of the ECtHR and other treaty monitoring bodies indicates that they would treat the current exemption systems in the UK as adequate to protect parents' rights to have their children educated in line with their belief systems. However, the failure to extend the opt-out system to children of sufficient understanding and maturity fails to comply with the UK's obligations under Article 12 UNCRC, and might be found to be a breach of the child's right to freedom of religion or belief. Questions also remain concerning discrimination against pupils for whom state-funded worship is not provided. More generally, it is suggested that there should be a more rigorous and child-rights-centric scrutiny of the arrangements for opt-outs before they are accepted as a complete solution to respecting the rights of parents and children.

References

Adhar, R., & Leigh, I. (2013). *Religious Freedom in the Liberal State*. 2nd edn. Oxford: Oxford University Press.

BBC (2016). Humanists' legal challenge to school religious observance. Retrieved April 13, 2017, from <http://www.bbc.co.uk/news/uk-scotland-37336340>.

Bradney, A. (1993). *Religions, Rights and Laws*. Leicester: Leicester University Press.

Committee on Economic, Social and Cultural Rights (1999). *General Comment 13: The Right to Education (Article 13)*. UN Economic and Social Council: E/C.12/1999/10.

Cumper, P. (2011). Religious Education in Europe in the Twenty-First Century. In M. Hunter-Henin (Ed.), *Law, Religious Freedoms and Education in Europe* (pp. 207–228). Surrey: Ashgate.

Eisgruber, C. L., & Sager, L. G. (2007). *Religious Freedom and the Constitution*. Cambridge, MA, and London, England: Harvard University Press.

Evans, C. (2001). *Freedom of Religion Under the European Convention on Human Rights*. Oxford: Oxford University Press.

Evans, M. (1997). *Religious liberty and international law in Europe*. Cambridge: Cambridge University Press.

Harris, N. (2007). *Education, Law and Diversity*. Oxford: Hart Publishing.

Human Rights Committee (1993). Summary of the 1209th Meeting, CCPR/C/SR. 1209.

Human Rights Committee (1993a). General Comment 22, Article 18. UN: CCPR/C/21/Rev.1/Add.4.

Humanist Society Scotland (2017). Young People given 'voice' but not 'choice' in new Religious Observance guidance. Retrieved April 17, 2017, from <https://

www.humanism.scot/what-we-do/news/young-people-given-voice-not-choice-new-religious-observance-guidance/>.

Joint Committee on Human Rights (2006). Twenty-eighth Report of Session 2005–2006. HL 247/ HC 1626.

Joint Committee on Human Rights (2008). Nineteenth Report of Session 2007–2006. HL 107/HC 553.

Kilkelly, U. (2001). The Best of Both Worlds for Children's Rights? Interpreting the European Convention on Human Rights in the Light of the UN Convention on the Rights of the Child. *Human Rights Quarterly, 23*, 308–326.

Langlaude, S. (2008). Children and Religion under Article 14 UNCRC: A Critical Analysis. *International Journal of Children's Rights, 16*, 475–504.

Lock, T. (2011). Of Crucifixes and Headscarves: Religious Symbols in German Schools. In M. Hunter-Henin (Ed.), *Law, Religious Freedoms and Education in Europe* (pp. 347–370). Surrey: Ashgate.

Lundy, L. (2005). Family Values in the Classroom? Reconciling Parental Wishes and Children's Rights in State Schools. *International Journal of Law, Policy and the Family, 19*, 346–372.

McCarthy, F. (2011). Prayers in the Playground: Religion and Education in the United Kingdom and Beyond. In J. Mair & E. Orucu (Eds.), *The Place of Religion in Family Law: A Comparative Search* (pp. 235–262). Cambridge: Intersentia.

McCrea, R. (2017). Rights as a basis for the religious neutrality of the state: Lessons from Europe for American defenders of non-establishment. *International Journal of Constitutional Law, 14*(4) 1009–1033.

Mawhinney, A. (2006). The Opt-out clause: imperfect protection for the right to freedom of religion in schools. *Education Law Journal, 2*, 102–115.

Mawhinney, A. (2015). Religion in Schools – A Human Rights Contribution to the Debate. In L. G. Beaman & L. Van Arragon (Eds.), *Issues in Religion and Education* (pp. 282–303). Leiden: Koninklijke Brill NV.

Mawhinney, A., Niens, U., Richardson, N., & Chiba, Y. (2010). *Opting Out of Religious Education – The Views of Young People from Minority Belief Backgrounds.* Belfast: Queen's University Belfast.

Mawhinney, A., Niens, U., Richardson, N., & Chiba, Y. (2011). Religious Education and Religious Liberty: Opt-Outs and Young People's Sense of Belonging. In M. Hunter-Henin (Ed.), *Law, Religious Freedoms and Education in Europe* (pp. 229–250). Surrey: Ashgate.

OSCE/ ODIHR (2007). *Toledo Guiding Principles On Teaching About Religions And Beliefs in Public Schools.* Warsaw: OSCE / ODIHR.

Taylor, P. M. (2005). *Freedom of Religion*, Cambridge: Cambridge University Press.

UN Committee on the Rights of the Child (2009). General Comment No. 12 – The right of the child to be heard. CRC/C/GC/12.

UN Committee on the Rights of the Child (2016). Concluding observations on the fifth periodic report of the United Kingdom of Great Britain and Northern Ireland. CRC/C/GBR/CO/5.

Cases

All ECHR cases may be found on the HUDOC database at: <https://hudoc.echr.coe. int/>. Therefore, only the ECHR Application number is given for the ECHR cases.

Belgian Linguistic case (No. 2), ECHR Application no. 1474/62, HUDOC.

Buscarini v San Marino, ECHR Application no. 24645/94, HUDOC.

C. J. v Poland, ECHR Application no. 23380/94, HUDOC.

Darby v Sweden, ECHR Application no. 11581/85, HUDOC.

Folgerø v Norway, ECHR Application no. 15472/02, HUDOC.

Gillick v West Norfolk and Wisbech Health Authority [1986] AC 112.

Hartikainen v Finland, Communication no. 40/1978, Human Rights Committee.

Kjeldsen v Denmark, ECHR Application no. 5095/71, HUDOC.

Kokkinakis v Greece, ECHR Application no. 14307/88, HUDOC.

Köse v Turkey, ECHR Application no. 26625/02, HUDOC.

Lautsi v Italy, ECHR Application no. 30814/06, HUDOC.

Sinan Işik v Turkey, ECHR Application no. 21924/05, HUDOC.

SP v UK, Application no. 28915/95, HUDOC.

Vojnity v Hungary, ECHR Application no. 29617/07, HUDOC.

Zengin v Turkey, ECHR Application no. 1448/04, HUDOC.

Zylberberg v Sudbury Board of Education (1998) 52 DLR (4th) 577.

PART III

Collective Worship and Religious Observance:
Educational Perspectives

JACQUELINE WATSON

8 The Contribution of Collective Worship to Spiritual Development

ABSTRACT

This chapter examines ways in which collective worship/religious observance/assemblies have been identified as contributing to the spiritual and moral development of children and young people (or the spiritual, moral, social and cultural development (SMSC) since the 1990s, when SMSC was (re-)emphasized). It is generally accepted that collective worship (and presumably religious observance) makes a strong contribution to spiritual and moral development. This chapter examines how it has been anticipated this contribution could be made in practice. The chapter also discusses the viability of using collective worship/religious observance for SMSC, as well as examining arguments for improving opportunities for SMSC by changing from collective worship to assemblies with spiritual content, as recommended in the recent Scottish model for religious observance.

Introduction

The statutory position of spiritual development

The spiritual development of pupils has been a consistent feature of school education in the UK, initially because of the Christian Churches' contribution to education. At the start of the last century, with greater government involvement in education in the United Kingdom, a commitment to the spiritual development of pupils, as part of a wider set of developmental aims, remained strong.

The 1944 Education Act for England and Wales (which was also hugely influential on the 1945 Education Act in Scotland and the 1947 Education Act in Northern Ireland) stated:

> [I]t shall be the duty of the local education authority for every area, so far as their powers extend, to contribute towards the spiritual, moral, mental and physical development of the community ... (Education Act, 1944: Part 2, Paragraph 7)

The 1988 Education Reform Act for England and Wales reaffirmed this commitment, although it changed the focus from the spiritual development of the community to the spiritual development of individual pupils and society:

> The curriculum for a maintained school satisfies the requirements of this section if it is a balanced and broadly based curriculum which -
> (a) promotes the spiritual, moral, cultural, mental and physical development of pupils at the school and of society ... (Education (Reform) Act, 1988: Part 1, Chapter 1, Section 1)

By the same token in Northern Ireland the 1947 Education (Northern Ireland) Act was closely modelled on the 1944 Education Act. Similarly, the Statutory Rules of Northern Ireland 2007 No. 46 Education provide that the statutory Northern Ireland Curriculum, from Foundation Stage to Key Stage 4, is a balanced and broadly based curriculum which 'promotes the spiritual, emotional, moral, cultural, intellectual and physical development of pupils at the school and thereby of society' (DoE, 2007, 3).

Since the Education (Schools) Act 1992 inaugurated the schools' inspectorates (Ofsted in England and Estyn in Wales), spiritual development has been presented by them as part of a group of development aims: 'spiritual, moral, social and cultural development' or 'SMSC'. For example, the *Ofsted Handbook* states that:

> Inspectors must evaluate and report on the strengths and weaknesses of the school's provision for the spiritual, moral, social and cultural development of all pupils ... [and] ... inspectors need to evaluate what schools actively do to promote pupils' development. (*Ofsted Handbook*, 1995, 5:3)

In England and Wales, in accordance with the Education Act 2005, school inspection authorities must currently report on schools' provision for spiritual development. According to the latest guidance from Ofsted and Estyn, inspectors must report on 'the spiritual, moral, social and cultural development of pupils at the school' (Estyn, 2010, Guidance for the inspection of secondary schools, 1) and that before making the final judgement on the overall effectiveness, inspectors must also evaluate 'the effectiveness and impact of the provision for pupils' spiritual, moral, social and cultural development' (*Ofsted Handbook*, 2015, 34).

The relationship between spiritual development and collective worship

In England and Wales, Circulars 1/94 (DfE, 1994) and 10/94 (Welsh Office, 1994), extant guidance clarifying the law, make a strong link between collective worship (CW) and spiritual development.

> Religious education and collective worship make an important, although not exclusive, contribution to spiritual, moral and cultural development. These activities offer explicit opportunities for pupils to consider the response of religion to fundamental questions about the purpose of being, morality and ethical standards, and to develop their own response to such matters. (Para. 4, 1/94 and para. 5 10/94)

In Scotland, rather differently, the 1980 Education (Scotland) Act does not refer specifically to spiritual development, but statutory guidance on religious observance (RO) was substantially updated in Circular 1/2005 (Scottish Executive, 2005a), and recently updated in March 2017 advice (Government of Scotland, 2017) (see Chapter 3). These advisory documents give the same wording for the definition of RO, and spiritual development features strongly:

> Religious Observance is defined as follows: '*Community acts which aim to promote the spiritual development of all members of the school's community and express and celebrate the shared values of the school community*'. (Ibid. 2017, 1)

This will be discussed further below and with reference to guidance which continues this approach to spiritual development.

In Northern Ireland, schools must develop pupils' 'spiritual awareness' (see, for instance, <http://www.nicurriculum.org.uk/docs/key_stage_3/ BigPictureKS3.pdf>), but there is no government guidance on the relationship between spirituality and collective worship. In practice, most publicly funded schools assume a generally Christian approach to collective worship.

In summary, it is intended that collective worship will make a strong contribution to pupils' spiritual development in all four countries, although this is not made explicit in Northern Ireland.

What is spiritual development?

Education in the UK has its roots in the Christian religion, but the authors of the 1944 (Butler) Education Act deliberately introduced the word 'spiritual' in preference to that of 'religious'. As Jack Priestley has explained:

> The first thing to say about the spiritual is that it is a wider concept than the religious. That is why it appeared as part of the preamble to the 1944 Education Act in the first place and why it has stayed there ever since. The author of that part of the Preamble was Canon J. Hall. ... Canon Hall was a sprightly 96 ... when I visited him a few years ago. 'Why,' I asked him 'did you use the word "spiritual" in the Preamble instead of the word, "religious"?' He laughed but did not hesitate. 'Because it was much broader,' he said and went on, 'If we had used the word "religious" they would all have started arguing about it.' (Priestley, 1997, 29)

Britain in the 1940s saw itself as essentially Christian and breadth was required to address interdenominational differences. When spirituality re-emerged in the 1988 Education Reform Act for England and Wales it was in the context of a common recognition of the principle of religious pluralism and the need for religious and racial tolerance (Swann, 1985). Accordingly it was widely accepted that spirituality could no longer be understood as an exclusively Christian concept but needed to be understood as something which crossed faiths, and had relevance even to the non-religious. As a result, the legal requirement for the 'spiritual development' of children and young people in schools was problematized and, since the 1990s also saw a more widespread social interest in spirituality, a new debate about spirituality generally, and spirituality in education in particular, was generated.

The re-introduction of spirituality to state education in the 1980s in England and Wales was a surprise, and led to much debate about the nature of spirituality in a multifaith and increasingly non-religious social context. This debate was embedded in a wider international discussion of spirituality in education (see e.g. Watson *et al.*, 2014) which impacted on all countries of the UK. From 1994–2003, Ron Best ran the *Education, Spirituality and the Whole Child* conference series (see Best, 1996) and, in 1997, Clive and Jane Erricker started the *International Journal of Children's Spirituality* and its conference series, both of which continue today. Since the 1980s, a new understanding of spirituality has emerged which sees spirituality as a shared human characteristic crossing sectarian and religious divides. Therefore most educationalists who endeavour to develop a theory on spirituality in education today seek to promote the spiritual development of *all* children (of every faith background, including those with no religion), and see spirituality underpinning all aspects of education. These essential characteristics were seen early on in the UK in influential statements from the National Curriculum Council (NCC) and Ofsted:

> The potential for spiritual development is open to everyone and is not confined to the development of religious beliefs or conversion to a particular faith. (NCC, 1993, 2)

> 'Spiritual' is not synonymous with 'religious'; all areas of the curriculum may contribute to pupils' spiritual development. (Ofsted, 1994, 8)

One of the most influential theorists in the field of spirituality in education has been David Hay. Originally a biologist, Hay collaborated and worked with the eminent British biologist Alister Hardy to run the Religious Experience Research Centre, which continues to collect and analyse accounts of spiritual experience at the University of Wales (<http://www.uwtsd.ac.uk/library/alister-hardy-religious-experience-research-centre/>).

Hay argued, like Hardy before him, that spirituality had evolved naturally in human beings and is essential to our survival. In the 1990s, Hay took the discussion into the field of education, arguing that spirituality should be disengaged from religion and seen as an innate awareness vital to all human beings and especially important to nurture in children. Hay worked with David Hammond and many other educationalists to produce an innovative handbook for teachers called *New Methods in RE Teaching*, which encouraged experiential learning for spiritual development in the RE classroom (Hammond & Hay *et al.*, 1990). He then worked with psychologist, Rebecca Nye, to develop highly influential theories of spirituality and education which were published in *The Spirit of the Child* (Hay with Nye, 1998). Hay identified three spiritual categories:

> Awareness sensing – with sub-categories, Here and now, Tuning, Flow and Focusing
> Mystery sensing (awareness of transcendence) – with sub-categories, Wonder and awe and Imagination
> Value sensing (affective/emotional response to others) – with sub-categories, Delight and despair, Ultimate goodness and Meaning.
> (Hay with Nye, 1998, 59–75)[1]

Hay and Nye argued that spiritual awareness could be encouraged in different subjects across the whole curriculum and therefore involved all teachers.

Some aspects of Hay's spiritual and educational theory are not shared by everyone in the field, and theorists such as Andrew Wright have argued that spiritual education should place a stronger emphasis on religious literacy and knowledge rather than over-emphasizing experiential learning and the affective. However, Hay and Nye's work has been highly influential in education. For instance, Hay's notion of 'sensing' can be seen in the current Scottish understanding of spirituality in the *Curriculum for Excellence* (Education Scotland, 2010). And, while there may not be agreement that spirituality has evolved biologically in human beings, there is agreement amongst educationalists that everyone is in some sense spiritual, and that spirituality is related to but different from religion.

Educationalists in this field, including Hay and Nye, also generally agree that a spiritual approach to education involves certain important

---

1   Notice that these three categories of spirituality are used and added to – with sensing meaningfulness, otherness, and challenge – in *The Report of the RO Review Group*, 2004.

pedagogical values. Both in the UK, and internationally, spiritual education signals concern for the *whole* child, and for a holistic education that is not limited by measurable performance outcomes. In England and Wales in particular, the discourse around spiritual development formed a critique of the Thatcher government's 'reforms' to education, which emphasized cognitive learning, content knowledge, and performativity. The educational literature giving advice to the UK teaching profession about spiritual development has in large part been an attempt to safeguard pedagogical values perceived as being devalued by consecutive governments' concerns with, for instance, the UK's performance in PISA (Programme for International Student Assessment) scores, a worldwide study of school pupils' scholastic performance in mathematics, science and reading, providing comparable data ostensibly to help countries improve education outcomes, but also meaning that these measures and schools subjects have gained a higher competitive value. The 1994 Ofsted discussion paper quoted above was authored by the first HMI for Ofsted, Sir Stewart Sutherland.[2] In the frontispiece to a set of books published soon after, Sutherland summarized what spirituality in education has come to mean for many.

> We talk of accountability and appraisal, SAT's scores and measurable outcomes, league tables and competition between schools. Somewhere, the pupil as a whole person is in danger of getting lost beneath the demands of all these outside constraints. (Charis, 1996, v)

The educational advice literature to emerge in the UK in the 1990s identified a broad set of concerns for spiritual development. In an article published in 2007, I summarized these as follows:

> *Creativity*: the celebration and encouragement of imagination and creative endeavour as well as aesthetic understanding and appreciation, so that education becomes more than merely acquiring factual, or scientific, knowledge and skills.

---

2   Stewart Sutherland was Head of Ofsted for only one year before the Thatcher government replaced him with Chris Woodhead, a man more to their taste.

Reflection: the inclusion in all subjects of space for reflection, rather than merely the acquisition of facts, and the encouragement of pupils to consider their own beliefs, values, opinions and feelings. Also providing opportunities for reflection on personal behaviour and, often, moral issues. Also periods of quiet and perhaps, on occasions, meditative thought.

Self-esteem: the encouragement of self-respect along with respect between pupils, between teachers and pupils, including permitting space for all pupils, and teachers, to find a voice and give expression to their feelings in a safe environment and for pupils' work and other contributions to school life to be celebrated.

Relationships: the fostering of good relationships within the school and of skills for sustaining good relationships in pupils' future lives. Also understanding community, difference, and the importance of rejecting prejudice in all its forms.

Relationship with the natural world: the fostering of positive responses to the natural world, including wonder at nature and the universe, in order to encourage in pupils positive behaviours toward the environment while at school and in their future lives.

Insight: the encouragement of insight, or understanding, alongside the acquisition of knowledge, so that education becomes more than merely acquiring knowledge and skills for the world of work. Also, insight that goes beyond the immediately obvious and, in some cases, the encouragement of an awareness that goes beyond the material.

Cohesion: making it clear that all subjects are related so that they become part of a holistic understanding of the world. Also relating all content and activities in lessons to the individual pupil in order that each pupil can engage in learning and in order that each pupil has opportunities to consider their own beliefs, values, opinions and feelings.

Challenge: encouraging questioning of received wisdom and knowledge and questioning of the status quo as well as challenging pupils to do their best, and, sometime, to show resilience and courage.

Wellbeing: the establishment of a safe environment in which all pupils are protected and do not suffer, and in which pupils who have suffered are able to seek help and reassurance.

Meaning: providing opportunities for pupils to learn from, as well as about, other pupils, other people, and other religions and world views, so that they enter the process of developing beliefs and values of their own to give meaning and value to their lives. (Watson, 2007, 130)

In summary, today, educationalists, domestically and internationally, share a similar understanding of spirituality for education (Watson, 2014). This includes a commitment to the idea that spirituality applies to children and young people from all religious or non-religious backgrounds, and that everyone is spiritual and should be free to explore and express their spirituality in their own way. A spiritual approach to education signals a recognition that education is not about unquestioningly learning content knowledge or propositional statements of truth; instead education is about enquiry, and must include space for reflection. In acknowledging the rights of the child, a spiritual approach to education includes listening to the voices of children and young people. Pedagogically, it values creativity and experiential learning, holistic education and education of the whole child. The discourse around spirituality in education also forms a critique of consumer-driven society, and of the impact of the neo-liberal agenda on current schooling systems, in the UK and internationally.

In England, Ofsted's most recent definition of spiritual development is as follows:

The *spiritual* development of pupils is shown by their:

- ability to be reflective about their own beliefs, religious or otherwise, that inform their perspective on life and their interest in and respect for different people's faiths, feelings and values,
- sense of enjoyment and fascination in learning about themselves, others and the world around them,
- use of imagination and creativity in their learning,
- willingness to reflect on their experiences. (Ofsted, 2015, 35)

While there are variations in the descriptions or definitions of spiritual development, the main features remain broadly similar and, in particular, have little to do with a religious understanding of spirituality, or of morality for that matter. The educational philosopher Terence McLaughlin made a key distinction between what he called tethered and untethered spirituality.

Religiously 'tethered' spirituality takes its shape from various aspects of the religion with which it is associated and which makes it possible to identify the nature and shape of 'spirituality' within that context, including criteria for spiritual

development. ... Religiously 'un-tethered' spirituality involves beliefs and practices that are disconnected from, and may even be discomforting to, religions.
(McLaughlin, 2003, 191–192)

In the context of publicly funded education, and public services generally, it is the 'untethered' form of spirituality that has come to dominate.
(See for instance the Royal College of Nursing's *Spirituality in Nursing
Care: a Pocket Guide* <https://www.rcn.org.uk/__data/assets/pdf_
file/0008/372995/003887.pdf>, or recent guidance from the NHS for
Chaplaincies <http://www.england.nhs.uk/wp-content/uploads/2015/03/
nhs-chaplaincy-guidelines-2015.pdf>.) Meanwhile, however, the understanding of CW has remained religiously 'tethered', *and* focused on
Christianity. Necessarily, then, there is a substantive tension in the relationship between CW and spiritual development: they do not readily map
on to each other.

Spiritual development through collective worship

As stated at the start of this chapter, Circular 10/94 for Wales and Circular
1/94 for England are clear that CW makes an important contribution to
spiritual development, while Scottish Circular 1/2005 is clear that RO promotes spiritual development. However, since the 1980s, considerations such
as the new educational discourse around spirituality (i.e. the untethering
of spirituality from religion), as well as the emphasis on children's voice
and the importance of inclusion, have made it increasingly difficult to map
spiritual development onto compulsory 'wholly or mainly Christian' CW.
Some of these tensions can be seen in the writing of four key authors in
the field of spirituality in education: John Hull; Terence Copley; Andrew
Wright; and Tony Eaude.

First, John Hull, writing well before the new educational discourse
around spirituality had become explicit, recognized the tension between
CW and spiritual development. In his seminal book, *School Worship: An*

Obituary (1975), Hull put the case for the replacement of CW with a reflective assembly, which he argued would be better able to offer a spiritual experience for pupils.

> The school assembly has considerable educational potential. When it is taken up with worship, something is being done which in the county school ought not to be attempted at all in that form, and in the meantime, the opportunity to do something more directly related to the tasks of the school is missed. Corporate, compulsory worship should be abandoned, and assembly then left free to relate in new ways to the curriculum. (118)

Although Hull did not use the term 'spiritual development' in this book, the language and ideas he used to describe the value of assemblies is close to that used for spiritual development today, as can be seen in the following extracts (the section would be too long to quote in full and some sentences have been removed):

> The objectives of school assembly will be to provide ceremonies, celebrations and other events which, while not assuming the truth of any one controversial statement, will present the issues to the pupils in a way so as
>
> 1. To widen the pupil's repertoire of appropriate emotional response. ... A person who is not moved by the beautiful and who never feels compassion is lacking in emotional breadth. It is, of course, impossible to avoid some degree of cultural definition of what an appropriate emotional response is, but the assembly would attempt to introduce the emotions and responses of other cultures. ...
> 2. To encourage a reflective approach to living, a way which transcends the immediacy of experience. Man's capacity for reflection upon himself and his worth is part of his distinctive existence [*sic*]. ... To live immersed in one's world instead of being in critical action and reaction with one's world is to lose part of being human.
> 3. To demonstrate the values which are not controversial and upon which democratic society depends. These values include freedom of speech, respect for the rights of minorities, the equality before the law and in education of all religious and ethnic groups, and responsibility for personal decision-making and for participation in community decision-making.
> 4. To provide some experience and understand of what worship is so that the way of worship, along with other life styles, will remain an option for anyone who wishes to follow it and so the all will have some insight into what it is like to live a religious life. But this provision will not require any one to worship and will certainly not commit the school to corporate acts of worship. (Hull, 1975, 118–119)

Second, Terence Copley, in his book *Spiritual Development in the State School* (2000), devoted a substantial section to the history of school worship. In the 1960s, he reported, teacher and head teacher attitudes, along with poor, over-crowded accommodation for CW meant the quality – and therefore the spiritual potential – of worship was difficult to achieve (2000, 86). By the 1990s, Circulars 1/94 and 10/94 tried to make schools in England and Wales take CW seriously, but 'no money was provided by government for training, research or in-service training of teachers in leading collective worship' (ibid. 94). Over these decades, understandings of CW had not much changed but meanwhile notions of spiritual development were 'emerging without reference to worship as a central activity' (ibid. 92). Copley lamented what he saw as the secularizing of spirituality and the consequent difficulty of reconciling spiritual development with religious worship.

> Worship has to be religious to be credible as worship, but in society in which compulsory religion is unacceptable, the future of compulsory school worship may be bleak. Spiritual development has dispensed with its religious, i.e. originally Christian, base in order to become acceptable among the communities of education. But in so doing it may have ceased to be spiritual in any sense which has continuity with UK or world religions traditions of understanding spiritual. (Ibid. 128–129)

Third, Andrew Wright, in *Spirituality and Education* (2000), put forward a brief but robust defence of CW as 'a crucial, though frequently neglected, dimension of the spiritual life of the whole school' (ibid. 122). Wright argued that CW is vital to spiritual development because of its contribution to communal relationship; a school must identify and articulate 'its core spiritual values' and ensure that in CW 'these values are celebrated with dignity and integrity' (ibid. 123). However, he also stated that this 'celebration may take the form of either a religious act of Collective Worship *or* a secular assembly' (ibid. my emphasis) and that critics of CW fail to 'acknowledge its in-built flexibility and accept the diverse range of religious and secular options it makes available' (ibid.). Wright criticized secular schools which put on 'mainly Christian' acts of worship 'with which only a minority can identify and about which few have any ultimate concern' as this 'introduces a spiritual vacuum in the very heart of the school community' (ibid.). He claimed:

> A school committed to a secular spiritual tradition is not justified in criticising the imposition of Collective Worship until it has taken up its right to apply for an exemption from this particular part of the legislation. (Ibid. 123)

This is a strange claim, since the law in England and Wales states that, where Christianity is not the main faith in the region, a 'headteacher can apply to the local SACRE to have the broadly Christian requirement disapplied and replaced by *CW distinctive of another faith*' (*Ofsted Handbook*, 2015, 10, my emphasis). There have now been several cases where schools have asked for a determination in order to have a neutral form of CW, for instance to have 'spiritual' worship or multifaith worship (see for instance, Brent, Ealing and Westminster SACRE guidance on CW). However, this wording does not appear to include the notion of a *secular* spiritual tradition, and a secular act of worship is patently a contradiction in terms – unless, of course, Wright is equating, and conflating, CW with school assembly.

The conflation of CW and the school assembly is common place in practice. The final figure of influence I examine in this area, Tony Eaude, writing for primary and early years teachers in *Children's Spiritual, Moral, Social and Cultural Development* (2006), deliberately chose to conflate the terms in his example of 'a memorable assembly' (ibid. 85–86).

> In primary schools, especially, collective worship, commonly thought of as assembly, offers many possibilities in relation to SMSC. 'Collective' recognises that those present may not all share a religious belief. For the whole school, or one section, to gather enables each child to see themselves as part of a bigger entity. The person leading the assembly can reaffirm positive values ... The chance to reflect together, with silence, music or a prayer, affirms the importance of taking a break from the busy-ness of life to ponder questions of deeper significance. (Ibid. 86)

Eaude's interweaving of the words 'worship' and 'assembly', and his explanation of the term 'collective' – which he uses to emphasize the importance of spiritual inclusivity rather than the requirement that the school gather together – demonstrate the flexibility with which CW is understood within the teaching profession. The key point for Eaude is that this event – whatever it is called – allows a short space for children, and staff, to slow down and be quiet and reflective within the otherwise frenetic school day. And while there is an emphasis on quiet and silence, Eaude is also keen to point out in his example the importance of ensuring children's voices are heard in discussion, another important aspect of spiritual development.

In summary, then, these key educational theorists demonstrate the problematics of attempting to map contemporary understandings of spiritual development onto CW.

Spirituality and collective worship in policy and practice

In policy and practice, these tensions have played out differently in the four countries of the UK. The tension is most acute in England and Wales, where the law requires schools to promote a broad and inclusive understanding of spiritual development across the whole curriculum, but simultaneously requires schools to promote spiritual development through daily acts of 'mainly broadly Christian' CW. This presents a contradiction which remains unresolved. In Northern Ireland, there is no guidance on the relationship between spiritual development and CW and most schools assume a generally Christian approach to CW. Educational tensions could be posed by the Council for Curriculum, Examinations and Assessment statement that spiritual growth also underpins the wider (secular) curriculum (CCEA, 2007). In Scotland the story is different again. Here, although CW in the form of religious observance remains statutory and continues to use the word 'religious', a great deal of work has been done to ensure RO is understood in terms of contemporary spiritual development. As this appears to present a fruitful way forward – or at least a way forward that seeks to reconcile this disrupted relationship – this approach is discussed in some detail in the following section.

Spiritual development through religious observance in Scotland

In 1998, the Scottish Joint Committee on Religious and Moral Education (SJCRME)[3] published a report (*RME and Religious Observance – a SJCRME position paper*) which, while it accepted that RO is legally required by statute, argued and concluded that RO in non-denominational schools need not and *should not* involve acts of worship. The report made the strong recommendation that assemblies should be clearly distinguished from acts of worship and 'that acts of worship should not be part of the formal activity of a non-denominational school either on a compulsory or voluntary basis' (Gray, 1999, 41) but only as part of the informal curriculum. It also recommended that RO in non-denominational schools should be assemblies and not acts of worship but, as such, can and should 'promote pupils' spiritual development', and 'provide opportunity for individual reflection on spiritual and moral concerns' (ibid. 40). Therefore, in their view, RO in non-denominational schools can contribute to spiritual development without involving acts of worship. The report stated that the two reasons generally given for acts of worship are that: schools should reflect the fact that Scotland is a Christian country through Christian acts of worship; and that pupils need to understand worship through experience. The first claim they refute because 'most people's lives in Scotland are not governed by commitment to the Christian faith' (ibid. 38). On the second point they argue that 'it is the role of religious education as a curricular subject to provide pupils with an understanding of the experiences which lie behind worship' (ibid. 37) and, therefore, there is no need for RO to provide this experience.

The SJCRME's revised 2005 position paper on religious and moral education (RME) and RO, currently available on their website, offers support to schools 'in developing their understanding of the complementary roles of Religious Observance (RO) and Religious and Moral Education (RME)' (SJCRME, 2005, 1). It does this by focusing on what they refer

---

3   The SJCRME was founded by the main teacher's union in Scotland and the Church of Scotland, but now represents a broad range of faiths, works to promote effective religious and moral education in Scottish schools.

to as 'the 'personal search' approach' and briefly suggests that RO might be better served by a different name.

> The personal search attempts to provide pupils with a means, through analogy and comparison, to relate to, and to an extent, enter, the world views of others with no confessional or worshipful commitment. (Ibid. 2)

In this light:

> Religious Observance is an opportunity for the individuals ... who make up a given school community to experience a common time of reflection ... on what the core beliefs and values of that community mean to them as individuals and how they, as individuals, contribute to and are influenced and shaped by those beliefs and values. (Ibid. 3)

The word 'spiritual' only appears once in this short document, but it is clear from much of the writing that a spiritual approach to RO is being advanced. It states that:

> The opportunity to engage in a personal search through RO can be described as the exploration of the spiritual dimension of human self awareness, a sense of the other, of mystery, awe and wander, of relationships with the self and with those around us, a capacity to be loved and to love others, a willingness to use how we feel about our life experiences as part of how we understand the meaningfulness of those experiences for ourselves and for any others involved. (Ibid. 4)

In 2004, the Scottish Executive set up a *Review of Religious Observance* and its final report continues to be highly influential today. The report is one of a number of key documents included on the website of the Scottish *Curriculum for Excellence* (CfE), which was introduced in 2010 (Education Scotland, 2010). The CfE website includes a substantial section on RO, and RO is strongly linked with spiritual development. Another key document on the website is a briefing document on RO which, in synchrony with the SJRME's recommendations, included a tentative new name for RO in the title of the document, *Religious Observance (Time for Reflection)* (Education Scotland, 2014). Issues around the re-naming of RO are discussed in greater detail in Chapter 3.

The most recent guidance on RO reiterates the importance of spiritual development for RO:

> Religious Observance is defined as follows: '*Community acts which aim to promote the spiritual development of all members of the school's community and express and celebrate the shared values of the school community*'. (Government of Scotland, 2017, 1)

The Report of the Religious Observation Review Group, set up by the Scottish Executive in 2004, included a section describing what it called the spiritual dimension as follows:

> *Sensing mystery*: experiences of awe, wonder and mystery about the natural world, human achievement and for some a divinity

> *Sensing values:* attitudes and feelings about what is really important, what really matters

> *Sensing meaningfulness:* the ability to make connections or to see potential patterns in one's life which give it meaning

> *Sensing a changed quality in awareness:* the feeling of being 'at one' with nature, oneself and others

> *Sensing 'otherness':* the sentiment that humans are more than their physical elements

> *Sensing challenge:* being challenged and moved by experiences such as love, beauty, goodness, joy, compassion, injustice, evil, suffering, death. (Scottish Executive, 2004, 13)

The inspection of collective worship's contribution to spiritual development

In 2000, I carried out a survey of Ofsted inspection reports in Norfolk secondary schools (as a sample of the national picture in England) to look at how Ofsted was inspecting spiritual development, and SMSC in general. The findings of my research, based on seventy-five inspection reports, was consistent with Ofsted Annual Reports in showing that, since 1993 when Ofsted began reporting, Ofsted inspectors had judged secondary school provision for spiritual development to be less successful than its provision for social, moral or cultural development (Watson, 2001, 206). Spiritual development was judged to be weak because inspectors considered that insufficient attention was being paid to spiritual development across the broader curriculum, and because half of the schools were in breach of their legal obligations for RE provision. In addition, like most secondary schools in the country, the majority of these schools were in breach of their legal obligation to provide a daily act of CW for all pupils, in particular because the replacement of whole school CW by classroom-based 'Thought for the Day' was a poor substitute.

In England and Wales today, this level of detailed information about school inspections is not available and consequently there is no data about Ofsted's or Estyn's perception of CW's contribution to spiritual development in school inspection reports, and very little detail in Ofsted and Estyn guidance documents or annual reports. In England, the value of SMSC was raised further when 'British Values' were introduced to the curriculum under the auspices of SMSC (DfE, 2014). The 2012 *Ofsted Handbook* had included SMSC in its subsidiary guidance only, whereas the 2015 *Ofsted Handbook* included SMSC in the main Handbook for the first time, giving it a much higher status. However, detailed information about the perceived links between SMSC and CW is absent from both. In the 2012 *Ofsted Handbook*'s subsidiary guidance, inspectors were told to gather evidence of SMSC through lesson observations, through observation of other activities 'such as tutorials, citizenship programmes and discussions with pupils about their work' (Ofsted, 2012, 19), and through evaluation of activities such as artistic, scientific, and international events: there is no mention of CW, or indeed of assemblies. The 2015 *Ofsted Handbook* makes clear that CW must take place in schools without a religious character, including academies, and schools must be effective in the provision of SMSC (32), but no link is made between the two. A link *is* made in the 2014 *Promoting British Values through SMSC* document, but without any detail:

> Meeting requirements for collective worship, establishing a strong school ethos supported by effective relationships throughout the school, and providing relevant activities beyond the classroom are all ways of ensuring pupils' SMSC development. (DfE, 2014, 4)

As explained in Chapter 4 on 'Collective Worship in Wales', the picture is more confusing here since Estyn does inspect CW on its ability to contribute to SMSC. However, Estyn's 2010 guidance (updated in 2014 according to the document itself) also states that:

> Although collective worship in a school may not comply with legal requirements, it may still make a significant contribution to pupils' spiritual, moral, social and cultural development. Conversely, collective worship may satisfy legal requirements yet make a limited contribution to pupils' spiritual, moral, social and cultural development. (Estyn, 2010, 3)

The situations are very different in Northern Ireland and Scotland. In Northern Ireland there is no guidance on the relationship between spirituality and CW, and in practice schools provide a generally Christian approach. In Scotland, on the other hand, the Scottish *Curriculum for Excellence* (CfE) continues to take RO's contribution to spiritual development very seriously. However, as the chapter on 'Religious Observance in Scotland' states, in spite of this we know little about how this plays out in schools as the Inspectorate does not look at RO, despite HMIE 2001 having expressed concerns that non-denominational secondary schools were failing to adequately provide RO.

Summary and Conclusions

The spiritual development of pupils has always been an implicit aim of education in the UK. However, the term 'spiritual development' was made explicit in the 1944 Education Act, as well as being re-stated in the 1988 Education (Reform) Act (for England and Wales) and the 2007 Statutory Rules of Northern Ireland.

Since the 1980s, theory and practice in relation to spirituality in education, both in the UK and internationally, have developed in such a way that spirituality is understood as a broader and more inclusive concept than religion, which is to be developed in all curriculum subjects. Spirituality

in education has also become strongly associated with a broad set of pedagogical values such as 'pupil voice', space for reflection, and the holistic
education of the child. As a result the contemporary understanding of
spiritual development has a wide and, some would say, a largely secular
set of concerns.

In all countries of the UK, collective worship/religious observance is
understood to make a strong contribution to pupils' spiritual development.
In England and Wales, collective worship must be 'wholly or mainly of a
broadly Christian character' (unless a school requests a dispensation). This
is in tension with the broad, inclusive and more secular understanding of
spiritual development. In Northern Ireland, the lack of guidance on the
relationship between CW and spirituality leaves this open to interpretation,
although in practice most schools assume a generally Christian approach.
In Scotland, religious observance is currently designed to follow the broad
and inclusive understanding of spiritual development and seeks 'to promote the spiritual development of all members of the school community
and express and celebrate the shared values of the school community'
(Circular 1/2005).

The Scottish model for religious observance offers a positive way forward. This model reflects John Hull's vision of a spiritual assembly: it is
inclusive, with the spiritual development of all members of the school as
its primary aim, and, as Andrew Wright has advocated, it seeks to celebrate
the shared values of the school community.

References

Best, R. (Ed.) (1996). *Education, Spirituality and the Whole Child*. London: Cassell.
CCEA (Council for the Curriculum, Examinations and Assessment) (2007). *The
    statutory curriculum at Key Stage 3*. Belfast: Council for the Curriculum, Exami-
    nations and Assessment.
Charis project (1996). *Charis Mathematics Units 1–9*. Nottingham: The Stapleford
    Centre.

Copley, T. (2000). *Spiritual Development in the State School*. Exeter: University of Exeter Press.

Department for Education (1994). *Collective Worship in Schools*. Circular 1/94. London: HMSO.

DoE (Department of Education, Northern Ireland) (2007). *The Statutory Rules of Northern Ireland 2007 No. 46 EDUCATION*. Stationary Office.

Eaude, T. (2006). *Children's Spiritual, Moral, Social and Cultural Development*. Exeter: Learning Matters.

Education England (1999). *1999 National Curriculum Handbook for Primary Teachers in England*. Retrieved April 12, 2017, from <http://www.educationengland.org. uk/documents/pdfs/1999-nc-primary-handbook.pdf>.

Education Scotland (2010). *Curriculum for Excellence*. Retrieved April 12, 2017, from <http://www.ltscotland.org.uk/understandingthecurriculum/>.

Education Scotland (2014). *CfE Briefing 16: Religious Observance (Time for Reflection)*. Retrieved April 12, 2017, from <https://education.gov.scot/Documents/ cfe-briefing-16.pdf>.

Estyn (2010). *Guidance for the inspection of secondary schools*. Retrieved April 12, 2017, from <http://www.estyn.gov.uk/english/inspection/inspection-guidance/ secondary-schools/>.

Government of Scotland (2017). *Curriculum for Excellence – Provision of Religious Observance in Scottish Schools – March 2017*. Retrieved May 30, 2017, from <http://www.gov.scot/Resource/0051/00516155.pdf>.

Gray, I. A. S. (1999). Religious Observance in Schools: A Scottish Perspective. *British Journal of Religious Education, 22*(1) 35–45.

Hammond, J., & Hay, D., *et al.* (1990). *New Methods in RE Teaching: An Experiential Approach*. Essex: Oliver and Boyd.

Hay, D., with Nye, R. (1998). *The Spirit of the Child*. London: HarperCollins.

Hull, J. M. (1975). *School Worship: An Obituary*. London: SCM Press.

McLaughlin, T. H. (2003). Education, spirituality and the common school. In D. Carr, & J. Haldane (Eds.), *Spirituality, philosophy and education* (185–199). London: RoutledgeFalmer.

NCC (National Curriculum Council) (1993). *Spiritual and Moral Development - A discussion paper*. York: National Curriculum Council.

Ofsted (Office for Standards in Education) (1994). *Spiritual, Moral, Social and Cultural Development: An OFSTED discussion paper*. London: HMSO.

Ofsted (The Office for Standards in Education) (1995). *The OFSTED Handbook: Guidance on the Inspection of Secondary Schools*. London: HMSO.

Ofsted (The Office for Standards in Education) (2012). *Subsidiary guidance*. Retrieved April 12, 2017, from <http://www.educationengland.org.uk/documents/pdfs/2013-ofsted-subsidiary-guidance.pdf>.

Ofsted (The Office for Standards in Education) (2015). *School inspection handbook: Handbook for inspecting schools in England under section 5 of the Education Act 2005 (as amended by the Education Act 2011)*. Retrieved April 12, 2017, from <www.ofsted.gov.uk/resources/120101>.

Priestley, J. (1997). Spirituality, Curriculum and Education. *International Journal of Children's Spirituality, 2*(1), 23–34.

Scottish Executive (2005a). Circular 1/2005 Provision of Religious Observance in Scottish Schools. Retrieved April 12, 2017, from <http://www.gov.scot/Publications/2005/03/20778/53820>.

Scottish Executive (2005b). *The Report of the Religious Observance Review Group*. Retrieved April 12, 2017, from <http://www.scotland.gov.uk/Publications/2004/05/19351/37052>.

SJCRME (Scottish Joint Committee on Religious and Moral Education). (2015). *RME and Religious Observance – a SJCRME position paper*. Retrieved April 12, 2017, from <http://www.sjcrme.org.uk/library.html>.

Swann, M. (1985). *Education for All: The Report of the Committee of Inquiry into the Education of Children from Ethnic Minority Groups (The Swann Report)*. London: HMSO.

Watson, J. (2001). OFSTED's Spiritual Dimension: an analytical audit of inspection reports. *Cambridge Journal of Education, 31*(2), 205–219.

Watson, J. (2007). Spiritual development: constructing an inclusive and progressive approach. *Journal of Beliefs & Values, 28*(2), 125–136.

Watson, J., de Souza, M., & Trousdale, A. (Eds.) (2014). *Global Perspectives on Spirituality and Education*. New York: Routledge.

Welsh Office (1994). *Circular 10/94 Religious Education and Collective Worship in Schools*. Retrieved April 12, 2017, from <http://www.wasacre.org.uk/publications/wag/E-circular10-94.pdf>.

Wright, A. (2003). *Spirituality and Education*. London: Routledge.

CLAIRE CASSIDY

9 Philosophy with Children: An Alternative to Religious Observance

ABSTRACT

In Scotland all schools must provide opportunities for religious observance. In 2004, the Religious Observance Review Group determined that time for reflection may be more appropriate for what is undertaken in some schools. While it is clear that religious observance/time for reflection should support the spiritual development of the school community, little, if any, advice has been provided for teachers, pupils or their parents regarding what might count as religious observance/time for reflection if not an act of worship. This chapter proposes that Philosophy with Children is a meaningful alternative to religious observance that is inclusive of all children and that it may usefully and meaningfully be employed in Scotland and the other jurisdictions in the UK, regardless of the curriculum followed.

Introduction

Scotland's education system and curriculum is different to the other jurisdictions in the United Kingdom. The curriculum, *Curriculum for Excellence* (Scottish Executive, 2004a), is for all children aged between 3 and 18. In every regard, bar one, the curriculum is consistent for all Scottish state schools. The one point of departure is the place of education about religion and how it is taught in schools. The non-denominational sector teaches what is known as religious and moral education (RME), while denominational schools, predominantly Catholic schools (see Chapter 3), teach religious education (RE). The difference being that the moral dimension in denominational schools is not taught discretely but that it permeates the whole ethos of the school, as noted by McKinney (2013) when he states that 'Catholic schools are perceived by the Roman Catholic Church to be a faith-formational approach to education and ... an integral component of the lifelong process of Christian formation' (301). The Scottish Catholic Education Service is clear that Catholic education is 'distinctive because of its focus on the faith development of children and young people within the context of a faith community. Its central purpose is to assist learners to make an informed, mature response to God's call to relationship' (Scottish Catholic Education Service, 2017). This is not to say that children in denominational schools do not, like their counterparts in non-denominational schools, learn about other religions, they do, but they do more than simply learn *about* the Catholic faith or the particular faith supported by the school. Aside from this distinction, there is much in common, most notably that religious observance is a facet of RE/RME shared by all schools.

Religious Observance or Time for Reflection

In Scotland the term 'Collective Worship' in schools is not used. Instead, schools have a statutory duty to provide children with opportunities to engage in 'religious observance'. The Religious Observance Review Group has provided a definition of religious observance as 'community acts which aim to promote the spiritual development of all members of the school's community and express and celebrate the shared values of the school community' (2004b, 12). In advice from the Scottish Government (2011) on the provision of RE/RME, head teachers were told that this element of children's education

> contributes to the development of the whole person, allowing children and young people to consider, reflect upon, and respond to important questions about the meaning and purpose of existence, the range and depth of human experience and what is ultimately worthwhile and valuable in life.

The advice goes on to acknowledge that 'this area of their education contributes to pupils thinking for themselves and making their own decisions about what they believe to be true about human living'. This latter statement was provided in acknowledgement of the Education (Scotland) Act 1980 (Part 1: 8(i)) which makes clear that schools should offer religious observance, but that parents may 'elect that their children should not take part in such observance'. Indeed, should parents decide to withdraw their child from religious observance, the note asserts that children should have as an alternative, the opportunity to participate in a 'worthwhile activity'. It is this element of RE/RME that has drawn the attention of Humanist Society Scotland (HSS) and the Church of Scotland. In early 2014, HSS and the Church of Scotland petitioned the Scottish Parliament that religious observance be amended to 'time for reflection' with HSS continuing with a further campaign for the right to withdraw from religious observance to be extended to children. The Church of Scotland later seemed to rescind their support for the move to time for reflection, seeing the shift as being more than a name change.[1] The important point here, though, is not the name change or what this disagreement between the two organizations might signify, but that something else is proposed for the occasions when religious observance is being undertaken in schools. Indeed, the advice to head teachers on the provision of religious observance suggests that rather than religious observance, non-denominational schools 'may' consider making 'time for reflection', in line with practice in public bodies such as the Scottish Parliament. This was originally proposed by the then Scottish Executive's Religious Observance Review Group Report (2004b) and subsequently appeared in letters to head teachers in 2011. Leaving aside the issue of denominational or non-denominational schools, there remains a question around the nature of time for reflection. Indeed, the advice on religious observance states that 'It should also provide opportunities for the school community to reflect upon and develop a deeper understanding of the dignity and worth of each individual and their contribution to the school and wider communities'. Interestingly, in 2014 Education

---

1 <http://www.scottish.parliament.uk/S4_PublicPetitionsCommittee/General%20 Documents/PE1487_PP_Humanist_Society_Scotland_28.01.14.pdf>.

Scotland published a briefing paper on religious observance with a view to sharing the aims of religious observance while offering guidance and information for practitioners, parents and pupils in this area. In 2017 the Scottish Government produced clarifying guidance on the provision of religious observance in Scottish schools (Scottish Government, 2017). What is of particular note is that there is a bracketed subtitle to the 2014 paper: *Curriculum for Excellence: Religious Observance (Time for Reflection).* The paper's authors retain the definition of religious observance provided above, but they suggest that 'Many non-denominational schools refer to Religious Observance as *Time for Reflection.* This helps to describe the type of experience that the learner can have through engaging with issues and events as part of RO' (Education Scotland, 2014, 2). This implies that time for reflection is only part of religious observance, but there is nothing within the 2014 paper or the 2017 guidance that expands more fully on the notion of time for reflection itself. The idea of 'worship', the paper notes, is perhaps more appropriate for denominational schools.

The paper highlights aspects of learning or experiences that pupils might have as part of religious observance and it emphasizes the importance of the development of beliefs, values and behaviour that promote the respect of others and that encourage the learner to consider her place in the world. Ideally this should engender an empathetic outlook to others and the range of perspectives they are likely to encounter. All of this is seen as '... central to their development as citizens in our modern, pluralistic society' (ibid. 3). Given what seems to be a now more all-encompassing view of religious observance, that it is more than worship, or that everything under the guidance might be construed as time for reflection, it may be suggested that there is no need of a religious affiliation in order to achieve the stated goals and that time for reflection is a notion that is more inclusive of those of faith and none. The question, though, is the manner in which one attains the aim of meaningful reflection. What is proposed in this chapter is that meaningful reflection that promotes empathy, understanding, respect and dialogue, regardless of having a faith or not, may be accomplished through Philosophy with Children (PwC). It is asserted that PwC is a sound approach for inculcating reflection on beliefs/non-belief, values and understanding. Importantly, too, it engenders in participants thinking that concerns itself with the world and one's place in that world from a philosophical perspective with a view to enacting and effecting positive impact on one's world. PwC offers an alternative to collective worship or religious observance, but it also has the potential to enrich the religious education experiences of all children.

Philosophy with Children

Philosophy with Children (PwC) is a generic term used to cover the range of approaches to structured, practical philosophizing done with children. PwC is used around the world, in a range of contexts and through varying practices. This range of approaches to PwC grew from Matthew Lipman's original Philosophy for Children (P4C) programme which was developed in the mid-1970s (Lipman, Sharp & Oscanyan, 1980; Lipman, 2003; Daniel & Auriac, 2011). From observing his university students' lack of criticality, Lipman created P4C with a view to encouraging more critical thinking in children before they reach higher education. From Lipman's P4C other practices have emerged, such as McCall's Community of Philosophical Inquiry (McCall, 1991; Cassidy, 2007), Cleghorn's Thinking Through Philosophy (Cleghorn, 2002), McCall's Guided Socratic Discussion (McCall, 2009), Brenifier's approach to philosophical practice (see <http://www.pratiques-philosophiques.fr/?lang=en>), and other variations on the P4C approach and the likes of Leonard Nelson's Socratic Method (Saran & Neisser, 2004). What these practices have in common is that rather than teach about philosophy in the traditional academic sense, they promote practical philosophy, the actual doing of philosophy in a collaborative context (Murris, 2000). In each approach the dialogue is structured to a greater or lesser extent and is facilitated by a chair or facilitator.

The structure relies on participants making connections with others' contributions and they have to do this by agreeing or disagreeing with the arguments presented while also providing reasons for that agreement or disagreement. In McCall's Community of Philosophical Inquiry (CoPI), for example, participants are provided with a stimulus, usually a short written text. Following the reading aloud of the stimulus, the participants are invited to pose questions arising from or prompted by the text. The facilitator selects the question with the most philosophical potential and the originator of the question is invited to start the dialogue. The rules are such that each speaker must raise her hand should she wish to contribute to the dialogue but she will not be selected to speak in turn, with the facilitator working to juxtapose the participants' perspectives by her selection of speakers. The participants begin their contribution by stating, 'I agree/disagree with [person's name] because ...'. Participants are not permitted to use technical jargon or language in their contributions as the process is inherently egalitarian; the dialogue should be conducted in everyday language, no matter the age or experience of the participants. Further, the participants are not permitted to refer to an authority, be that a book, the internet, a television programme or a relative, for their reasons for agreement or disagreement. The reasons must come from the participant's own thinking, but it need not be her own opinion. There is no search for consensus or conclusion in CoPI as this would imply an end to the questioning, that the matter had been resolved (Cassidy, 2007, 2012a; McCall, 2009).

Within PwC generally there are certain factors that would suggest that it is an appropriate means of offering children meaningful time for reflection. Lipman's P4C has three core elements: critical, creative and caring thinking (Lipman, 2003). McCall's approach has four main underlying assumptions: there is an external reality into which we can inquire; everything is open to question; as humans we all have the capacity to reason; and as humans we are all fallible (Cassidy, 2007; McCall, 2009). Taking together Lipman's types of thinking and McCall's foundations of CoPI, it is clear that time for reflection might easily be addressed through PwC.

The importance of being reasonable

McCall's suggestion that humans all have the capacity to reason is fundamental to any reflective activity. There has been some argument around whether or not children are able to philosophize but this criticism is easily addressed by Murris (2000) who dismisses the argument by asserting that we do not refuse to teach children mathematics or writing because they are not mathematicians or authors, and in the same way any suggestion that we avoid doing philosophy with children because they are not academic philosophers is foolish. There is also empirical evidence that children do engage in philosophical dialogue (see, e.g., Matthews, 1980, 1984; Topping & Trickey, 2007; Trickey & Topping, 2008; Gregory, 2008; Daniel, 2008; Cassidy and Christie, 2013). Certainly children and adults do not necessarily share the same range of vocabulary, but they are all able to engage with the philosophical ideas at hand to a greater or lesser degree. The extent to which they are able to engage with the ideas has less to do with age than may at first be imagined. There is much evidence to illustrate that children engage with the same philosophical ideas and arguments as their adult counterparts (Cassidy, 2012a; Cassidy & Christie, 2014). The question of children's reasoning, particularly their moral reasoning or reasoning related to ethical issues, is pertinent to the discussion around using PwC as an opportunity to allow for reflection.

Lipman (1995) identifies the challenges in moral education. He suggests that to consider it as simply determining the difference between good and evil is too simplistic. He suggests that children may see the range of alternatives presented as possible goods and that the work of moral education is in supporting children to 'distinguish greater goods from lesser ones' (Lipman, 1995, 61). He goes on to question whether there is an approach to moral education, and time for reflection fits squarely in this realm, 'that can knit together emotions and reasoning, facts and values, intuition and argument, desires and values, beliefs and dispositions ... so as to form one single, unified approach to the improvement and enrichment of human life' (ibid. 62). He proposes that the answer is via inquiry. He is clear that this is not just in the area of moral reasoning, but that approaches are required in order to prepare 'the child to be as flexible and resourceful as needed, seeking to respond appropriately whatever the circumstances, whatever the provocation' (ibid. 63), and that what is demanded is critical, creative and caring thinking. Lipman is clear that moral education cannot be simply presented to children; they need to have opportunities to engage in inquiry related to ethical matters. He sees that this is possible through doing philosophy with children, the key being that engagement in philosophical dialogue prepares children for the democratic society of which they are a part. He correctly points out that 'We cannot expect people who have been passive and assimilative until they are of voting age to go through a sudden and inexplicable metamorphosis which enables them to be politically active and productive once they are adults' (ibid. 70). This political dimension of the ethical life is clear in Scottish education.

The Scottish curriculum, *Curriculum for Excellence* (CfE) (Scottish Executive, 2004a), promotes interdisciplinary learning, and though it retains clear subject guidelines, it has four central planks that run across these subjects. The curriculum has been written for all children between the ages of 3 and 18 with a view to supporting them to become Successful Learners, Confident Individuals, Effective Contributors and, importantly here, Responsible Citizens with the goal of developing attributes for learning and children's knowledge and skills to prepare and support them in their life and work (Scottish Executive, 2004a). The notion of the responsible citizen is relevant to any discussion of children's reasoning, in considering society generally and ethical concerns more specifically. The curricular documentation makes clear that children as responsible citizens will have 'respect for others [and a] commitment to participate responsibly in political, economic, social and cultural life' (Scottish Executive, 2004a, 12). This is further elaborated upon. These responsible citizens will be able to:

> develop knowledge and understanding of the world and Scotland's place in it; understand different beliefs and cultures; make informed choices and decisions; evaluate environmental, scientific and technological issues; and develop informed, ethical views of complex issues. (Ibid. 12)

As one would anticipate, this resonates well with the Education Scotland briefing and guidance provided for religious observance/time for reflection where much is made of the need for children to have opportunities to 'broaden their understanding of the world', to consider their cultures and that of others, to think critically and creatively, to be curious about their environment, to consider issues around equality, and to consider and reflect upon topical social and moral issues (Education Scotland, 2014, 2).

In a study by Cassidy and Christie (2014), 133 children between the ages of 5 and 18 in Scotland, in a range of formal and non-formal educational settings, were provided with three short vignettes that presented them with moral dilemmas. The children were asked for a resolution to the dilemmas, but they were also asked for a reason for that decision. It was the reason-giving that was of interest to the researchers. After the initial vignettes, the children participated in McCall's Community of Philosophical Inquiry (CoPI) for an hour a week for up to ten weeks. At the end of that period the children were given three similar, but different, vignettes with moral dilemmas to resolve. Again the children had to provide reasons for their decisions. The reasons offered by the children were scored by the researchers to gauge whether there had been any improvement in their reason-giving as a consequence of participation in CoPI. The study found that 'significant improvement was shown across both primary and secondary school sectors and that the pattern of improvement was consistent across seven diverse classroom settings' (ibid. 47).

Reflective dialogue

There is much to support the use of PwC to engender reflection and inquiry as an approach to time for reflection. It is important to make clear the distinction between PwC and philosophy more generally, in its academic sense. Gazzard (1996) identifies three ways of thinking about philosophy. The first is in a traditional sense, that it is a search for meaning, a move towards an examined life as Socrates would have it, that the individual is searching for wisdom. The second view of philosophy is what might be considered academic philosophy, the history of ideas, with the third view being reflective thinking where one strives for 'the elucidation and critical appraisal of virtually any problem from any discipline' (ibid. 9). The second, academic notion of philosophy has its place in terms of encouraging children to see that philosophical pursuit is a worthwhile approach to life, but it is perhaps of less significance in relation to providing children with time for reflection. Under the first consideration of philosophy as a search for meaning or to support one in striving towards what Gazzard calls a 'more reasonable, more meaningful life' (ibid. 9), the role of the teacher is vital. In the Aristotelian tradition, the teacher ought to model the type of life one should live, that she should evidence her reasoning through 'thoughtful action' (ibid. 9). Indeed, Cassidy (2012b, 2017) proposes that doing philosophy with children supports them in their learning to 'live well' and to their well-being or being well.

This aligns with Gazzard's third view of philosophy, that of reflective thinking. Gazzard makes clear that philosophical thinking pertains to a range of problems that cut across disciplines, but that it is different from the likes of scientific reflection. She posits an example of the issues surrounding abortion. Scientific reflection, she says, would consider the likelihood of the foetus' survival or the probability of the unwanted child to be adopted. Philosophical reflective thinking, on the other hand, would concern itself, in Gazzard's view, with questions around rights, or notions of murder, or of choice, and so on. She is clear that the practice of philosophizing should not be an end in itself as such discrete thinking skills activities have limited bearing on experience and the aspirational meaningful life; the application of the thinking is required. Cassidy (2012b), when discussing the notion of practical wisdom, asserts that doing PwC is when children are learning how to examine their lives in order to live wisely. Thought and action are inextricably linked. Lunenberg and Korthagen (2009) suggest that possible action is revealed through careful deliberation. Similarly, Wivestad (2008) recognizes practical wisdom as a connection between reflection and action in order to do what is good for oneself, while also promoting the good life more generally. Gazzard (1996) discusses a 'reflective habit of mind' and suggests that this is used as a tool to facilitate critical engagement with the world around one as opposed to engaging in endless analyses to no purpose. The reflective habit of mind allows the individual to abstract herself from the issue at hand, while, at the same time, staying engaged with it. Being able to see the problem from a range of perspectives is vital in the promotion of the reflective individual. PwC, she continues, will inculcate opportunities to broaden children's minds, that they might encounter others' perspectives and will support them in building their own views and arguments and that these will be stronger for that deliberation.

Cassidy (2012b) echoes this and adds that this will, in turn, breed respect for the views of others, though it need not lead to agreement.

What is important in all of this is that the dialogue is not internal. Certainly one might assume that time for reflection implies individual search for meaning, but this need not be the case. Indeed, in articulating views one is able to experiment with ideas, to be offered counter arguments and supporting arguments, and to gauge which reasons fit with the problem being considered. In PwC children are given the opportunity to learn from others' thinking. Indeed, in McCall's Community of Philosophical Inquiry (CoPI), participants need not present their own opinions; they can experiment with ideas with a view to coming to their own understanding via shared meaning making. McCall's (2009) proposition that we are all fallible is important here, particularly when considering time for reflection for those of faith or none. While she acknowledges that we can all share the same view or opinion, we can all be wrong about that view. She suggests that we are more likely to be accurate in our thinking if we test our views with others through philosophical inquiry. Indeed, as McCall notes, some participants not only agree/disagree with others, it is commonplace for participants, after reflecting on other contributions, to state, 'I disagree with myself because ...'. This, says McCall (2009), is part of an internal dynamic within CoPI where ideas are articulated, reasons are provided, examples are offered and counter-examples are presented with contradictions being highlighted in the reason-giving or in the examples themselves. It is in reviewing one's thinking, reflecting upon it, that moves the dialogue, the reasoning, the reflection and the thinking forward.

Exposing individual reflection, reasoning or thinking through PwC can only be achieved with a group or community of philosophical inquiry or philosophical community of inquiry, as it is variously called. PwC is a collaborative activity; it demands other participants in order to work. Lipman (2003), in writing about community in relation to inquiry, notes that not all communities engage in inquiry. A philosophical community of inquiry, though, has a goal or purpose. In the context of time for reflection this may be to explore beliefs or values or ethical or social issues. Lipman also identifies that the inquiry itself has a direction. There is a movement to the inquiry; it tacks back and forth, but always going forward, with each new contribution opening further possibilities for agreement or disagreement or both. McCall (2009, 13) illustrates this by explaining that after the first child speaks the next to speak has four options: to agree with the idea and reason presented; to disagree with the idea but agree with the reason; to agree with the idea but disagree with the reason; and disagree with the idea and disagree with the reason. It is not just the second speaker who is considering these four possibilities, all others in the community are reflecting on the contribution and the four possibilities. If the second speaker chooses the first, second or third option then she has offered the others at least one new element to consider. If she opts for the fourth possibility of disagreeing with the idea and the associated reason, she will be creating a new idea and a new reason. This means, as McCall shows, that the third speaker has sixteen options available to her, assuming, of course, that she chooses only to speak about one previous contribution since it is perfectly normal for a participant to make links between several contributions. For example, 'I agree with Aileen because ... but disagree with Donald because ... and this means I also disagree with Julie because ...', making it is easy to see how the opportunities for taking the inquiry further magnify quickly.

This relates to another of the key points raised by Lipman (2003) in relation to community of inquiry, that of dialogue and reasonableness. He is clear that dialogue is different to discussion in that it follows rules such as those outlined previously for McCall's CoPI and that, unlike discussion, it is not self-serving, the speaker is contributing to the inquiry and not engaging for what she might gain. Indeed, Lipman (1993) notes that a conversation or discussion 'may be brittle and superficial, with evasion of anything resembling a problem. There is shared chatter rather than shared inquiry' (ibid. 302) and inquiry is what is desired. In addition, logic is involved in the reasoning. With each new contribution participants must

> explore what was being assumed or taken for granted that led to that particular inference ... Each move sets up a train of countering or supporting moves. As subsidiary issues are settled, the community's sense of direction is confirmed and clarified, and the inquiry proceeds with renewed vigor. (Lipman, 2003, 92)

The community never comes to a final conclusion, since each temporary conclusion raises further questions to be explored, a feature highly pertinent when considering time for reflection. The shared endeavour for creating meaning is seen clearly through the notion of community when the participants become less personally invested in the dialogue in the sense that they lose ownership of their contributions, they offer agreement/disagreement with the aim of taking the dialogue further rather than seeing it as an opportunity to score points or to win an argument. In Gregory's 2011 interview with Ann Sharp, a close colleague of Lipman in the development of Philosophy for Children (P4C), Sharp elucidates some of Lipman's thinking when he designed the P4C programme: 'the art of making judgments that might improve that [everyday] experience ... as a quest to help us to lead qualitatively better lives' (200). What is important is the participants' thinking rather than a desire to pursue and persuade others to their own personally held opinions (McCall, 2009). It is this willingness to engage in inquiry for the benefit of the whole community that offers much to time for reflection.

Building a collaborative Community of Inquiry

Millett and Tapper (2012) highlight the social practice of paying attention by listening and responding that is important within PwC. They emphasize the social endeavour of thinking together as being important to developing positive social behaviours since, in their view, by thinking together children will think better. Talk, notes Fisher (2012), supports children in both their social and cognitive learning, but the type of talk promoted with children is important. In this instance, Fisher identifies dialogue as being crucial to meaningful learning and this dialogue should promote the attentive listening and responding to others' ideas as Millett and Tapper propose. However, it also involves asking questions, being able to think about the topic critically and creatively, and making a link between what is thought and what is done through the exercise of good judgement. This, for Fisher, is not possible with only one or two individuals; it demands a community approach, a group of people engaged in a common endeavour with the purpose of better understanding or to create meaning in relation to the topic at hand. Engaging in collaborative philosophical inquiry should empower children and this will, in turn, lead them to think carefully about how they act (Burgh & Yorshansky, 2011). This ultimately has a bearing on others as it is not possible to practise such habits in a vacuum; it demands others who are similarly disposed if it is to have a positive effect. It may be suggested that time for reflection is a solitary activity. However, while introspection has its place, one does not exist in isolation. If one's reflections determine one's actions, it would be wise to reflect with others in what is a supportive context, with a view to practising one's views, thinking and reasoning.

In PwC each contribution is equally valued in adding to the dialogue, for without these there would be no foundations upon which to build other contributions. McCall (2009) exemplifies this when she shares an extract from a CoPI dialogue to show that one child is pushed further in his thinking because of the reasoning provided by a previous speaker in the dialogue. This, in turn, drives the other participants further in their thinking because they have more to consider, challenge, support and extend. The collaborative sharing and shaping of one another's thoughts is important in establishing a community. This does not mean that the participants need all agree; indeed, without disagreement there would be no philosophy. The 'community' in Community of Philosophical Inquiry is significant. The community works together. There is not always agreement, but there is a reliance on others to ensure that the community thrives and works towards a common goal. McCall (2009) suggests that the community relationship in CoPI is like a family, and she cites a participant who sees the relationship as being very much like that of a family: 'At first I couldn't stand X, but then it began to feel like when you have an annoying cousin, you get really annoyed with him, but he is part of your family and you don't let other people disrespect him' (86). Indeed, it is clear in CoPI that when a participant is absent for some reason, she is missed; the perspectives usually provided by that individual are also absent and this is detected by the participants. The social dimension cannot be overstated.

Caring thinking

It is here that Lipman's (2003) notion of caring thinking is important, though not divorced from the critical and creative, his other modes of thinking. Indeed, the caring, creative and critical are equally important and inter-related for Lipman. Juuso (2007) summarizes Lipman's notion of caring thinking as 'the ability to value what has value' (145). The caring community of inquiry articulates well with the aims of time for reflection; it is 'one that cultivates the appreciation of values, is likely to study how such cultivation can best be accomplished and how to live so that the values of what is worthwhile will be disclosed for all to perceive' (198). One may care about understanding and so may ask many questions, one may care or be concerned about inquiry itself and work for precision in reasoning, one may care about language or express enjoyment of some activity, but this is all seen as caring. For Lipman, the more perceptive individual will be more caring. Let it be clear that the careful listening, the respect shown to others and any empathy for views espoused do not necessitate that these views are shared or even tolerated by other participants. Caring thinking demands that the respect shown means that others' ideas are considered seriously and critically with a view to making informed judgements about them (Bleazby, 2011). In time for reflection time for reflection it is easy to see how respect might be shown to others but that this reflection should lead to a considered position, whether this is an acceptance or rejection of the issue at hand. For Lipman, that we care about something is a judge-ment; we are judging that it matters. So, in investing in caring thinking during time for reflection through PwC we are stating clearly that certain issues matter and because they matter we care about them. Lipman goes on to state that 'Caring is a kind of thinking when it performs such cognitive operations as scanning for alternatives, discovering or inventing relation-ships, instituting connections among connections, and gauging differences' (2003, 264), but that this is still not a satisfactory definition. The realm of caring thinking involves other elements such as: appreciative thinking in the sense of attaching value or worth to something; affective thinking that links emotion with reason; active thinking that aligns acts with reasoning and the idea that one might care for something; normative thinking that pertains to how one wants to live and how one ought to live; and empathic thinking being the ability to put oneself in another's position. This is vital in the promotion of time for reflection and it can be achieved through philosophical dialogue that allows pupils, as Schertz (2007) suggests, to engage with others' subjectivities in a social context that engenders prosocial behaviour. It is this connection between thinking and behaviour that is important in time for reflection.

Thinking and action

Without an impact on actions or behaviour there seems little point in thinking or reflecting. It is evident, then, that what one thinks, reflects or cares about is important. McCall (1991, 2009) makes it clear that in Community of Philosophical Inquiry there is an external reality, independent of humans, and that this therefore means that everything is open to question. This is closely aligned to the idea of fallibilism, mentioned earlier. McCall (2009) suggests that there is a world that exists independently of our thoughts and because it is independent of our thoughts, we can be wrong about it. She continues, the external world is constituted of material objects and non-material objects such as ideas, theories, institutions, language, and so on, and that once these things have been created they are no longer dependent on humans for their existence. Indeed, once created, these entities can be put to different uses. McCall asserts that we can be wrong about these immaterial entities and that they need to be tested conceptually through the likes of PwC. This leads one to see that everything must be open to question. In time for reflection, questioning or conceptual testing may revolve around conceptions of the good by engaging in inquiry about how to deal with people that break the law or what can be done to address inequality. It is important that in supporting children in their development as active, political and participative individuals they are given the tools with which to engage (Cassidy, 2007).

Indeed, in time for reflection there should be no topic out of bounds, everything should be open to question. If children are to be fully engaged in the world around them, and this is what is meant by Cassidy when she suggests that they ought to be active and political and that their participation in the world beyond the playground should be facilitated, then they have to be enabled to question and to challenge the people and the world around them. Questioning and challenge need to be taught and this can be addressed through PwC. The safe, structured environment where ideas are shared and considered allows for caring in thought, but it also permits critical and creative thinking. McCall (2009) contends that to engage in PwC demands creativity since, in order to be understood by the other participants, one must create meaning. Similarly, in order to consider and understand what is being said, and to reflect upon one's views in relation to these ideas, one must create meaning for oneself. Daniel and Auriac (2011) offer a list of features that belong to creativity; they say that 'Creativity presupposes skills such as inventing, associating, suggesting alternatives, making analogies, formulating hypotheses, etc' (418).

Critical and creative thinking

Lipman's (1995) notion of critical thinking demands that individuals pose problems as well as working to solve them. It is bound by rules or applies criteria to engage with issues or questions, but with individual instances of ambiguity or bias, as Lipman would say, being the focus. This is unlike creative thinking in the sense that it requires the individual to apply criteria but across the range of problems within the issue. He notes, too, that critical thinking is concerned with a search for truth while creative thinking aims towards the creation of meaning. Both, though, are applied in practical contexts, for '[t]hey always involve a push that goes beyond process and eventuates in some sort of product or judgment' (Lipman, 1995, 65). Judgement, though, 'involves the making of finer and more useful discriminations in the course of expressing one's self and appraising one's world' (Lipman, 1993, 303). It is through this practice of self-correction that one becomes more reasonable and it is this that is practised and perfected through philosophical inquiry. The practical application of refined judgement and considered reasoning resonates with the demand for time for reflection and the need for it to impact upon action. In applying this to living one's life, it would be wrong to see problems or the inquiry as discrete or abstracted from one's life; the context in which one is situated is important. It is necessary, holds Lipman (1993), that inquiry is not solely about self-correction, taking the context into account is key and this holistic thinking, as he calls it, is an essential element of creative thinking. Juuso (2007) makes clear the aspects of critical thinking and creative thinking that complement one another: critical thinking is thinking that (1) facilitates judgment because it (2) relies on criteria, (3) is self-corrective, and (4) is sensitive to context ... Creative thinking, on the other hand is the thinking that it is imaginative, holistic, inventive and generative' (70). Juuso recognizes the Aristotelian notion of practical reason in Lipman's view of critical, creative and caring thinking, that it links with activity, with one's actions and behaviour.

Philosophy for all

Garside (2013) argues that PwC 'should facilitate the formation of judgement as a way of engaging with the world and self' (146); in other words, reflection. The implication of this position is that it is impossible to separate the idea of reflection from being. Therefore, in proposing time for reflection in place of religious observance in schools, the inextricable relationship between what one is reflecting upon and that one's reflections ought to impact on one's actions is recognized. Such reflection need not depend upon an individual having a particular faith or belonging to a religious group. Reflection should be encouraged for all. Indeed, allowing children time to reflect on values, beliefs, ideas, and so on, is not teaching them specific values but, crucially, teaching them about values. Through this thinking and collaborative reflection they will come to recognize their own values. Even more importantly, it is anticipated that they will learn to question and challenge themselves, that they will not allow themselves to sit comfortably with their views, and that they will continue to assess, probe and evaluate their thinking and their behaviour.

In speaking about moral education Lipman (1995) suggests that we are 'projecting ... an image of the kind of world one would like to inhabit' (70). It is essential, though, that if the discussion is really about the kind of world we would like to inhabit, then the voices of children must be heard, since they too are part of this world. Indeed, a recent study by Conrad, Cassidy and Mathis (2015) used McCall's CoPI for just that purpose. They asked children what kind of society they want to live in and found that children engaged with a wide range of issues around topics such as rights, poverty, health care, equality, friendship, and so on. It is clear from these philosophical dialogues that children are able to reflect on social and ethical issues and that their thinking was influenced by the world they inhabit, but also permitted them to see how they might influence or impact upon that world. The time for reflection that these dialogues afforded was, it may be argued, more meaningful and worthwhile than prayer, worship or some other form of religious observance. The engagement with the issues, and with others about the issues, may be more likely to promote what Westheimer and Kahne (2004) call 'justice-oriented' citizenship where the participants recognize the importance of the activist potential of the community and that they are moved to act after reflecting on issues, unlike the 'personally-responsible citizen' who may not be as prompted to act.

The different practices that constitute the field of Philosophy with Children all strive towards a common goal, and for the proponents of PwC there is agreement that the promotion of Lipman's trinity of critical, creative and caring thinking is important. There is agreement, too, that children should be taught to think philosophically in order that they can act positively in the world. Following the 1995 UNESCO Paris Declaration for Philosophy, in 2007 UNESCO published its report, *Philosophy: A School of Freedom*, which clearly stated that

> by training free, reflective, minds capable of resisting various forms of propaganda, fanaticism, exclusion and intolerance, philosophical education contributes to peace and prepares everyone to shoulder responsibilities in the face of the great challenges of the contemporary world, particularly in the field of ethics. (Ibid. xiii)

Indeed, the report recognizes the important role PwC can play in supporting children in their lives in relation to ethical reasoning and decision-making, and raises questions about the fact that PwC is not available to all children 'so that it can be applied within all other disciplines and enable the keen analysis of the problems faced by the world today' (UNESCO, 2007, 240).

In proposing PwC as time for reflection, it is worth considering UNESCO's (2007) findings:

> When philosophy wants to contribute to freedom, it does not offer to replace ethical, cultural or political contents by others of the same nature, but offers a strict and radical criticism of any closed corpus of beliefs, precepts or dogma. When the teaching of philosophy is reduced to an ethical indoctrination, it betrays its liberating function. This is why philosophy teaching remains the decisive field of battle between formal knowledge, with the free and open morality that accompanies it, and dogmatic knowledge, with its authoritarian moralizing. (115)

It is essential that for time for reflection to be the meaningful experience that will encourage children 'to grow and develop their own sense of themselves, to be confident in expressing their own beliefs and values, and to develop an understanding of and empathy towards others' (Education Scotland, 2014, 1), they must be afforded opportunities to reflect. Children need to be furnished with the tools and given opportunities to practise their thinking. It is not enough to assume a quiet moment or even a prayer will facilitate children's thinking or reflection, and that in encouraging prayer or a quiet moment that children will think about themselves, the world and how they interact with the world and its inhabitants. It is suggested here that in order to inculcate thinking that will impact positively on children and their lives, they are given space and time to explore their own and others' ideas, and that this is best done collaboratively, using a philosophical approach, which permits experimentation with ideas. Lipman (1993) is correct when he suggests that there is a problem when practitioners try to teach children skills before they allow them to practise these in a situation that encourages inquiry. It is in this realm that many children experience learning, it is not until adulthood that they are permitted to apply skills they have learned while at school. Engaging in philosophical dialogue is the activity, says Lipman, that allows children to acquire the necessary skills for engagement; it is not, he says, 'the skills that generate the dialogue' (303). These skills are ones that will enable the child, and the future adult, to have 'confidence in making their own minds up about important issues and help them to express their own views reasonably and securely ... [while allowing them to develop] respect for the beliefs and values of others as well as by developing empathy with a wide variety of perspectives' (Education Scotland, 2014, 2). In proposing PwC as the approach to time for reflection for all children, regardless of them belonging to a religion or having a faith or none, Lipman (1995) deserves the final word:

> The expectation many or most children have of 'moral education' is of a regimen that is joyless and repressive. And yet, they are puzzled as to what society expects of them and how they are to deal with the dark ambiguities that surround them. A moral education approach that enables them to learn from one another's experience, to share one another's understandings and to feel a sense of belonging to a larger community is bound to be greeted by them with joy and warmth and enthusiasm rather than with suspicion and diffidence. (70)

References

Bleazby, J. (2011). Overcoming Relativism and Absolutism: Dewey's ideals of truth and meaning in philosophy for children. *Educational Philosophy and Theory, 43*(5), 453–466.

Burgh, G., & Yorshansky, M. (2011). Communities of Inquiry: politics, power and group dynamics. *Educational Philosophy and Theory, 43*(5), 436–452.

Cassidy, C. (2007). *Thinking Children*. London: Continuum.

Cassidy, C. (2012a). Questioning children. *Thinking: the Journal of Philosophy for Children, 20*(1&2), 62–68.

Cassidy, C. (2012b). Philosophy with Children: learning to live well. *Childhood & Philosophy, 8*(16), 243–264.

Cassidy, C. (2017). Wellbeing, being well or well becoming: who or what is it for and how might we get there? In M. Thorburn (Ed.), *Wellbeing and Contemporary Schooling*. (pp. 13–26). London: Routledge.

Cassidy, C., & Christie, D. (2013). Philosophy with Children: talking, thinking and learning together. *Early Child Development and Care, 183*(8), 1072–1083.

Cassidy, C., & Christie, D. (2014). Community of Philosophical Inquiry: citizenship in the classroom. *Childhood & Philosophy, 10*(19), 33–54.

Cleghorn, P. (2002). *Thinking Through Philosophy*. Blackburn: Educational Printing Services.

Conrad, S.-J., Cassidy, C., & Mathis, C. (2015). Encouraging and supporting children's voices. In J. Tremmel, A. Mason, P. Godli, & I. Dimitrijoski (Eds.), *Youth Quotas and Other Efficient Forms of Youth Participation in Ageing Democracies*. Switzerland: Springer.

Daniel, M.-F. (2008). Learning to philosophize: Positive impacts and conditions for implementation. A synthesis of 10 years of research (1995–2005). *Thinking, 18*(4), 36–48.

Daniel, M.-F., & Auriac, E. (2011). Philosophy, critical thinking and Philosophy for Children. *Educational Philosophy and Theory, 43*(5), 415–435.

Education Scotland (2014). *CfE Briefing 16. Curriculum for Excellence: Religious Observance (Time for Reflection)*. Glasgow: Education Scotland. Available at <https://education.gov.scot/improvement/Documents/rme26-cfe-briefing-religious-observance.pdf>.

Garside, D. (2013). *Edifying Judgement: Using Rorty to Redescribe Judgement in the Context of Philosophy for Children*. PhD thesis: University of Bath, England.

Gazzard, A. (1996). Philosophy for Children and the discipline of philosophy. *Thinking, 12*(4), 9–16.

Gregory, M. (2008). Philosophy in schools: ideals, challenges and opportunities. *Critical and Creative Thinking, 16*(1), 5–22.

Gregory, M. (2011). Philosophy for Children and its critics: a Mendham dialogue. *Journal of Philosophy of Education, 45*(2), 199–219.

Juuso, H. (2007). *Child, Philosophy and Education. Discussing the Intellectual Sources of Philosophy for Children*. PhD thesis: University of Oulu, Finland.

Lipman, M. (1993). Promoting better classroom thinking. *Educational Psychology: An International Journal of Experimental Educational Psychology, 13*(3–4), 291–304.

Lipman, M. (1995). Moral education higher-order thinking and Philosophy for Children. *Early Child Development and Care, 107*(1), 61–70.

Lipman, M. (2003). *Thinking in Education (2nd edition)*. New York: Cambridge University Press.

Lipman, M., Sharp, A. M., & Oscanyan, F. S. (1980). *Philosophy in the Classroom (2nd edition)*. Philadelphia: Temple University Press.

Lunenberg, M., & Korthagen, F. (2009). Experience, theory, and practical wisdom in teaching and teacher education. *Teachers and Teaching: Theory and Practice, 15*(2), 225–240.

McCall, C. (1991). *Stevenson Lectures on Citizenship*. Glasgow: Glasgow University Press.

McCall, C. (2009). *Transforming Thinking. Philosophical Inquiry in the Primary and Secondary Classroom*. London: Routledge.

McKinney, S. J. (2013). Catholic Education in Scotland. In T. G. K. Bryce, W. M. Humes, D. Gillies, & A. Kennedy (Eds.), *Scottish Education Fourth Edition: Referendum* (pp. 298–307). Edinburgh: Edinburgh University Press.

Matthews, G. B. (1980). *Philosophy and the Young Child*. Cambridge, MA: Harvard University Press.

Matthews, G. B. (1984). *Dialogues with Children*. Cambridge, Massachusetts: Harvard University Press.

Millett, S., & Tapper, A. (2012). Benefits of Collaborative Philosophical Inquiry in Schools. *Educational Philosophy and Theory, 44*(5), 546–567.

Murris, K. (2000). Can children do philosophy? *Journal of Philosophy of Education, 34*(2), 261–279.

Saran, R., & Neisser, B. (Eds.) (2004). *Enquiring Minds: Socratic Dialogue in Education*. Stoke-on-Trent: Trentham Books.

Schertz, M. (2007). Avoiding passive empathy with Philosophy for Children. *Journal of Moral Education, 36*(2), 185–198.

Scottish Catholic Education Service, <http://www.sces.uk.com/religious-education-2.html>, accessed May 2017.

Scottish Executive (2004a). *A Curriculum for Excellence*. Edinburgh: Scottish Executive.

Scottish Executive (2004b). *The Report of the Religious Observance Review Group*. Edinburgh: Scottish Executive.

Scottish Government (2011). *Curriculum for Excellence – Provision of Religious and Moral Education in Non-denominational Schools and Religious Education in Roman Catholic Schools*. Available at <http://www.gov.scot/resource/doc/920/0113849.pdf>.

Scottish Government (2017). *Curriculum for Excellence – Provision of Religious Observance in Scottish Schools – March 2017*. Available at <http://www.gov.scot/Resource/0051/00516155.pdf>.

Topping, K. J., & Trickey, S. (2007). Collaborative philosophical enquiry for school children: cognitive effects at 10–12 years. *British Journal of Educational Psychology, 77*(2), 271–288.

Trickey, S. (2008). 'More than cognitive': reflections on the components of the Clackmannanshire Thinking Project. *Critical & Creative Thinking, 16*(1), 23–43.

UNESCO (2007). *Philosophy: A School of Freedom*. Paris: UNESCO Publishing.

UNESCO (2012). *Philosophy: A School of Freedom*. Paris: UNESCO Publishing.

Westheimer, J., & Kahne, J. (2004). What kind of citizen? The politics of educating for democracy. *American Educational Research Journal, 41*(2), 237–269.

Wivestad, S. M. (2008). The educational challenges of *agape* and *phronesis*. *Journal of Philosophy of Education, 42*(2), 307–324.

JULIA IPGRAVE AND FARID PANJWANI

10 Collective Worship and Theology: Issues and Questions

ABSTRACT

Using *teacher perspectives* this chapter investigates the difficulties entailed in retaining the benefits to community of collective worship while giving due consideration to the divergent religious (and non-religious) outlooks of pupils and integrity of the religious content. Questions and assumptions behind these challenges and responses to them are often rooted in different religious and theological understandings of the issues. The chapter shows how teachers are often led to ignore religion altogether or else impose new theological frameworks on their material and pupils. It then applies more nuanced understandings of the terms 'collective' and 'worship' from inter-faith theology and practice to suggest other approaches to collective worship that avoid these outcomes but combine shared experiences and intentions with diversity of response. Giving prominence to the implications of Circular 1/94, the chapter largely relates to the English context although its arguments also have relevance to collective worship/religious observance in other nations.

Introduction

The Collective Worship Network has explored the issues and questions raised by current legislation, official guidance (as in the Department for Education Circular 1/94) and provision from a number of different angles, legal, pedagogical, sociological. The business of this network is to delve below the surface and provide a more nuanced understanding of the issues surrounding the legislation, principles and practice of collective worship. This chapter investigates the religious and theological issues pertaining to collective worship, in acknowledgement of the fact that controversies tend to focus on its *religious* content and that criticisms (including secular criticisms) of the current arrangement often rest on assumptions about theology, the relationship between worship and belief and the inappropriateness of collective worship where belief is not shared. This chapter seeks to test some of those claims and assumptions and in doing so puts forward a case that, provided due attention and respect is given to the nature of received tradition, it is possible to interpret the idea of worship in a manner that is compatible with a religiously plural and secular gathering of people such as might be found in many UK schools. The religious perspectives investigated in this chapter are largely Christian and Muslim reflecting the cultural backgrounds of the authors.

Contextual factors and questions

Some of the critics of the collective worship requirement for schools treat it as axiomatic that collective worship cannot take place in a religiously plural context. For example, the British Humanist Association declares that 'a school can do many things collectively, but, lacking a shared religious faith, it cannot worship collectively' (BHA). While on the surface this seems like a potent critique, we contend that forceful arguments can be found to respond to it. The chapter will show that such arguments can be constructed by giving due consideration to the spectrum of faith positions that might be found in a regular congregational act of worship; by attending to the breadth of meanings of the term 'worship'; and by analysing the descriptor 'collective' carefully chosen as distinct from 'corporate' in legislation and guidance.

There is plenty of evidence of schools side-lining religion in their collective worship provision in an effort to respect the religious and non-religious diversity of the pupil population or because this is how they understand the secular ethos of the state community school (Cheetham, 2004, 76, 105); as one teacher said of collective worship at his school, 'we have various themes in the school, but nothing relating to religious topics, just making them a better person, moral issues, etc.'[1] In such cases, worship is often understood in its etymological sense of 'worth-ship' and so the term's meaning is broadened to include celebrations of or reflection on anything deemed to be of worth or concern whether or not it has religious reference. This movement away from religion in the public arena of school assembly is guided by an interpretation of religion as belonging to the private sphere (ibid. 27–28, 39, 76, 145). The logic of the collective worship statutory requirements and the guidance found in government Circular 1/94 points in a different direction. When Circular 1/94 employs the term 'worship', it gives the word its 'natural and ordinary meaning' of 'reverence or veneration paid to a divine being or power'. However, in the same paragraph, the circular also requires that 'subject to the right of withdrawal' collective worship 'should be appropriate for and include all pupils attending the school' (DfE, 1994, para. 54). This chapter explores the challenges and possibilities of meeting these two requirements in the current situation. It begins by outlining some contextual factors (pupil religion, civic religion, teacher worldviews) that feed into the theological questions the situation raises. This discussion is informed by perspectives of teachers involved in the delivery of collective worship, including teachers who have participated in recent research on religion in schools undertaken by Warwick Religions and Education Research Unit,[2] teachers whose voices have been reported in Richard Cheetham's 2004 study of collective worship in English schools, and respondents to a questionnaire delivered to Muslim teachers in community schools in 2015 in preparation for this chapter. The chapter then considers the position of religious content and religious activity within the context of worship in schools

---

1   This comment was contributed by a Muslim teacher responding to a questionnaire administered to Muslim teachers in order to inform this chapter (see below).

2   Including the research projects, 'Materials Used in Schools to Teach World Religions in English Schools' funded by the Department of Children, Schools and Families 2009–2010 (Robert Jackson *et al.*, 2010); and the AHRC/ESRC funded research project 'Young People's Attitudes towards Religious Diversity' (2009–2012) involving studies in schools across the UK (Elisabeth Arweck, 2017).

without a designated religious character, with a particular interest in the state of tension between diversity and inclusivity.

Responding to diverse context

Throughout the UK young people represent a wide divergence of experience of religion (Ipgrave, 2012b). The presence in our schools of large numbers of students with no religious background, and of some with atheist worldviews, has prompted questions about the validity of school collective worship (BHA). At the same time, alongside pupils with predominantly secular worldviews, schools serve many other young people who see their faith (as one teacher said of her Muslim pupils) as 'a living, breathing entity' and the interpretive principle of their lives (Ipgrave, 2010). In the UK these young people may be more likely to come from minority populations – in a 2006 DfES survey (working with an ethnically mixed sample of 15,450) 85 per cent of Pakistani and Bangladeshi students and 71 per cent of black African heritage students claimed that religion was '*very* important' in their lives – but they are in the majority in many of our schools and a minority whose needs should not be overlooked in others. The 1992 Church of England guide for multifaith worship points out that it is often difficult for secular perspectives to appreciate the extent to which 'life in much of the rest of the world' – and, we might add, in many communities and families in Britain today – 'is lived with a continual consciousness of the dimension of divinity' to which worship comes naturally (The Inter-Faith Consultative Group, 1992, 29). For schools that seek to recognize and build on the family and cultural background of their pupils, pupil religion is an important factor to take into consideration and several teachers expressed the view that collective worship served this purpose. This is so with teachers responding to Cheetham's research and with the Muslim teachers of the 2015 questionnaire mentioned above. One of the latter declared that through collective worship in his school, 'all students feel that their religious background is valued and celebrated'.[3] Religion's performative value as a source of energy and motivation, and of reassurance at times of pressure is also of interest to the subject of school worship.[4] At one school (participating in Warwick research) with a predominantly Christian, African-heritage student population, the deputy head reported her pupils' expressions of regret at the interruption to collective worship occasioned by the use of the school hall for GCSE examinations, as, these girls claimed, they particularly needed the support it gave them at this time. The presence of pupils with such an outlook suggests a need for them at least to have opportunities for worship at school, but it does not answer the question whether that worship should be an expectation for all, or what value such opportunities might have for those without religion in their lives.

While the case for collective worship outlined above argues from the religiosity of (some of) the pupils involved, another case for collective worship is based on the lack of religious experience of many others. Whatever the background of the children or their eventual stance with regards to religious belief and practice, the argument goes, their understanding of human experience and their ability to relate to the religious expressions in their society and wider world and develop their own response (their 'religious literacy') would be diminished without this opportunity. The large majority of UK school children are positioned somewhere between the very religious and the completely non-religious. Most of these, figures suggest, have little experience of organized religion in their lives outside school, though only a few may hold completely atheistic views of reality.[5] It is in response to this context of lack of experience but not outright negativity towards religion that two head teachers (interviewed for a Warwick

---

3   As the data collected for this questionnaire has not been published citations in this text are not referenced. The same is true of some of the data collected from the Warwick research.

4   Cheron Byfield's research study has shown the positive effect of religion on the achievement of black pupils. She uses the term 'religious capital' to describe this effect (Byfield, 2008).

5   The European Values Survey of 2012 found only a small minority who espoused outright atheism in the UK as in most of the continent.

University study) expressed their understanding of collective worship as providing opportunities for prayer and adoration without enforcing participation. For these heads, collective worship has potential to create new awareness and open up new opportunities for their pupils. In both cases the head teacher himself was a practising Christian and the collective worship was conducted upon fairly traditional lines with religious songs and readings. The junior school liturgy included moments of quiet reflection the head expressing his hope that some might be led through this activity into 'prayerfulness' and 'a spiritual dimension'. At the secondary school the declared intention was that pupils would develop 'through instruction, exposition and imaginative appeal, a sense of the beauty of holiness'. It could be contended that the provision of such experiences at school is even more important for religiously non-practising students who do not have such opportunities elsewhere. This was the argument made by an infant school head teacher (participating in the same study), for the significance given to collective worship and religious education in her school. She explains that though there is no intention to 'evangelize' the pupils, 'we do like to make sure that we do bring God and Christ into school in a way that we feel we need to acknowledge the children perhaps not having that experience outside school'. It is a question of enabling breadth of experience and understanding. The understandings of the head teachers outlined above conform to Circular 1/94's requirement that an act of collective worship should be 'capable of eliciting a response from students, even though on a particular occasion some of the students may not feel able actively to identify with the act of worship' (1/94, 1994, para. 59). They described cases where the collective worship event brings students to the threshold of religious experience, but cannot take them over it (Ipgrave, 2012a). This formula relates to a fundamental question for this chapter, the nature of worship.

Community aspect of collective worship

So far in this discussion of collective worship the faith and response of individual pupils has been the subject; teachers interviewed also showed a strong interest in community aspects of this worship, an interest that has particular implications for a community whose population is so diverse. The language used by several of Cheetham's respondents reflected this interest as they spoke of 'community', 'togetherness', 'belonging', and 'sharing' (Cheetham, 2004, 62). One of the Muslim teachers in the 2015 survey declared that in collective worship, 'pupils felt a deeper sense of being part of a wider family and this in turn encompasses a sense of security'. Many teachers thought that collective worship mirrored the traditional role of institutional religion in the establishment and maintenance of community identity and the expression of solidarity and witness at times of heightened significance – celebration, remembrance, crisis – at national, local and family level. Some teachers saw collective worship as a way of teaching the behaviours and responses often deemed appropriate within wider society at such times. Thus, one infant school head teacher spoke of the importance of learning through school worship how to be quiet and thoughtful, and in other schools pupils learnt the ritual and symbolism of lighting candles. In three institutions participating in Warwick University research projects, teachers reported how the experience and format of collective worship had enabled the school communities to respond appropriately and meaningfully to the recent deaths of a pupil in one school, and of teachers in the others. These examples encourage consideration of the significance and nature of the 'collective' that is brought together in worship when that collective is not defined by religious identity or faith.

Another way in which collective worship expresses the community theme is in the tradition of using the opportunities it provides for a celebration of the diversity of the school community and/or of wider society. Thus, schools taking part in the research mentioned made use of collective worship to mark Christmas, Diwali, Eid, Vaisakhi, Chinese New Year and other celebrations, and we find at school level a reflection of the shared communal celebrations of each other's festivals that frequently takes place at the local civic level. Indeed, these collective worship events are more than a reflection. In the training and expectation they give to young people growing up in our school system they contribute to the promotion and continuation of such activity in the wider community. Festivals are recognized not just through the academic learning of the RE lesson but through the experiential and empathetic learning of collective worship. This is especially the case at primary school level. One infant head teacher described her school as 'a community in celebration' and set great store by its celebrations of the diversity of faiths within the school community. A junior school teacher found that his weekly 'multifaith' assembly made his contribution to the school 'much more colourful and much more meaningful' (ibid. 84). In its mirroring of civic services and participation in the festivals of different faith communities, collective worship raises questions about multifaith worship, about religious integrity, about fidelity to one's own faith, or to one's God, about the relative value given to different faiths and the theological implications. It is an area where wider experiences in and theorizing of inter-faith relations can be instructive. The relevance of these to collective worship will be explored later in the chapter.

Interpreting religious content of collective worship

Selection and interpretation of content

Not just the overall purpose of collective worship but the content and its interpretation is of interest to the perspectives of this chapter. We recognize that much of the material used in school collective worship is secular in character but, as our interest is the possibility and validity of a collective worship that, in accordance with current legislation and guidance, has religious reference, *religious* content of collective worship is the focus here. The variety of views and practices recorded from school to school and within schools, highlights the determining influence of the teacher over selection and interpretation of religious content and also reveals some of the issues involved when the teacher is lacking in the confidence or awareness needed to rise to the challenges posed by collective worship. While some taking a secularist stance may object to the use of religious content in assemblies of children from religiously plural and non-religious positions, others speaking from religious perspectives may object to what they see as the misuse of religious material by those not qualified or insufficiently committed to the content to convey the power and significance of their subject matter to the young people. There is some resistance to handing over this precious material to the keeping of the secular teacher and school.

Whatever the language of legislation and guidance, there has been a decline in the influence of Christianity in school worship (outside church schools) and a move away from the traditional hymn/prayer format. In 2004, Cheetham noted the eclectic nature of collective worship provision, his teacher respondents acknowledging 'a lot of personal leeway' in their selection and presentation of material (Cheetham, 81–82). The teacher's personal thoughts become the content of worship: 'I just like to keep things floating around in my mind and collecting little bits, little thoughts', and teachers confessed to 'twisting' religious material, especially religious stories, to suit their own needs (ibid. 82, 83). A junior school teacher admitted that in his choice of stories for collective worship, it did not matter where the story came from as long as it illustrated the point he wanted to make. Termly collective worship plans show an eclectic mix of themes with no external authority to recommend them (ibid. 83). What Cheetham identifies in his research is the 'dominance and authority of the individual teacher over any corporate tradition'; he uses Disraeli's phrase to describe teachers as the 'new sacerdotal class' (ibid. 81f). These findings raise questions about the ownership of religious material and its potential distortion (seen from point of view of the believer) by the school.

Against this concern about 'ownership' and 'distortion' is recognition of the interpretive nature of religious understanding and the responsiveness of faith traditions themselves to the changing circumstances of believers' lives. Meanings of religious texts and rituals are constructed and reconstructed by members of religious groups creating both the internal diversity of interpretations and a shared sense of history and symbolism rooted in sacred texts (Lindof, 2002; Panjwani, 2014). At the same time the internal variety within a tradition leads to a diversity of interpretations of its texts and their import. The recognition of this interpretive flexibility and internal diversity within Islam, for example, is seen as particularly important at this time by educators with a Muslim background wanting to counter static and authoritarian presentations of their faith with a pedagogy that values both communal identity and individual autonomy (Panjwani, 2015, 122).

An understanding of a religion as internally diverse and evolving rather than as circumscribed 'finished product' or 'inert body of knowledge' (ibid. 133), is something that can be usefully conveyed through collective worship events, and that allows some flexibility in the adaptation of its resources to the perspectives and experiences of the pupils. It does not, however, grant unlimited licence to teachers to use or interpret religious material for their pupils in whatever way seems fit for their personal understanding and pedagogical and institutional purposes. A distinction needs to be recognized between the way teachers interpret religious material for themselves and the way they interpret it for their pupils. There is also an essential difference between the school community that assembles around the religious content selected for a collective worship event in a non-denominational setting, and the faith community that gathers around the received scriptures, rites and teachings that it holds sacred. In the former case the content employed is borrowed content and though its use in school worship might support the development of a collective identity for the school, it does not in itself constitute that identity. In the latter case the contents of religious tradition are bound to the interpretive community in a mutually constitutive relationship; the interplay between community and tradition expands and creates new meanings while also setting boundaries within which the hermeneutic activity takes place.

In the *Religion in the Service of the Child RE* project for primary school children, developed at the University of Birmingham in the 1980s and 1990s, a clear distinction was maintained between what religious artefacts might signify to pupils of the traditions from which they derive and what they might signify to pupils not of those traditions (Grimmitt *et al.*, 1991). In the former case a relationship of 'belonging' was recognized; in the latter, where this relationship of 'belonging' did not exist, great care was taken to maintain a respectful distance between child and artefact, so that, while the children could learn from and be inspired by the object, they were not required to venerate it in their acts and words. The Hindu child, Kedar, in one of the project resource books, lights lamps and sprinkles petals over the Ganesha in his family shrine, but the non-Hindu children are not allowed by their teacher to imitate his actions with the Ganesha set up in their classroom; 'You cannot sprinkle the rose petals because you do not belong to

Ganesha. You must stay in your seat' (Hull, 2000, 121).[6] This project and its resources, it should be stressed, were designed for the RE lesson not collective worship and for the classroom not the assembly hall. Nevertheless, the distinction between closeness to and distance from religious content that they are guarding here has evident relevance to non-denominational collective worship contexts too.[7] This chapter will later explore further opportunities for differentiated response ('practised' and 'experienced', 'performative' and 'non-performative') among young people in collective worship according to their diverse religious or non-religious positions. It will consider how all might be able to respond to the religious content of a collective worship event when that content has faith significance to some and not to others. The distinction is not just between religious belief and non-religious belief but between faiths and different denominations within a faith. The fear of idolatry in the Abrahamic traditions makes sensitivity about the use of artefacts within collective worship particularly important. The issue is not just the special relationship of believers from a tradition with content that tradition has generated or holds sacred. For many outside a tradition being represented in a given collective worship event, it is important that their fidelity to their own faith, or to God, or their integrity as someone without religious faith is not compromised by any action that appears to recognize divinity in the object of veneration of another faith or acceptance of its beliefs.[8] These considerations add to the challenges of collective worship.

Questions of 'ownership' are less straightforward where religious content is held to be divine revelation. The conviction within many (though

---

6 The fact that the distinction between closeness to and distance from religious content was made in the context of RE is symptomatic of a common blurring of the boundaries between the worship space of collective worship and the pedagogical space of the RE lesson (in primary schools in particular).

7 It is a debatable question whether or not the teacher should choose for the child what nature and degree of involvement he or she should have with the religious content rather than letting the child (or parent) decide.

8 Some faith traditions welcome the engagement of 'outsiders' in their own religious ceremonies. For example some Hindus inviting non Hindus to make offerings to their gods.

by no means all) faith communities of the universal application of their holy scriptures – God's revelation to humankind rather than to a specific community – suggests that they have been given for the benefit of those outside their traditions as well as to those within. Again, different traditions within faiths countenance varying degrees of freedom for the individual in their interpretations of these texts. However, as suggested above, the teachers leading collective worship are not free agents in the interpretation of religious scripture for their students. Cheetham found his respondents considered themselves subject to a number of restraints imposed not so much by the faith traditions whose material they were using as by their idea of what was or was not appropriate to their non-confessional school setting. There are twin concerns involved: not to indoctrinate and to teach. Several teachers expressed the view that the expression of their personal religious beliefs was inappropriate in the context of collective worship (Cheetham, 2004, 87–91, 119). At the same time they needed to feel 'comfortable' with the messages conveyed through their material – 'if they are not "comfortable" with what is being done then it will not happen' (ibid. 91). It may be this combination of avoiding reference to personal faith and finding a 'comfortable' message in the scriptural content that led to the sanitized versions of Biblical stories that Terence Copley found in research for his Biblos project, versions where reference to God and faith was replaced by what he describes as mundane 'do-goodery' (Copley & Sawani, 1998). It is perhaps not surprising that one of the common sensations associated with collective worship by its critics is boredom, or that religious critics fear that through collective worship children will be 'inoculated against' religion (Oldfield, 2015). A sense of the inadequacy of school treatment of religious material and a perceived need by faith communities to reclaim their scriptures can be read into the Bible Society's *Open the Book* project which involves volunteers from churches across the UK presenting Bible stories in primary school assemblies. Although this input has been appreciated by many – for 2,000 schools were reported as taking part in its programmes in 2015 – schools do not have to rely for good collective worship on visitors from outside to do it for them. The goodwill and honest efforts of teachers leading collective worship should be recognized, as should their frequent success. It is perhaps significant that some of the most exciting collective worship events observed during research in schools, or recalled by pupils (a Diwali assembly, a Christingle, a series recounting the events of Holy Week), have been those events that have placed the content firmly within its faith context, linked it to particular communities and used it as an opportunity to recognize and celebrate the diverse religious traditions of society and school communities. In such cases there was often greater emphasis on the experience than the message in keeping with the stipulation of Circular 1/94 that collective worship should be something 'special' and capable of 'eliciting response' (Department of Education, 1994, para. 57; para. 59). As the infant school head teacher cited earlier declared, the collective community identity being formed through such worship events was an identity of celebration ('a community in celebration') and of plurality, rather than an identity bound to any of the narratives shared in this way. The nature of the 'collective' gathered together in 'collective worship' will be explored further at the end of this chapter.

Theological framework

The influence of the teacher is felt not just in the presentation of specific content but also in the overarching theological framework within which collective worship is conceived. The tension noted earlier between diversity and inclusivity has led, in several of the schools researched, to a shift in the delivery of collective worship, from the ethical (human rights) principle of treating people of different religious persuasions as equals (for example by giving a more balanced weighting to different religious traditions within collective worship) to a theological position that assumes the equal value of those beliefs – a position founded on a commendable desire to be even-handed and inclusive, but perhaps not fully cognizant of the implications. There are parallels with debates in the sphere of inter faith dialogue. While some see pluralist theologies of religions (such of those of John Hick 1980 and Paul Knitter 1985) as the foundation of inter religious engagement, critics argue that, by implying that different religions are equally valid interpretations of divine reality, these theological positions actually exclude from interreligious engagement those who hold that their own tradition

guards a truth not found in other religions (the oneness of God, the unique-
ness of Christ, the special status of the Qur'ān (D'Costa, 1987; 2000).[9] A
challenge for collective worship is to be doubly inclusive in content and in
response; to encourage respect for a diversity of faith traditions through
the content delivered while allowing a differentiated response from the
students according to their particular relationships to the religious material and their positions in relationship to its truth.

Cheetham's research found that teachers delivering collective worship often resorted to a promotion of pluralistic theologies. There was a
tendency to focus on commonalty and downplay difference. One primary
school teacher (interviewed for a Warwick research project) showed how
concern to present them as fundamentally the same could lead to a superficial, lowest-common-denominator presentation of religious traditions
in collective worship and in religious education: 'As I keep saying to the
children, religions are basically very similar ... all the gods are basically
saying the same thing of how we must be patient and how we must be
respectful' (Ipgrave et al., 2010). Another, related tendency among several
of the respondents was to present religions as options from which the
young people could make their own autonomous choice based on reason
or preference, thus a liberal concept of religion (as private and constructed)
is being promoted (Cheetham, 2004, 113f). This is in line with John Hull's
suggestion that assemblies should, from time to time, be used to impart
some understanding of other religions 'not to secure commitment nor to
profess faith but to deepen understanding and facilitate choice' (Hull, 1984,
15). However, it sits uneasily with much religious teaching that emphasizes
the given nature of faith, such as the idea in Islam that one is born Muslim,
or, for example, the inherited nature of Jewish identity and the special
relationship with God it entails, or, for Christians, Jesus' pronouncement,
'You have not chosen me, but I have chosen you' (John 15:16).

Another move towards inclusivity in collective worship is the search,
in the name of universality and impartiality, for something beyond and

---

9   One obstacle to involvement for many Muslims is the (mistaken) idea that it
     involves subscribing to the views that 'your faith is mine and there is no difference'
     (Muhammad Shafiq and Mohammed Abu-Nimur, 2007, 7).

outside religion (and often outside reference to a divine source) to which religions hold a subordinate place, a kind of tradition-less spirituality. One junior school policy declared that 'spiritual development ... transcends the potential barriers of religious and cultural difference ... spiritual development relates to that aspect of inner life through which pupils acquire insights into their personal existence which are of enduring worth' (Cheetham, 2004, 150; 148f). The teacher here is expressing a view that is often found in educational circles influenced by the University of Nottingham's Children's Spirituality Project directed by David Hay and Clive and Jane Erriker's Children and Worldviews Project (Chichester Institute of Higher Education) which were in turn enthused by the theories of zoologist Alastair Hardy (*The Spiritual Nature of Man*) and Mircea Eliade's *The Sacred and the Profane* (Erriker and Erriker, 2000; Hay and Nye, 1998; Hardy, 1979; Eliade, 1959). Others in the field have noted tensions between these interpretations of the relationship between spirituality and religion and theologies (including the hermeneutics of Christian philosopher, Paul Ricoeur) that emphasize humankind's relationship with and dependency on a personal God, or seek to balance what they see as overvaluing of spiritual experience, with reminders of the importance to religious understanding of the revelation of God's Word (Ricoeur, 1995; Wright, 2000; Ipgrave 2013). In Hebraic religion, Ricoeur reminds us, 'the word outweighs the numinous'; the numinous is just 'the underlying canvas from which the word detaches itself' (Ricoeur, 1995, 56). Thus while the concept of universal, extra-religious spirituality has wide purchase in community schools, it is not uncontested. It remains important to give the traditional strong and organic connection between religion and spirituality its due and to avoid the danger of tradition-free spirituality becoming a light-weight affair.

In both cases (religion as personal choice between equally valid options, or a spirituality that is both internal and transcends religion) theological positions are being taken. One question to be asked is whether, in their concern to make the message of collective worship universally applicable, teachers are being led by the logic of the requirement to promulgate a new theology; Cheetham suggests teachers who lead collective worship have become 'high priests of a new spirituality' (Cheetham, 2004, 91). Another question is how collective worship might attain that universal applicability while catering for the divergent religious (and non-religious) beliefs held by the different groups and individuals who make up British society and the communities of its schools. The answer to this last question is crucial for the continuance of collective worship. Clarity about the provenance within traditions of the varied religious resources, customs, stories, texts introduced in collective worship, and the explicit allowance of differentiated responses from the young people according to their own religious (and non-religious) positions might go some way towards meeting the challenges that have been discussed. Teachers have received very little guidance, however, on how this might be achieved.

Interpreting collective worship

'Worship'

Much of the controversy about collective worship hangs on interpretations of the term 'worship', a term that is perceived by some to be too religious for the context of the community school. In Scotland the term 'worship' is not used for collective gatherings of this nature but 'religious observance' is used instead. In some quarters this term in fact has a stronger association than 'worship' with following traditionally prescribed rites, ceremonies and disciplines, and so its adoption is further evidence that clarity is not to be found in terminology alone but depends on interpretation and use. To confuse the field further, 'worship' is sometimes employed to translate words in other languages where the correlation is not exact. In the case of Islam the mismatch between concepts of 'worship' commonly engaged in collective worship or religiously plural worship and *ibadah* (the Islamic term commonly translated as 'worship') has been viewed by some Muslim teachers as both an obstacle to and legitimization of such activity. One of the Muslim teachers in the 2015 questionnaire demonstrated the difficulty of translation when he declared, 'Worship in Islam has specific meaning and is done through prescribed manners such as the daily prayers and *zikr*. Calling school gatherings as worship may not be appropriate in Islamic terms and can be confusing for the students'.[10] While use is important, it is not helpful for different schools to adopt completely open 'meaning-in-use' understandings of collective worship, whereby the meaning of the term is determined by the practice that is so described in each institution. Such an understanding could, for example, turn an assembly consisting of little more than sharing school information into 'worship' should the school choose to use the collective worship period in this way. Instead, it is evident that, in legislation and guidance, the term is taken to denote an activity which, though it might vary according to context and circumstance, is nevertheless intended to fit within certain parameters, to be something 'special or separate' from ordinary activity and have reference to 'a divine being or power' (DfE, 1994, para. 57). Getting the right degree of openness within these boundaries is a challenge. Difficulties achieving this balance between contextually sensitive flexibility and religious reference can lead to the kind of confusing contrasts in collective worship experience noted by one teenager; 'At primary school ... they always lit a candle and said, "God said, let there be light! Jesus said 'I am the light of the world!'" And every assembly after it we said a thankful prayer. At high school the assembly says something like "Rugby is cancelled"' (Ipgrave & McKenna, 2008, 137).

The British Humanist Association has declared that worship is not possible without shared religious faith, but, despite the confidence with which it states its claim, this is not a self-evident truth relying as it does on a particular, restricted understanding of what constitutes 'worship'. While the legislation and guidance of Circular 1/94 recognizes different forms of worship in the distinction between 'corporate worship' (the activity of 'a group with beliefs in common') and 'collective worship' that does not require this commonalty, the debate over collective worship in schools often lacks a differentiated definition. It should also be acknowledged that there

10	The authors of the Church of England's 1992 guidance on multifaith worship observe that 'some Muslims would regard only the ritual Islamic prayer of *salat* and *namaz* as real worship and so may feel more free to join in other religious activities without compromise' (Inter-Faith Consultative Group, 1992, 28).

is no common concept of 'worship' differently translated into different languages and expressed in different faiths (CTBI, 2000). The specific context of schools within our education system that do not have a designated religious character, or that have a mix of religious and non-faith positions among its pupils and teachers, requires a more nuanced understanding of what worship can or does entail. The school context is not unrelated to some other situations where the intentions, religious beliefs and identities of attendees at worship vary widely: civic occasions and memorial services that involve worship; weddings, baptisms and funerals. Christmas celebrations and traditional choral evensong also attract a variety of religious and non-religious attendees, as do Buddhist meditation sessions. In some of these cases only certain people attending will be fully involved in all the rituals and ceremonies, but others are not excluded on account of faith identity and belief. If, then, it is 'all right' for the non-believing to attend these events, what makes it 'all right'?[11] To what extent are those attending actually participating in worship and what is the nature of that participation? These are questions that have exercised those involved in the field of inter-faith dialogue and relations with their concern to bring people of different faith communities and backgrounds together in a meaningful way. Inter-faith literature that explores the possibilities and parameters of shared worship is therefore relevant to our theme. There are differences with general inter-faith practice, however, in that school collective worship is not (or by law should not be) occasional and only linked to special events but is frequent and regular and organized with the intention that the whole student community attends and all are able to respond meaningfully to its content. The student attendees are to be something more than mere witnesses or observers at another's theatre. In this section's exploration of worship, distinctions between *cultic* and *non-cultic* worship, the concept of *performative* worship, the difference between worship as *practice* and worship as *experience*, will be applied, and some of the problems and possibilities considered for a school collective worship that is aware of and sensitive to its import for those taking part.

---

11   It may be that there are some minority religious groups for whom such attendance is not 'all right'. In collective worship the withdrawal clause caters for their needs.

Following the example of theologian, Gavin D'Costa, a useful distinction can be made in several major faith traditions between *cultic* and *non-
cultic* worship.[12] The former cannot be fully shared by those outside the
faith as the prayers and rituals form part of public self-identification within
that faith (D'Costa, 2000, 147). One obvious example of *cultic* worship
is the Christian Eucharist which in a real sense is about the formation of
a body – expressed in the words, 'although we are many we are one body
because we all share in one bread'. It is thus essentially *corporate* rather than
collective. Other examples with *cultic* reference, reserved for a particular
faith community, are the recitation of the Christian creed in worship or
salat prayers for Muslims. They are not activities in which religiously mixed
assemblies of people can be expected to participate. A reported example
of a misunderstanding of the parameters of *cultic* worship and of school
collective worship is an instance where a local imam was invited to lead a
collective worship session in a community secondary school with a large
majority of Muslim pupils. Mistaking his brief, he chose to lead the assembly in praying *salat*. Most of the gathered assembly, being Muslims, made
the accompanying actions bowing down to the floor, while the minority
non-Muslim (Christian and Hindu) students were left standing dotted
around the school hall embarrassedly looking across room at each other as
the worship took place. Neither they nor their Muslim peers would have
felt it appropriate for them to join in. While this example from a school
in Leicester happened fifteen years ago, present concerns (expressed in
the media and political circles) about an 'Islamization' of certain public
schools, mean greater clarity about distinctions between *cultic* and *non-
cultic* worship would be valuable. The inappropriateness of this example of
collective worship does not preclude the worshipping together of Muslims
and non-Muslims however.

   Non-cultic worship differs from *cultic* in that it is does not have the
character of set rituals and ceremonies but is more spontaneous or is tailored
to a particular occasion (ibid. 147). Its possibilities for shared worship were

---

12   Here the term 'cultic' (related to a particular system of traditional religious worship
     with distinct rites and ceremonies) is not linked to the concept of 'cult' as a minority
     religious sect with novel or deviant beliefs and practices.

recognized back in 1969 by the then Vatican Secretariat for Non-Christians in its *Guidelines for a Dialogue between Muslims and Christians*:

> Some people ask if we can pray with Muslims. Although it is evident that we must not take part actively in the cult of another religion, we can be associated with spontaneous prayer. Nevertheless, apart from special and very rare occasions, when certain prayers drawn from one or other religious heritage could be said in common, it would seem preferable to compose, or better still get others to compose, special prayers, which can express the religious sentiment of all those taking part. (Secretariat pro Non-Christianis, 1969, 140)

The document goes on to recommend some psalms or selected texts from Muslim mystics as providing material of generally acceptable content. Against this idea of mutually acceptable prayers is concern that the result will be a watered-down, lowest-common-denominator expression of faith, for example, Christians praying without reference to the triune God because this would be unacceptable to their Muslim co-worshippers. Worship in accordance with such multi-religious formulae is not then a substitute for prayer within the worshipper's own tradition, but is designed for specific non-denominational/inter-faith contexts. A common approach to multi-religious worship in schools is to adopt phrasing that leaves the identity of the addressee open for the worshipper to direct it according to their own faith, whether the prayer is a prayer of thanksgiving ('we thank you for ...'), penitence ('I am sorry for ...'), petition ('help me to ...'), intercession ('look after ...', 'may the people of the world ...'). Prayers of adoration and praise for God, or of oblation (offering oneself to God) may be less appropriate in such settings. The question to whom those without a religious belief direct their thoughts in a collective worship context is, perhaps, less straightforward than it would be for their religious peers, but solutions might be found even if it is for them to thank the world for being, or mentally to address their entreaties to those within their own lives who give them strength and support. Some schools adopt an approach of using silent reflection rather than prayer because of sensitivities about imposing inappropriate formulae on the young people, though in such cases the pupils are often given little guidance about what to do during these moments of reflection other than keep silent (Cheetham, 2004, 113).

Another concept that has value for determining what is and what is not appropriate for school collective worship, is the concept of *performative* worship, informed by linguist John Austin's distinction between words that *describe* (constative) and words that *do* (performative) (Austin, 1962). *Performative* speech, that does not just describe, but changes reality, has particular importance within religious contexts. In these contexts actions too may have a greater significance in terms of what they actually perform than the immediately obvious consequences. To refer again to the example of Eucharistic worship, what the priest visibly does at the altar – takes the bread and wine, recites Jesus' words at the Last Supper – is quantitatively different from the great mystery of Christ's presence and unity with Christ's Church, that, in Christian understanding, his/her words and actions (met by God's grace) actually initiate. Outside church schools and independent schools the Eucharist is rarely incorporated into collective worship, but the difference between surface words and actions and what they in religious understanding actually perform, works at multiple levels and in multiple circumstances. Within a multi-religious and non-denominational collective worship setting, the teacher needs to be aware that the use or imitation of particular words, formulae and actions from religious traditions may have significance for pupils or their parents beyond what they intended. One teacher discovered this when she chose to illustrate the *haj* pilgrimage in collective worship by getting a child to walk seven times round a chair (representing the *kabbah*), only to be told by a Muslim mother that this act was paramount to venerating the chair, giving it sacred significance.[13] For many Muslims certain acts and words of prayer may have the *performative* role of taking away sins or purifying the soul. In Christianity, sacraments (including the Eucharist, absolution, baptism and marriage) have a *performative* character, putting people into a new relationship with God and with each other. Pledges and acts of dedication, as *performative* speech acts, are common elements in Christian worship whether as prayers or in hymns ('Take my life and let it be, consecrated lord to thee';

13   From a conversation with a Warwick University researcher.

'O Jesus, I have promised to serve thee to the end').[14] These liturgical acts and promises are understood in Christian theology as the 'return-gift' of the people in response to the action of the Holy Spirit preparing them to receive God's grace (Duffy, 2005, 242). To engage in them is to allow oneself to be taken into a relationship with God or into the community that is the Church. *Cultic* worship fits into a *performative* category, but *non-cultic* worship, for example where the dedication of self is involved, may also have a *performative* force.

Most would agree that the purity of souls, covenantal relationships with God and growing the Church are areas beyond the expectations and deliberate intentions of collective worship in schools outside the faith sector. Some schools acknowledge these parameters in the advice teachers give on the use of 'Amen' at the end of prayers, for example, several schools adopt the formula recommended by the Essex and Cumbria and other SACREs; 'I would like you to listen to this prayer, and if you would like to make the prayer your own, you can do so by saying "Amen" at the end' (Essex SACRE, 2013, 18; Cumbria SACRE, 2014, 9). The *Open the Book* project makes use of the same formula. Making the prayer one's own is to accept a *performative* function for that prayer, positioning oneself within the community to which it belongs and the relationship with God that it signifies. It is not dissimilar to writing one's signature at the end of what has been said. What is of interest in this collective worship strategy is that this formula sets up a distinction between *performative* and non-*performative* engagement, a distinction that mirrors that made by the junior school head teacher cited above when he allowed that, in a given collective worship event, some of his students would be engaged in reflection while others might be engaged in prayer.

---

14   For some what is viewed as *performative* covers a very wide range of activities, to enter the place of worship of another faith, to read or hear their scriptures or their music, to view their images, is to affect negatively in real terms one's standing with God or one's purity. There may be accommodations that cannot be made within collective worship without having a negative impact on the opportunities provided for other students. In such rare cases the withdrawal clause may be the only alternative.

In his chapter on worship, in *Theology Remixed*, Adam English, makes a useful distinction, for our purposes, between *experiencing* and *practicing* worship (English, 2010, 188). According to Circular 1/94, school collective worship should both be concerned with reverence or veneration to a divine being or power *and* be capable of eliciting response from all pupils (Department of Education, 1994, para. 57); '"Taking part" in collective worship implies more than simply passive attendance' (ibid. para. 59). This combination (within the same collective worship events) of opportunities to worship God for religiously believing pupils and the engagement of the non-religious presents a challenge but not an impossibility for schools. Directing his work to a Christian audience, English's prime interest is in the *practice* of worship which he characterizes as *performative* because in it 'we return the *whole self* to God'. The *practice* of worship may be more than the 'emotional high', 'the cathartic cleansing', 'a psychological release', 'the rush of adrenaline when singing', 'the soothing calm of praying', than 'pious thoughts', 'than a stirring in the heart', but these responses – these non-performative *experiences* of worship – also have a value (English, 2010, 188–189). They might be student responses to the emotional drama and cognitive challenge of religious narratives and scriptures, to the inspiration and example of religious lives, to the words, rhythms and meanings of religious prayer, to the sights and sounds of religiously inspired art, music and theatre, to the natural wonders that for religious believers tell of God's creation. They speak to the aim of the secondary school cited above that its students, should gain 'through instruction, exposition and imaginative appeal a sense of the beauty of holiness'. They also include powerful elements to be found in secular understandings of spirituality that are often used as non-religious justifications for collective worship. Although it might entail a challenging balancing act, the combination of *practising* and *experiencing* worship incorporates the sense of direction towards an object of worship recognized in the 'reverence or veneration paid to a divine being or power' of Circular 1/94 paragraph 57, and the subjective response of paragraph 59, religious and secular orientations being catered for.

'Collective'

This chapter has unpicked the term 'worship' to explore what understandings and forms of worship might be appropriate to schools without a religious character or with a religiously plural student population and retain the
religious reference. The emphasis has been on differentiated understandings
of worship that enable individual worshippers of different religious and
non-religious backgrounds and beliefs to participate in a way meaningful
to their respective positions. In this section the emphasis will be on what it
might be that unites and so gives value to the *gathering* of school members
in the worship event. It has already been seen how important the sense of
'community' and 'togetherness' is to the teachers involved. The term 'collective' will be examined for its significance to our theme, the exploration
supported by the discussions of those involved in guidance for inter-faith
relations. The 1944 Education Act made an intentional choice to require
'collective' rather than 'corporate' worship in acknowledgement of the
fact that those collected for worship will not share a religious faith or faith
identity in the way those participating in 'corporate' worship might. The
question remains what it is that unites the 'collective' around this act of
worship. To understand this we explore the concept of 'co-intentionality'
as employed by Gavin D'Costa and explicated in a guidance document,
Christian Parameters of Multi- Faith Worship for Churches Together, produced by Churches Together in Britain and Ireland (D'Costa, 2000; CTBI,
2000). This guidance points out that unless there is found underlying a
gathering for worship some spirituality of shared intentionality inclusive
of all present, the ideology of 'pick and choose' 'bourgeois consumerism'
can come to dominate multifaith worship (CTBI, 2000, 8).

   D'Costa posits three levels of intentionality, heart, mind and action,
which together provide a holistic context for speaking about intention.
At the level of the heart is the desire to worship, though one's intentions
may not be explicitly known or finely articulated (D'Costa, 2000, 155). It
is an intention unaffected by propositional correctness but is more akin
to the sighs of the Spirit ('for we do not know how to pray as we might')
in Paul (Rom. 8:26). The second level concerns the mind and explicit conceptual knowledge (ibid. 156), an area where the irreducible differences of

propositional truth claims between religions, as well as varying understandings of worship, have an impact on the degree to which, at this level, *co-intentionality* can be attained. The third level is that of action emphasizing the point that prayer (and worship) is not pure interiority but is related to other aspects of life. Arguments against the practice of collective worship in schools have often focussed on propositional beliefs and the irreconcilability between them, but D'Costa's model aims to show that praying (or for our purposes, worshipping) with 'one accord' is not exclusively a doctrinal matter, but 'a complex interplay between head, heart and practice' (ibid. 158). In the school context the level of the 'mind' is the one at which divergence might be acceptable provided some convergence at the other two levels is aimed at. A translation of these levels to the context of school collective worship looks something like this:

> HEART – intention of the heart is a desire to worship OR desire to commit ourselves to respect for and openness towards each other in the presence of that which is significant/sacred to us OR a desire to celebrate X or commemorate Y.

> MIND – intention of the mind engages with propositional beliefs and is the place where commonalty in a combined multi-faith and non-faith gathering is least likely to be achievable and so should not be expected.

> ACTIONS – intention of action can involve living out one's life together as influenced by the collective experience OR could relate to the actions of worship and ask 'how these might be patterned to express and enable some measure of co-intentionality between people of different faiths' and none who make up the collective. (CTBI, 2000, 5)

Conclusion

To sum up the arguments of this chapter it can be noted that a number of key questions and issues have been identified that require consideration before recommendations can be made about the future of collective worship in non-religious and religiously plural schools. These include the appropriateness of a religiously informed collective worship to the religious background of the pupils, its value to the community of the school and as preparation for wider society, the ownership and use of the religious content of collective worship, the implications of different understandings of 'worship' and 'collective' experience that might legitimize and support the continuation and improvement of provision.

For context, this chapter has stressed the importance of recognizing and valuing the backgrounds and perspectives of pupils for whom religion is a key element in their lives, while considering what might be gained from religiously informed collective worship individually for those without religious background as well as collectively for the religiously mixed community of the school. For content, this chapter has recognized the role of the teacher in the use of the religious material in collective worship. It relates this role to the continuing interpretive activity that always underpins any use of religious texts and objects, resulting in the rich plurality of interpretations from within the faith traditions. At the same time, the chapter recommends that, as far as possible, teachers be sensitive towards the significance of texts and objects to the identity and deeply held convictions of the faith communities. Above all the chapter seeks to counter simplistic interpretations of 'worship' that either widen its scope so far as to make it meaningless, or so restrict it as to make it impossible within a school setting. It stands on the principle that the challenges posed by collective worship are not sufficient reasons for getting rid of the requirement for schools; rather they provide the stimulus for the more detailed exploration and consideration of the practice initiated by this Collective Worship Network. In this exploration it has been found valuable to engage with the theologically informed theories and practice of those who recognize the civic and relational value (as well as the parameters) of joint opportunities for worship in our religiously plural society, and through this engagement to develop a nuanced understanding of 'worship' that allows for shared experience and commonality of intention and action while respecting the individual pupil's integrity and freedom of response.

References

Arweck, E. (Ed.) (2017). *Young People's Attitudes to Religious Diversity*. London: Routledge.

Austin, J. L. (1962). *How to Do Things with Words. The William James Lectures Delivered at Harvard University in 1955*. J. O. Urmson & M. Sbisá (Eds.). Oxford: Clarendon Press.

BHA. *Collective Worship*. Retrieved May 3, 2017, from <https://humanism.org.uk/campaigns/schools-and-education/collective-worship/>.

BHA. *'Collective Worship' and School Assemblies: your rights*. Retrieved May 3, 2017, from <https://humanism.org.uk/education/parents/collective-worship-and-school-assemblies-your-rights/>.

Bible Society (2015). *Open the Book Reaches 2000 Schools*. Retrieved May 3, 2017, from <http://www.biblesociety.org.uk/news/open-the-book-reaches-2000-schools/>.

Byfield, C. (2008). The Impact of Religion on the Educational Achievement of Black Boys: a UK and US Study. *British Journal of Sociology of Education, 29*(2), 189–199.

Cheetham, R. (2004). *Collective Worship: Issues and Opportunities*. London: SPCK.

Copley, T., & Savini, H. (1998). The State of the Bible in State Schools. *The Bible in Transmission*, The Bible Society, 5–8.

CTBI (2000). *Christian Parameters of Multi-Faith Worship for Churches Together*. Churches Together in Britain and Ireland. Retrieved August 25, 2015, from <http://www.ctbiarchive.org/pdf_view.php?id=93>.

Cumbria SACRE (2014). *Best Practice in Collective Worship: Guidance from Cumbria SACRE*. Cumbria SACRE.

D'Costa, G. (1987). *John Hick's Theology of Religions, A Critical Evaluation*. Lanham/New York/London: University Press of America.

D'Costa, G. (2000). *The Meeting of Religions and the Trinity*. Maryknoll: Orbis Books.

Department for Education (1994). *Collective Worship in Schools*. Circular 1/94. London: HMSO.

DfES (2006). *Ethnicity and Education: The evidence on minority ethnic pupils aged 5–16*. London: Department for Education and Skills.

Duffy, Mn. (2005). *How Language, Ritual and Sacraments Work: According to John Austin, Jürgen Habermas and Louis-Marie Chauvet*. Rome: Georgian University Press.

Eliade, M. (1959). *The Sacred and the Profane*. Orlando: Harcourt Inc.

English, A. C. (2010). *Theology Remixed: Christianity as Story, Game, Language and Culture*. Illinois: IVP Academic.

Erriker, C. & J. (2000). The Children and Worldviews Project: A Narrative Pedagogy of Religious Education. In M. Grimmitt (Ed.), *Pedagogies of Religious Education* (pp. 188–206). Great Wakering: McCrimmons.

Essex SACRE (2013). *Guidance on Collective Worship in Schools*. Essex County Council.

Grimmitt, M., Grove, J., Hull, J., & Spencer L. (1991). *A Gift to the Child: Religious Education in the Primary School*. Hemel Hempstead: Simon and Schuster.

Hardy, A. (1979). *The Spiritual Nature of Man: Study of Contemporary Religious Experience*. Oxford: Clarendon Press.

Hay, D., & Nye, R. (1998). *The Spirit of the Child*. London: Harper Collins.

Hick, J. (1980). *God has Many Names: Britain's New Religious Pluralism*. Philadelphia: The Westminster Press.

Hull, J. (1984). *Studies in Religion and Education*. Lewes: Falmer Press.

Hull, J. (2000). Religion in the Service of the Child Project: the Gift Approach to Religious Education. In M. Grimmit (Ed.), *Pedagogies of Religious Education* (pp. 172–188). Great Wakering: McCrimmons.

Inter-Faith Consultative Group (1992). *Multi-Faith Worship?* London: Church House Publishing.

Ipgrave, J. (2010). Including the Religious Viewpoints and Experiences of Muslim Students in an Environment that is both Plural and Secular. *Journal of International Migration and Integration, 11*(1), 5–22.

Ipgrave, J. (2012a). Conversations between the Religious and Secular in English Schools. *Religious Education, 107*(1), 30–48.

Ipgrave, J. (2012b). Relationships between local patterns of religious practice and young people's attitudes to the religiosity of their peers. *Journal of Beliefs and Values, 33*(3), 261–274.

Ipgrave, J. (2013). From Storybooks to Bullet Points: Books and the Bible in Primary and Secondary RE. *British Journal of Religious Education, 35*(3), 264–281.

Ipgrave, J., & McKenna, U. (2008). English Students' Perspectives on Religion and Religious Education. In T. Knauth, D. P. Jozsa, G. Bertram-Troost, & J. Ipgrave (Eds.), *Encountering Religious Pluralism in School and Society* (pp. 113–148). Münster: Waxmann.

Ipgrave, J., Miller, J., & Hopkins, P. (2010). Responses of Three Muslim Majority Primary Schools in England to the Islamic Faith of their Pupils. *Journal of International Migration and Integration, 11*(1), 73–89.

Jackson, R., Ipgrave, J., Hayward, M., Hopkins, P., Fancourt, N., Robbins, M., Francis L., & McKenna, U. (2010). *Materials Used to Teach about World Religions in Schools in England*. London: Department for Children, Schools and Families.

Knitter, P. (1985). *No Other Name? Critical Survey of Christian Attitudes towards the World Religions*. Maryknoll: Orbis Books.

Lindlof, T. R. (2002). Interpretive Community: An Approach to Media and Religion. *Journal of Media and Religion, 1*(1), 61–74.

Oldfield, E. (2015). *Abolishing the Collective Act of Worship.* Retrieved August 25, 2015, from <http://www.theosthinktank.co.uk/comment/2015/06/15/not-worship-at-all-should-we-abolish-the-collective-act-of-worship-in-schools>.

Panjwani, F. (2014). Faith Schools and the Religious Other: the Case of Muslim Schools. In J. D. Chapman, S. MacNamara, M. Reiss, & Y. Waghid (Eds.), *The International Handbook on Learning, Teaching and Leading in Faith-Based Schools* (pp. 139–156). Dordrecht: Springer.

Panjwani, F. (2015). Educational Reform. *Critical Muslim*, July-September, *15*.

Ricoeur, P. (1995). *Figuring the Sacred: Religion, Narrative, Imagination.* Minneapolis: Augsburg Fortress.

Secretariat pro Non-Christianis (1971). *Guidelines for a Dialogue between Muslims and Christians.* Rome: Edizion Ancora (1st edn 1969).

Shafiq, M., & Mohammed. A. (2007). *Interfaith Dialogue: A Guide for Muslims.* Herndon: The International Institute of Islamic Thought.

Wright, A. (2000). *Spirituality and Education.* Abingdon: Routledge.

NORMAN RICHARDSON AND AIDEEN HUNTER

11 Educational Perspectives on School Collective Worship: Beyond Obituary

ABSTRACT

Much has changed in education in all parts of the United Kingdom over the period since the post-war Education Acts of the 1940s prescribed 'a daily act of collective worship' in England, Wales and Northern Ireland. While religious education in most of the UK has changed significantly in response to a much more diverse and plural society, collective worship/religious observance now appears to many people, including educational professionals, to be anachronistic. This chapter will analyse this changed situation and review some of the discussions and proposals from religious, educational, secular and political perspectives. While three main approaches seem to be evident in the current debate – maintaining the status quo, reform, abolishing the requirement – some attention will be given to the view that a modified activity might focus on 'spiritual development' and inclusive 'shared values'.

Introduction

In the title of a major early work published in 1975 the eminent writer on religious education, John Hull, pronounced an obituary on school worship. Over forty years later Hull's verdict may seem to be deserving of the same remark that Mark Twain made when he read his own obituary in *The New York Times*, namely that it was 'greatly exaggerated'! Yet a close re-reading of Hull's detailed discussion of the issue suggests that notwithstanding the significant changes in educational legislation and practice since the mid-1970s his analysis still offers much that is helpful in the contemporary debate. Hull's work stands out as probably the major contribution on this issue and he was undoubtedly ahead of his time; more recent developments, notably s. 7 of the 1988 Education Act (England and Wales) and the subsequent Circular 1/94 which required that school worship should be 'wholly or mainly of a broadly Christian character', appear regressive on this issue by comparison.

In order to understand the current place of collective worship in the education system, it is important to examine how educational thinking and practice has changed considerably over the past half-century. Taking into account these changes along with the analysis of Hull and others, this chapter will map the transition (or lack thereof) of collective worship in order to attempt to understand its current and future role in education. Due to the similarities in collective worship legislation in England, Wales and Northern Ireland, much of the discussion in this chapter will relate primarily to those parts of the UK, although many of the broader educational issues are no less relevant to the situation of religious observance in Scotland.

Terminology and reservations

Across the jurisdictions of the United Kingdom different terminology is employed to discuss and refer to this dimension of school activity. In England, Wales and Northern Ireland the legally correct term is 'collective worship', though 'School Assembly' (sometimes 'assembly for worship') is commonly employed in everyday use. Statutory collective worship was set into legislation by the post-war 1944 Education Act in England and Wales and the similar 1947 Act in Northern Ireland. Acts of worship – or 'observances' (Hull, 1975, 12) – had taken place in many schools prior to this but were not legally required and were generally perceived as a dimension of religious instruction. In Scotland, the terminology of 'religious observance' was retained and remains in use up to the present. While the 1944 and 1947 Acts in England, Wales and Northern Ireland stipulated daily worship in all state-funded schools, Scotland remained less prescriptive in the nature of its 'observances' and this has changed little over successive decades. Scotland's 'religious observances' are distinct from school assemblies and happen at regular intervals – 'sufficiently frequently to have an impact on the spiritual development of the school community' (Curriculum for Excellence, 2017). Their focus ('Community acts which aim to promote the spiritual development of all members of the school's community and express and celebrate the shared values of the school community' (ibid.)) is also different from practice in the other three regions. Unlike other UK jurisdictions, in Northern Ireland over the past thirty years there has been no significant examination of collective worship and almost a complete absence of reference to it in policy documents and Department of Education advice. Minor changes to legislation in the various regions over the years have permitted assemblies for worship to take place in non-whole-school groupings (year groups, single classes or other smaller combinations), in recognition of the difficulty of larger schools providing a space for all pupils together. While the 1988 specification that collective worship should be of a 'broadly Christian nature' only applied to England and Wales, the general assumption throughout the UK has continued to be that collective worship/religious observance is perceived or intended to be Christian worship. Yet despite the close association between religious education (RE) and collective worship in legislation, the significant changes in most of the UK towards a multifaith approach to RE have seemed to many people to be increasingly at odds with the legal requirement for confessional (implicitly Christian) collective worship.

It is striking to note that authors in the past who accepted the assumptions of a confessional approach to RE had no difficulty in referring to the links between teaching and school worship (e.g. see the writings of James Smith, 1936, the National Society, 1939, and Doris Starmer Smith, 1945). However, over the past half-century, many or most of the writers promoting open or inclusive approaches to RE have steered well clear of such a link. Terence Copley made the point well when he wrote:

> If any activity connected with education looks on paper like religious indoctrination, this has to be it. ... School worship is an orphan in curriculum terms. Outside faith schools, nobody on the staff 'owns' it. Collective worship is frequently not resourced from the school budget. No teachers are trained to lead it. ... No one should be

surprised in the light of all this that worship in schools lacks friends and that it can easily be perceived as obsolete and unviable. (Copley, 2005, 128)

Geoff Teece has also picked up on this issue in a book designed for primary teachers, who are normally expected to teach the whole curriculum including RE. Despite the title *A Primary Teacher's Guide to RE and Collective Worship*, the worship section is left to a short chapter at the end of the book and he starts with a warning:

> Some RE advisers discourage their teachers from thinking of RE and collective worship as two sides of the same coin. This is understandable ... confusion can arise about the distinctiveness of each. ... Another reason ... is the fairly common perception that one activity (RE) is relatively non-controversial and the other (collective worship) is highly controversial. Maybe this is because, in the words of John Hull, people understand RE to be concerned with 'speaking about God' while collective worship is concerned with 'speaking to God'. (Teece, 2001, 114)

The complete absence of any reference to collective worship in some recent RE writing confirms the impression that many contemporary RE teachers prefer to keep clear blue water between their professional outlook and the perceived dubious territory of school worship. Some other teachers, not necessarily from the subject area of RE, have preferred to approach school worship from a 'spiritual development' perspective. Teachers in England are expected to provide opportunities to promote Spiritual, Moral, Social and Cultural (SMSC) education, and similar expectations are found in other UK jurisdictions. While they may take a wide range of views on the desirability and the nature of school worship, some teachers involved in SMSC do not appear to exhibit the same set of professional reservations as their RE colleagues, as evidenced, for example, in the quote from Tony Eaude at the end of this chapter. By contrast, many RE teachers and academics have clearly had to make a professional judgements about the extent to which they wish to be seen to be associated with worship in schools.

Religion, education and cultural diversity: Changed perceptions and practice

For many, collective worship is a nebulous concept difficult to define and therefore difficult to influence or direct. Frequently seen as a 'separate' part of school life which sits outside the mainstream, trends, changes and influences in educational thinking have often bypassed collective worship, leaving it as a relatively unchanged and unexamined part of the education system. As a result of this isolation, collective worship has largely been unrepresented in educational research though, from time to time, debates emerge about its purpose and relevance. Not only does collective worship appear to be in a different place from most other educational practice, research and dialogue, but it has also arguably remained aloof from changes and influences in social structure and demography (Leonard, 1988).

While it is closely linked to educational legislation and many people's perceptions with religious education, collective worship often seems to have stood still while RE has undergone many changes associated with cultural pluralism. Kincheloe and Steinberg (2002) identify various approaches towards a multicultural society on a spectrum beginning with 'conservative multiculturalism', or monoculturalism. Parekh (2000, 19) describes what he refers to as monism as 'the tendency to argue that only one way of life is the best and that all others can be judged and even graded'. This monoculturalist approach to education, and indeed to society at large, is typified in the 1944 Butler Education Act whereby the exploration of religion (solely Christianity) was housed within *religious instruction*, which was assumed to be complemented by school collective worship. In educational terms religious instruction is understood to include doctrinal or confessional teaching and devotional observances in relation to a particular faith or belief, with the intent of inculcation (which some would describe as 'indoctrination') to that faith. While religious instruction and collective worship faith schools could be delivered in a catechetical model, they were to be non-denominational in state schools. Non-denominationalism, however, remained based on Christian assumptions and did not include the examination or contemplation of other faiths, beliefs or practices. In this assimilative approach to multiculturalism other faiths and cultures were not represented in the daily workings of school life.

The social revolution experienced in society during the 1960s saw similar experimentation and examination of the purpose and method of state education – a liberalization of social values reflected in what McLaren (1999) terms a 'liberal humanist' approach and a move away from mono-culturalism. Increasing migration into the UK altered the demographic profile of the country and gave rise to a liberal multiculturalism agenda in policy, if not always in practice.

Various developments in educational thinking in much of the UK during this period led to a widening of the gap between religious education and collective worship, and a questioning of the once taken-for-granted link between the two as represented in 1940s legislation. Key influences on this change included Kohlberg's (1958, 1984) work on the stages of moral development, Goldman's (1964, 1965) research on stages of religious development (both of these significantly influenced by Piagetian ideas) and Loukes' (1961) examination of the religious attitudes of young people in which he called for more 'realism and relevance' (1961, 11) in the curriculum. Further change resulted from the popularization of Ninian Smart's phenomenological approach to religious study (1969) and the growing movement during the 1970s towards the inclusion of the study of world religions other than Christianity (notably reflected in the 1975 Birmingham RE Agreed Syllabus). It was during this period that John Hull, a major player in the changing approaches to RE, delivered his 1975 'obituary' for collective worship, which must have seemed an inevitable consequence of the thinking of the time.

The 1988 Education Reform Act in England and Wales officially renamed 'religious instruction' as 'religious education', belatedly acknowledging the move from an instructional and confessional RE towards a more objective and plural approach. While the 1988 Act stated that programmes of work should reflect 'the fact that religious traditions in the UK are in the main Christian', it did encourage pupils to learn from different religions, beliefs, values and traditions. It reflected the fact that RE had moved into a more plural approach and thereby highlighted how the perceived incompatibility with collective worship was becoming significantly more marked, notwithstanding the government's attempt in the same Act to re-emphasize the Christian nature of collective worship (as will be discussed below). Within a few years this plural and experiential approach had become mainstream, as reflected in various curriculum statements in England and Wales. For example, as the Qualifications and Curriculum Authority says:

> Religious education encourages pupils to develop their sense of identity and belonging. It enables them to flourish individually within their communities and as citizens in a pluralistic society and global community. (QCA, 2007)

As the multifaith curriculum increasingly required the study of contested worldviews, pupils were presented with the opportunity to evaluate, critically, their own and others' belief systems and to engage in intercultural encounters (Jackson, 2004; Keast, 2007). This emerging phase of critical multiculturalism has also impacted on the teaching of RE and other religious expressions in schools, as well as on the growing significance and influence of citizenship education (Gearon, 2004). As a result, and as highlighted by Teece (2001, 114–115), collective worship has seemed increasingly removed from progressive philosophy, at odds with the rest of the education system, and existing in something of a time warp.

Pluralism, equality and inclusion

Beyond the relationship with religious education, other changes impacting on perceptions of collective worship stem from debates on pluralism, equality and inclusion in the education system in general and everyday practice within schools. An emphasis on human rights principles and the introduction into the various UK jurisdictions of equality legislation have highlighted the importance of promoting a fair and more equal society; for example, the Equality Act of 2010, covering England, Wales and Scotland (separate equality legislation exists in Northern Ireland) was introduced to provide 'a legal framework to protect the rights of individuals and advance equality of opportunity for all' (Equality and Human Rights Commission). Within this context it is generally assumed and expected that schools will model and promote such values so that pupils will carry them into adulthood and into the restructuring of society. In 1997 the government established an Advisory Committee to examine 'the teaching of citizenship and democracy in schools', under the chairmanship of Professor Bernard Crick, leading to the introduction in England in 2002 of the Citizenship curriculum (linked to Personal, Social and Health Education (PSHE)). This was a direct attempt by policymakers to explore issues of equality, governance and political empowerment with young people. The emphasis was on citizenship as a life-skill in which

> [c]itizenship is more than a subject. If taught well and tailored to local needs, its skills and values will enhance democratic life for all of us, both rights and responsibilities, beginning in school and radiating out. (Crick, 1999)

Similar curriculum initiatives have been included in different ways, and under different terminology in other parts of the UK – such as *Local and Global Citizenship* in Northern Ireland post-primary schools; *PDMU* (Personal Development and Mutual Understanding) in Northern Ireland primary schools; *Active Citizenship* and *PSE* (Personal and Social Education) in Wales; and *Social Studies* in Scotland – in order to pursue similar aims. Across these four regions social and civic education has become part of the explicit curriculum. For example, schools in England must also provide SMSC (Spiritual, Moral, Social and Cultural Development) and related concepts operate elsewhere in the UK. By means of these initiatives pupils are exposed to, and participate in, experiences which are intended to foster tolerance, inclusion and equality. In this changed landscape, where does collective worship now sit?

Collective worship: John Hull's 'Obituary'

Having examined the broader context, it is worth looking in some detail at Hull's 1975 discussion on collective worship, which is important not least because he was eminently able to analyse it from both educational and theological perspectives. Beginning with an outline of the development of worship in schools from 1870 to the mid-1960s, Hull cited a circular sent out in 1878 requesting information on worship in the various school board areas which indicated that 'in very many maintained schools at this time there was, as in the church schools, little or no distinction between worship and religious instruction'. But '... [i]n many of the regulations governing worship and instruction there was a kind of strict neutrality' (Hull, 1975, 12) which at that time would have been understood in the sense of non-denominationalism. According to Hull, 'The neutrality of the period following 1870 gives way to the vigorous instruction of the period following 1944' (ibid. 46). He also noted that after the 1944 Act 'the word 'worship' began to take the place of the word 'observances' and 'the duties of personal and corporate religion take the place of the formal teaching of liturgy and ecclesiastical practices without regard for the spiritual growth of the individual' (ibid. 15).

It is clear, Hull argued, that after 1944 'there is no doubt at all that the school assembly was understood to be worship in the full sense of the word', citing, for example, the Herefordshire Agreed Syllabus of 1954: 'all religious instruction is part of the preparation for school worship' (ibid. 31). Worship, according to Hull, is always a response to God (in some form), conferring 'supreme value on the divine caller' (ibid. 35–60). Christian worship entails certain beliefs and 'requires the allegiance of the worshipper' (ibid. 36). This is the perception of worship that emerges from the period leading up to and following the 1944 Act, in keeping with an orthodox Christian understanding of worship, but, Hull suggests, it fails 'to give sufficient consideration to the relationship between worship and education' (ibid. 37).

Rejecting the notion of 'secular worship', which would clearly not be true worship in the sense understood by a religious believer, Hull wondered if schools could approach 'the threshold of worship' – a term he returns to later. Children may not understand much of what goes on in worship, according to their age, whether in church or in school, but the difference in church is that learning to experience worship can validly be regarded as part of the process of religious nurture, whereas schools (other than church/faith schools) have no such role (ibid. 42–43).

In Hull's analysis there are clear tensions between worship and education, not least in their attitudes towards controversy. In education everything is up for discussion and enquiry. As Hull put it, 'Religious education is ... not concerned with belief or dis-belief but with the grounds for belief and dis-belief' (ibid. 56). Moreover, for Hull, the religious educator 'is neutral about the truth claim of a given religion ... in the sense that it is not his object to secure commitment to or rejection of that religion ... he wants his pupils to understand them, to realize upon what they are based, to compare them with other claims, and to go on enquiring after them' (ibid. 59). Thus, Hull concluded that while it may be possible to learn through worship, 'worship and education cannot take place concurrently' (ibid. 59):

> To worship intelligently, as worship understands it, is to worship the Lord God and not Baal and to worship in spirit and in truth. But to worship intelligently, as education understands it, is to pass through a period of reflection in which you are exposed to the possibility that there might be neither God nor Baal to worship, or if they be, then they might not be worthy of worship. Education necessarily puts the possibility of worshipping at risk. (Ibid. 62)

In an age when the school can no longer be seen as 'an alleged Christian community' (ibid. 76), Hull suggested that 'school worship is left without support ... the aims and methods of classroom teaching are no longer compatible with the assumptions of worship' (ibid. 88–89). Moreover, he added that '[w]orship cannot be open; classroom teaching in religion must be open' and that '[t]he secularization of religious education has thus driven a wedge between the assembly and the classroom (ibid. 99).

Possible alternatives, according to Hull, might be to: (a) use a selection of materials from different faiths; (b) find materials that express the common values of all faiths; (c) adopt a broad definition of worship and incorporate a variety of religious ceremonies from all faiths (ibid. 90–91). But these are not really worship as such, and 'it is important to insist that religious education, having only just escaped from the clutches of one religion, must not be allowed to fall into the embrace of all of them together' (ibid. 91).

Hull also considered how worship has remained resistant to change or academic scrutiny, while RE has significantly changed and is inspected for its educational effectiveness. This conservatism may in part be due to the association between school worship and assembly as a means of reinforcing the hierarchy and discipline of the school. As Hull put it: '[t]he effect of all this upon the religious attitude of young people is rather negative ... School assembly can be thought of as an institutional form of child control through coalition with God. One begins to wonder whether religious education, already not one of the strong subjects of the curriculum, can afford the alliance with school assembly' (ibid. 102).

Finally, Hull proposed a non-worship approach to the school assembly with educational aims:

1. To widen the pupil's repertoire of appropriate emotional response ...
2. To encourage a reflective approach to living which transcends the immediacy of experience ...
3. To demonstrate the values ... upon which democratic society depends ...
4. To provide some experience and understanding of what worship is ... But this provision will not require any one to worship and will certainly not commit the school to corporate acts of worship. ... The first three objectives relate to central concerns of education and the last one is a contribution from religious education. (Ibid. 118–119)

This would be 'a time of sharing of ideals and visions' and for Hull such assemblies would 'not seek to secure commitment, not to profess faith but to deepen understanding and to facilitate choice' (ibid. 135–136). But Hull made clear that such occasions should not compromise the conscience of staff or pupils and that the motivations must be educational, not evangelistic:

> It is possible for Christians and those interested in religious education to understand these assemblies as being a threshold to worship, i.e. ... as being a preparation for an appreciation of what worship involves ... This interpretation is not required by the sort of assemblies we have described but it is a possible one. (Ibid. 125)

Hull returned to the issue in 1995 following the debates and concerns resulting from Section 7 of the 1988 Education Act and the Department of Education Circular 1/94, making a strong critique of the government's attempt to tighten the definitions around collective worship, namely that it should be 'wholly or mainly of a broadly Christian character'. Hull clearly believed that the new legislation was 'wrong in principle' and 'divisive':

> In its intention to strengthen collective worship so as to make a more effective contribution to the spiritual development of pupils and of the school, the Education Reform Act has overreached itself and become counterproductive. A gulf has opened between the search for spirituality in education and the function of collective worship in satisfying that need. ... The set of complex problems facing us will yield to a simple solution: repeal of Section 7 of the Education Reform Act 1988. ... The expression 'collective worship' should be removed and replaced by 'collective spirituality'. (Hull, 1995)

Terence Copley also expressed regret at the impact of the worship provisions of the 1988 Act:

> ... whatever impact the Act made upon the teaching profession in regard to its provision for RE was overshadowed by the negative reaction to the provision for collective worship. ... Head teachers saw the potential divisiveness of these requirements in their staffrooms and among their pupil populations, especially in multi-ethnic schools. It seemed as if years of work to make school worship a community occasion had been challenged by attempts legally to enforce Christian observance on school children. (Copley, 2008, 150)

Elsewhere Copley came to a similar conclusion to that of Hull and argued for a 'Thought for the Day' approach – not passive, but with responses from the children – though he expressed fears that teachers lack the confidence to talk about religion and spirituality with their pupils. He indicated support for the idea of assembly as a holistic approach to spiritual development and as a corrective to an education which 'has been reduced to the acquisition of a product' (Copley, 2005, 132). Noting that 'worship' understood in this way 'has the potential to be de-indoctrinatory because it offers a window into a different 'take' on life and is capable of looking at the whole', he suggested that:

> Those schools that are making links between collective worship and cross-curricular theme of spiritual development are making most progress here, as the act of collective

worship is being integrated into the life of the school and not left outside, the orphan in the cold. (Ibid. 131)

In the early years of the 2000s in England there was some evidence that the kind of approach proposed by Copley and Hull was regarded positively by Ofsted inspectors, as observed by Gill (2004, 195–196): 'Ofsted reports ... replace earlier statistical references to collective worship with similarly quantified comments in respect of spiritual development, perhaps quietly acknowledging current practice.'

A surprisingly strong defence of a more traditional approach to collective worship by an Ofsted Inspector, Margaret Warner, was published in a symposium (Best, 2000) on SMSC (Spiritual, Moral, Social and Cultural Development). In contrast to Hull and others writing from a religious education perspective, her position was overtly confessional and based on an interpretation of spiritual development that is fundamentally religious. Spirituality, in her definition, means 'that God is in all His creation and we see and begin to understand him through the subjects we learn, the experiences we have and the worship we offer, be it collective or personal worship' (Warner, 2000, 204). She appeared to be critical of a call by the National Association of Head Teachers for the requirements of collective worship to be lifted and stated:

> To start each day either offering the day to God or reflecting on how one is going to use it, is hardly something which should be controversial, but embraced as a move towards leading a worthwhile and positive life. Such daily experiences should not only serve pupils well at school, but also equip pupils for their lives outside school when they leave. (Ibid. 202)

Warner also offered criticism of those teachers who do not fully carry out the letter of the law, suggesting that 'the law should not bend to those who wish to ignore it', but that such teachers should 'support the head who is doing all in his power to fulfil it' (ibid. 204). The law, she argued, must be kept, even where lack of adequate accommodation makes it difficult:

> To me it is a simple offering of the day to God. This may be in the form of a well-prepared assembly ... or it may be in the form of a quiet time of reflection or prayer

before going to lessons. To meet the requirements, however, God must be addressed. (Ibid. 207)

In the context of an education system serving a plural society in the twenty-first century, Warner's position appears rather patronizing, reaching back more than a half century to a period that seemed to enjoy much greater religious certainty. To state that such an approach 'is hardly something which should be controversial' suggests an unwillingness to acknowledge the impact of social change and demography on educational and cultural practice. Likewise, to simply assert that 'the law should not bend ...' implies an absolutist attitude whereby change is inadmissible.

Towards a 'new way forward' for collective worship

Alongside Hull's analysis, one of the more thorough educational investigations into collective worship was carried out in the mid-1990s by the Religious Education Council (REC) for England and Wales, in association with the National Association of SACREs (Standing Advisory Councils on Religious Education) and the Inter-Faith Network for the UK. This process involved a research report, a series of three conferences, a consultation and a publication. Participants and delegates included representatives of a range of Christian denominations plus Jews, Muslims, Sikhs and other faith communities and also the British Humanist Association, together with various professional bodies and teaching unions.

The initial REC Report, entitled 'Collective Worship in Schools' (REC, 1996), surveyed the development of statutory collective worship since 1944 and examined the issues around its definition, the possibility of its educational and theological justification, its frequency, its variable practice and in particular the UK Government's attempts to 'tighten' the Christian nature of the activity through the 1988 Act and the 1994 Circular (as referred to above). An early conclusion of the report was that this subsequent legislation 'had raised very difficult theological, educational and practical issues' (37–38). Many of the points made echoed Hull's significant work of two decades earlier.

In a paper prepared in advance of the third of the three conferences, it was suggested that:

> There are substantial doubts about the viability of the concept of 'collective worship'. In most schools it is difficult to fulfil, on a regular basis, a requirement for acts of worship which are also collective in the sense of involving the committed and participative worship of pupils who are likely to come from a wide variety of backgrounds. ... There is a need to ensure that the rights and concerns of minority communities in different school situations are safeguarded ... [and] There is widespread concern that the present requirement for daily collective worship is excessive. (Culham, 1998, 18)

A wide range of views on the value and future of collective worship was evident from the series of conferences which formed the heart of this REC-led project, but there was some degree of consensus towards the need for 'a new approach' (ibid. 11ff) that would take account of cultural and religious diversity and respect the integrity of pupils, teachers and parents. The details and practicalities of any new approach were explored but there was not full agreement among those taking part. At the end of the process it was recommended that the government 'should now take over the baton and establish a governmental review of collective worship' (ibid. 14), but this suggestion was not taken up by government, for reasons best known to themselves.

The current debates on collective worship

The current range of educational opinion on collective worship tends towards three main positions, although variations and nuances are evident between the several expressions of these views. Perhaps the strongest voice is that which argues for the removal from legislation of compulsory worship, which we may call the 'No' campaign. Others argue for an amended

approach, a radically altered assembly time with the removal of the requirement for a 'broadly Christian Character' and greater flexibility, including
opportunities for reflection relating to a range of faiths or spiritualities.
A third group, perhaps more muted, wishes for a retention of the status
quo, though with a desire for clearer guidance, organization and direction
on the content and format of collective worship. These key positions are
reflected in a recent study on collective worship and religious observance
in UK schools (Cumper & Mawhinney, 2015), though in a different order
(Option 1: Maintain; Option 2: Abolish; Option 3: Reform).

Those situated in the 'No' camp – particularly represented by bodies
such as Humanists UK (formerly the British Humanist Association) and
the National Secular Society (NSS) – contest the appropriateness of enforcing 'worship' of any kind especially that of a selected faith, arguing that
fundamental human rights such as the freedom to thought, conscience
and religion are challenged by the current situation.

The Chief Executive of Humanists UK, Andrew Copson (in a personal
communication to the authors) has commented:

> In our increasingly diverse society, the requirement for schools to hold a daily act of
> 'broadly Christian' collective worship represents an unacceptable affront to a child's
> freedom of belief. Parents don't want it, teachers are uncomfortable with it and
> pupils have very little choice in the matter. What's more, surveys suggest that almost
> two-thirds of schools don't even enforce it. (A. Copson, Humanists UK, personal
> communication, 2015; used by kind permission of the author)

It is often pointed out by proponents of this view that there is a gulf in
time and social composition between the post-war era (when the Act was
initiated) and today's multicultural society. According to Stephen Evans
from the National Secular Society:

> The law as it stands is an anachronism; the legacy of a society unrecognisable from
> the diverse and pluralistic Britain of today where citizens hold a wide variety of reli-
> gious beliefs, and increasingly, no religious beliefs'. (Evans, 2015)
> Moreover, as Evans puts it:
> Any law that requires worship is incompatible with genuine commitment to
> religious freedom. Even with limited withdrawal rights, requiring a daily act of wor-
> ship, in which pupils by law are required to 'take part', undermines young people's

freedom of religion or belief and impedes parents' abilities to raise their children in accordance with their own religious or philosophical convictions. (Evans, 2014)

The legal responsibility to ensure that collective worship takes place falls ultimately with a school's board of governors. Many school governors, however, may have limited awareness of this responsibility, while others clearly feel ill at ease with the requirement and in 2014 the National Governors' Association (England) called for collective worship to be 'non-mandatory' for all non-faith schools (NGA, 2014).

In two recent prominent reports, a similar range of views has been expressed. In their 2015 Westminster Faith Debates paper, Charles Clarke and Linda Woodhead note that what is needed is 'a healthy and up-to-date legal framework which reflects modern religious and educational life and practices' (Clarke & Woodhead, 2015, 22). They recommend that 'the current requirement in statute for an Act of Collective Worship should be abolished, and the decision about the form and character of school assemblies should be left to the governors of individual schools' (ibid. 27). They also propose that 'school community assemblies', as a dimension of SMSC, should be inspected by Ofsted. Just a few months later the Report of the Commission on Religion and Belief in British Public Life (CORAB) took a very similar view, commending in particular the proposals by the Church of Scotland and the Humanist Society Scotland for a 'time for reflection' as 'an example for the rest of the UK' (CORAB, 2015, para. 4.17).

Following several debates and discussions on collective worship and other issues around religion in education, the Liberal Democrats political party, at their York conference in March 2017, voted overwhelmingly in favour of abolishing the legal requirement for state-funded schools to hold acts of collective worship. They agreed that such acts could continue voluntarily so long as adequate provision was made for pupils to opt out (Accord Coalition, 2017).

Voices of discontent on collective worship do not always emanate from expected sources, however. Prior to his retirement in 2014, the Church of England's Bishop of Oxford, the Rt. Rev. John Pritchard, publicly announced his wishes to see the current requirement for collective worship replaced by an opportunity for 'spiritual reflection'. This period of reflection would, he argued, allow for the inclusion of world religions other than Christianity, although this would apply to state schools only and not faith schools. A similar proposal from the Church of Scotland (in the form of a parliamentary briefing) urged consideration of a change of name from 'religious observance' to 'a time of reflection'. Describing contemporary religious observance as 'a pluralist approach in a pluralist society', the briefing suggests that 'a change of name for Religious Observance events can often have a very positive effect on the sense of inclusion and is to be encouraged' (Church of Scotland, 2013). Such views, however, remain contentious within these denominational communities.

Noting the disconnect between legal requirements and actual practice in many schools, Gill (2004, 194) has highlighted the need for greater clarity and direction in terms of the form and function of collective worship, indicating that '[a]n advisory document to supersede "Religious Education and Collective Worship" (Circular 1/94 DFE) which recognised the actual situation in schools would be welcome'.

Many of those who argue for an amended approach express a desire for more diverse representation of the many faiths represented within the UK, arguing that the focus on one faith is not representative of the demographic of a multicultural society. Yet as Hull and others have pointed out, there are theological and practical concerns over whether this could, in any real sense, be called 'worship'. Quite apart from the question of the appropriateness of worship in schools, can 'multifaith worship' ever be possible in the context of the very different truth claims to be found within the religions and beliefs that are currently present in the UK?

Those who set out a case for maintaining the status quo in relation to collective worship or religious observance sometimes cite Article 9 (1) of the European Convention on Human Rights (1950) which includes the right to freedom of thought, conscience and religion and the right to manifest one's religion or beliefs (subject to some democratic legal constraints and the protection of others' rights, as in Article 9(2)) 'in worship, teaching, practice and observance'. Others may, of course, object that the legal requirement for collective worship is a form of imposition which thereby goes beyond the mere 'manifestation' of religion or beliefs. The larger Christian denominations, including those which have their own 'faith schools', have also made a case for retaining the status quo on the grounds of the importance of religious insights and spiritual development in education in general, and not just in faith schools. This point of view is often expressed in denominational reports/publications, and is also represented in the work of the School Chaplains and Leaders Association (SCALA), which promotes the fostering of faith across the curriculum and the delivery of inclusive quality collective worship (especially, though not exclusively, in England). In the view of SCALA, collective worship for many pupils may be the only opportunity they have to explore their spirituality:

> School worship can be a significant and powerful ingredient in enabling pupils to develop a thoughtful and reflective understanding of the world around them, and a sense of meaning and purpose. (SCALA, n.d.)

SCALA does, however, acknowledge the importance of respect for multifaith contexts and urges that schools 'should seek the greatest degree of commonality' (ibid.). Similar views have been expressed by many of the English and Welsh SACREs (Standing Advisory Councils on Religious Education, established following the Education Act of 1988 in each local authority area to monitor the provision and quality of religious education and collective worship), suggesting that there would be an educational deficit if collective worship were to be removed from the school day.

Yet even among those who continue to take a more traditional view of collective worship, few appear to be arguing for a full-on return to the confessional assumptions of the 1940s. There is a general acceptance of the importance of openness and inclusivity and of the realities of a plural society, though for some this is tied in with ambiguities around a desire to promote 'traditional Christian values', as is evident in some of the collective worship statements issued by many local authorities and individual schools.

Collective worship in a bubble of isolation?

The transformation of educational and social philosophy since the mid-twentieth century has led to a situation in which collective worship now finds itself in a bubble of isolation, remote from many of the other changes in education that have taken place in educational practice. The realities of social and cultural pluralism have contributed to radical changes in the curriculum subject of religious education, but for many of that subject's practitioners collective worship has become an incompatible bedfellow. Sharpened attitudes towards equality issues and changes in the wider educational curriculum, such as the introduction of citizenship education, have also appeared to leave collective worship outside of the mainstream processes of the education system. Moreover, the lack of direction and the very limited professional attention that is available to influence the nature and content of collective worship, has increased practitioner uncertainty and made for extremely variable practice. These issues have led to increasing calls to abandon or significantly review collective worship in schools. Regional variations, issues around cultural and religious identity in schools, greater awareness of human rights, and changing views on the fundamental purpose of education all contribute to this debate, making consensus potentially hard to achieve.

It has nevertheless been shown in this discussion that there are positive voices proposing constructive alternatives to collective worship that do not require its complete abandonment. If some, or even many, RE professionals are wary of collective worship, some other educators may feel less conflicted or potentially compromised by activities of this kind. Setting aside the controversial terminology of 'collective worship', the concept of 'spiritual development', not necessarily understood in a religious sense, appears to be helpful to many educators. Schools in England and Wales are required to provide opportunities in SMSC (Spiritual, Moral, Social and Cultural Development), the Northern Ireland Curriculum designates 'spiritual awareness' as a 'Curriculum Objective' (CCEA, 2007) and a similar concept is evident in references to 'spiritual development' by the Scottish Government (Curriculum for Excellence, 2017). These developments may offer a generally more helpful way forward in providing a more holistic understanding of the positive potential of a reflective assembly focused on spiritual development in its broadest sense. This is evident in the thinking of Hull, Copley and others as indicated above, and also in the writing of Tony Eaude:

> In primary schools, especially, collective worship, commonly thought of as an assembly, offers many possibilities in relation to SMSC. 'Collective' recognises that those present may not all share a religious belief. For the whole school, or one section, to gather enables each child to see themselves as part of a bigger entity. The person leading assembly can reaffirm positive values, maybe with a story, using a symbol such as a candle or a flower, or celebrating the successes of individuals or groups. The chance to reflect together, with silence, music or a prayer, affirms the importance of taking a break from the busy-ness of life to ponder questions of deeper significance. (Eaude, 2006, 86)

Conclusion

In the context of significant educational and social change over the past half-century, debates about the educational appropriateness of collective worship and religious observance continue to evoke strong opinions, but calls for abolition or radical change appear to be increasing. Hull's 'obituary' has clearly not been realized, though his thoughtful analysis and the argument that worship and education are not compatible remain compelling, especially outside the 'faith schools' sector.

This chapter has reviewed the continuing discussion and analysed some of the arguments for the main approaches: abolition, reform or maintenance of the status quo. Broad consensus does not appear to possible, though many educational observers appear to favour a moderate position that moves away from 'worship' in its traditional sense but retains opportunities for reflection and spiritual development in the life of schools. It is frequently emphasized that such opportunities should be inclusive, respectful of diversity and not involve any form of coercion. Amidst intensifying calls for changes in legislation, however, it remains to be seen if a moderate position will be possible or whether it will be swept aside in favour of a much more radical abolitionist approach.

References

Accord Coalition (2017). *Lib Dems call for end to religious discrimination in faith school admissions.* Accord Coalition website. Retrieved June 18, 2017, from <http://accordcoalition.org.uk/2017/03/31/lib-dems-call-for-end-to-religious-discrimination-in-faith-school-admissions/>.

Best, R. (Ed.) (2000). *Education for Spiritual, Moral, Social and Cultural Development.* London: Continuum.

CCEA (2007). *Northern Ireland Curriculum: 'The Big Picture'.* Council for Curriculum, Examinations and Assessment. Retrieved June 19, 2017, from <http://ccea.org.uk/sites/default/files/docs/curriculum/area_of_learning/ks1_2_bigpicture.pdf>.

Church of Scotland (2013). *Religious Observance in Schools – why opt-in is the inclusive model* (parliamentary briefing). Edinburgh: Church and Society Council of the Church of Scotland.

Clarke, C., & Woodhead, L. (2015). *A New Settlement: Religion and Belief in Schools (Westminster Faith Debates).* Lancaster University: Economic & Social Research Council; Arts & Humanities Research Council.

CORAB (Commission on Religion and Belief in British Public Life) (2015). *Living With Difference: Community, Diversity and the Common Good.* Cambridge: The Woolf Institute.

Copley, T. (2005). *Indoctrination, Education and God: the struggle for the mind.* London: SPCK.

Copley, T. (2008). *Teaching Religion: Sixty Years of Religious Education in England and Wales.* Devon: University of Exeter Press.

Crick, B. (1999). *National Curriculum: Citizenship.* London: DfEE & QCA.

Culham College Institute (1998). *Collective Worship Reviewed: Report of the 1997 Consultation.* Abingdon: Culham College Institute.

Cumper, P., & Mawhinney, A. (2015). *Collective Worship and Religious Observance in Schools: An Evaluation of Law and Policy in the UK.* An AHRC Network Report. Retrieved April 20, 2017, from <http://collectiveschoolworship.com/

documents/CollectiveWorshipReligiousObservanceAHRCNetwork Report-13November2015.pdf>.

Curriculum for Excellence (2017). *Provision of Religious Observance in Scottish Schools – March 2017*. Scottish Government website. Retrieved June 18, 2017, from <http://www.gov.scot/Resource/0051/00516155.pdf>.

Eaude, T. (2006). *Spiritual, Moral, Social and Cultural Development – Primary and Early Years*. Exeter: Learning Matters.

Equality and Human Rights Commission. *An Introduction to the Equality Act 2010*. Equality and Human Rights Commission website. Retrieved June 14, 2017, from <https://www.equalityhumanrights.com/en/equality-act-2010/what-equality-act>.

Evans, S. (2014). *Challenging Religious Privilege: New petition calls for an end to compulsory worship in schools* (10 July 2014). National Secular Society website. Retrieved June 30, 2015, from <http://www.secularism.org.uk/collective-worship.html>.

Evans, S. (2015). *Challenging Religious Privilege: Collective Worship*. National Secular Society website. Retrieved June 30, 2015, from <http://www.secularism.org.uk/collective-worship.html>.

Gearon, L. (2004). *Citizenship through Religious Education*. London: Routledge.

Gill, J. (2004). The act of collective worship: pupils' perspectives. In *British Journal of Religious Education 26*(2), 185–196.

Goldman, R. (1964). *Religious Thinking from Childhood to Adolescence*. London: Routledge & Kegan Paul.

Goldman, R. (1965). *Readiness for Religion: A Basis for Developmental Religious Education*. London: Routledge & Kegan Paul.

Hull, J. (1975). *School Worship: An Obituary*. London: SCM Press.

Hull, J. (1995). Collective Worship: the Search for Spirituality. In *Future Progress in Religious Education: The Templeton London Lectures at the RSA* (pp. 27–40). London: RSA.

Jackson, R. (2004). *Rethinking Religious Education and Plurality*. London: Routledge Falmer.

Keast, J. (Ed.) (2007). *Religious Diversity and Intercultural Education: a reference book for schools*. Strasbourg: Council of Europe.

Kincheloe, J., & Steinberg, S. (2002). *Changing Multiculturalism*. Buckingham: Open University Press.

Kohlberg, L. (1958). *The Development of Modes of Thinking and Choices in Years 10 to 16*. PhD Dissertation, University of Chicago.

Kohlberg, L. (1984). *The Psychology of Moral Development: The Nature and Validity of Moral Stages (Essays on Moral Development, Volume 2)*. New York: Harper & Row.

Leonard, M. (1988). *The 1988 Education Act: A Tactical Guide for Schools*. Oxford: Blackwell Education.

Loukes, H. (1961). *Teenage Religion: An Enquiry into Attitudes and Possibilities among British Boys and Girls in Secondary Modern Schools*. London: SCM Press.

McLaren, P. L. (1999). A Pedagogy of Possibility; reflecting upon Paulo Friere's politics of education. *Educational Researcher, 28*(2) 49–54.

National Society (1939). *Worship and Education*. London: National Society and SPCK.

NGA (2014). *NGA responds to Telegraph article on collective worship*. Birmingham: National Governors' Association. Retrieved July 9, 2015, from <http://www.nga.org.uk/News/NGA-News/May-Sept-14/NGA-responds-to-Telegraph-article-on-Collective-Wo.aspx>.

Parekh, B. (2000). *The Future of Multi-ethnic Britain*. Exmouth: Profile Books /The Runnymede Trust.

QCA (2007). *Religious Education Programme of study (non-statutory) for key stage 3 and attainment targets* (Extract from the National Curriculum 2007). Retrieved July 7, 2015, from <http://webarchive.nationalarchives.gov.uk/.../QCA-07-3350-p_RE_KS3_tcm8-411.pdf>.

REC (1996). *Collective Worship in Schools – Research Report*. London: Religious Education Council of England & Wales.

SCALA (n.d.). *Worship*. From the website of the School Chaplains and Leaders Association (SCALA). Retrieved July 3, 2015, from <http://www.scala.uk.net/>.

Smart, N. (1969). *The Religious Experience of Mankind*. Englewood Cliffs, NJ: Prentice Hall.

Smith, J. (1936). *The Teachers' Handbook to the Syllabus of Religious Instruction for use in Scottish Schools*. Edinburgh: The Church of Scotland Education and Youth Committees.

Starmer Smith, D. (1945). *The School Service*. London: REP.

Teece, G. (2001). *A Primary Teacher's Guide to RE and Collective Worship*. Oxford: Nash Pollock Publishing.

Warner, M. (2000). Reflections on Inspections. In R. Best (Ed.), *Education for Spiritual, Moral, Social and Cultural Development* (pp. 199–209). London: Continuum.

PART IV

Collective Worship and Religious Observance: International Perspectives

MARY ELIZABETH MOORE

12 Collective Worship and Religious Observance in UK Schools: Questions and Possibilities

ABSTRACT

This chapter argues that engaging communal religious practices is part of holistic learning. Recognizing contextual differences, the author analyses diverse purposes and approaches to collective worship and religious observance. Purposes include: the cultivation of human integrity, holistic interreligious knowledge, and human relationships with self and other. Potential approaches are wide-ranging: engage practices of one tradition; offer choices to opt out of religious practices; develop collective experiences without religious content; engage in shareable practices from multiple traditions; and cultivate a sense of wonder. The conclusion includes heuristic visions for UK schools, including specific goals from personal development to reflection to collective sensibilities. The discussion culminates with qualities of holistic education: intersubjective learning, engaging religions religiously, ritualizing, moving from dominance to multiplicity, dignifying, and revering.

The underlying hope is for a comprehensive, engaged education that is meaningful for human lives and communities, while preparing good citizens.

Introduction

The question posed in this book – collective worship and religious observance in schools – is a high-stakes query. Collective worship is communal ritual practice, veneration, and reverence, which lies at the heart of most religious traditions. Religious observance is the full range of shared practice among religious adherents. Both worship and other observances stand at the heart of religious traditions and cultures, which is why decisions about including or not including them in state-funded schools is so challenging. Even with long traditions of worship in United Kingdom schools, the increasing pluralism in the society and in the schools themselves poses challenging questions. The three most obvious responses are to continue practices of Christian worship while also teaching about world religions, to expand the opportunities for worship and religious observance in multiple traditions, or to eliminate worship and religious observance altogether, perhaps replacing these practices with other forms of ritual gathering.

Any of these three options opens new questions. How can students learn the complexities of any tradition – their own or others – if they are not engaged in some way with the rituals and collective observances of the tradition? The seemingly easy divide between learning (or being formed) *within* a tradition, and learning *about* religious traditions is fraught. How are students to learn about a religious tradition if they do not encounter the communal practices of that tradition? What will they miss if they study only descriptions of the history, beliefs, and values of each tradition? What kinds of encounters are needed if deep knowing is to emerge? How can such encounters be respectful and non-invasive to adherents and non-adherents alike? At the same time, we need to ask what can and cannot be understood by observing or participating in religious practices that are outside one's own tradition? These are only a few of the questions posed by the issue of collective worship and religious observance in schools.

In comparison with the United States public education system, where the separation of religion and state is largely assumed, the UK is well situated to wrestle with these important educational questions in the contemporary pluralistic context. The questions viewed from the experience of other countries can be instructive, but only with consideration of comparative complexities, such as the structural, social, and missional diversities in the religion-education relationship. For example, the US structures are neither centralized (as in Austria and Prussia) nor decentralized (as in The Netherlands and Belgium), but a complicated alternative that blends aspects of both (Glenn, 2012). At the same time, US educators address complexities that resonate with those of other countries as regards the teaching of religion in relation to educational goals, cultural and religious pluralism, and issues of citizenship and freedom (Hunt & Carper 2013; Bankston & Caldas, 2009; Greenawalt, 2007; Kunzman, 2006).

Such comparisons provide a contextual background for this chapter, though the focus here is not on the comparative or structural issues themselves. The chapter focuses on questions of worship and religious observance in schools, recognizing that worship and religious observance are shaped by the structures of religion and education in diverse countries and regions. With this recognition in the background, we turn to the primary themes of this chapter: the *purposes, approaches, and visions of worship and religious observance in schools.* The themes emerge differently in varied contexts, but many educational questions and insights thread across structural differences and speak to the heart of teaching and learning religion.

Considering purpose

At all levels of education, the question of purpose is strong, and the question is particularly intense when one asks the purpose of worship and religious observance in schools. In teaching religion and theology at any level, purpose questions can be hotly contested, often framed as dichotomies, such as the dichotomy between information and formation. This particular dichotomy of purposes has been debated in higher education as well as in education for children and youth. In one debate on this subject, John Thatamil (2011) argues that all education involves some form and degree of formation, while Amanda Porterfield (2011) argues that any mixing of formation goals into education undermines the effort to engage religions historically and critically. In the same journal, I make a case that education best proceeds as an interactive endeavor aimed toward formation, information, reformation, and transformation (Moore, 2011). These authors teach, and reflect on religion and teaching, from diverse social locations in the United States. Thatamil, as a comparative theologian, argues that education across religious traditions requires participatory teaching and learning, aiming toward some key virtues:

- An empathetic appreciation for and even love of traditions other than their own and a willingness to learn from them.
- A theological desire to know more about the nature of ultimate reality by learning from Hindu and Buddhist texts and practices.
- An interhuman and theological desire to meet persons from other traditions with more than a narrowly anthropological or reductive gaze. (Thatamil, 2011, 370)

In Thatamil's point of view, communal religious practice has a role to play, even in interreligious education. It contributes to empathic development, knowledge, and interreligious appreciation and relationships.

Such a view is echoed and expanded by global educators and religious leaders who see a relationship between religious knowing and the cultivation of human values and practices in young lives. Values include: empathy (de Souza, 2016, 35–56, esp. 55–56); connectedness (de Souza, 84–108; Buber, 1971); gratitude (Schnall and Schnall, 2017); and humility (Resnick, 2017; Heschel, 1965), among others. Marian de Souza (2016) who writes from an Australian context, makes a case that these values and practices relate to the deep spiritual nature of human beings; thus, they are critically important for education that fosters full human development (4–34). De Souza has done an extensive review of the global literature on education, concluding that both Eastern and Western cultures, and both religious and secular cultures, acknowledge spirituality as a human trait, reflected in objective and subjective experiences. She concludes further that 'spirituality is an innate human trait which pertains to the relational dimension of life and may be observed and experienced through the expressions of connection between the Self and Other' (33). From this perspective, education calls for engagement with diversity in an interspiritual way (ibid. 135–143), thus requiring multidimensional and holistic education – intellectual, emotional and spiritual (ibid. 110–134).

One sees a similar accent in Robert Jackson, who agrees with the Delors Report of UNESCO in saying that religious education 'should include learning to know, learning to do, learning to live together and learning to be' (Jackson, 2007, 27). Jackson adds: 'It is arguable that religious education should be concerned with all of these, especially the fourth' (ibid.). He makes this case in a context in which he is himself emphasizing the third, responding in a particular historical moment to pressing political and social issues. Jackson's position is a reminder that different moments call for different emphases, even while holding a comprehensive vision for religion in schools. Like Thatamil, de Souza and Jackson understand the value of educating whole persons through holistic education, seeking to enhance empathic development, knowledge, and interreligious appreciation and relationships with others.

The purposes identified in this brief span of literature can be summarized as the cultivation of human integrity, holistic interreligious knowledge, and human relationships with self and other. *Integrity* is an interweaving of knowledge and experience into a meaningful whole that shapes and reshapes a person or community over time. Integrity is thus an interweaving of rational, emotional, aesthetic, physical, and spiritual ways of knowing. *Holistic interreligious knowledge* draws upon a similar wholeness in the study of religious traditions, a wholeness that is found within religious communities themselves and in their relationships with the larger society. These first two purposes point to the third – enhancing *human relationships* through respectful encounters with the self and others. Such education enhances mutual appreciation and dignity, and it magnifies opportunities for shared human action for the common good.

These comprehensive goals for education tap many ways of human knowing, thus engaging students with the breadth and depth of religious traditions and experiences. What then might be the role for collective worship and religious observance in schools of the United Kingdom? My own proposal is that students need opportunities to engage religions religiously – to draw upon their own capacities to engage religions in some degree of their fullness and depth.

Considering purpose in the United Kingdom

The United Kingdom is itself quite diverse in educational, religious, cultural, and political traditions; thus the purposes of worship and religious observance in the schools are inevitably complex. The key question is what are the appropriate purposes (if any) for including collective worship and religious observance in the practices of schools. The question has been much debated for four decades (Hull, 1975, 1989; Parker & Freathy, 2012; Freathy & Parker 2012, 2013), and other authors in this volume elucidate the debates and moments of decision in some detail. Some build upon the arguments of John Hull (1984) for religious education that is critically open and creates space (as in school assemblies) for free expressions by diverse religious groups, rather than worship led by one religious community. These discussions will continue in the internal UK networks.

My role here is not to advise the UK decision-makers, but to pose critical questions and fresh perspectives for consideration. Some of the purposes identified in the UK discussions to date are for education to: encourage worship of God; engage spiritual and moral issues; enable students to explore their own beliefs; encourage students to participate in and respond to religious traditions; develop a community spirit, common ethos, and shared values; provide time for reflection; encourage and reinforce positive attitudes; and enhance learning, confidence, and responsibility in students. These purposes are not mutually exclusive, but they do reveal some tensions.

In a world where religious communities are fighting one another on every continent and often compete to win people's souls, the suggestion that religions might meet religiously seems absurd, as does the idea of studying the inner life and everyday practices of religious people. People often feel that the most they can hope in such a world is to avoid clashes, to promote tolerance, and to study other religions at a distance so people can live in peace with one another. Many people do not even dare to hope for that, but rather turn to their own religious communities for hope or turn completely away from religion and the study of religion. In such a world, what is the role of educators who seek to educate persons with all of these hopes and reservations, and more?

I have proposed above that religious education has the purpose to cultivate human integrity, holistic interreligious knowledge, and human relationships with self and others. I have further proposed that such religious and interreligious education can best be done by offering opportunities for students to engage religions religiously. This does not mean that students will engage in religious practices as adherents or devotees, but that they will engage religious traditions deeply and will develop some understanding and appreciation of the fullness of multiple traditions and communities. Such an approach is multidimensional, but neither confessional nor coercive.

The decisions about religious education in the UK lie within the appropriate local and regional governing bodies, but I can elaborate here on initial goals to consider. One important educational goal is to *explore the religious teachings and practices of diverse traditions and to reflect on the meanings* these teaching and practices hold for the people who participate in them. A second educational goal is to *engage in interreligious relationships*, moving beyond superficiality, curiosity and comparative beliefs to more complex communication of the textures of diverse religions, and the difficult questions that emerge in such engaged learning. A third goal is to *reflect critically and appreciatively on the teachings and practices of diverse religious traditions*, identifying contributions of those traditions to human and ecological well-being. All three practices promise to enrich religious understanding and nurture justice and peace in our tormented world. They cultivate the soil in which human beings can grow in knowledge and integrity and in which they can come to greater appreciation of one another and greater willingness to work together across difference for the flourishing of the world we share.

Probing these goals, the key words are explore, engage, and reflect deeply and appreciatively. These goals are similar to those found in the study of history, literature, or chemistry. In chemistry, students *explore* concepts, empirical research, and meta-theories. Students can also *engage* in the work of chemistry, learning to do simple and increasingly complex experiments. Finally, students *reflect* on the connections that they and others have discovered, and they often discover the wonder of chemical facts and interactions. The study of religion is not so different from that; ideally, it involves similar goals in the study of religious and spiritual traditions – exploring, engaging, and reflecting. To make such a case is to acknowledge that the world and global educational movements have changed since John Hull's earlier reflections (1979, 1984, 1989). This does not mean that his earlier plea for critical openness and freedom are outdated, but only that we can now consider the option of engaging in religious practices as *part* of an education that is critically open and that frees students to explore and express themselves.

Such learning can actually be enriched by the inclusion of collective worship and religious observance that engages students with the embodied life practices of religious communities. The purpose is not to coerce people into worship or other forms of observance within a particular tradition, but to explore, to engage religious practices, and to reflect. The hope is that young people would not only develop a more comprehensive understanding of religions and their historic and ethical significance, but they would also develop an honest appreciation of diverse religious traditions as they seek to discern the meanings and concerns that lie beneath the surface of religious communal life. Appreciation does not replace critical thinking about religious traditions and their historical actions, but rather opens pathways toward more nuanced and fair-minded critique. Such education has potential to minimize religious prejudice and discrimination and to maximize mutual respect, critical conversations across traditions, and shared work for the common good.

Being alert to hidden intentions

The proposal that I have offered has a shadow side, as it can be distorted to support and advocate for one particular religious tradition; to borrow inappropriately from religious traditions; or to avoid religion as a subject of human history, culture, and meaning-making for fear of distortion. For this reason, decision-makers need to reflect honestly on their hidden intentions in order to critique and refine their purposes. They also need to develop safeguards against practices that could close critical openness rather than open it. For example, decision-makers need to ask if their hidden purposes may be to re-inscribe the dominance of Christianity, or to re-inscribe colonial-type power in any form. As to the latter, Freathy and Parker (2012, 8) note that, in the parliamentary debate in 1944, clerics and politicians expressed concern about 'a spiritual and moral crisis threatening the Christian foundations of civilisation, freedom and democracy'. The desire to preserve the Christian character of the nation was a major intention of the actions during that era. To what extent does this desire linger? Can this desire to preserve a precious inheritance be held alongside other values and traditions? These are honest and difficult questions.

Some intentions may be less hidden and also less bound to one particular religious tradition. The desire to nurture good citizens with a shared set of values or to build a spirit of community can be enacted without any expectation or requirement of religious hegemony. These motivations are also part of UK educational history. Shared values may cross many trditions, albeit with complexities, diverse expressions, and subtle differences. The study of shared values is actually enriched by the complexities, expressions, and differences. In reality, a spirit of community can include experiences of similarity and dissimilarity, moments when students are stirred to curiosity and appreciation for difference. The community spirit is thus fed by the richness of difference and a growing awareness that differences are a reason to celebrate and wonder rather than to worry.

Considering approaches to worship and religious observance

Educational purposes are intricately woven with educational approaches. The range of approaches is wide, though a robust and well integrated education would press for a still wider range of approaches to collective worship and religious observance. For example, the assumption that education will include worship and observance in a more or less hegemonic way, or conversely choose not to include these practices at all is a faulty assumption. Other alternatives exist. The potential approaches may be wider than typically assumed when asking questions about including or not including collective worship and religious observance in schools. One challenge is to identify the alternative approaches and values embodied in them. Educators in the UK and many other countries across the globe have been addressing these challenges for some time, including research on diverse approaches

(Jackson, Miedema, Weisse, & Willaime, 2007; Engebretson, de Souza, Durka, & Gearon, 2010) and on student and teacher attitudes in diverse contexts (Jackson, 2012; Arweck, 2016; Kuusisto, Poulter, & Kallioniemi, 2017). The global picture of pedagogical approaches is complex, but the potential for drawing upon multiple approaches is itself promising for educational practice, offering new possibilities for exploring, engaging, and reflecting (as discussed above).

Some common approaches have long been present in UK schools and in schools worldwide. For example, one set of approaches that is strongly represented in the educational history of the UK is to *engage in collective practices that are grounded in one particular religious tradition*. In the UK, the common majority tradition has been Christianity, albeit with diverse ecumenical expressions in different parts of the land. Such approaches to collective worship and religious observance usually accentuate formation. Yet they are expressed and enacted with varied goals: to create opportunities for students to revere or venerate a divine being or power; to instill particular beliefs, as belief in Jesus Christ; to inspire and guide Christian character; to provide an ecumenical or non-denominational experience; and/or to communicate the country's Christian heritage. Such approaches usually assume some degree of homogeneity in the community, which can contribute to community bonding (at least for the majority in many schools) while simultaneously raising questions regarding diversity and respect for all students.

Because schools are increasingly heterogeneous, another set of approaches have been developed to accent choice and *allow families and communities to adapt the dominant practices or to opt out of them altogether, thus allowing for diversity*. These approaches permit families and schools to request allowances so they can revise the dominant approaches or choose not to participate for reasons of conscience or religious difference or rejection of religion. Such approaches also allow for schools that are established with a particular religious character to provide their own distinctive worship. These options are clearly respectful of difference, though they can place a burden on families and communities to take initiative in making requests, a burden that is particularly challenging for persons in a small or less-than-powerful minority. These approaches do have merit, however.

Recognizing the extent of diversity in UK schools, school leaders will always need to provide such alternatives, either to adapt or opt out of the predominant approach, whatever it is.

In addition to the religion-specific and opt-out approaches, another common approach is to *create opportunities for collective actions that are not explicitly religious or not explicitly tied to one religion*. John Hull's (1984) encouragement of school assemblies is one example. Another is to create opportunities for a school community to participate in acts of service, explorations into values, and/or rituals that promote spiritual development and shared values. Students can be given opportunities to participate in community service on a regular basis, working together in teams and with people in the local community. They can be offered special events with films, presentations, discussions and debates on value questions that are urgent for them and the larger society. They can also be given opportunities to mourn and celebrate in rituals that are not explicitly religious. These are important options whether or not schools also provide opportunities for collective worship and religious observance.

I would suggest two other options that are not as explicit in the discussions of religion in UK schools, thus adding a fourth and fifth option to the more common approaches. The fourth option is to *study and engage in 'shareable' practices of multiple traditions*. Shareable practices are those deemed appropriate for sharing with people who are not adherents of a particular religious tradition. Many meditation traditions are so identified, as are many practices of thanksgiving. To engage this approach with full respect and counsel, educators need the wisdom of practitioners in each tradition. Religious leaders themselves need to identify shareable practices and offer guidance as to how the practices might best be communicated and practiced with persons in other traditions, or with persons who do not identify with any particular religion or worldview. Educational leaders and curriculum designers need to conduct consultations and engage in research to undergird such an approach, producing curricular materials and training to support and guide schools and teachers, many of whom will also have resources in their local communities. This kind of work is well underway in the UK and elsewhere in the world, as noted above, and far more is needed. To engage students with shareable practices is a rich alternative to ignoring collective religious practices or focusing on only one and allowing people to opt out. Shareable practices carry meanings in their originating religious context(s) and also in public spaces. Further, they can enhance the process of meaning-making in students, especially as they seek to know themselves and others.

One vivid example of shareability is found in the traditional Buddhist practices of mindfulness and compassion meditation. Thich Nhat Hanh (1999, 2005) and His Holiness the Dalai Lama (2002, 2016) have actively sought to share these practices with others, drawing from their Vietnamese and Tibetan Buddhist traditions respectively. Their sharing does not assume that non-Buddhists will experience meditation with all of the meanings that a Buddhist would experience; however, these practices are often significant for non-Buddhists, both in their efforts to understand Buddhism and in their personal explorations of the phenomena of religious experience. Thich Nhat Hanh has travelled the world speaking and leading people in walking meditation and other mindfulness practices. His Holiness the Dalai Lama has encouraged the widespread practice of compassion meditation, as well as research into its physiological and psychological effects. Both recognize the potential of meditation for human wellbeing, and they seek to share the gift from their traditions with the larger human family. Both also speak and write to explicate Buddhist worldviews and values. Their contributions to educational thinking are thus two-fold – the sharing of practices and the explication of those practices within their larger traditions.

One last approach is similarly not a major theme in discussions of religion in UK schools, but it is a common practice in many classrooms. This is the effort to *cultivate a sense of wonder and, simultaneously, appreciation for the unique gifts and practices of diverse religious traditions.* On the subject of wonder, Abraham Joshua Heschel is particularly inspiring, as this theme runs through much of his writing, influenced by his uniquely Jewish life and his engagement with people of many different traditions and non-traditions. In his long life, he understood wonder and awe as critical to human wellbeing: 'There are three ways in which we may relate ourselves to the world – we may exploit it, we may enjoy it, we may accept it in awe' (1975, 34). Heschel clearly encouraged the path of engaging the world with awe, seeing this practice at the heart of religious faith as well as human flourishing. He also connected the repeated themes of wonder, or radical amazement, with education: 'We teach children how to measure, how to weigh. We fail to teach them how to revere, how to sense wonder and awe' (ibid. 35). For Heschel, the cultivation of awe is critical in all aspects of human life and human interaction, and thus critical for education.

Wonder is a quality of life that crosses religious traditions. Thich Nhat Hanh describes a similar phenomenon in terms of 'awareness', and he links awareness with the practice of meditation:

> Meditation is to be aware of what is going on – in our bodies, in our feelings, in our minds, and in the world. Each day 40,000 children die of hunger. The super-powers now have more than 50,000 nuclear warheads, enough to destroy our planet many times. Yet the sunrise is beautiful, and the rose that bloomed this morning along the wall is a miracle. Life is both dreadful and wonderful. To practice meditation is to be in touch with both aspects. (Hanh, 2005, 8)

Similar themes thread through the Dalai Lama's writing. Thus, drawing from diverse traditions, Abraham Joshua Heschel, Thich Nhat Hanh, and the Dalai Lama see the potential of religious practice to awaken wonder or awareness, attuning to beauty and tragedy in religious observance, stirring both religious and human understanding of the world, and cultivating ways of being in the world.

This array of educational approaches is at once generative and daunting. The challenge is to identify the purposes that are most significant for the UK school systems and then to identify approaches that best fit those approaches. The remainder of this chapter will suggest directions for consideration.

Considering visions for the future

The final section provides an opportunity to weave themes together and draw visions for the future. As an outsider to UK schools, I offer what I hope will be a compelling picture of promising ideas and practices rather than definitive advice. The focus in these conclusions is on expanding educational purposes and approaches and drawing major themes into a generative map of possibilities.

Expanding purposes

The educational analysis of this chapter suggests possibilities for educational leaders to consider in evaluating and planning for collective worship and religious observance. I earlier suggested three overarching purposes for education and its engagement with religion: the cultivation of human integrity, holistic interreligious knowledge, and human relationships with self and others. These purposes point to the value of collective worship and religious observance, especially when they take place within contexts that are educationally rich in other ways. Worship and observance cannot stand alone and be well integrated into the school's educational processes and into the lives of students. However, they can be very meaningful in contexts that encourage exploration, engagement, and reflection. When they are interwoven with the full educational enterprise, they can contribute to critical openness and appreciation of religious traditions as they play influential roles in human history, in global cultures, and existentially in human lives.

What is needed is holistic education, which engages many forms of knowing combined with in-depth reflection. Holistic education enhances multifaceted knowledge of religious traditions in diverse contexts, and it cultivates values of self-awareness, empathy, interreligious appreciation, and respectful relationships with others. These are lofty purposes but, if they are to be entertained seriously, they can be parsed into more specific goals that offer practical guidance for educational administrators and teachers. Elaborating on the goals can stir practical imagination regarding the future of religious education and the place of collective worship and religious observance in UK schools.

Human integrity

The first purpose of education articulated in this chapter is the cultivation of human integrity. As described above, integrity is an interweaving of knowledge and experience into a meaningful whole that shapes and reshapes a person or community over time. Thus, integrity has to do with providing opportunities for personal development in many forms, exploration of values, and experiences of wonder and awareness. Each of these might be parsed into goals.

(1) Personal development goals

At the heart of education is personal development, which is not to say individualistic development but rather *opportunities for personal growth in relation to the larger community, past and present*. The value of personal development has traveled through the ages as an essential goal of education, espoused by philosophers and social scientists, as well as educators. The philosopher Alfred North Whitehead described education as a process of 'self-development', calling attention to the human and personal element of education (Whitehead, 1967b, 1). Another helpful reminder is the complementary work of Michael Polanyi, who reflects on personal knowing and social relationships. Polanyi – a chemist, social scientist, and philosopher – originated in Budapest, Hungary, and immigrated to England where he spent much of his teaching life at the University of Manchester from 1933 forward. Polanyi was convinced that knowing and creative discovery are permeated with personal passion or commitment, and that reason combines with 'tacit knowing' to produce insights and lead to new discoveries. Thus, knowing is a process by which one's internal passions interact with one's experiences in the world – human relationships, reading, artistic endeavors, and so forth – to yield knowledge (Polanyi, 1958).

Personal development goals enhance human integrity by providing opportunities to weave one's inner life and unique life experience with all that one encounters in the educational process. These encounters, and reflections upon them, enable persons to form new insights and develop new capacities. Thus, the goals of education need to include opportunities for students to examine themselves and their inner passions in relation to new knowledge encountered in the exercise of multiple ways of knowing. Such goals will encourage both internal reflection and the stretching of boundaries of knowledge.

(2) Value goals

Closely related to personal development goals are value goals. Education is always more than facts and theories; it involves every aspect of a human life. As Marion de Souza (2016) has said, education taps into intellectual, emotional and spiritual forms of knowing (110–134), and thus into goals that encompass all three. Also cited above, Robert Jackson describes the ideals of religious education as 'learning to know, learning to do, learning to live together and learning to be' (Jackson, 2007, 27). Both of these theorists urge educators to be comprehensive in their approaches to teaching and learning. Comprehensive goals move educators to see their role in cultivating values, *cultivating the capacity to appreciate the worth of others and to make ethical judgements.*

Similarly, Alfred North Whitehead warned against education that perpetuates 'minds in a groove' (Whitehead, 1967a, 197), critiquing educational methods that only emphasize the collection of information and intellectual analysis. He argued that these methods fail to 'strengthen habits of concrete appreciation of the individual facts in their full interplay of emergent values' (ibid. 198). Thus, he connected values with the stretching of educational boundaries, inviting teachers and learners to engage with one another and with the subject matters at hand with a spirit of appreciation.

Educational goals that tap multiple ways of knowing are more likely to shape students' values. Collective worship and religious observance are opportunities to expand the range of knowing and subjects for reflection. Collective rituals and practices that arise from the community without religious specificity can also contribute to the cultivation of values. Religious rituals and more public (non-religious) rituals of mourning and celebration, together with other shared practices, such as community service, can all enhance personal meaning-making and public citizenship.

(3) Wonder goals

Religious educators are uniquely situated to study the experiences of wonder that religious people share, however differently they experience and interpret the mysteries they encounter. As discussed above, the goals of wonder can contribute richly to education by *cultivating awareness of self and world and a sense of awe and appreciation.* The philosophical theologian Bernard Meland (1953) addresses these goals in higher education, identifying them with what he calls 'appreciative consciousness', and I would argue that appreciative consciousness is relevant for all ages in different ways. Appreciative consciousness requires holistic teaching and learning that equip students to integrate critical and aesthetic thinking, analysis and feeling. Such learning interweaves analytic, embodied, and affective dimensions of human experience. It includes the acts of analysing and critiquing, but also moves beyond these ways of knowing. Appreciative consciousness 'invites a sense of wonder and an awareness of the depth of relations that inform thought and judgment' (Meland, 1953, ix). It is an opening of the mind that moves beyond learning facts and even beyond problem-solving to evoke the full humanity of learners (ibid.).

Educational goals of wonder are vital, drawing upon the riches of diverse religious traditions while evoking awe and awareness. Such goals are relevant to the study of history, literature, and science as well as religion, for all learning is filled with wonder. Wonder can also be enhanced through interdisciplinary study as students discover fascinating connections between literature and history, science and religion, and all of these with cultural studies and current events.

Holistic interreligious knowing

The second purpose of education described in this chapter is holistic interreligious knowing. This one focuses especially on religious education. Holistic interreligious knowing again requires multiple ways of learning, which opens students to the wholeness of religious traditions and their larger historical and social relationships. Holistic learning requires both knowledge and reflection goals, drawing upon the wide capacities of students to learn in diverse ways and to integrate their discoveries into ever-emerging insights.

(1) Knowledge goals

Knowledge goals are obvious in religious education, but the more specific nature of those goals is far less obvious. What do you hope that children and youth will come to know? What forms of religious knowledge are especially important for their lives. I propose that goals should include *opportunities to know the complexity of lived religions.* Such a goal requires exploration, engagement and reflection, as reiterated throughout this chapter; however the goal is not as obvious as it may seem. I propose that religions can best be understood if they are viewed as active movements rather than static essences. This requires a non-essential approach to religious traditions, which would be a welcome relief to many religious communities. For example, Islam is particularly subject to being essentialized and over-simplified in popular culture and educational settings. Carl Ernst and Bruce Lawrence (2005, xi) argue that 'the study of Islam and Muslim societies is marred by an overly fractured approach that frames Islam as the polar opposite of what "Westerners" are supposed to represent and advocate'. They elaborate that 'Islam has been objectified as the obverse of the Euro-American societies' (ibid).

Further, much interreligious study is dry and lifeless because it focuses on finding and comparing the presumed essences of diverse religious traditions. Even if one were to assert that all religions have an essence (a debatable assumption), the static reality of a religion is probably far less interesting and less helpful for understanding the pulse of the tradition than the movement quality of its passions, commitments, practices, and questions. The goal or religious learning is to know the pulse of traditions in all of their lived complexity.

(2) Reflection goals

The knowledge goals lead naturally to reflection goals, recognizing the reflective component of all education and the value of John Hull's (1989, 1984, 1979) accent on critical openness and freedom in the practice of religious education. *Reflection goals require multiple forms of interpretation – analytic, critical, aesthetic, existential, contextual, and meditative to name a few.* These forms of interpretation parallel the forms of knowing described above. The potential of reflective activity is limitless, inviting personal and communal reflection and drawing upon diverse forms for the sake of opening new insights. A learning community needs opportunities to ponder their own responses to religious traditions and practices and the interplay of those traditions and practices with their distinctive passions and worldviews. They also need opportunities to ponder the *meaning* of those traditions and practices for adherents. This is why reflection requires many forms, and why it can best be done when students engage with religious practices as well as beliefs, historical influences, and cultural forms. All forms of reflection are at their best when they take account of the wholeness of religious traditions and practices.

Reflection goals also require opportunities to *reflect on the dynamic process of religious life*. Teachers and students need opportunities to study religious life over time and in its many different forms. They need opportunities to explore the interconnections of religious traditions and practices within local and global contexts. Such goals require the study of many different forms of interconnection: intermingled histories, interwoven lives on a threatened planet, and shared experiences of awe before the Holy. To study shared histories is to uncover patterns of peaceful co-existence, intimate sharing, disintegration, and conflict. All of these are important to reflection on religion.

Human relationships with self and others

Finally, the third purpose of education described in this chapter is to enhance human relationships as people engage in respectful encounters with themselves and others. This purpose is critical if education is to contribute to mutual appreciation and dignity, and to shared human action for the common good. Donna Hicks (2013), a leader in international conflict resolution, argues that dignity is at the center of meaningful and peaceful relationships, whether in families and local communities or in international relations. She also argues the converse: that violations of dignity are at the center of aggression, abuse, and violence. Drawing upon her own professional experience in dialogue with interdisciplinary study, she concludes that leaders need to develop their capacities to cultivate dignifying cultures and human relationships. This insight resonates with many educators, emphasizing the educational importance of building relationships with self and others. The question for educators is how can we contribute to this urgent need. At least two kinds of goals are important to this work: practical engagement and collectivity goals.

(1) Practical engagement goals

The study of diverse religious traditions can easily reinforce a sense of the exotic and strange nature of religions different from those of the students. Education in the fullness of these traditions includes *participation in the collective practices of religious traditions, thus cultivating understanding, empathy and respect for the values of the traditions.* Such education contributes to a dignifying culture and to the dignifying of human relationships. The teaching-learning process will be multi-form, drawing upon the fullness of the traditions and the capacities of learners to know in cognitive, affective, aesthetic, embodied, and spiritual ways. The potential of collective worship (or ritual) and religious observance is considerable for this kind of learning. The discussion above about shareable religious practices is relevant to the identification of goals that encourage practical engagement and reflection thereon. In addition to Buddhist meditation practices, educators might consider Jewish Shabbat; Muslim celebrations of Eid-al-Fitr; Christian contemplation; and prayers, narratives, music, art and alms-giving from many traditions. These practices are only a few that are commonly shared by religious practitioners with others.

Practical engagement is more than experimentation. It also involves exploring, asking questions, and reflecting on the meanings of these practices for religious adherents and for others. In some cases, as in Thomas Merton's (1998) experiences with Eastern religious practices, the practices will become meaningful for students – a part of their own practice or meaning-making. Consider, for example, how Buddhist meditation and yoga (originating in Hinduism, Buddhism, and Jainism) have had meaning for many peoples across diverse worldviews and religious orientations. In other cases, also seen in Merton (1998), the practices of traditions different from one's own will lead students into new explorations and discoveries in their own tradition. Consider how Jewish Sabbath practices often inspire Christians to rediscover their own Sabbath traditions. The intrigue of new traditions and the rediscovery of one's own tradition are not antithetical movements. Afterall, religious narratives, beliefs, values, and practices exist side-by-side in history, often interacting and interweaving with one another. Further, traditions can be resonant with one another even when they are quite different in many respects. Such discoveries are made when schools provide opportunities for practical engagement goals.

(2) Collectivity goals

Human relationships with self and others are also furthered by collectivity goals. These are goals for *bringing people together for shared and mutual learning, shared experiences, and communal work in the school and community*. Collectivity goals may include school events, communal learning projects, sharing circles, ritual occasions without specific religious content, pauses for silence, moments for deep breathing, and aesthetic practices with the arts. They may also focus on the study of interreligious activist work as diverse religious groups focus collective effort on global issues and local issues of global import. Such work is documented in films, broadcast interviews with religious leaders, and in-person engagement with local leaders. The range of that work can also be suggestive of activist projects in which a school or a group of students might engage. The approach to such collective knowing and collective practice will necessarily be broad. Certainly, the most appropriate approaches and sensitivities will vary from context to context, but the range of options is vast.

Expanding approaches to collective worship and religious observance

The potential approaches to collective worship and religious observance have been presented above, so this concluding section will focus instead on qualities that educators might keep in mind as they implement the approaches described.

Intersubjective learning

One important quality in school life is intersubjective learning. I have written elsewhere about the myth of objectivity (Moore, 1995), arguing that the subjective dimensions of education are inevitable. What *is* possible is to create spaces for each person and book and film to speak for itself, and I would argue that is the intent of objectivity, namely to attend to the messages and meanings of others. What is also possible is to create a context for genuine listening and mutual engagement. In relation to collective worship and religious observance, schools can enhance intersubjectivity by sharing religious traditions and practices, and then reflecting on the meaning of those practices for adherents and others.

Meeting religiously

Another quality of education – meeting religiously – was named above as an important value in the study of religions. Schools can enhance interreligious understanding by providing opportunities for people to encounter the diversity of religions religiously, engaging with the full range of religious beliefs, values, and practices. Multidimensional study respects the fullness of religious traditions and opens opportunities for students to learn about those religions in a more holistic way, glimpsing the religious passions and hopes within them.

Ritualizing

A third quality of education is ritualization. Ritual is an important aspect of human experience and culture-building; thus, it is important to many of the educational goals named above, such as personal development, value, and wonder goals. By including collective worship and religious observance in school life, educators have opportunities to encourage a broad experience of ritual, as well as opportunities to reflect on them. They can also encourage practices of ritual without explicit religious content, creating shared ritual activities that are binding and meaningful for the whole community.

Moving from dominance to multiplicity

A challenge for educators in making decisions about worship and other forms of religious observance is to enact religious observances without inscribing the dominance of one tradition. Even the 'opt out' option accedes to dominance when one religious tradition is the focus and the people who do not fit that worldview need to request an exception. Though options for choice need to continue, schools can also seek a more comprehensive approach by selecting religions traditions and practices that represent the multiplicity of religions in each school and by providing opportunities to engage with at least a few other religions of the world.

Dignifying

A fifth important quality in education is to cultivate a sense of the worth and dignity of all peoples. The purposes and approaches discussed in this chapter serve that end. If teachers and learners are engaging the subject matter and one another with respect, they have already begun to cultivate dignity. What is also important is to study the religious and cultural practices of diverse peoples in order to encounter values important to them. When you participate in a Muslim gathering and people pause for prayer at the appointed hour, you discover the power of prayer and praise in Islamic tradition. When you engage in peacemaking practices with people from diverse traditions, you discover the power of meditation for Buddhists and verbal analysis for Jews and Christians; thus, you discover a fuller range of peacemaking possibilities. Such approaches not only dignify the people and traditions you are studying, but also broaden students' perspectives on the subject under study, whether prayer practices or peacemaking.

Revering

One final quality in education is to inspire and encourage reverence. The earlier discussions of wonder relate here. To revere is to recognize the more-ness of an educational moment or a religion under study. Collective worship and religious observances call attention to these moments as people engage the practices of diverse religious communities. Evelyn Underhill (1946), for example, encouraged teachers to teach all subjects in a 'spirit of worship', describing the spirit of worship as a 'deep reverence for life' (189–190). Such teaching can enliven education, whether in history, the sciences, literature, religion, or other subjects.

Underhill's emphasis calls us back to the theme of wonder, found in people as disparate religiously as Abraham Joshua Heschel and Thich Nhat Hanh. The theme is also important to my work, both in relation to Christian communities and to secular or interreligious settings (Moore, 1998, 2004). The value of awe-filled approaches to education is far more than passing delight; it enriches the depth of human lives. Heschel recognizes that these approaches to life and to education foster wisdom and connection with the universe: 'The beginning of awe is wonder, and the beginning of wisdom is awe ... Awe is a way of being in rapport with the mystery of all reality' (1975, 37). The educational quality of revering calls us back to the importance of wonder.

The qualities of education described here provide a synthesizing summary of values that emerge when schools include collective worship and religious observance. I have also argued that the inclusion of religious practices is vital for a full-bodied religious and humanistic education. Yet the approaches to religious practice need to be chosen with care to enhance the central purposes of education. I have proposed three guiding purposes in this chapter – integrity, holistic interreligious knowing, and human relationships with self and others. I have also named approaches and qualities that could guide these decisions. Whether educators adopt these proposals or others, they need to make intentional decisions about purposes and approaches as they engage with religious practices in schools. The underlying hope is for a comprehensive, engaged education that is meaningful for human lives and communities, at the same time preparing good citizens for local and global communities.

References

Arweck, E. (2016). *Young people's attitudes to religious diversity*. Abingdon: Routledge, Taylor & Francis.

Bankston III, C. L., & Caldas, S. (2009). *Public education – America's civil religion: A social history*. New York: Teachers College Press.

Buber, M. (1971). *I and Thou*. New York, NY: Touchstone.

De Souza, M. (2016). *Spirituality in education in a global, pluralized world*. Abingdon: Routledge.

Engebretson, K., de Souza, M., Durka, G., & Gearon, L. (Eds.) (2010). *International Handbook of Inter-religious Education*, International Handbooks of Religion and Education 4. London: Springer Science+Business Media B. V.

Ernst, C. W., & Lawrence, B. B. (2005). Foreword. In M. Cooke & B. B. Lawrence (Eds.), *Muslim networks from Hajj to Hip Hop*. Chapel Hill, NC: University of North Carolina.

Freathy, R., & Parker, S. G. (2012). Freedom from religious beliefs: Humanists and religious education in England in the 1960s and 1970s. In S. G. Parker, R. Freathy, & L. J. Francis (Eds.), *Religious education and freedom of religion and belief: Religion, education and values* (pp. 7–27). Oxford: Peter Lang.

Freathy, R., & Parker, S. G. (2013). Secularists, humanists and religious education: Religious crisis and curriculum change in England, 1963–1975. *History of Education: Journal of the History of Education Society*, 42(2), 222–256.

Glenn, C. L. (2012). *The American model of state and school: An historical inquiry*. New York: Continuum.

Greenawalt, K. (2007). *Does God belong in public schools?* Princeton: Princeton University Press.

Hanh, T. N. (1999). *The miracle of mindfulness: An introduction to the practice of meditation*. Boston, MA: Beacon.

Hanh, T. N. (2005). *Being peace*, 2nd edn. Berkeley: Parallax.

Heschel, A. J. (1965). *Who is man?* Redwood City, CA: Stanford University.

Heschel, A. J. (1975). *The Wisdom of Heschel* (selected by R. M. Goodhill). New York: Farrar, Straus & Giroux.

Hicks, D. (2013). *Dignity: Its essential role in resolving conflict.* New Haven, CT: Yale University.

His Holiness the Dalai Lama (2002). *How to practice: The way to a meaningful life* (trans. J. Hopkins). New York: Pocket Books, Simon & Schuster.

His Holiness the Dalai Lama (2016). *The heart of meditation: The art of discovering inmost awareness* (trans. J. Hopkins). Boulder, CO: Shambhala.

Hull, J. M. (1975). *School worship: An obituary.* London: SCM Press.

Hull, J. M. (1984). *Studies in religion and education.* Abingdon: Taylor & Francis.

Hull, J. M. (1989). *The Act unpacked: The meaning of the 1988 Education Reform Act for Religious Education* (Birmingham Papers in Religious Education). Derby: CEM.

Hunt, T., & Carper, J. (Eds.) (2013). *Religion and schooling in contemporary America: Confronting our cultural pluralism.* New York: Routledge.

Jackson, R. (2007). European institutions and the contribution of the study of religious diversity to education for democratic citizenship. In R. Jackson, S. Miedema, W. Weisse, & J. P. Willaime (Eds.), *Religion and education in Europe: Developments, contexts, and debates* (pp. 27–55). Münster: Waxmann.

Jackson, R. (Ed.) (2012). *Religion, education, dialogue and conflict: Perspectives on religious education research.* Abingdon: Routledge.

Jackson, R., Miedema, S., Weisse, W., & Willaime, J. P. (Eds.) (2007). *Religion and education in Europe: Developments, contexts, and debates.* Münster: Waxmann.

Kunzman, R. (2006). *Grappling with the good: Talking about religion and morality in public schools.* Albany, NY: State University of New York Press.

Kuusisto, A., Poulter, S., & Kallioniemi, A. (2017). Finnish pupils' views on the place of religion in school. *Religious Education, 112*(2), 110–122.

Meland, B. E. (1953). *Higher education and the human spirit.* Chicago: University of Chicago.

Merton, T. (1998). *The seven-storey mountain: An autobiography of faith,* 50th Anniversary Edition. New York: Houghton Mifflin Harcourt Publishing Co. (Original work published 1948).

Moore, M. E. (1995). The myth of objectivity in public education: Toward the intersubjective teaching of religion. *Religious Education, 90*(2), 207–225.

Moore, M. E. (1998). *Teaching from the heart: Theology and educational method.* Valley Forge, PA: Trinity.

Moore, M. E. (2004). *Teaching as a sacramental act.* Cleveland: Pilgrim.

Moore, M. E. (2011). (In)formation and beyond: Religious and theological studies, *Teaching Theology and Religion, 14*(4), 376–381.

Parker, S. G., & Freathy, R. J. K. (2012). Ethnic diversity, Christian hegemony and the emergence of multi-faith religious education in the 1970s. *History of Education: Journal of the History of Education Society, 41*(3), 381–404.

Polanyi, M. (1958). *Personal knowledge: Towards a post-critical philosophy*. Chicago: University of Chicago.

Porterfield, A. (2011). The problem of 'formation' for historians teaching religion, *Teaching Theology and Religion, 14*(4), 371–376.

Resnick, D. (2017). A place for shame in religious education. *Religious Education, 112* (2), 149–159.

Schnall, E., & Schnall, D. (2017). Positive psychology in Jewish education: Gratitude in the school and synagogue classroom. *Religious Education, 112*(2), 160–171.

Thatamil, J. (2011). Comparative theology and the question of formation, *Teaching Theology and Religion, 14*(4), 367–370.

Underhill, E. (1946). Education and the spirit of worship. In L. Menzies (Ed.), *Collected Papers of Evelyn Underhill*. London: Longmans, Green and Co. (Paper was originally presented as the Winifred Mercier Memorial Lecture, Whitelands College, Putney, November 1937).

Watson, J., de Souza, M., & Trousdale, A. (Eds.) (2014). *Global perspectives on spirituality and education*. Abingdon: Routledge.

Whitehead, A. N. (1967a). *Science and the modern world*. New York: McMillan, The Free Press. (Original work published 1925).

Whitehead, A. N. (1967b). *The aims of education and other essays*. New York: The Free Press. (Original work published 1929).

INA TER AVEST

13 Embracing Otherness in Supporting Community: A Plea from a Pedagogical Perspective for Experiential Learning in Dialogicality

ABSTRACT

Plurality in relation to secular and religious worldview orientations requires educators (typically parents and teachers) to prepare their children or pupils for encounters with 'the other'. In this chapter the British educational context is compared with the Dutch context regarding this preparation for 'living together in peace'. As well as 'knowing *about* the other', a precondition for such an encounter seems to be the experience of 'otherness' by way of 'living *with* the other', resulting in 'learning *from* the other'. As a consequence the skill of dialogicality will grow, the ability to embrace 'otherness' will intensify, and the awareness on one's own positionality regarding different worldview traditions will increase. This chapter ends with a recommendation for teacher training, preparing trainee teachers for their task to support the community by means of experiential learning in dialogicality. The term dialogicality is understood as meaning the competency to engage into a dialogue, a constructive and meaningful conversation requiring an open attitude paired with a genuine curiosity, and the willingness to change one's mind (Benson *et al.*, 1997).

Introduction

Today's children are the constructors of tomorrow's world, in which people of different ethnicities, class, gender and religious identities have to live with 'the other'. A precondition for this is a combined process of cognitive learning (i.e. knowing the characteristics of 'the other', knowing about different ways of 'living together') and affective learning (i.e. how does it feel to have an encounter with 'the other' or what kind of emotions are evoked meeting 'the other'). In this chapter I will present interReligious

Education (iRE) as a possible way of teaching and learning about religious diversity, embracing religious otherness and, as such, supporting collectivity. The focus is on dialogicality as the key for community and, in this process, every child matters.

In the first part of my chapter I will give my understanding of the concepts of 'collective worship' and 'religious observance', the key concepts in the context of religious education (RE) in the United Kingdom. Then I will explain the legal situation in the Netherlands, and focus on the way we in the Netherlands interpret and practise 'collective worship and religious observance' in primary schools. In the second half of my chapter I will seek to offer some fresh thinking on collective worship and religious observance in schools, elaborate on a child-centered approach, and take account of children's and parents' rights to educate their children in accordance with their beliefs and traditions.

Collective worship and religious observance

To explore what is meant by a term such as 'collective worship' in schools, I start with definitions of the verb 'worship', which is commonly thought of as being associated with the showing of one's respect (The BBI Dictionary of English Word Combinations, 1997). The word 'respect' refers to the Latin verb *respicere* which means 'being focused (at something)' or 'attentive observing or listening'. The dictionary definition of respect provides that 'if you worship someone or something you love them or admire them very much'. Following this clarification of terms, *collective worship* refers to attentive observing and listening, or loving and admiring someone or something that is shared by the members of a *community*. By the same token, in relation to religious observance, 'observance' is associated with 'obeying or following a custom or habit'. Accordingly, the interpretation of religious observance is 'entering into a familiar space of which the rules and habits – regarding religion – are known and obeyed, and such rules constitute the boundaries of the 'safe place of encounter'; encounters that may be 'contentious and risky, yet playful, pleasurable and ripe with educational possibilities' (Stengel and Weems, 2010, 506; see also Du Preez, 2012, 58).

On the basis of these definitions (from the dictionary) it can be seen that a key characteristic of 'collective worship' is 'attentive observing and listening, loving and admiring what people have in common', and that the focus of 'religious observance' is on 'entering in the space of and obeying to given and known (transmitted and/or experienced) religious rules'. Following this line of thought 'collective worship' in schools first of all needs such a marked space and the capacity to offer opportunities to discover and explore what people have 'in common', by 'attentive observing and listening' of what can be 'loved and admired' together. Similarly, the concept of 'entering in a space of and obeying given religious rules' urges people to get to know and acknowledge what exactly are the given religious rules for this space of exploration; rules that transform an ordinary space into a safe place of encounter, allowing not only for the pleasure of enriching aspects but also giving space to contentious and risky moments in intercultural and interreligious encounters.

Collective worship and religious observance: A journey

In seeking to set out on the road of exploring what is meant by the concept of 'otherness' a point of departure is needed. People start their journey – a real journey or an imagined one – from a certain place, which is typically a place that one is familiar with. It is important that it is a safe place (i.e. a place where one can return to in case the experiences of the 'journey' are less than pleasant), and a place that one knows well. Heinz Streib, in his essay in honour of the late John Hull, has emphasized the importance of the classroom being seen as a safe place where one feels free and able to encounter 'the other' (Streib, 2006, 191–204).

In this regard, Streib describes a variety of emotional experiences that can meet the encounter with 'otherness' or 'strangeness'. It can, for example, be 'coupled with anxiety or fear, with the desire to assimilate and abandon strangeness ... or with curiosity and an openness to its challenge, opposition and demand' (ibid. 193). According to Streib there is a hierarchical order in the emotional responses of a person meeting 'the other', and that this constitutes 'a movement of declining anxiety and increasing curiosity' (ibid. 193). This process is accompanied by moments of recognition of 'sameness' in 'the other', by feelings of (stronger) commitment to one's individuality, and by periods of acknowledgment and toleration[1] of the principal differences with 'the other'. This may result in collective endeavours, and the fostering of a new constructed experiential knowledge of the other's personal religious or secular worldviews. Collective endeavours crystallize different conceptions of tolerating 'the other', and this toleration may, on occasion, lead to the embracing of 'otherness'. As a consequence, making collective endeavours to tolerate can be the key to the building and fostering of community.

The Dutch and living apart together

The need for toleration of principal differences with 'the other' brings me to the Dutch pillarized educational context. In the Netherlands in the second half of the twentieth century 'the other' was housed in its own 'pillar'. The concept of 'pillarization'[2] was coined to describe the situation in which several religious subcultures existed side by side and were, in effect, 'Living Apart Together' (LAT). Accordingly, 'pillarization', whereby people were divided into several segments or 'pillars' based on different faiths or

---

1   See, for an extensive discussion about the concepts of 'tolerance' and 'toleration', M. Walzer, 1999.
2   'Pillarized' education is enacted by law, and allows for equal financial support for state schools as well as (religiously based) private schools. The financial support is the same for state as well as private schools, as is also the regular inspection of the quality of the education provided.

ideologies, has been termed to describe the Dutch model of responding to religious diversity (ter Avest *et al.*, 2007; ter Avest & Bakker, 2017).

For some Dutch Christian and Islamic schools (and, in particular, their principals/head teachers, teachers and parents) religious customs, habits and rules are a 'safe space', being, for example, clearly outlined in mission statements and ready to be implemented in the classroom by way of deductive reasoning in religious instruction. These are schools with a Christian (i.e. Protestant or Catholic), Islamic, or Hindu identity and ethos, which are all financed and controlled by the Dutch government. In different ways these schools empathize and practise their Christian, Islamic or Hindu identity as a *lived* identity (by the staff and the teachers) and as an *experienced* identity (by the pupils and their parents). In these practices the position and status of 'the other' is responded to in a variety of ways.

Encountering 'the other'

With the arrival of 'the other' in the school (i.e. in the Netherlands Muslim children from Turkey and Morocco), some Christian schools held on to their Christian practices of praying, singing hymns and reading Bible stories. Principals and teachers in some of these schools expected 'the other' simply to join in their practices, because in such schools 'teaching in' and 'teaching about' Christianity is dominant. However, some other Christian schools took as their starting points the *similarities* between these two religious traditions, and in such schools this 'teaching about' the Christian and the Islamic traditions was paramount. Moreover, some other types of school aimed to prepare their pupils for *inter-religious dialogue* (ter Avest, 2017), and in such schools they focused on 'teaching about' and 'teaching from' the tradition(s) of each other.

By law since 1985 all schools in the Netherlands (e.g. public schools, religious schools, and schools that adhere to a particular pedagogy such as Montessori and Steiner schools) have been obliged to teach and learn about other worldviews in a subject called *Geestelijke Stromingen* (Philosophical and Spiritual Orientations). In that subject information about 'other' religious or secular/humanistic traditions, as represented in Dutch society, is given from the school's own perspective – a (secularized) Christian, Islamic or Hindu perspective.

In addition to the religious schools (i.e. Christian, Islamic and Hindu) in the Netherlands there are public and independent schools – the former based on a humanistic/liberal perspective and the latter based on certain pedagogical views (e.g. Waldorf-schools and Montessori-schools). In public schools, where *teaching and learning about* religion is practised, information is given from a so called neutral perspective, giving room, on an equal basis, to the adherents of different traditions. In public schools, because of the challenges of neutrality and objectivity in the classroom, the strategy that is adopted is one of 'active plurality'. Thus, by way of example, schools' principles of association typically stipulate that every child is welcome, irrespective of the religious or secular worldview of their parents, because the school is 'a mini society' which mirrors the plural nature of Dutch society, in which difference is to be tolerated and respected.

Where parents in public schools wish for religious instruction in the tradition to which they adhere, Christian, Islamic and Hindu classes can be organized during school hours. This means that these children, for one hour a week, leave the classroom for religious instruction in accordance with the wishes of their parents, or receive instruction in accordance with a specific worldview.[3] In practice Christian and Humanistic instruction is routinely organized. In contrast, the extent to which Islamic instruction is organized depends on the educational views and perspective of the principal and the team of the school, while Hindu instruction is hardly ever organized in public schools. The organization of RE in this way has been a response to parental convictions that religious/worldview education at school should be in line with the way in which they themselves adhere to a particular system of beliefs or faith traditions.

---

3   See, for an extensive description of the Dutch educational system, ter Avest *et al.*, 2007.

The times, they are a changing

Bob Dylon wrote, in 1964, that 'the times they are a changin' and half a century later, they continue to change. Today a significant number of parents no longer adhere to a traditional or rigid belief system. As a result the views of some parents currently represent the process of 'bricolage' – in the sense of adhering to flexible belief systems constructed from a diverse range of sources – and this has resulted in what has been termed 'believing without belonging' (Davie, 1994). Whereas in former years a common question asked by parents was 'How to raise my children in my own tradition', this question nowadays is often reformulated in terms such as 'how to raise my children in a diverse world', or 'how to teach them to participate as citizens in a plural society' or 'how to raise my children to appreciate difference without becoming indifferent'. In tackling such questions this chapter now turns to focus on child centered RE, with particular reference to the challenge of responding to 'the other', who is different from me but with whom I must learn to live with in the public domain of the Dutch society.

Child-centred RE

A useful starting point here is the United Nations Convention on the Rights of the Child (UNCRC), a human rights treaty which documents the rights of children and was adopted by the General Assembly of the United Nations on 20 November 1989. The UNCRC, and international human rights law more generally, stipulates that parents (and guardians) have the right to educate their children in line with their beliefs and philosophical convictions. Moreover, according to the UNCRC, each government has to respect the rights and responsibilities of parents regarding the practice of the child's rights (article 5), and each child has the right to be educated (article 28). The aim of education should be identity development in the broadest sense, and this includes the development of the child's talents, as well as their psychological and physical skills. Education should prepare each child to participate as an active adult in a free society, and it is expected to respect a range of human rights including others' cultural backgrounds, native languages and value orientations (article 29).

The United Nations has long taken the view that it is the right of every child to be educated, and that this is more than merely being socialized in the tradition of one's parents. Besides learning to respect other peoples' human rights and their cultural backgrounds (e.g. their religious or secular worldviews), teachers should also familiarize their pupils with commonly held goals such as the Earth Charter (2000), which is an international declaration of fundamental values and principles about the need to protect the environment and build a just, sustainable, and peaceful global society in the 21st century. Indeed, school is there to enlarge the child's world (Bronfenbrenner, 1999) and to familiarize pupils and students with different world views – such matters being the essence of 'living in difference'!

Living in difference

A good example of what constitutes 'living in difference' can be seen from the beginning of the twentieth century. Janusz Korczak, who was born in 1878 as Henryk Goldszmit, was educated as a medical doctor and experiential expert as a coach in summer camps with youngsters of different social, cultural and religious backgrounds. He developed a form of 'practical wisdom', which is now known as the 'pedagogy of respect' (Berding, 2016, 42). His conscientious and assiduous note taking in his diary about his experiences with the children and subsequent reflections enabled him to develop his characteristic pedagogical approach. Moreover, this 'pedagogy of respect' was practised in the two orphanages he founded in (what is now) Poland.

In Korczak's line of thought, based on a pedagogical strategy of trial and error in the summer camps, four aspects come to the fore. First,

Korczak's contact with the children is not characterized by monologues, but by a dialogical approach. He does not tell the children what they have to do according to him, but time and again he 'creates a new world together with the children' (ibid. 46). Second, there is the recognition of children's rights. In Korczak's view every child has the right to promote their interests, based on what, according to them, is the best thing to do. As a result, others should respect this person's view on 'the best to do'. At the same time Korczak points to the fact that this right is limited by the right of the other also to aspire to what s/he thinks is the best thing to do. A particularly striking aspect of this is the right of the child to 'death'. With this 'right to death'[4] Korczak points to the need of each child to make their own mistakes, to learn by taking risks, by trial and error, and he addresses parents and warns them not to choke their children by their all-loving and caring attitudes. Third, is the clear and carefully arranged organization of the daily round, a structure in which each child participates. The structure is created regarding certain tasks and the responsibility for their accomplishment.

To resolve different points of view or conflicting interests, Korczak held meetings of the Children's Tribunal on a regular basis. At the Children's Tribunal problems were discussed and judged in public by a chosen group of pupils, presided over by a child, 'problems that apparently only touch upon individuals but that in everyday life always influence the community' (ibid. 54). Not punishment but forgiveness is central in the tribunal's discussions. Korczak's pedagogy breathes an atmosphere of democracy, of which respect, justice and participation are the core concepts (Berding, 2011, 78–80). The Children's Tribunal can be seen as a way of learning by doing (Dewey, 1999), experiential learning '*avant la lettre*'. Last but not least, and closely related to the above mentioned characteristic of recognition, is Korczak's 'law of respect', stressing equality of people (Berding, 2016, 57). The voice of a child according to Korczak should not be looked down on as if it were of minor importance; the voice of a pupil, expressing sorrow,

---

4   With the 'right to death' Korczak uses the word 'death' metaphorically. With the 'right to death' Korczak points to the right of children to find out for themselves which of their investigations lead to nothing, and appear to be dead-ended.

opinion and successes, should be considered as the same importance as the voice of a teacher (Berding, 2011, 78–79).

In the UN Convention on the Rights of the Child, aspects of Korczak's line of thought are clearly recognizable. With the characteristics of dialogue, children's rights and the limits thereof, Korczak's 'pedagogy of respect' can be seen as a forerunner of today's views on citizenship education. It must be said, though, that Korczak's point of view – highly idealistic – did show clear signs of realism. He stopped his repeated efforts to ban all fights between the children the moment only one daily fight was reported. Apparently Korczak was convinced that even in a world where people live together respectfully not all conflicts will have died away, as highlighted in his Children's Tribunal where the discussion about fights were included in the process of 'learning by doing' in response to conflicts.

Citizenship education

Korczak's ideas find their way in conceptions of citizenship education. With regard to citizenship education in a Dutch publication of 2004 three sub-concepts are distinguished: assimilative citizenship; individual-oriented citizenship; and critical democratic citizenship (Leenders & Veugelers, 2004). Assimilative citizenship focuses on the community to which a person belongs. The citizen has certain obligations to this community, and a person's identity is closely related to their position in this community. This position guarantees each person's rights and the protection thereof. The community is based on shared values. To be (or to become) an appreciated citizen in this community, one has to adhere to the shared value orientation. The transfer of the community's shared value orientation is the aim of education. Discipline and social commitment are central; homogeneity in the community is pivotal.

For individual-oriented citizenship the focus shifts from the community to the individual and each person's rights. These rights are seen as the basis of the individual's autonomy. The aim of education in this conception of citizenship is on skills of communication to enable pupils to enter into a dialogue on different ideas about their participation in society and the worldviews that these ideas stem from. Self-discipline and autonomy are central; social commitment has a lower position in the hierarchy of values as promoted in individual-oriented citizenship education which relates to education that focuses on autonomy.

In critical democratic citizenship, which is the third concept of citizenship identified by Leenders and Veugelers (2004), the strengths of the above mentioned other two conceptions of citizenship are brought together. Respect for the autonomy of each person is important, as is social cohesion. This social cohesion is not an unquestioned given (as it is in the conception of assimilative citizenship), but rather is creatively constructed through cooperation between citizens and dialogue about issues bothering them.

Ideas about citizenship and citizenship education on 'minimal and maximal citizenship' are expressed by McLaughlin (1992), and elaborated upon by Miedema (2012), and Miedema and Bertram-Troost (2014). Minimal citizenship, according to McLauglin, is knowledge based: knowing *about* the legal aspects of citizenship. In education according to a 'knowing about' approach, critical reflection and personal identity development is not seen as being of the utmost importance, since identity is written down and (by consequence) is given in legal terms. In maximal citizenship the active participation of persons is required and the focus is on inclusion and interaction. According to Miedema, maximal citizenship education opens up for the inclusion of different religious and secular worldviews. By consequence, in citizenship education, the focus should be on personal identity development, and the development of students' skills of dialogicality stimulating the development of one's own position regarding different views on living together in a plural society. Thus, for Miedema, such 'an embracing concept of citizenship education should imply that religious education and development is an inclusive part of citizenship education' (Miedema & ter Avest 2011, 414; Miedema, 2012).

Inclusive citizenship education

Inclusive citizenship education '*avant la lettre*' is central in an innovative
model that was developed in the last decades of the twentieth century in the
Netherlands as a model for teaching and learning in difference. From a growing awareness of the permanent stay of the so called children of 'guest work-
ers', in a Protestant Christian primary school the principal (together with his
team of teachers, parents, and Christian and Islamic theologians) developed
an interreligious RE model (iRE). This was a model in which every child
mattered irrespective of whether they were children with Christian parents,
Islamic parents, or parents who did not adhere to a specific faith tradition.

Starting in the 1980s, in a small village in a rural area of the Netherlands,
interReligious Education (iRE) was constructed (ter Avest, 2003, 2009).
The point of departure was the search for what the religious traditions
involved had in common, and the relation of the core of these narratives
to a child's everyday life. The psychological development of the child determined the level of the teaching materials, for which a Vygotskian point
of view regarding 'comfort zone' and 'zone of proximal development' was
decisive. The group of experts (i.e. teachers, theologians, parents) developed teaching material for Christian classes and Islamic classes separately
in which identification with the parental tradition was central, and this
included shared lessons ('lessons of recognition and dialogue') that constituted teaching *about* and *from* religion.

Every Monday the week started with a meeting of all classes in the
central hall of the school. In this meeting the principal or the teacher on
duty introduced to the children the theme of the week, a theme related to
a well-known narrative in the Christian and Islamic traditions. In my view
such a meeting is an astonishing parallel with my understanding of collective worship and religious observance. During this time Islamic classes
were taught by an Imam to children with an Islamic background (Turkish
or Moroccan), and Christian classes were taught by their class teacher.

One day a week there were so called 'classes of recognition' with peers
in their own classrooms. These 'classes of recognition' focused on the practice of dialogue. Commonalities in narratives from the traditions involved

were central, and differences were explored. The closure of the week took place in a gathering of all pupils with a central meeting in which learners from different ages showed how in their classes they made religion 'happen', and demonstrated how religion was present in pictures, songs, hymns, and texts (e.g. from the Bible and the Qur'ān) or theatre plays (Meyer, 2012, 7).

The core of interreligious education by way of narratives, fairy tales, songs, movies, and texts from Bible and Qur'ān has been described by Meyer in the following terms: It is 'making or fabricating something [that] is not simply an instrumental act in which the maker is unaffected and in control; it is a generating process in which subjects and objects are mutually constituted, becoming enmeshed and indistinguishable from one another, and which also creates surplus or excess. Humans are shaped by and shape the material world in such dynamics (ibid. 21).

Experiential teaching and learning in difference

Teaching and learning to live together cannot be successful without *practising* to live together, to start with in the classroom. This is an important area of concern: in case we aim at 'living together in difference', then the practice of separated religious classes might usher segregation (see also ter Avest & Miedema, 2010). We must become aware of implicit or explicit processes that lead to segregation; we must oppose not only exclusion but even or more so processes of expulsion (Sassen, 2014). Inclusion can be practised by way of training our pupils in different degrees of awareness of 'otherness' and tolerating 'otherness' (Walzer, 1997). Expulsion can be fought by putting into words what in general goes without saying, and challenge pupils to take the perspective of the other to understand the implicit discrimination and exclusion that accompanies what is seen as 'normal' for 'our kind of people'.

The Surinam-Dutch scholar Gloria Wekker in her 'assumption analysis', points to the implicit ways of discrimination – the so called 'everyday common discrimination' ('*alledaags racisme*'). This particular form of racism is originated in the 'cultural archive', a concept Wekker takes from the writings of Edward Said. The 'cultural archive' according to Wekker is 'a storehouse of ideas, practices, and affect that which is in between our ears, in our hearts and minds, regarding race, based on four hundred years of imperial rule' (author's translation from the original, Wekker, 2016, 30). It is a way of thinking, feeling and living that goes viral, for whites and blacks, be it with different consequences. Thus, for Walzer this requires having an awareness and recognition that 'others' have rights, even if they exercise those rights in strange or unattractive ways, as well as having a willingness to listen to and learn from 'the other'. This willingness to listen to and learn from the other is consistent with the Juliana van Stolberg (above) model for iRE, which is a sort of inclusive citizenship education.[5]

Teachers' qualifications

I am very much aware of the variations on the theme of dialogicality, practised in a variety of classrooms all over the world. I appreciate that a teacher can never be totally neutral or objective in the teaching and learning process. One's reaction to, or contribution to, a dialogue is always imbued with knowledge and opinions coming from our own religious or secular perspectives. But is this necessarily a 'problem'? Just imagine the scenario where a teacher brings into the classroom conversation a perspective that is deviant in some degree from what a pupil or student is socialized in. Rather than merely assuming that this is a 'problem', should we not reframe the situation and say, what an interesting point of departure for the subsequent classroom conversation?

In his recent publication 'Signposts', based on extensive research with teachers and students all over Europe, Robert Jackson (2014) describes a

5   In a recent publication (ter Avest, 2017) the concept of 'normative citizenship edu-
     cation' is coined, referring to the normativity of (inclusive) citizenship education.
     It relates to normativity in the sense of it being based on the standards to which the
     school and its teachers adhere.

variety of ways in which teachers have adopted to responding to the plural situation in their classrooms, mirroring the diversity in the religious and secular worldviews that are represented to a greater or lesser degree in contemporary Europe. It is particularly interesting if and how a teacher responds to the dissonant voice(s) in the classroom. Does s/he perceive the dissonant as a voice that disturbs a peaceful classroom conversation, or as a challenging voice that contributes to a dialogue on difference? Jackson stresses the need for well qualified teachers, with a good knowledge of worldviews and the relevant technical skills, to teach about these worldviews and to guide the pupils in learning from these worldviews.

A precondition for pupils being able to enter into dialogue with peers socialized in other religious or secular worldviews is knowledge about the variety of ways worldview traditions are represented in teaching materials and in the media. An interesting perspective on the urge for knowledge as a precondition for development is offered by John Hull in a book chapter entitled 'The education of the religious fanatic' (Hull, 2007). Following Hull's line of thought, the key for religious development is in knowledge about people's different beliefs and faiths. Hull favours a historical approach on the inner-religious, the intra-religious and the inter-religious developments, making pupils and students aware of the different interpretations of holy texts, as well as their context and relation to time and place. It is in the exchange of multiple ideas in a dialogue with a range of beliefs that pupils can arrive at a reflective and authentic position regarding (religious or secular) worldview traditions. According to Hull a lack of knowledge hinders dialogue and, as a consequence, hampers development. Indeed, for Hull, a key element of good religious education is the art of asking questions.

A well-equipped teacher, according to Jackson's and Hull's perspectives, is someone who can represent the diverse worldviews which constitute the 'cultural archive' of our society, as well as the 'cultural archive' of the relevant school, and is someone who can reflect on their own subjective positionality in the field of religious and secular worldviews. In short, they need to be appropriately qualified as normative professionals (Van den Ende and Kunneman, 2008; elaborated upon for teaching and learning by Bakker, 2014; and Bakker & Wassink, 2015; and Bakker & Montesano Montessori, 2016).

Conflicts widening pupils' horizons

In my view the main pedagogical task of the school is in widening the horizon of the child. As a result a subjective point of view of the teacher as a normative professional is exactly what is needed for the development of the child. One should keep in mind that, from a Vygotskian point of view, what is needed for development in general and by consequence also for citizenship education (including religious or secular worldview development) is 'difference'. In other words, a different point of view of 'the other' who is different from me – a 'conflict' that invites students to leave their comfort zones, explore what has been said, and a willingness to learn from and with 'the other'.

Nowadays, however, it is frequently the case that 'the other' is often seen as posing a threat to one's identity. However, this need not be necessarily so and the differences and tensions that might occur between persons adhering faithfully to a different system of beliefs can create an opportunity for learning, as is shown above in the iRE-model of the Juliana van Stolberg primary school. It is important to keep in mind that to trigger the curiosity of children and to invite them for the encounter with 'the other', the difference with 'the other' should be proportionate – being neither too big, because that might be threatening, nor too small, since then the child might think 'It's similar to what I know already, there's no need for exploration' (Vygotsky, 1997; Streib, 2006).

The Pope's materialized religion

In the twenty first century the boundaries of religious traditions are not as rigidly defined as they were in the past. In the Dutch context many people neither define themselves as 'Christians' nor do they obey so called Christian duties, while many Muslims – although they self-define as Muslims – do not obey all of the customs and habits of Islam. It is however striking that

Christmas is celebrated by all Christians – uniting in some way conservative and secularized Christians, as Ramadan in the same way unites all Muslims. In addition, many people in the Netherlands practise what is called 'whatever-ism' (a term coined by the Dutch former Minister of Education, Ronald Plasterk)', or what is in a more positive way and more clearly related to religious traditions coined as 'believing without belonging' (Davie, 1994), or 'multiple religious belonging' (Kalsky & Pruim, 2014). It is in concrete societal issues that people discover what they have 'in common', what can be 'respected, loved and admired' together. It is in their habits and customs that their religious or secular worldviews are materialized (Meyer, 2012).

Materialized religion: A starting point for dialogue

A recent interview with Pope Francis in '*Straatnieuws*' (the Dutch 'Big Issue') provides a good example of 'materialised religion', offering a possible starting point for teachers and pupils to reflect upon our collective worldviews (Pope Francis, 2015). In the interview the Pope informs us about an experience he had as a child. He writes:

> I remember very well the women who came to our house to assist my mother in cleaning the house, washing the cloths. ... She was poor, but she was such a nice women, I'll never forget her.

For the little boy who later became the Pope, this woman was to be respected, loved and admired, and to him her way of cleaning and washing must have been like rituals of purification. But the Pope is not alone in being inspired by the actions of others. Everybody knows somebody who is respected, loved and admired – somebody who epitomizes faithful dedication to their religion or equivalent system of belief. Such an example can provide a perfect starting point for a classroom conversation about what makes somebody respected, loved and admired, and this can foster dialogue about the relevance of shared values.

In his 2015 interview Pope Francis also said, 'I want a world without poverty. We need to fight for that'. Poverty, in whatever sense, can be a theme of 'materialized religion' to be explored as a starting point for dialogue, awakening a longing for a new and better world – a world in which the child can potentially become the co-constructor. For example, possible questions to be asked include, what makes you feel 'poor', or what do you experience when you reflect upon a 'poor' encounter? These are questions to be explored, the different interpretations being seen as challenges that can sharpen (or possibly change) convictions, or trigger the development of new dreams.

The interview with Pope Francis is an example of how to invite children to explore the concept of 'poverty'. This can help to generate discussion about who can be loved, respected and admired by them, and by whom they themselves feel loved, respected and admired. Daily experiences, in which abstract concepts are present in a 'hidden' way, can give us the starting points for exploration of (and reflection upon) our own/the teacher's own positionality with regard to religious and secular worldviews, which in turn provide the starting points for classroom conversations about reaching common ground on what can be tolerated, respected, loved or admired.

Normative professionalism

It is only through the process of reflection that daily experiences can become learning experiences (Dewey, 1999). Moreover, reflection is, according to the Scandinavian scholar Sharon Todd, the process by which a person systematically answers the following questions: What am I doing, why do I do what I do, why do I do it this way, what is my aim by doing this, and, last but not least – in the current context and in relation to educators – what are the consequences for my teaching? Reflection, as an external or internal dialogue, is the systematic reinterpretation or reframing of experiences and knowledge. It involves making a person aware of their actions and consequences, as well as adding to the technical skills of teaching and (as such) improving previous actions (Todd, 2007) – a process that has been described as reflection breadthwise (Kelchtermans, 2006).

To facilitate the development of normative professionalism – that is professionalism based on values, norms and standards of the professional her/himself (Bakker & Montesano Montessori 2016) – the reflection process is intensified by confronting teachers with the following three questions. First, what does the situation mean to me in the context of my biography? Second, what is the purpose of my actions against the background of (religious) values shared with significant others? Third, what if for example the hierarchy of (religious) values of my employer (the school/ institution) differs profoundly from my own value orientation? This also is coined as reflection in depth (Kelchtermans, 2009). A characteristic of reflection in depth is that it challenges one's own and others' beliefs, values and cultural practices, as well as historical, social, political and power structures. This raises the issue of contextual awareness, which means that we realize that our assumptions are socially and personally created in a specific historical and cultural context. What is needed in this process of reflection in depth is imaginative speculation, which is the potential to imagine alternative ways of thinking. Last but not least, suspense is of pivotal importance, because suspense points to the ability to suspend available evidence or reject it temporarily in order to establish new ways of acting (cf Brookfield 1988, see also Hatton & Smith, 1995).

The process of reflection hardly can be standardized, since unique situated experiences are at the start of each reflection process. Of decisive importance in the school environment are the voices of teachers, pupils and their parents, either as voices of persons present, or as characters in narratives (e.g. religious and folk narratives, or fairy tales). In case these voices are internalized, Driessen (2008) speaks of voices in the 'society of mind', being of greater or lesser importance for a person, depending on the context. For example, a child 'hears' the voice of the teacher telling her to be an autonomous person at the moment she turns to her best friend for advice. In another situation the teacher's voice will be pushed into the background or even be silenced. In a similar way the voice of a character

in a narrative or fairy tale can come to the fore or be silenced, depending
on the context in which the child finds herself.

Conclusion

To stimulate reflection and fresh thinking on collective worship and religious observance, and prepare for innovative 'collective worship' and 'religious observance', we need not start from scratch. In Robert Jackson's
'Signposts' there are many examples of good practice and of embracing
otherness. In John Hull's work we find challenging notions about 'teaching and learning in difference' from a range of different perspectives (e.g.
inner-religious, intra-religious and inter-religious ones). Indeed Hull, in
offering advice for novice teachers, has written about the need 'to come to
terms with the religious archetypes and to develop a mature understanding
of the ways in which religion has (or has not) interacted with their own
life' (Hull, 2007, 61).

It is suggested that we need to take up the examples from the workplace, as presented in Jackson's 'Signposts'. It is also important to support
the collective endeavours crystallizing the different concretizations of tolerating 'the other', by training students' skills for dialogicality and by doing
so to support the community. It is important that teachers, lecturers, and
other relevant stakeholders develop their sensitivity for 'examples of good
practice' and continue at their workplace what has already been started
as work-in-progress: they need to awaken in our pupils the longing for
a new world, and educate on the basis of what implicitly is already practised regarding our dreams of responding to diversity. This latter aspect
is of utmost importance: they must educate in regard to what is already
practised in the school as a miniature society – following Korczak – and
address the school community with a reasonable sense of reality! By way
of inductive reasoning these practices will find their way in policy documents – not as practices merely followed or copied but rather as inspiring
examples of learning by living together in a diverse community.

References

Arendt, H. (1994). *Oordelen, lezingen over Kant's politieke filosofie*. Den Haag: Krisie/ Parrèsia.

Bakker, C. (2014). *Het goede leren. Leraarschap als normatieve professie*. Utrecht: Hogeschool Utrecht.

Bakker, C., & Montesano Montessori, N. (Eds.) (2016). *Complexity in Education. From Horror to Passion*. Rotterdam/Boston/Taipei: Sense Publishers.

Bakker, C., & Wassink H. (2015). *Leraren en het goede leren; Normatieve professionalisering in het onderwijs*. [Teachers and good teaching; Normative professionalization in education]. Utrecht: Hogeschool Utrecht.

Bakker, C., & ter Avest, I. (2010). Self-understandings of RE-teachers in Structural Identity Consultation; Contributing to School Identity in a Multi-faith Context. In K. Engbertson, M. de Souza, G. Durka, & L. Gearon (Eds.), *International Handbook of Inter-religious Education* (pp. 415–424). Dordrecht/Heidelberg/ London/New York: Springer Verlag.

Benson, M., Benson, E., & Ilson, R. (1997). *The BBI Dictionary of English Word Combinations*. Amsterdam/Philadelphia: John Benjamins Publishing Company.

Berding, J. W. A. (2011). Opvoeding, participatie en burgerschap. De inspirerende visie van Janusz Korczak [Education, participation and citizenship. The inspiring vision of Janusz Korczak]. In N. Broer, H. de Deckere, M. Meer, T. Notten, & J. Stakenborg (Eds.), *Grenzeloze pedagogiek tussen wetenschap en praktijk* [Borderless pedagogy in between science and practice] (pp. 75–84). Gouda: VBSP.

Berding, J. W. A. (2016). Ik ben ook een mens: opvoeding en onderwijs aan de hand van Korczak, Dewey en Arendt [Me too, I am human: education and teaching inspired by Korczak, Dewey and Arendt]. Culemborg: Uitgeverij Phronese.

Bronfenbrenner, U. (1999). Environments in developmental perspective. In S. L. Friedman & T. D. Wachs (Eds.), *Measuring environment across the life span: Emerging methods and concepts*, 3–28. Washington, DC: American Psychological Association Press.

Brookfield, S. (1988). Developing Critically Reflective Practitioners: A Rationale for Training Educators of Adults. In S. Brookfield (Ed.), *Training Educators of Adults: The Theory and Practice of Graduate Adult Education*. New York: Routledge.

Davie, G. (1994). *Religion in Britain Since 1945: Believing Without Belonging*. Blackwell: Oxford.

Dewey, J. (1999). *Ervaring en opvoeding. Vertaald en ingeleid door G. Biesta en S. Miedema*. [Experience and education. Translated and introduced by G. Biesta and S. Miedema]. Houten/Diegem: Bohn Stafleu Van Loghum.

Hatton, N., & Smith, D. (1995). Reflection in teacher education: towards definition and implementation. *Teaching & Teacher Education, 11*(1), 33–49.

Hull, J. (2007). The education of the religious fanatic. In J. Astley, L. J. Francis, & M. Robbins (Eds.), *Peace or Violence: The Ends of Religion and Education?* (pp. 46–63). Cardiff: University of Wales Press.

Jackson, R. (2014). *Signposts – policy and practice for teaching about religions and non-religious worldviews in intercultural education.* Council of Europe Publishing: Strasbourg.

Kalsky, M., & Pruim, T. (2014). *Flexibel geloven. Zingeving voorbij de grenzen van religies.* [Flexible Faith; Sense giving beyond religious boundaries]. Vught: Skandalon.

Kelchtermans, G. (2006). Capturing the multidimensionality of teacher professionalism: Broad and Deep Reflection. In *Postgraduate Programs as Platform: An Interactive and Research-led Approach* (pp. 97–109). Dordrecht: Sense Publishers.

Kelchtermans, G. (2009). Who I am in how I teach is the message: self-understanding, vulnerability and reflection. *Teachers and Teaching: theory and practice, 15*(2), 257–272.

Leenders, H., & Veugelers, W. (2004). Waardevormend onderwijs en burgerschap. Een pleidooi voor een kritisch-democratisch burgerschap. *Pedagogiek, 24*ᵉ jaargang, 4, 361–375.

McLaughlin, T. (1992). Citizenship, Diversity and Education: A Philosophical Perspective. *Journal of Moral Education, 21*, 235–250.

Meyer, B. (2012). *Mediation and the Genesis of Presence. Towards a material approach to religion.* Public Lecture, October 19, 2012, Universiteit Utrecht.

Miedema, S. (2012). Maximal citizenship education and interreligious education in common schools. *Commitment, character, and citizenship. Religious education in liberal democracy.* 96–102.

Miedema, S. (2014). Learning to Live with Religious Plurality in Personhood Formation. *Philosophy Study, 4*(1), 28–35.

Miedema, S., & ter Avest, I. (2011). In the flow to maximal interreligious citizenship education. *Religious Education, 106* (4), 410–424.

Miedema, S., & Bertram-Troost, G. D. (2008). Democratic citizenship and religious education: Challenges and perspectives for schools in the Netherlands. *British Journal of Religious Education, 30* (2), 123–132.

Pope Francis (2015). 'I want a world without poverty. We need to fight for that', *The Big Issue*, December 2. Retrieved June 15, 2017, from <http://www.bigissue.com/interviews/pope-francis-interview-i-want-world-without-poverty-need-fight/>.

Sassen, S. (2014). *Expulsions. Brutality and Complexity in the Global Economy.* Cambridge: Harvard University Press.

Sinclair, J., Fox, G., Bullon, S., & Manning, E. (1998). *Collins Cobuild English Dictionary*. London: Collins.

Stengel, B. S., & Weems, L. (2010). Questioning Safe Space; An Introduction. *Studies in Philosophy and Education, 29*, 505–507.

Streib, H. (2006). Strangeness in inter-religious classroom communication. In D. Bates, G. Durka, & R. Schweitzer (Eds.), *Education, Religion and Society* (pp. 191–204). London: Routledge.

Ter Avest, I. (2017). Levensbeschouwelijk onderwijzen en leren [Teaching and learning in worldview(s)]. *Tijdschrift voor Religie, Recht en Beleid, 8*(1), 57–77.

Ter Avest, I., & Bakker, C. (2017). Religious education in the Netherlands. *RE Today, 34*(2), 56–60.

Ter Avest, I., Bakker C., Bertram-Troost, G. D., & Miedema, S. (2007). Religion and Education in the Dutch post-pillarized education system: historical backgrounds and current debates. In R. Jackson, S. Miedema, W. Weisse, & J. P. Willaime (Eds.), *Religion and Education in Europe, Developments, Contexts and Debates* (pp. 203–221). Münster: Waxmann.

Ter Avest, I., & Miedema, S. (2010). Noodzaak tot recontextualisering van onderwijsvrijheid vanuit (godsdienst) pedagogisch perspectief [The urge to recontextualize freedom of education from a pedagogical perspective]. *Tijdschrift voor Onderwijsrecht en Onderwijsbeleid.* 77–88.

Todd, S. (2007). Teachers judging without scripts, or thinking cosmopolitan, *Ethics and Education, 2*(1), 25–38.

Unicef (2001). Verdrag inzake de Rechten van het Kind [Universal Declaration of Children's Rights], aangenomen in de Algemene Vergadering van de Verenigde Naties op 20 November 1989. Den Haag: Unicef Nederland.

Van den Ende, T., & Kunneman, H. (2008). Normatieve professionaliteit en normatieve Professionalisering [Normative professionalism and normative professionalization]. In G. Jacobs, R. Meij, H. Tenwolde, & J. Zomer (Eds.), *Goed werk. Verkenning van normatieve professionaliteit* [Good work. Exploration of normative professionalism] (pp. 68–87). Amsterdam: SWP.

Vygotskij, L. S. (1997). *Educational Psychology*. Florida: CRC Press.

Walzer, M. (1999). *On Toleration*. New Haven: Yale University Press.

Wekker, G. (2016). *White Innocence. Paradoxes of Colonialism and Race*. Durham and London: Duke University Press.

GEIR SKEIE

14 Common Symbols in a Diverse School for All: Collective Worship Seen from a Scandinavian Perspective

ABSTRACT

The issues arising from the debate over collective worship in United Kingdom challenge us to consider the role and function of school in the local community as well as on a national level. This chapter considers some parallel issues and developments in Scandinavia, including the changes in the place of religion in Norwegian schools based on human rights law and considerations about collective celebrations in Swedish schools. It is argued that it is important for schools to have collective practices that reflect the general aims of education in a way that is accessible for students.

Introduction

This chapter addresses the issues of collective worship and religious observance in UK schools. An evaluation of the law and policy surrounding these activities was recently undertaken and presented in a report by an interdisciplinary network of academics funded by the UK Arts and Humanities Research Council (AHRC) (Cumper & Mawhinney, 2015). Rather than providing further discussion as to how this issue should be dealt with in a UK context, this contribution approaches the issues from the perspective of a Scandinavian researcher in religion and education. It is an attempt to reflect on a distinct UK phenomenon, by drawing on examples from two other national contexts and overviews (Osbeck & Skeie, 2014; Skeie & Bråten, 2014).

For a Scandinavian reader, the AHRC report appears as informative, interesting, thought-provoking as well as well-argued. Many reports on educational policy and practice tend to be voluminous and, in their efforts to present the complexity of the issues, they sometimes drown the reader in detailed information. However, I find this report to the point and, at the same time, able to concretize its issues in a way that brings even the non-UK reader straight into the concrete, spatial and bodily aspects while ensuring the legal perspectives are kept to the fore. A key part of the report refers to the possible rationale of collective worship/religious observance. It takes the reader back to the Second World War and the need to 'ensure the nation's future well-being', and asks whether the situation in the UK today, including the relationship between State and Church, can provide a contemporary rationale for the practice. The key elements in such a rationale are referred to as the needs of the individual pupil, the needs of the school and the needs of a wider society. These elements are not necessarily to be seen as alternatives, but it is certainly possible to imagine that by putting a particular emphasis on one of them, another could be hampered. The original justification focused on the state and the national ethos, and certainly this could be seen as a conscious step to diminish or suppress individual and group-oriented identities that could challenge the collective loyalty to the nation. Here, the situation at present is different from 1944, but even if it is not a war situation, recent debates show that issues such as EU membership, European integration, migration, diversity and postmodern relativism carry references to imagined collective threats. It is not too far-fetched to argue that these or other examples could be used to argue for the same priority of 'British values' that was relevant when the moral crisis was on the agenda in 1944.

By highlighting the issues mentioned above, the AHRC report therefore challenges the reader to consider how one can balance and manage the individual, educational and societal aims of education. Are they possible to conceptualize in a way that is universally accepted, or does this simply open up political divisions? As if this is not enough to sort out, we must ask whether religion and belief can have any place in a collective worship context when pupils, parents and teachers belong to different traditions. These questions are certainly appropriate, but they threaten the possibility of placing an appropriate value on 'community' in schools. It is certainly difficult to imagine running a school without a common ethos. On the other hand, what are the legitimate resources to draw on in order to meet the individual and collective needs for communal harmony and a good learning environment? Can they be drawn from religions and beliefs? If not, from where?

Without stating this explicitly, the AHRC report indicates that any kind of event that plays a similar role to today's collective worship/religious observance would face the same questions. The fact that religion has a history of underpinning the national heritage and ethos does not mean that (other) ideologies cannot play a similar role, and this certainly must have been part of the background in 1944 when knowledge about Nazi Germany was widespread. Then Christianity was used to perform that role; but today the report is a sign that this must be up for negotiation with the possibility that there may be potential for something like an 'overlapping consensus' (Rawls, 1987).

A final aspect worth mentioning in regard to this section of the report has to do with the role of school subjects in relations to collective worship/religious observance. At times when 'knowledge' is a catchword in educational policy and much attention is directed to the performance of pupils, schools and national educational systems in some core subject areas, it is not always easy to focus attention in a discussion about the 'soft' aspects of education. The learning environment and well-being of pupils, social relations and personal development are important issues both to teachers and parents, but often this is overshadowed by a focus on related learning outcomes and evaluation systems. It is therefore an important question to ask whether there is a need to have a 'distinct and designated period of time' allocated for pursuing the type of aims that a collective worship/religious observance may reasonably do.

When considering the pressing practical issue, namely the question whether the existing practice is acceptable, the AHRC report presents the concerns around its current form, concerns that will continue into the future should the status quo be maintained. In a situation where the actual practice often seems to be problematic, and the rationale appears outdated, a reconsideration certainly seems appropriate. However, to abolish the practice altogether appears to be a too easy a way out of the dilemma. It seems justified to expect that the effect of this would be to open up for disparate and local practices with limited transparency. A suggestion to let the governors of individual schools decide the form and character of future acts of collective worship may lead to some of these weaknesses (Clarke & Woodhead, 2015). It seems fruitful to take the complex and contested issues into the public arena, to process it politically and to decide on a renewed practice based on a reformed rationale. This would ensure a continuing reflection on practice and policy, including inspection. The AHRC report does not go in detail about the content of this, but it rather recommends a set of rules for the process. It is difficult for an external observer to be more specific about future regulations. What can be done, however, is to reflect further on some of the issues raised above, and to bring in some issues from the Scandinavian scene that can add perspective to discussions in the UK.

Nation and education

There are reasons to believe that the Scandinavian context may have some relevance for discussing the situation in the UK regarding collective worship/religious observance. The wider socio-cultural settings are marked by features such as secularization, combined with increasing diversity and the residual position of the main Christian churches. As indicated in the AHRC report, the relationship between religion and nation plays an important role in the historical origins of collective worship (Cumper & Mawhinney, 6). The Christian religion, particularly through a dominant national church, has played a significant role in forming and maintaining a national ethos in all countries. Secularization started to reduce some of the aspects of this function long ago, but the echo from former times it is still very present in both institutional and functional ways. This can be detected in national celebrations, the status and performance of the head of state, and in situations of national crisis. It can therefore be argued that the close connection between (Christian) religion and the nation state is not obsolete but rather is still very relevant, even though they are perceived and analysed in different ways than was previously the case.

Additionally, public education should be included in the deliberation about how national identity and ethos are negotiated and produced today. In the light of the above, public education can be interpreted as a vital institution for maintaining the national ethos and for passing it on to future generations, even if this is articulated differently in contemporary educational acts and regulations. For example, in each of England, Norway and Sweden the nation plays a role in the formulation of the overarching aims of education. In the English national curriculum, this is presented in the following way:

> The national curriculum provides pupils with an introduction to the essential knowledge that they need to be educated citizens. It introduces pupils to the best that has been thought and said; and helps engender an appreciation of human creativity and achievement. (The National Curriculum 2013, 6)

In Norway, similar issues are voiced in the Education Act:

> Education and training shall help increase the knowledge and understanding of the national cultural heritage and our common international cultural traditions. (Norwegian Education Act, § 1–1)

The Swedish Education Act links the nation closely to international human rights, claiming that this is the value foundation of Swedish society:

> Education shall teach and anchor respect for human rights and the basic democratic judgements, which the Swedish society rests upon. (Swedish Education Act § 4, translated by author)

By anchoring of the aims of education in some broad national ethos, the local school also becomes committed to the same ethos. Further, the local school can be seen as a society in miniature, where the diversity of the local community to some extent mirrors the national diversity. In the light of this, events such as collective worship can be seen as a ritualization and manifestation of the social community that the school is representing, while at the same time connecting this to the larger, national community.

The problems that arise in relation to the practice of collective worship today, which are briefly but distinctly discussed in the report, can be read to problematize the basis or composition of this 'community'. I read this as asking on what grounds a symbolic collective celebration of community and society can be justified in a school for all. The report unpacks the issues involved in a fruitful way by differentiating between personal, educational and social needs as separate dimensions. On the other hand, one reason for installing and keeping the practice seems to be the ambition to let all these three dimensions work together on a daily basis in school. It is therefore interesting to approach the possible relationship between the dimensions. Is there a priority of concerns? Is there an internal dynamic, meaning that one impacts on the other two?

Another observation to be made from reading the report is that when discussing primary considerations about rationale, this is phrased in terms of 'needs'. This may imply that there are certain deficits that should be met. This tends towards a certain view of children and young people as being (mainly) in need of certain things instead of doing or acting on their own behalf, and being seen as more resourceful. Alternatively, one could interpret 'needs' as referring to constant cycles of needs and satisfaction that are not valued, but only registered, like need for food, shelter or meaning. This is a way of 'naturalising' the needs, making them appear as 'basic' or 'human'.

Finally, the report frames its discussion in a particular way by introducing the rationale as something coming from the past. This is exactly what comes to the fore in the examples presented by the report, following the 'need'. However, here it is clear that the report focuses less on the logic of 1944, where the focus was on threats, and instead concentrates on visions for a future school and society. Visions for the individual, the school and the society are taken together to cover the general aims of education. It locates the question of collective worship in a deliberation about what we want education to be. Therefore, the specific aims of 1944 are less relevant but yet the question as to what the nation requires today remains even if the focus is not solely on these needs. Such a location of the issue makes it possible to discuss collective worship also across national borders, even if the phenomenon itself is not found all over. What we are looking to compare are situations or practices of collectively formulating, celebrating and remembering aims of education, with an emphasis on the individual, a school or society generally, or the three combined. This can be seen as a ritualization of school ethos, or memory politics. As an example of collective memory and ritualization, collective worship also raises the issue as to the nature of the role that religion plays or may play in this context.

In the following, I will present some perspectives from a Scandinavian context, which while not arising from the same type of practice as collective worship, I find to be of relevance for the UK. This discussion deals with issues of human rights, the national and school ethos, as well as collective, symbolic gatherings in schools.

The Scandinavian context

Today, both Norway and Sweden have similar types of religious education in school(s). The subjects are compulsory for all students, with broad, knowledge-oriented subjects covering religions, secular worldviews and ethics. In Norway philosophy is also included. There is no general right of exemption, but some activities may be optional. In Sweden this type of religious education subject has a longer history than in Norway: in the 1960s religious education was 'secularized', while a similar process started in Norway in the late 1990s. To some extent, these developments have paralleled the changes in relationships between Church and State, but this is only part of the picture (Osbeck & Skeie, 2014; Skeie & Bråten, 2014). Both countries have a long history of Lutheran kingdoms and absolutism, but today each has a separation between State and Church, although this process has been gradual and is ongoing, particularly in Norway. Heads of state, in both cases kings, maintain a relationship with the national church, although this seems to be stronger in Norway than in Sweden where the Norwegian Constitution demands that the king is Lutheran.

The long history of state religion and the fact that a large majority of the population still belongs to the Lutheran church means that to account for the formal and legal relationship between State and Church does not give sufficient knowledge to understand the present situation (Breemer, Casanova, & Wyller, 2014). One oft-discussed aspect of this has been called the 'Nordic paradox', referring to highly secularized societies' low-church attendance combined with their high participation in life rituals (Bäckström, Edgardh Beckman, & Pettersson, 2004). Furthermore, in situations of national crisis, the Church of Norway has had a central position, from the resistance against the German occupation during the period 1940 to 1945 to the crisis management and memory rituals after the terror attacks on 22 July 2011.

In addition, in the case of religion in education, it is possible to detect the same paradox in the practice of church-based celebrations by local schools. In both countries, it is quite common, especially in the countryside and smaller towns, for the end of term celebration for the whole school (either before Christmas or before the summer holidays) to be held in the local church. This is in spite of there no longer being a formal relationship between church and school. This practice is, however, as controversial as collective worship and it seems that the debates in both Norway and the UK are partly following the same lines.

Human rights debates about religion and education in Norway

The AHRC report refers to the possibility of withdrawing pupils from acts of collective worship/religious observance. One important reason for having this right is to ensure protection of the right to freedom of religion or belief. The report refers to the case-law of the European Court of Human Rights in order to clarify the relevant norms in this matter. In the case of *Folgerø vs. Norway*, the court stated:

> The Court notes in particular that for a number of activities, for instance prayers, the singing of hymns, church services and school plays, it was proposed that observation by attendance could suitably replace involvement through participation, the basic

idea being that, with a view to preserving the interest of transmitting knowledge in accordance with the curriculum, the exemption should relate to the activity as such, not to the knowledge to be transmitted through the activity concerned (see paragraph 48 above). However, in the Court's view, this distinction between activity and knowledge must not only have been complicated to operate in practice but also seems likely to have substantially diminished the effectiveness of the right to a partial exemption as such. Besides, on a purely practical level, parents might have misapprehensions about asking teachers to take on the extra burden of differentiated teaching (see paragraph 29 above). (ECHR 2007, 100)

The European Court made the remark in a case that challenged the then curriculum for religious education in Norway and therefore is not directly applicable for the practice of collective worship/religious observance. The case had to do with situations where some students or parents felt that participation in school activities or lessons would breach their right to freedom of religion or belief. Certain activities are mentioned that could be part of religious education lessons, and the European Court ruled that it is not easy to establish whether this should be seen as some sort of participation in religious activities or whether it was merely observing a practice for educational purposes. Therefore, the practice was judged to be problematic. Of practical relevance for collective worship is the list of activities that should be considered relevant for exemption. Following the case, the common interpretation by Norwegian educational authorities was that pupils could be exempted from certain (religious) activities, but not from knowledge (about religions). The focus of interest was therefore on the type of situations that tended to be seen as religious activities. In the view of the court, these included:

> Prayers, creed and other important religious texts; hymn singing; attendance at rituals/visits to churches or other religious assembly buildings; excursions; school services; illustrations; the prohibition of images, especially challenging stories, parallel figures; dramatizations. (ECHR 2007, 77–81)

In a religious education teaching and learning context, these activities are seen as examples that may lead to concerns around religious freedom. Here it is foreseen that parents and pupils may feel that the learning activity is inappropriate given their religion or belief. Therefore, it can reasonably be argued that these are situations where (partial) exemption should be an option. The court said that information about forthcoming activities should be sufficiently detailed so as to afford parents a realistic opportunity to request an exemption if they so wished. In order for the procedure to be easy and efficient, and to avoid stigmatising students, the formalities were reduced as much as possible. When the first non-confessional religious education subject for all was introduced in 1997, a main aim was to include all students in the class. It was considered to send the wrong message if students could not learn about religions and beliefs in joint classes, since this could communicate that diversity was a problem. At that time, 5 to 6 per cent of the students were exempted from religious education classes and it was a clear intention to include these students (NOU, 1995) Therefore the general right to exemption was removed. Ten years later, after the case in the European Court of Human Rights, the aim of one subject for all had strong support both nationally and in local schools. There seemed to be a search for inclusive practice and parents seldom used the partial exemption. One reason for this has probably been that schools tended to avoid those activities that could lead to requests for exemptions. Therefore, one could conclude that the aim of inclusive religious education in a diverse classroom requires the monitoring of activities so as to avoid forcing certain students to ask for exemption. On the other hand, the possibility that someone might ask for exemption does not mean that any such activity is necessarily problematic.

Since many of the activities mentioned above might be relevant also for collective worship/religious observance, it would certainly be wise to differentiate a collective school assembly from religious activity by naming it differently. This would mean avoiding both 'worship' and 'religious' in the title. Further, it may also be wise to consider the types of activities mentioned above with some care, in order to avoid too many negative reactions. It is clear that some pupils may wish to be exempted anyway from time to time and this should be provided for. If it is not, the nature of the activity will be closely scrutinized. Rules for the right of exemption in the Norwegian Education Act are formulated generally for the school and not targeting religious education in particular:

> Following written notification by parents, pupils shall be exempted from attending those parts of the teaching at the individual school that they, on the basis of their own religion or own philosophy of life, perceive as being the practice of another religion or adherence to another philosophy of life, or that they on the same basis find objectionable or offensive. It is not necessary to give grounds for notification of exemption pursuant to the first sentence. Exemption cannot be demanded from instruction in the academic content of the various topics of the curriculum. If the school does not accept a notification of exemption on such a basis, the school must deal with the matter in accordance with the provisions concerning individual decisions laid down in the Public Administration Act. (Norwegian Education Act, Section 2–3a)

Even if this is a whole school regulation, the intention is also specifically reflected in the syllabus of the religious education subject in a way. Here the need to be sensitive towards different reactions among students and parents is formulated as follows:

> Care must be used when selecting working methods. The careful choice of working methods is especially important when considering parents, guardians and pupils so that they feel their own religion or philosophy of life is respected and that the subject be experienced without seeming to exercise another religion or forming an affiliation to another philosophy of life. Respect for the views of individuals and local communities should be paramount. (Curriculum for knowledge of Christianity, religion, philosophies of life and ethics (rle1-02) 2015, 1)

One important change in the Norwegian policy on religion in education following the judgement of the European Court of Human Rights – and which is reflected in the above quotation from the Education Act – was that religion in school became an issue that was treated separately from religious education. For this reason all regulations to do with exemptions refer to teaching in schools in general and therefore apply also to religious education. One reason was to relieve some of the pressure from religious education, which had been through significant scrutiny for ten years. Another was the knowledge that issues of freedom of religion or belief did not only apply to religious education. In a school for all, there may be activities that certain parents and pupils do not want to take part in because of their basic convictions. This should not automatically be seen as a failure from the school to be inclusive, but exemption should be provided. The principle could therefore be applied, for example, with respect to sports, literature classes, collective assemblies, excursions or religious education classes. In addition, the regulation requiring detailed and sufficient information to be provided in ample time before an activity took place was made universal. This seems to be relevant for the UK debate in that it shows how the issue of exemption always has to be taken into account in a school with a diverse student population. Even if this means a temporary exclusion from the community of students, it does not imply that it should be avoided altogether. For some, the right to be excluded from certain activities can be of vital importance and in the end aids inclusion because they are not forced to take on a battle nor act in a manner that conflicts with their beliefs.

Collective celebrations in Swedish and Norwegian schools

An interesting example of religion in education that has relevance to the UK situation of collective worship is the rather common but not universal practice in many Norwegian and Swedish communities that the entire school goes to a school service in the local church either before Christmas or at the end of spring term. This service is usually specially designed for the purpose and prepared in advance in cooperation between church and school. Here, pupils usually participate in the performing of the service by reciting poems or other texts, singing and playing instruments. Both in Norway and in Sweden these practices have caused debates and school inspection agencies have given their rulings or advice in certain cases.

The background and rationale for these services are probably not that different from the history behind collective worship/religious observance. The practice has roots that go back to former times when school was as a matter for the state church and confirmation was the final examination, which means that it is part of collective memory in the local community, going back generations. The modern practice is possibly reinforced by the war experiences, when the majority of Church of Norway clergy strongly opposed the German occupation. This strengthened relations between the Church and the national heritage after the war and, in particular, it contributed to a mellowing of the rather tense relationship between the Church and labour movement that existed during the 1920s and 1930s. This was important because of the long reign by the Labour Party after the war. Nonetheless, during the 1950s, the ties between the state and the majority Church of Norway were criticized, in particular, by the growing Norwegian Humanist Association and eventually this and other criticisms led to the separation of Church and State, a process which is ongoing. However, the above mentioned 'Nordic paradox' seems to be relevant also for understanding the continued support in many communities for school services in church, even today. Regular debates about such services, often stimulated by the Norwegian Humanist Association, have raised issues of religious freedom, parental rights and ritualization within school communities. Sometimes local 'silent majorities' have been even more keen to support these services than either humanists or local parishes. In these cases, school leaders may be caught between the wishes of a number of strident parties (Hovdelien & Neegaard, 2014).

Sweden is often described as even more secularized country than Norway, with a less strong official emphasis on national identity. Nonetheless, school services play a role in local communities here also and have generated much debate. In some cases when there have been complaints about such services, the Swedish school inspection has issued rulings. An example of such a case concerns the local school in Hässeholm. In this instance parents brought the practice to the attention of the inspectorate who looked into the question of whether the service was 'religious', and, if so, was it was possible to interpret the event as insufficiently religious to warrant concern? The following quotation gives an impression of the reasoning and conclusion:

> Even if the church space itself, pastors and psalms in themselves are religious elements, no religious element in an end of school year celebration is in conflict with the law and regulations. The School Inspection has decided that end of term celebration can happen in church if the emphasis is on traditions, hallow atmosphere and being together, and not on religious elements like prayer, blessing or confession'. (Skolinspektionen, Dnr 41-2011:3039, translated by author)

According to this, the end of term gathering may happen in a church if the event is designed in a particular way. Awe and religious atmosphere in terms of space is acceptable, but religious elements or activities like prayer, blessings or professing of creed, sermon or other type of preaching are not. The rulings in the inspection case are based on the regulations of the national educational authority, Skolverket, which has dealt with end of term events in churches in a legal advice document (Skolverket, 2012). Here, issues of principle are discussed and the main line drawn is that a non-confessional school should not include religious activities. As shown above, the division line between 'religious' and 'non-confessional' is not always easy to draw. The sometimes subtle dividing line is illustrated by the legal advice document, when it takes the example of a particular psalm, which can be sung because it is so 'commonly associated with tradition and end of term in school' (Skolverket, 2012, 5). It is further mentioned that religious festivals may be given attention in the school, provided the regulations are followed. The example mentioned is that of lighting candle(s) in the Advent period before Christmas.

The Swedish regulations differ from the Norwegian ones, in that the Norwegian regulations deal with religion in school as a general feature. This means that exemption is possible at any point in the school day and for any kind of activity if it is seen as interfering with the right to freedom of religion. In Sweden, the regulation says that the right to be exempted is applicable only to teaching situations and not to other parts of the school day. Therefore, the end of term event in a church is not something students can be exempted from; the only alternative is to claim that the entire event is in conflict with freedom of religion. It could be argued that this course of action would result in greater exclusion and stigmatization for those parents or students who pursue such a claim.

The general impression in both the Swedish and Norwegian context is that the regulation of religious elements in school practice are somewhat problem-oriented, but this should not overshadow the fact that there is strong support for doing things together in school that may support positive elements like tradition, awe and fellowship (community). The challenge is that the elements used to build such celebrations of school community and social cohesion in a wider sense may be contested. It is tempting to argue that we are here referring to 'imagined communities' and that both local practices as well as national regulations are part of negotiations about these imagined communities (Anderson, 2006). Perhaps because of this 'contestedness', there is a certain shyness or anxiety toward collective celebrations in schools. A further search at the website of Swedish National Agency for Education with focus on terms related to community and collectivity shows that in spite of a significant emphasis on values in education and the value foundation of the Swedish education system, much of the rhetoric is dominated by a focus on the individual. This may reflect trends in educational policy that already have been noticed and discussed by educational research (Bergström, 1999).

Concluding reflections

In addition to what has been said above about the situation in Norway and Sweden, it should also be underlined that much takes place in the local school context that goes unnoticed. Looking at schools' websites in both countries, one gets the impression that many collective events are going on that may look similar to collective worship in the UK context. Elisabet Haakedal, one of the few to have studied this to some degree in Norway, claims that there are developments in what she terms 'ritualization' of the school day. Earlier many of these events did have some kind of connection to the local church or to the Christian religion, but this is changing. One of her conclusions is that:

> There is an intriguing relationship between the place and status in Norwegian primary schools of 1) particular religious commemorative practices, 2) the nation's commemorative practices with the aim of constructing and sustaining a national identity, and 3) mediated action intended to support universal values of solidarity and caring. (Haakedal, 2009, 13)

I think it is well worth reflecting on the question of rationale for the practice of collective worship/religious observance as set out in the AHRC report and to take into this reflection the complexity of changing traditional practices without careful consideration. As Haakedal shows, any change to ritual events in local schools is complex and involves several intersecting influences in addition to local agency. She also discusses how the role of the principal can differ from the staff in this respect. The situation in the UK is that the regulations are national and not local, and this means that it is possible and useful to have a broader reflection. It also means that the relationship between nation and education, the national level and the school level needs to be addressed. I will conclude with some normative remarks taking this as departure point.

There is a need to reflect on the basic issues of general education in the local school. The nation state is the structure that guarantees the legal, political and economic status of local schools while securing education for all. This is not a given situation, but a result of political struggles and decisions in the recent past. Education is also a vital part of democratic citizenship and this needs to be represented and practised on local school level. One important precondition for securing collective commitment to democratic citizenship is to embrace diversity in the celebration of equal opportunities and dignity. This therefore needs to be represented in terms of symbolic ritualization, if not 'worship' in a public context.

Education for all can be conceptualized as a basic necessity for life in society, which at a minimum involves educating individuals for the world of work. It is also, as mentioned above, a means of socialization into the role of a democratic citizen and, finally, education is a means of allowing an individual to understand her/himself as a responsible human being. These three aims of education (Biesta, 2004), are connected to the teaching of school subjects, learning to live together and learning about oneself. These three dimensions can be cherished, celebrated and mirrored through collective events in the school. The basic values of education are not national, they are international and universal and should be celebrated as such.

Finally, the local school ought to strive for becoming a community of human beings, a community of learning and a public space for all where the diversity of values, world-views, religions and convictions are included. While diverse positons may be considered, compared, contrasted and critiqued, there is also a time for celebrating the school as a community of resourceful diverse people. Collective events are necessary to symbolize this community in diversity. It is also necessary to experience community as something that stretches out of the local context and points towards both the national and international level. Here, collective events have a particularly important role to play by being inclusive and by balancing the representation of diversity with the celebration of community and fellowship. While this role may be one that is played out and experienced locally, it should be acknowledged and formulated on a national level.

References

Anderson, B. (2006). *Imagined communities: reflections on the origin and spread of nationalism.* London: Verso.

Bäckström, A., Edgardh Beckman, N., & Pettersson, P. (2004). *Religious Change in Northern Europe : The Case of Sweden : from State Church to Free Folk Church : Final Report.* Stockholm: Verbum.

Bergström, Y. (1999). Föreställningar av en gemenskap. *Utbildning och demokrati, 8*(1), 21–50.

Biesta, G. (2004). Against learning. Reclaiming a language for education in an age of learning. *Nordic Studies in Education, 24*(1), 70–82.

Breemer, R. v. d., Casanova, J., & Wyller, T. (Eds.) (2014). *Secular or Sacred? The Scandinavian Case of Religion in Human Rights, Law and Public Space.* Göttingen: Vandenhoeck & Ruprecht.

Clarke, C., & Woodhead, L. (2015). *A New Settlement: Religion and Belief in Schools.* Westminster Faith Debates. Retrieved April 20, 2017, from <http://faithdebates. org.uk/wp-content/uploads/2015/06/A-New-Settlement-for-Religion-and-Belief-in-schools.pdf>.

Cumper, P., & Mawhinney, A. (2015). *Collective Worship and Religious Observance in Schools: An Evaluation of Law and Policy in the UK.* An AHRC Network Report. Retrieved April 20, 2017, from <http://collectiveschoolworship.com/ documents/CollectiveWorshipReligiousObservanceAHRCNetworkReport 13November2015.pdf>.

Curriculum for knowledge of Christianity, religion, philosophies of life and ethics (rle1-02) Retrieved April 2017, from <http://www.udir.no/klo6/rle1-02/Hele/?lplang=eng> (English version)

ECHR 2007: Reports of Judgments and Decisions 2007-iii. Registry of the Court, Council of Europe. Strasbourg: Carl Heymanns Verlag. Retrieved April 20, 2017, from <http://echr.coe.int/Documents/Reports_Recueil_2007-III.pdf>.

Haakedal, E. (2009). School festivals, collective remembering and social cohesion: A case study of changes in Norwegian school culture. *Journal of Religious Education, 57*(3), 46–55.

Hovdelien, O., & Neegaard, G. (2014). Gudstjenester i skoletiden – rektorenes dilemma. *Norsk Pedagogisk Tidsskrift, 98*(4), 260–270.

National Curriculum in England Key Stages 1 and 2 Framework Document, September 2013. Retrieved August 15, 2016, from <https://www.gov.uk/government/uploads/system/uploads/attachment_data/file/425601/PRIMARY_national_curriculum.pdf>.

Norwegian Education Act. Retrieved August 15, 2016 from <https://lovdata.no/dokument/NL/lov/1998-07-17-61/KAPITTEL_6#§5-7>. English version, retrieved April 20, 2017, from <https://www.regjeringen.no/contentassets/b3b9e92cce6742c39581b661a019e504/education-act-norway-with-amendments-entered-2014-2.pdf>.

NOU (1995). *Identitet og dialog : kristendomskunnskap, livssynskunnskap og religionsundervisning : utredning fra et utvalg oppnevnt av Kirke-, utdannings- og forskningsdepartementet i August 1994; Avgitt 3. Mai 1995.* Oslo: Statens forvaltningstjeneste (NOU, 1995:9).

Osbeck, C., & Skeie, G. (2014). Religious Education at Schools in Sweden. In M. Rothgangel, M. Jäggle, & G. Skeie (Eds.), *Religious Education at Schools in Europe. Part 3: Northern Europe* (pp. 231–260). Göttingen: Vienna University Press.

Rawls, J. (1987). The Idea of an Overlapping Consensus. *Oxford Journal of Legal Studies, 7*(1), 1–25.

Skeie, G., & Bråten, O. M. H. (2014). Religious Education at Schools in Norway. In M. Rothgangel, M. Jäggle, & G. Skeie (Eds.), *Religious Education at Schools in Europe. Part 3: Northern Europe* (pp. 203–230). Göttingen: Vienna University Press.

Skolinspektionen, Dnr 41–2011:3039. Retrieved April 20, 2017, from <http://www.skolinspektionen.se/globalassets/0-si/07-beslut-och-rapporter/spara-2011/hasslehoma-20011-3039.pdf>.

Skolverket (2012). Skolverket Oktober 2012, juridisk vägledning om Skol- och förskoleverksamhet i kyrkan eller annan religiös lokal [Legal advice concerning school and preschool activities in churches or other religious places]. Retrieved

August 25, 2016, from <http://www.skolverket.se/polopoly_fs/1.162944!/Menu/ article/attachment/Skolan%20och%20kyrkan%20121016_granskad121018.pdf>.

Swedish Education Act. Skollag; utfärdad den 23 juni 2010. Svensk författningssamling, SFS 2010:800. Retrieved August 15, 2016, from <http://rkrattsdb.gov.se/ SFSdoc/10/100800.PDF>.

PETER CUMPER AND ALISON MAWHINNEY

Conclusion

Few issues in the field of education generate more passion and acrimony than that of collective worship and religious observance. As can be seen from the previous chapters, this is an area where consensus, both nationally and regionally, is evidently in short supply. Indeed, to the extent that common ground exists, it could be said that the most obvious area of agreement is a common perception that the law which currently governs collective worship and religious observance is far from satisfactory. So what can be done? Or more particularly, what are the various options for the UK in the coming decades?

Obviously there are numerous possibilities that might exist in relation to the possible future direction of law and policy in this area but, for reasons of brevity and clarity, we will focus on three. The first of these is to maintain the status quo by continuing with the current arrangements. The second is to abolish the collective worship/religious observance requirements. Finally, the third one is to reform the current duty on schools relating to collective worship/religious observance. Each of these possible options will now be briefly examined in turn.

Maintaining the status quo

Whilst there are doubtlessly those who would resist *any* changes to the current law and policy governing collective worship/religious observance, such a view is evidently very much a minority one. On the contrary, it is usually difficult to find scholars who express the opinion that the present

arrangements are operating satisfactorily. Indeed, to the extent that a persuasive argument can be made for maintaining the status quo, it seems likely
to be based less on principle and more on a pragmatic acknowledgment that
any attempt to reform the current system would be extremely problematic.

At present the most common view is that the case for maintaining
the status quo is completely unsustainable. In this regard the following
three arguments can be made against the contention that the current law
and policy on collective worship/religious observance should remain
unchanged.

First, the law in this area, as it currents stands across the UK, lacks a
coherent rationale. This absence of a clear and accepted rationale for the
duty of collective worship and religious observance arguably leads to both
non-compliance owing to uncertainty as to what is actually expected in
regard to the activity, and non-compliance on the grounds of principle.
What is more, it could be argued that there is a risk that this widespread
non-compliance will continue until the rationale for such activities is coherently articulated and properly acknowledged.

A second argument against maintaining the status quo is that the
law currently sits uneasily with human rights obligations. For example,
it may risk undermining the rights of those who wish not to participate
in acts of collective worship/religious observance. Similarly, the existing
legal arrangements may also risk discrimination against those who, whilst
supportive of collective worship/religious observance in principle, are not
from a Christian tradition. While the right to withdraw from such classes
exists, the current law and policy in this area is open to criticism on the
ground that it fails to comply with some key principles of international
human rights law. These include whether schools always provide sufficient
information about the nature of acts of collective worship/religious observance for parents (*Folgerø*, 2008, para 84) and whether clear procedures are
necessarily in place for the exercise of this right, so as to enable parents to
make informed choices about their rights of withdrawal in regard to such
lessons (*Folgerø*, 2008, paras 96–102).

A third argument against keeping the current law on collective wor-
ship/religious observance unchanged relates to the nebulous nature of
terms such as 'collective worship' and 'religious observance'. Ambiguity in

legislation and official guidance, coupled with weaknesses in accountability structures, may result in a wide diversity of interpretations and practice. This lack of clarity and accountability can give teachers considerable discretion and it means that they may, on occasion, exercise undue or inappropriate personal influence over the content and style of collective worship/religious observance. Moreover, this self-same lack of clarity and accountability may lead to situations where such teachers are at times forced to – or are equally unwilling to – make decisions about the content of collective worship/religious observance for which they are inadequately prepared.

Abolition of the duty

A second option is to abolish the duty on schools to hold acts of collective worship/religious observance. This option may be chosen where a country concludes there is no rationale for it to continue to obligate its schools to hold such activities. Such a decision may be bolstered by the fact that a high proportion of people in the UK appear to have eschewed traditional religious beliefs (National Centre for Social Research, 2017), thus reinforcing the lack of justification for continuing to impose such statutory requirements on schools. However, the abolition of the current duty on schools would not necessarily prevent schools from continuing to hold collective gatherings if they so wished. These may take the form of what may be called 'school assemblies' where school news and activities are reported and celebrated. Alternatively, some schools may choose to extend these assemblies to promote certain educational, moral and social values, a gathering that can be termed 'extended assemblies'. Each approach raises issues worthy of consideration.

First, if the duty on schools to hold acts of collective worship/religious observance were to be abolished, some schools may legitimately decide not to hold 'extended assemblies'. Arguably, this might mean that an opportunity would be lost for the transmission and sharing of positive moral, social and spiritual values within the school community in a way that is ordinarily not realizable through curriculum subjects. Additionally, it is possible that the abolition of any form of collective worship/religious observance duties could prompt some parents to remove their children from the (non-religiously designated) state sector and opt rather to place them in schools of a religious character, thereby increasing the division between faith and community sectors.

Secondly, were some schools to hold 'extended assemblies' in place of the current arrangements, these events could potentially be controversial and problematic. In the absence of a statutory duty, there would still need to be a mechanism, such as non-statutory guidance, to ensure that 'extended assemblies' were inclusive and respectful of the integrity of pupils, parents and teachers. Inspection bodies would have an important role to play in ensuring that schools adhered to such guidelines. In addition, if 'extended assemblies' were to resemble 'religious assemblies', the risk that schools could become increasingly divided along religious/belief lines would have to be recognized. Moreover, in the absence of a statutory duty, problems could exist in devising the means by which schools were to reach decisions on the nature of their 'extended assemblies', not least because certain decision makers (e.g. head teachers and teachers) could at times be seen as exercising undue influence. These concerns highlight the need for governments to set out clear guidance for such assemblies as well as provide an extensive range of good practice models.

Thirdly, the human rights concerns highlighted under Option 1 above (Maintaining the Status Quo) would be equally applicable to 'extended assemblies'. In particular, it should be noted that the right of individuals to opt out of 'extended assemblies' would exist if the nature of these assemblies was such that they did not offer and convey information and knowledge in an objective and pluralistic manner.

Reform of the duty

The 'reform option' may have the advantage of being seen as something of a compromise between the previous two, but the challenges in the articulation and realization of a reformed duty should not be underestimated.

First and foremost, the nature of any reform must be fundamentally driven by a clearly identified rationale. And this rationale will be derived from the requirements, aspirations and priorities of each country. Secondly, if a government considers reform of the existing duty to be the best option, – rather than abolition or maintaining the status quo - then it must be confident that the rationale for any reform has widespread support and that schools are clear in what is expected of them. Obviously there are numerous potential reforms that could be initiated, and many of these have been teased out in the earlier chapters. Rather than merely rehearsing all of these previously made arguments we will now, briefly, touch on some of them by identifying three possible suggestions for reform.

First, in relation to Scotland, an alternative way forward would be for schools to replace the statutory term 'religious observance' with 'time for reflection'. There have been calls on the part of some non-religious organizations, as well as the Church of Scotland, for such a change to be made. After all, the term 'time for reflection' could be seen as being more inclusive of Scotland's diverse, multifaith community, for it symbolically reflects the diversity of Scotland's children, which obviously includes those with no religion or faith. Any such change would necessitate the revision of the current guidance for these matters in Scottish schools. However, objections to reform in this area would be likely to be forthcoming from some quarters – especially those who would almost certainly view any such change as constituting a dilution of the role and status of organized religion in public life.

A second possible reform would be for England and Wales to remove the requirement that acts of collective worship must be of 'a broadly Christian character'. The removal of this requirement would return these countries to a pre-1988 position, because the 'broadly Christian' requirement was introduced by the Education Reform Act 1988, and the original duty (as set out in the Education Act 1944) only required that 'the school day in every county school and every voluntary school shall begin with collective worship on the part of all the pupils in attendance'. Any attempt to introduce such a reform would almost certainly attract strong criticism from some quarters (e.g. conservative Christian groups), and could also provoke acrimonious discussion of what is meant by 'worship' and the extent to which it may ever bring school communities together.

A third possible reform would (in relation to England, Northern Ireland and Wales) be for the current requirement to provide an act of collective worship to be replaced by a duty on schools to introduce a 'time for reflection'. A time for reflection could closely resemble aspects of the current Scottish model, which explicitly aims to promote the spiritual development of all pupils and to celebrate shared values. Indeed, such a duty might additionally, or alternatively, choose to focus on the provision of Philosophy with Children in the classroom, which aims to encourage and promote the facilitation of critical learning. Based on the principle of inclusiveness, the proposal for a 'time for reflection' takes account of the importance of affording recognition to the increasingly secular, yet also multifaith, nature of the UK. But the creation of a duty of a time for reflection would almost certainly cause disquiet on a number of fronts. These might, for example, include concerns that a time for reflection would: pose a threat to the distinctiveness of collective worship; risk emphasizing individual development at the expense of communal development; and, have a negative impact on religious literacy.

Future directions

The fact that education is a devolved matter within the UK means that when it comes to the specific issue of collective worship/religious observance, it is up to the law and policymakers of each of the four constituent countries of the UK to choose the most appropriate path for their nations. It is our hope that the essays in this collection will give them food for thought. Now is surely the time for serious attention to be devoted to an area that, for all too long, has been neglected by those in government.

References

Folgerø v Norway (2008) 46 EHRR 47.

National Centre for Social Research (2017). British Social Attitudes: Record number of Brits with no religion. Retrieved October 2, 2017, from <http://natcen.ac.uk/news-media/press-releases/2017/september/british-social-attitudes-record-number-of-brits-with-no-religion/>.

Contributors

CLAIRE CASSIDY is Senior Lecturer in the School of Education at the University of Strathclyde. Her research interests are in the areas of Philosophy with Children; children's rights and human rights education; and concepts of child and childhood. Her publications include C. Cassidy (2017), Philosophy with Children: a rights-based approach to deliberative participation, *International Journal of Children's Rights* 25(2), 320–334, and C. Cassidy, S-J. Conrad, M-F. Daniel, D. Garside, W. Kohan, K. Murris, M. Rego, X. Wu, & T. Zhelyazkova (2017), Being children: children's voices on childhood, *International Journal of Children's Rights*, 24(3–4), 1–26.

PETER CUMPER is a Professor in the School of Law at the University of Leicester. His research interests are in the areas of law, religion and human rights. His publications include P. Cumper (2015), Freedom of religion and human rights laws – awkward bedfellows, in M. Van den Brink, S. Burri, & J. Goldschmidt (Eds.), *Equality and human rights: nothing but trouble?* (pp. 283–304), Utrecht: SIM, Netherlands Institute of Human Rights; and P. Cumper (2014), Multiculturalism, human rights and the accommodation of sharia law, *Human Rights Law Review*, *14*, 31–57.

AIDEEN HUNTER is a Lecturer in the School of Education at Ulster University. Her research interests are in the areas of religious education; integrated and shared education in Northern Ireland; and special educational needs. Her publications include A. Hunter, J. Bates, A. McCully, & O'Connor-Bones (2014), Primary Integrating and Enriching Education (PIEE) Project: Report on the Shared teacher role in the PIEE project, North Eastern Education and Library Board (NEELB); and A. Hunter, J. Bates, A. McCully, & O'Connor-Bones (2012), Evaluation of the Primary Integration and Enriching Education (PIEE) Project, Final Report: A legacy of Partnership, NEELB.

JULIA IPGRAVE is Honorary Research Fellow in the Department of Humanities at the University of Roehampton. Her research interests are in the areas of religion and education; young people's understanding of religion; and interreligious engagement at community level. Her publications include J. Ipgrave, T. Knauth, A. Körs, D. Vieregge, & M. Von Der Lippe (Eds.) (2018), *Religions and Dialogue in the City: Case Studies on Interreligious Encounter in Urban Community and Education*, Münster: Waxmann Verlag; and S. Hirsch, M. McAndrew, G. Audet, & J. Ipgrave (Eds.) (2016), *Judaïsme et éducation: enjeux et défis pédagogiques*, Québec: Presses de l'Université Laval.

ROBERT JACKSON is Emeritus Professor of Religions and Education at the University of Warwick and Founding Director of Warwick Religions and Education Research Unit. He is Visiting Professor in the Department of Humanities and Social Sciences Education at Stockholm University, and an Expert Adviser to the Council of Europe in Strasbourg and the European Wergeland Centre, Oslo. His publications include R. Jackson, '*Signposts*': *Policy and Practice for Teaching about Religions and Non-Religious Worldviews in Intercultural Education*, Strasbourg: Council of Europe Publishing (<http://www.theewc.org/Content/Library/ COE-Steering-documents/Recommendations/Signposts-Policy-and-practice-for-teaching-about-religions-and-non-religious-world-views-in-intercultural-education>).

ALISON MAWHINNEY is Reader in Law in the School of Law at Bangor University. Her research interests are in the areas of freedom of religion or belief in schools, religious discrimination in employment and the human rights obligations of non-state service providers. Her publications include A. Mawhinney (2016), Coercion, oaths and conscience: conceptual confusion in the right to freedom of religion or belief, in F. Cranmer, M. Hill, C. Kenny, & R. Sandberg (Eds.), *The Confluence of Law and Religion Interdisciplinary: Reflections on the Work of Norman Doe* (pp. 205–217), Cambridge: Cambridge University Press; and Mawhinney, A. (2016), Claims of Religious Morality: The Limits of Religious Freedom in International Human Rights Law, *Law and Ethics of Human Rights*, *10*(2), 341–365.

FRANKIE MCCARTHY is Senior Lecturer in the School of Law at the University of Glasgow. Her research interests are in family law, property law and human rights. Her publications include F. McCarthy (2017), Protection of property and the European Convention on Human Rights, *Brigham-Kanner Property Conference Journal, 6*, 299–328; and F. McCarthy (2015), The rights of the child in Scotland, in O. Cvejic-Jancic (Ed.), *The Rights of the Child in a Changing World: 25 Years after the UN Convention on the Rights of the Child* (pp. 235–250), Switzerland: Springer.

MARY ELIZABETH MOORE is Dean of the Boston University School of Theology and Professor of Theology and Education. Her research interests are youth and culture, interreligious relationship building, and education and leadership for just peace. Her publications include M. E. Moore (2015), Youth navigating identities: charting the waters through narrative, in P. Couture, R. Mager, P. McCarroll, & N. Wigg-Stevenson (Eds.), *Complex Identities in a Shifting World: Practical Theological Perspectives* (pp. 65–76), Lit Verlag; and M. E. Moore (2017), A collage of contexts: young people and religious diversity in the United States, in E. Arweck (Ed.), *Young People's Attitudes to Religious Diversity* (pp. 263–274), London and New York: Routledge.

FARID PANJWANI is Director of the UCL Institute of Education, University College London. His research interests are in the areas of religion and education; Islam and education; intra-religious diversity; and education and imagination. His recent publications include F. Panjwani, L. Revell, R. Gholami, & D. Diboll (2017), *Education and Extremisms: Rethinking Liberal Pedagogies in the Contemporary World*, London: Routledge; and F. Panjwani (2017), No Muslim is just a Muslim: Implications for Education, *Oxford Review of Education 43*(5), 596–611.

NORMAN RICHARDSON is Senior Lecturer Emeritus at Stranmillis University College, Belfast. His research interests are in intercultural religious education; integrated education in Northern Ireland; and religion, education and human rights. His publications include N. Richardson (2016), Issues and Dilemmas in Religious Education and Human Rights:

Perspectives on applying the Toledo Guiding Principles to a divided society, in M. Pirner, J. Lähnemann, & H. Bielefeldt (Eds.), *Human Rights and Religion in Educational Contexts* (pp. 295–306), Switzerland: Springer International Publishing; and R. Greenwood, N. Richardson, & A. Gracie (2017), Primary Humanities: A Perspective from Northern Ireland, *Education 3–13: International Journal of Primary, Elementary and Early Years Education, 45*(3), 309–319.

ANN SHERLOCK is Senior Lecturer in the Law School at Aberystwyth University. Her research interests are in human rights, especially children's rights; the law of devolution in Wales; and the Older People's Commissioners in Wales and Northern Ireland. Her recent publications include A. Sherlock & J. Williams (2017), The Children's Commissioner for Wales and the Older People's Commissioner for Wales and the Administrative Justice System, in S. Nason (Ed.), *Administrative Justice in Wales and Comparative* Perspectives (pp. 125–143), Cardiff: Gwasg Prifysgol Cymru /University of Wales Press; and A. Sherlock (2015), Human rights in the National Assembly for Wales, in M. Hunt, H. Hooper, & P. Yowell (Eds.), *Parliaments and Human Rights: Redressing the Democratic Deficit* (pp. 239–254), Oxford: Hart Publishing.

GEIR SKEIE is Professor in Religious Education at the University of Stavanger and Stockholm University. His research interests are in the theory and practice of religious education. His recent publications include G. Skeie (2017), Transforming local places to learning spaces in religious education. Revisiting a collaborative research project, in M. Rothgangel, K. v. Brömssen, H.-G. Heimbrock, & G. Skeie (Eds.), *Space and Place in Religious Education* (pp. 115–130), Münster: Waxmann Verlag; and G. Skeie (2017), Impartial teachers in religious education – a perspective from a Norwegian context, *British Journal of Religious Education 39*(1), 25–39.

INA TER AVEST is Emeritus Professor at Inholland University of Applied Sciences and an Emeritus Assistant Professor of Religious Education at the Vrije Universiteit in Amsterdam. Her research interests are in the areas of the religious identity construction of pupils/students, teachers and

institutions. Her publications include D. Wielzen & I. ter Avest (Eds.)
(2017), *Interfaith Education for All. Theoretical Perspectives and Best Practices
for Transformative Action*, Boston/Rotterdam/Taipei: Sense Publishers;
and I. ter Avest (2017), 'I Experienced freedom within the frame of my
own narrative'; the contribution of psychodrama techniques to experiential
learning in teacher training, *International Review of Education, 63*(1), 71–86.

JACQUELINE WATSON is Honorary University Fellow at the University
of Exeter and was formerly the Director of the Centre for Spirituality and
Religion in Education at the University of East Anglia. Her research interests are spirituality in education, including connections between spirituality
and religious education. Her publications include J. Watson (2017), Every
Child Still Matters: interdisciplinary approaches to the spirituality of the
child, *International Journal of Children's Spirituality, 22*(1), 4–13; and M. de
Souza, J. Bone, & J. Watson (Eds.) (2016), *Spirituality across Disciplines:
Research and Practice*, New York: Springer.

Index

Religion, Education and Values

Debates about religion, education and values are more central to contemporary society than ever before. The challenges posed by the interaction between these different spheres will continue to increase as the effects of globalization and cultural pluralization impact on educational settings. Our radically changed and rapidly changing environment poses critical questions about how we should educate individuals to live in increasingly diverse societies.

Books in this series offer the most recent research, from a variety of disciplinary perspectives, on the interface between religion, education and values around the world. The series covers such themes as the history of religious education, the philosophies and psychologies of religious and values education, and the application of social science research methods to the study of young people's values and world-views.

Books within the series are subject to peer review and include single and co-authored monographs and edited collections. Proposals should be sent to any or all of the series editors:

Professor Stephen G. Parker (s.parker@worc.ac.uk)
The Rev'd Canon Professor Leslie J. Francis (Leslie.Francis@warwick.ac.uk)
Professor Rob Freathy (r.j.k.freathy@ex.ac.uk)
Professor Mandy Robbins (mandy.robbins@glyndwr.ac.uk)